AAKAR BOOKS CLASSICS

HISTORICAL PREMISES FOR INDIA'S TRANSITION TO CAPITALISM

AAKAR BOOKS CLASSICS

HISTORICAL PREMISES FOR INDIA'S TRANSITION TO CAPITALISM

(Late 18th to Mid-19th Century)

V.I. Pavlov

Historical Premises for India's Transition to capitalism
V.I. Pavlov

First Aakar Edition 2016

ISBN 978-93-5002-407-2

Published by
AAKAR BOOKS
28 E Pocket IV, Mayur Vihar Phase I, Delhi 110 091
Phone : 011 2279 5505 Telefax : 011 2279 5641
aakarbooks@gmail.com; www.aakarbooks.com

Printed at
Mudrak, 30 A Patparganj, Delhi 110 091

CONTENTS

INTRODUCTION

Subject-matter—There is a growing body of research in historical writings throughout the world into the problem of the general regularities and concrete ways of transition from one socio-economic formation to another. Interest in this subject (rather, an involved complex of problems) springs from various circumstances, the chief of which appear to be two: first, the struggle to fill the global historical process either with a socialist or a capitalist content, and, second, the urgent need, in this context, for a comprehensive scientific analysis of the succession of formations as a multifaceted process, which cannot be understood without the use of all modern methods of research.

Accordingly, one will readily understand the dissatisfaction with what has been done in this field up to now. Indeed, the rapid spread of more precise and objective methods of analysis has led to a review and even to the elimination of many well-established views and conceptions. This applies not only to the works of writers of earlier generations, but even to the conceptions expressed in earlier works by scientists still alive. Some of my own earlier works have had to be reappraised as well.

This book is a continuation of my study of India's economic history which I began over 25 years ago with a work on the specific formation of some national groups of the Indian industrial bourgeoisie. When I decided to make a study of the Indian bourgeoisie, one important consideration was that this class had found itself in power in a sovereign state, which made it very pertinent to study its formation, structure and role in the country's economic and political life. I also tried to consider some general aspects of the genesis and development of capitalism in India, such as the periodisation of these processes.

There remained the question of India's socio-economic level (especially in industrial production) just before she was conquered by the British, a question that had to be answered if one was to gain a clearer understanding of the drag exerted by colonial oppression and to establish the tendencies of the country's independent development. Because it was believed that progressive potentialities lay above all in the genesis of capitalist relations, I concentrated on discovering these in the industrial production of pre-British India. Together with E. N. Komarov, and under the general guidance of our teacher Igor Reusner, an article was written in 1954 describing some pockets of capitalist prodction in the 18th century and early 19th century. Today, the article is perhaps of historiographic interest, because subsequent studies by K. A. Antonova, L. B. Alayev and especially A. I. Chicherov brought to light much more crucial evidence than that contained in the article, which had, however, drawn attention to the problem and, besides, brought into circulation a unique source like F. Buchanan's inquiries.

My 1958 book, "The Formation of the Indian Bourgeoisie", presented the new assessments[1] which had appeared after the 20th Congress of the CPSU, and this made it possible to revise a number of definitions which had an air of dogmatism about them. But in that book I did not overcome the main methodological defect, namely, consideration of the capitalist sector as a separate self-developing entity of socio-economic relations and a corresponding production basis.

As I have already said, the attempt to bring out the capitalist sector from the system of socio-economic relations in industry and then, having divided it up into successive stages, to study it along an upgrade—from early capitalist production to monopolistic concerns—led one unwittingly to exaggerate the historical potentialities of capitalism in contemporary India. Until 1960, accelerated development of capitalism along the most democratic lines was still regarded as the immediate historical prospect. But the choice of socialist orientation by the then leadership of the ARE, Algeria and Burma, India's growing economic difficulties and new research into Indian economy gradually led to a reappraisal of the earlier views about the ways of development for the young African and Asian states, including India. In 1963, I reached the conclusion that at the present stage general democratic changes, rather than helping to clear away the medieval survivals from the path of capitalism actually blocked its way. This idea was subsequently elaborated in detail in a number of publications as part of the general conception of bypassing the stage of monopoly capitalism in the emergent countries.[2]

My views were greatly influenced by the further research studies which have shown very well the specific features of capitalist development in independent India: the narrow sphere (chiefly in the social sense) of large-scale enterprise; the enlivening of the medium generating capitalism in the form of the manufactory* and the small factory, that is, a kind of historically retarded emergence of the second, "manufactory", stage of capitalism in industry, which had earlier been almost missed; the existence of sections (vast in terms of employment) of pre-capitalist small-scale production, partially retaining direct (non-commodity) bonds with agriculture. In other words, there arose this problem: to what extent capitalism in India has already succeeded or would succeed in the historically foreseeable future in transforming in its own way (the "Japanese" way) the pre-capitalist sectors and, with them, the country's whole socio-economic structure.

Over the past few years, the genesis of capitalism in agriculture and industry has quite naturally become the subject of growing research and theoretical generalisation. This covers a vast period of roughly five centuries—from the 14th-15th centuries to the present day. The study of the genesis of capitalism, consisting of numerous works of individual countries, has been assuming global proportions and serves as a premise for the appearance of generalising works.

Historians today are faced with the key scientific and political task of analysing the gradual fade-out of the socio-transformatory potentialities of capitalism in the African and Asian countries as it moves into its highest stage of development on a world scale. Naturally, this does not imply any refurbishing of the vulgar voluntarist conception about capitalism having lost its potential for boosting the productive forces and carrying out technical improvements in production.

Still, in the economically lagging countries capitalism has now displayed a relatively lesser capacity than it did in its early stages in the West European countries to transform the social structure, to overcome the multisectoral make-up and to secure dominant positions not only in the volume of production but also in the social interrelations. In a sense, the technical achievements of state-monopoly capitalism in the industrially advanced countries have, for their reverse side, the signs of stagnation in the social processes of the African and Asian countries. In other words, in the economically lagging countries it is becoming ever more difficult to transform the capitalist sector into a sphere of production providing employment or a majority of the population. There is no doubt that countries which have lagged in entering upon the capitalist way have shown less and less capacity for providing such employment on the technical level of modern

* Here and further on, the term "capitalist manufactory" is used to mean a capitalist workshop with a detailed division of hired manual labour.

capitalism. Even Japan and Italy, which have been highly active in boosting the productive forces in the post-war period, have failed in these 30 years to solve their social problems in the structure of the employed population. The African and Asian countries are in an especially (difficult position. Thus, in India's large-scale industry employment has been growing at a rate which is just above the rate of the natural population growth.

Historically, the most favourable conditions for the formation of the class structure of capitalist society took shape in Britain, where the process of society's bourgeois transformation began in the pre-manufactory and manufactory periods at a low rate of capital per capita. Besides, considerable funds flowed into Britain from outside. In India, the very opposite situation obtains. There is now need for vast investments per worker, which are hundreds of times in excess of the investments required in the period of society's capitalist transformation in Britain. The influx of funds along conventional external economic channels either does not exist or constitutes a negative magnitude. The difficulties of accumulating capital to the extent necessary for society's capitalist integration have been growing with the improvement and higher cost of capitalist technology and the weakening of the positions of the countries that have been late in entering the world capitalist market and the world capitalist economy.[3]

Some Aspects of the Study of Multisectoral Society—A central problem is to determine the place of the capitalist sector in the whole national-economic structure and also within the system of world economic relations. When elaborating the methodology of research in concrete terms for the individual countries, one should bear in mind that in his "Capital" Marx has made a study of British society which had gone through the processes of capitalist transformation in the purest form and which had already solved its own multisectoral problem by the mid-19th century. That is why Marx confines himself chiefly to examining the relations between the lower and higher forms of capitalist production, and this was indicated by V. I. Lenin, when he wrote: "Marx speaks of one 'economic formation of society' only, the capitalist formation, that is, he says that he investigated the law of development of this formation only and of no other." [4]

In "The Development of Capitalism in Russia", Lenin set a model for studying the petty-commodity sector and various subsections of the capitalist sector in their interaction, without tackling every aspect of the general multisectoral problem. This will be readily understood because this work of Lenin's had a definite scientific and political purpose, which was to refute the assertions of the Narodniks concerning the limited development of capitalism in Russia. His subsequent agrarian studies contained an elaboration of his conception of the multisectoral nature of Russian society and the place of the capitalist sector in it. The problem of the multisectoral nature of Russian society was tackled in the most generalised form in Lenin's writings about the New Economic Policy.

In view of the fact that the multisectoral problem has become central to this study, there is need briefly to formulate what we mean by formation and sector, especially because this subject has become controversial. By formation we mean the basis, the internal essential regularity of production and social processes, and by sector, a concrete expression of these regularities. These are not, of course, full-scale definitions of formation and sector, which have been thoroughly elaborated by the founders of Marxism-Leninism, but merely a comparison of the two categories in principle. When making a study of the sector as a concrete historical, economic and social phenomenon, we gain a deeper insight into the concept of formation as the essence comprising more general, permanent and abstracted conceptions of these same processes. In fact, Engels asked whether feudalism had ever corresponded to its conception, remarking on the lack of identity between the historically concrete reality and its abstracted conception.[5] In other words, through a study of the sector and multisectoral structure we advance to a knowledge of formation as such, and also in combination with relicts or, on the contrary, emergent elements of other formations.

In the Russian text of this book use is made of the Russian term u k l a d, which was first proposed by V.I. Lenin. Because there is no adequate English term I have used "sector" as the nearest one to u k l a d. But one should bear in mind that u k l a d has a much broader connotation, for, apart from its economic aspect, it also has socio-class, socio-psychological, political, ideological, cultural, institutional and other aspects, which make it possible to regard u k l a d-sector as a structural subdivision of society. The term u k l a d itself is being further discussed in Soviet writings. In the light of the historical approach, I have taken as the main criterion in identifying u k l a d certain stages in socio-economic formations and also intermediate, inter-formational stages. Accordingly, among the u k l a d-sectors considered in this book are the following: (1) early and (2) developed feudalism, (3) petty-commodity, (4) early or manufacture capitalism, and (5) industrial capitalism (which up until the mid-19th century had taken shape only in Britain). The views of Soviet Indologists the multi-sectoral structure of India society in the subsequent stages of its development will be found in the work: V. Pavlov, V. Rastyannikov, G. Shirokov, "India: Social and Economic Development (18th-20th Centureis)" (see note 3).

The approach to the study of society as being mainly a multisectoral structure does not in itself provide an answer to the question but merely paves the way for its understanding, and, let us add, not through any enlargement or reduction, but through a complexification and enlargement of the gamut of research. It is, of course, easier to study a single component or even an important unit of a mechanism than the whole mechanism in its entirety, to say nothing of studying it as a functioning entity with its component parts in interaction. First of all, the introduction into usage of definitions of the u k l a d, which are already known or which have been variously analysed on the strengths of other facts, tends to produce the illusion that we operate with well-known categories, so that the task is to determine the concrete relationships between the various u k l a d s (sectors) in the given socio-economic structure.

But the point is that the specific features of a given structure spring not only from the unique intrasectoral proportions but also from the national concreteness of each sector individually and its corresponding interaction with other sectors. It was Marx who observed that events which were remarkably similar but which occurred different historical environments tended to produce totally different results. It is easy to understand this when studying each of these evolutions separately and then comparing them, but it is never possible to reach such an understanding by making use of the universal skeleton key of some general historico-philosophical theory. Putting the finishing touches to this idea towards the close of his life, Engels stressed that the laws of the development of society do not have "any reality, except as approximation, tendency, average, and never as immediate reality".[6]

Thus, when we define the economy of the rural èlite strata in India in the 18th-19th centuries as being feudal or the economy of the urban handicraftsmen as being petty-commodity or petty-capitalist, we are merely carried to the point of research into their actual socio-economic content and internal economic relations. Indeed, the "sector-wise" definition does not in itself allow us to draw a distinct line between the various types of relations of production. When, for instance, does the village-community carpenter become a petty-commodity producer, and the well-to-do community member a small farmer or a feudal land-owner leasing out land? Similarly, if we start only from the quantity of the labour involved and its detailed division in the manufacture of sugarcane products in the Indian countryside, the establishments concerned would have to be classified as capitalist. But the data on the remuneration of the labourers and the element of patronage in their relations with their employers suggest that such establishments were perhaps ancillary lines of production carried on by feudal-type householding proprietors among the rural èlite.

By contrast, in another socio-economic context an establishment based on the personal labour of the owner may be classified as capitalist. Thus, under-developed capitalist production, according to Lenin's definition, even simple commodity production becomes not only a reserve of capitalism but also one of its minor varieties. The category of the small rural bourgeoisie "includes every small commodity-producer who covers his expenditure by independent farming, provided the general system of economy is based on the capitalist contradictions".[7] This kind of situation can hardly be discovered in India in the period under review, but what Lenin says provides yet another important methodological criterion for typisation.

The Place of the Individual Sectors in a Mixed Economy.— But even if we have established that a given type of economy belongs to a definite sector, we have merely reached the problem of indicators which are to determine the place and role of the individual sectors—in particular, which of them has the formation-shaping function. Two indicators are usually regarded as being crucial: the share of the given sector in the gross national product, and its share in the gainfully employed population. But the experience of research and the theoretical propositions of the Marxist-Leninist classics show these two indicators to be inadequate.

The first indicator becomes highly imprecise and unreliable because of the different conditions of price-formation in the various sectors. But what is even more important is that the volumes of the national product which are comparable in terms of value may differ sharply in their concrete material form, notably, the presence and the quality of the material elements of reproduction. What is also essential is the extent to which these elements are part of the necessary product or the surplusproduct. Marx observed that "surplus-value is convertible into capital solely because the surplus-product, whose value it is, already comprises the material elements of new capital".[8]

In a footnote to this formulation, Marx says something that does much to show his methodology and also has a direct bearing on our subject: "We here take no account of export trade, by means of which a nation can change articles of luxury either into means of production or means of subsistence and vice versa. In order to examine the object of our investigation in its integrity, free from all disturbing subsidiary circumstances, we must treat the whole world as one nation, and assume that capitalist production is everywhere and has possessed itself of every branch of industry."[9] Here, the scale of the allowance is obvious, if only because the "whole world" included British India as well. Because this was a deliberate abstraction, Marx's model for the conversion of surplus-value does not embrace a number of concrete processes of reproduction in multisectoral structures.

Obviously, if a sector under consideration commands a large share and volume of the surplus-product, its importance in the life of society is enhanced. But the distribution of the surplus-product between the accumulation fund and the consumption fund of its producer or of the one who appropriates the surplus-product, is equally important. Concerning the temptations of the latter, Marx makes this ironic remark: "The world still jogs on solely through the self-chastisement of this modern penitant of Vishnu, the capitalist."[10] India's example shows very well that the volume of the surplus-product is not at all adequate to the scale of extended reproduction in the sector in which it has been produced. Moreover, under a concrete system of redistribution and consumption, the bulk of the surplus-product may predetermine stagnation both in the given sector and in the whole national structure, or may be largely expended on rapid expansion of production in another sector (for instance, the flow of funds from the petty-farm sector into large-scale industry).

In some instances, the redistribution system, while falling short of the needs of extended reproduction, helps to maintain stable domination of society by sections feeding off the surplus-product of the given sector. Where the volume and material elements of the surplus-product are balanced out with the numerical strength, demographic dynamics and living standard (demands) of the ruling class, that class will have little incentive for a long time to effect any changes in the mode of production.

In this context, let us note that in some feudal countries the ruling class had a system of usages and traditions regulating its natural reproduction. In Western Europé it was the busy life of the society ladies, the military service and the duels of the gentlemen, and the celibacy of the clergy; in Japan the sanguinary strife among the samurai clans; and in India the marital regulations for women of the higher castes. Finally, all feudal-type societies had barriers to the recognition of the hereditary rights of children born out of wedlock to women of an inferior social estate, of another creed, caste, clan, etc. For all the national distinctions in the mechanism of demographic regulation it did, undoubtedly, help to maintain a balance between the requirements of the ruling class and the possibilities of satisfying these, and in that sense enhanced the conservative character of that class. (It is quite another matter when, as during the War of the Roses in England, the aristocracy was carried away in its self-destruction, thereby creating something of a vacuum which was filled with new social elements.)

In stagnant societies with traditional technology, the relative numbers of the ruling sections depend on the size of the surplus-product they appropriate and this, in turn, depends on the natural conditions of labour. Marx said that "should labour-power be minute, and the natural conditions of labour scanty, then the surplus-labour is small, but in such a case so are the wants of the producers, on the one hand, and the relative number of exploiters of surplus-labour, on the other, and finally so is the surplus-product, whereby this barely productive surplus-labour is realised for those few exploiting land-owners." In India, there was apparently a situation with social derivatives that were the opposite of those considered by Marx (with the exception of the small wants of the producers)

When considering the conditions for the formation of a ruling class over a lengthy historical period, the division of the surplus-product it appropriates into that part which is consumed and that which is turned to extended reproduction runs into a definite contradiction with the reproduction of the class itself: the larger the surplus-product personally consumed by this class, the more numerous it is today, but by failing to put away a necessary part for extended reproduction, the ruling class in a sense eats away its own future, dooming its own lower sections to proprietory degradation (although in traditional societies this does not entail immediate loss of social privileges). That is why excessive non-productive consumption by the ruling classes of the whole or almost the whole of the surplus-product led to a kind of population explosion in its midst (barring extraordinary military and other constraints) and bred a host of have-nots who were all the more conservative in laying claim to the traditional volume of the good things of life (to Sancho Panza's dismay, the totally disinterested Don Quixote received the good things of life from the Duke and the Duchess as a legitimate recompense for his professions of allegiance).

Recognition of a society as being multisectoral entails a more complicated approach to its super-structural institutions. Of course, any society needs a system of social rules of law and morality and the corresponding super-structural institutions to regulate the given mode of production, to govern the relations between its members, the social micro-elements (family, community, caste), production units and macro-entities (the state, nation, the national economy as a whole). In stagnant (rather, slowly evolving) societies, the ideological and institutional aspects of this mechanism come to be regarded by man as everlasting, complete and sanctified by divine reason and will. This attitude on the part of society to its institutions and rules of morality and law invests both with additional independence, giving some historians ground to insist on the self-contained nature of the institutional-legal complex in the East.

Of course, every society is dominated by the state super-structure of the sector which determines the socio-economic formation to which the whole of society belongs. But the system of superstructural institutions also includes, as its subordinate components, social institutions of obsolescent or, on the contrary, emergent sectors. In the course of long coexistence these are subjected to mutual influence, and in the conditions of general social stagnation this tends to approximate their formal organisation and functional load. For instance, India's system of caste institutions shows signs of tribal cohesion, slavish servility, and organisation along guild and social-estate lines. These features are differently represented, or are totally absent, in the various tiers of the caste hierarchy, but even in the upper echelons of the administrative and military personnel there was extensive practice of the master-and-servant relations intrinsic to the tribal or slave-holding system. In this sense, India has never had a vassal hierarchy of the ruling class that was homogeneous in terms of social estate, like the one in feudal Europe (although even there alien elements did intrude into the system). The widespread practice in the East of recruiting (frequently impressing) persons of alien ethnic origin (and now and again of other creeds) into the military and administrative apparatus on terms of slavish allegiance to the despotic ruler is evidence, I think, that the feudalisation of the ruling class and its machinery of administration and coercion was incomplete gauged according to the norms of the late-feudal, absolutistic society.

The balance between the individual groups of the exploiting classes in pre-British India was not a mere reflection of their numerical strength or their role in the country's economic and ideological life. Indeed, the Mogul élite did not match up in these indicators to the Hindu land-owner sections in their aggregate, but for over a century and a half it held sway because of its greater cohesion, centralisation and military-political activity. That is why the feudal tendencies represented by the interests of the local Hindu land-owners were not embodied for a long time and the corresponding changes in the socio-economic structure were delayed.

Nor should the place of the working classes in a country's economic, political and ideological life be determined solely by their numerical proportions. The growing costs of reproduction and the technical equipment of producers employed in a higher mode of production tend rather to limit (under a given volume of productive accumulation) the volume of manpower in transition from archaic to historically advanced sectors. The growing labour productivity of individual producers from different sectors also operates in the same direction. But those employed in the more productive sphere are able to make good their relatively smaller numerical strength by greater cohesion, higher cultural standards, more vigorous activity and other qualitative advantages. In this sense, there is the widest gap between the modern proletarians and the working men in the patriarchal subsistence economy, with a string of working men of different production types and social standards running between the two. This is another point that is relevant to any definition of the place of a sector under study in the internal structure.

Indicator of the Distribution System Engendered by the Mode of Production.—When considering the intranational and international division of labour and through these the process of accumulation, I have been guided by the following proposition: "The so-called distribution relations, then, correspond to and arise from historically determined specific social forms of the process of production and mutual relations entered into by men in the reproduction process of human life."[12] Marx goes on to bring out capitalist distribution and to distinguish it from other, pre-capitalist forms of distribution, which disappear only with the corresponding form of production,[13] that is, the given aggregation of modes of production engenders a corresponding system of forms of distribution. The multiplicity of distribution systems in Asian societies corresponds to the unparalleled complexity and peculiarity of their socio-economic structures.

The remaining Indian and British-introduced super-structural institutions continued to play an active social role until Independence in the redistribution and consumption of the national product even while both took a relatively insignificant part in productive accumulation. This mixed system of redistribution was superimposed upon, and influenced, an even more intricate system of product movement along the channels of the social division of labour, which combined in contradictory terms and embraced the circuit of the product within the limits of the micro-region (the jajmani type unit, the village community, the rural locality), the emergent nationwide market and, finally, the world capitalist market.

With the emergence of factory production in India, the interaction between the multisectoral structure of production relations and the various modes of distribution became unusually contradictory. The new type of production engenders a corresponding mode of distribution, as Engels pointed out: "The method of distribution essentially depends on how much there is to distribute, and ... this must surely change with the progress of production and social organisation, so that the method of distribution may also change."[14] Of course, the quantity of the product turned out by the average production unit of capitalism (factory) was a thousand times greater than the volume of production of the typical tradition-bound unit. That is why, alongside the fairly rapid displacement of the fiscal apparatus of the Indian princely states by the Treasury of the British administration, there was a gradual formation of the capitalist machinery of redistribution (banks, agency houses, commercial companies, etc.). In this way, the new multisectoral quality of production was reflected and carried on in the multisectoral and specific character of the sphere of commodity-money circulation (although in India's conditions the latter was much narrower than the aggregate system of redistribution).

The consequences of the multisectoral structure of the sphere of circulation are evident in the fact that the bulk of commodities is heterogeneous not only in the range of products (which is inevitable), but also in the conditions in which its elements are produced, and this means also in the mass and rate of profit built into the various commodities which are comparable in price. Accordingly, loan capital differs in origin and application, and this is expressed in the diversity of the rates of interest, terms of credit, and, what is most important, in the extent to which it is tied with production and is able to reorganise it on a new technological basis. Of course, in the sphere of circulation the boundaries of the sectors appear to be eroded and are not as pronounced as they are in the sphere of production (for instance, the activity of trading and moneylending capital in petty-commodity and early capitalist production). Still, the use of a criterion like the forms and conditions of connection with production provides a sufficiently obvious intersectoral guideline.

The mobility of capital in the sphere of circulation, its "inclination" to this or that sector, the extent and conditions of its involvement in production largely predetermine the proportions and dynamics of the multisectoral structures. Here, capital in the sphere of circulation itself can be transformed into a different qualitative state, by being connected with this or that type of capitalist industry, thereby representing a fundamentally new, capitalist principle of redistribution. That is understandable, for, as Marx observed, pre-capitalist production was aimed chiefly at the production of use-value, and this had two implications: "On the one hand, that circulation has not as yet established a hold on production, but is related to it as to a given premise. On the other hand, that the production process has not as yet absorbed circulation as a mere phase of production. Both, however, are the case in capitalist production."[15]

Under pre-capitalist modes of production, Marx goes on, "merchant's capital appropriates an over-whelming portion of the surplus-product partly as a mediator between communities which still substantially produce for use-value, and for whose economic organisation the sale of the portion of their product entering circulation, or for that matter any sale of products at their value, is of secondary importance; and partly, because under those earlier modes of production the principal owners of the surplus-product with whom the merchant dealt, namely, the slave-owner, the feudal lord and the state (for instance, the oriental despot), represent the consuming wealth and luxury which the merchant seeks to trap...."[16] Consequently, consuming wealth in pre-capitalist society is personified chiefly by the sections which extract the surplus product without joining in the process of its production and circulation as a necessary element. In these conditions, merchant's capital operates as a go-between not so much between the various spheres and types of production as between the owners of large concentrations of the surplus product withdrawn from these spheres of production. That is why merchant's capital does not, as a rule, intrude into the lower echelons of the system of distribution and concentrates at the higher ones. The redistribution of the necessary product (in the broad sense of the term), including the elements of reproduction, occurs mainly on the basis of direct subsistence consumption, exchange and remuneration. I have, naturally, ignored the intrusion of usurers into small-scale subsistence production.

Summing up this line of reasoning about the socio-economic indicators of the formation-shaping sector, these should apparently be brought out for the time being as the most important ones: a higher level of technical equipment, organisation of labour and corresponding productivity; production (in this sphere) of the bulk of the surplus-product; the maximum flow of this product into the higher, centralising echelons of the system of redistribution; its materialisation in the most perfect types of consumer objects, weapons and, what is most important, means of production; the prevailing influence of the productively used part of the surplus-product of this sector on the nation-wide processes of extended reproduction, that is, on accumulation (the latter indicator is especially acceptable for the factory sector); the leading role of the product of the given sector in the maintenance of the ruling classes, the personnel of super-structural institutions, and the machinery of coercion and ideological influence; the role of the ideology of the class dominating the given sector in the traditional ideology and social ethics from which spring the intensity of vital—above all labour—efforts and the volume of claims to material benefits.

Concerning the Comprehension of Social Being under Multisectoral Structures.—Above I brought out the socio-economic indicators with emphasis on their qualitative aspects. However, one cannot do without a consideration of the quantitative elements which, by their very massive inertia, communicate to historically new movements a corresponding—and mainly retarding and frequently regressive—correction in terms of pace and vigour of progress. Thus, among the criteria which help to determine the role of the given formation-shaping sector (even if it meets the above-mentioned and other indicators) are the distribution of the working population by modes of production, the living conditions of the corresponding groups, sections and individuals and their comprehension of these conditions as being standard or, conversely, as running counter to their well-established notions of the necessary aggregation of material and spiritual benefits.

This comprehension is in no sense objective, to say nothing of its being scientifically exhaustive. By the mid-19th century, for instance, this kind of comprehension was yet to be gained by the British working class, then the most advanced contingent of the world's proletariat and of the contemporary working population in general. In 1844, Engels wrote that social calamities need to be studied and comprehended, and the mass of workers had yet to do that.[17] In the light of this, the social self-assessment of the labouring sections in the India of that period could hardly have been objective.

It is the ruling classes of the leading sectors that claim to comprehend social being and to interpret it. Quite naturally, they seek to impose their own ideological conception primarily on the labouring mass of "their own" sector: the slave-owners on the slaves, the feudal lords on the serfs, and the bourgeois on the proletarians. At the same time, the ruling class of the leading sector usually seeks to subordinate the whole of society to its own ideology, presenting it as being universal "allnational", etc. In India, the efforts of the ruling class to implant its own ideology among the labouring sections had a number of specific features.

While the sectoral structure of India in the late-medieval period is still being studied, it appears fairly obvious that sizable relicts of slave-holding and tribal relations, which in some areas constituted sectoral formations, continued to coexist alongside the dominant feudal sector. It is also obvious that elements of the petty-commodity sector (including some pockets of capitalism), primarily in the urban handicrafts, were also there. Indeed, Indian feudalism was itself multiform. All of this produced an unusual diversity in the conditions of the social being of the labouring masses of India and in the levels of their material and spiritual culture.

The long historical period in which labouring sections with different living conditions coexisted with each other may have resulted in a situation in which the diversity of social ethics engendered such a rigid religious fixation of it in the caste regulations of Hinduism, which, however, allowed various interpretations, sectarian trends and philosophical lines. At any rate, there is need for a historical and sociological explanation for the two clear-cut distinctions between Hinduism, on the one hand, and Judaism, Christianity and Islám, on the other: the open and direct establishment of social specifics in the rules of social behaviour and vital claims, and tolerance of ideological pluralism among its adherents.

The socio-economic processes which started in India after the British conquest, notably, the extension of the petty-commodity and the formation of the capitalist sector, led to a further dichotomy of social being and consciousness. In the new conditions, labour and the products of labour to use Marx' words, took the shape, "in the transactions of the society, of services in kind and payments in kind" (as under feudalism), but increasingly assumed "a fantastic form different from their reality" (as under capitalist commodity production).[18] Indeed, in his ordinary life the Indian land cultivator or handicraftsman appropriated or, conversely, alienated his product not only through the mechanism of immediate and understandable personal relations but also through commodity exchange, where he was faced with "the whole mystery of commodities, all the magic and necromancy that surround the products of labour as long as they take the form of commodities".[19] In this respect, British rule confronted the Indian labouring man with a two-fold aspect: the personal—in the much too familiar form of the tax collector who appropriated a part of his product, and in the mystical—as the depersonified owner of the product produced by an unknown labourer in unknown conditions and at unknown costs.

Accordingly, the unpaid surplus-labour here could be expressed either in the form of rent or of profit. That is why extra-economic, coercive (taxes, rent and levies), trade and moneylending, and more or less purely capitalistic methods of exploitation were applied to Indian working men. Para-phrasing what Marx once said, it is safe to say that from the mid-19th century the social relations of the Hindus in the sphere of labour appeared both as their own mutual personal relations and "under the shape of social relations between the products of labour".[20] In Christianity, the dualism of social consciousness in the period of transition to capitalism was given a more or less adequate, even if contradictory, ideological reflection in the course of the bourgeois Reformation. But neither of the two great religions of India has ever gone even through the initial stages of bourgeois Reformation (and it is noteworthy that in India even Christianity has maintained its pre-Reformation forms). Moreover, the maturity of Hinduism as the ideology of full-scale feudalism is not beyond doubt. Jainism, Sikhism and Nestorian Christianity have remained socially and geographically localised ideologies, and their very readiness for bourgeois Reformation has been far from proved. In short, by the mid-19th century India had no classes or large social groups equipped with an advanced ideology combining the demands of that class or that largest social group and the all-national interest.

In effect all the ideologies existing in the country fundamentally substantiated the existing system or redistribution of the product and sought to modify it only in exceptional circumstances. That is why the regulation of consumer claims and with them of the very way of live of the Indians belonging to various social sections has always been an integral part of India's traditional ideologies. Indeed, the system of regulations included—at the head of the list—the deductions going to the maintenance of the vehicles and exponents of the ideologies (Hinduism, Islam, etc.), and this intensified their social conservatism and their adherence to traditional institutions.

In the new historical situation, when the most acute social conflicts were already expressed through the medium of intruding capitalism, the traditional religious consciousness could serve as a basis only for conservative reactions to the emergent phenomena and processes. At the same time, no single narrow-class secular ideology, including bourgeois nationalism in a more or less pure form, could be a substitute for the religious ideology as an "operating" day-to-day ideology for a majority of the population. In these circumstances, the emergence of Gandhism, as an ideology laying claim to all-national acceptance, appears to have been quite natural. Let us note that for a time the weaker aspects of such an ideology—vagueness, eclecticism, its indifference to class contradictions—proved to be its strongest aspects, which is why its socio-economic programme was widely accepted, at any rate at the stage of the struggle for independence.

Comprehensive and Imperative Nature of Incentives to Progress.—In ideological life, the objectively contradictory character of a situation when the leading sector, which, according to a number of indicators, has already become formation-shaping but has yet to provide employment for the bulk of the population, that is, has yet to prevail in the social structure, becomes especially obvious. In this kind of situation, coercive ideological expansion frequently serves as a kind of extra-economic battering-ram used to take possession of the social sphere of archaic sectors (for instance, the conversion of the patriarchal peasantry to Christianity or Islam by the feudal or feudalised nobility). In such instances, the top sections of the archaic sectors frequently undertake to champion the ageold creed and traditional institutions whose destruction would mean their removal from control of the redistribution of the social product and loss of their habitual social status.

The all-round approach to an understanding of the socio-economic structure and its functional interconnections predetermines the more complex Marxist view of historical progress. In this context there arises the problem of a situation which in Marxist writings is designated as formation leap, that is, a comprehensive transition of all the basic elements of a given socio-economic structure to a historically new qualitative entity. It is essential to emphasise the universality of this transition because some bourgeois conceptions of leap tend to reduce its content to a technical-and-production "take-off" (as Walt Rostow does) or to some other one-sided change.

The Marxists hold that a formation-leap is law-governed when it is preceded by an accumulation of crisis phenomena in the basic elements of the dominant (formation-shaping) sector, that is, in the sphere of the productive forces, relations of production, social institutions, ideological conceptions, cultural values etc. But the necessity for such accumulation does not imply that the transformative process begins simultaneously and proceeds at the same pace and with equal depth in every sphere of social life. This unevenness of the revolutionary process in the change of formations results in various disproportions and even deformations, which constitute the birth-pangs of history.

The Marxist view of the general and constantly operating stimulus to progress differs greatly from, say, Gunnar Myrdal's valuations precisely because it starts from objective and inexorably operating factors, instead of selected criteria. The internationalist-minded Marxist finds the difficult part of the problem consisting in the establishment of the relationship between these factors in their specific, national-regional, and in their general, global expressions. Here, we are guided by this formula of Lenin's: "...The historic events that are unfolding before our eyes can be understood only if we analyse, in the first place, the objective conditions of the transition from one epoch to the other. Here we have important historical epochs; in each of them there are and will always be individual and partial movements, now forward now backward (My emphasis.—V. P.), there are and will always be various deviations from the average type and mean tempo of the movement.... Only a knowledge of the basic features of a given epoch can serve as the foundation for an understanding of the specific features of one country or another."[21]

Thus, for the Marxist historian the initial conceptual position is unusually complexified and made difficult by the need to analyse a whole complex of internal and external imperative relations. "A knowledge of the basic features of a given epoch" is Lenin's starting point for understanding the national situation in concrete terms. This formula, we believe, provides the scientific approach to a study of the socio-economic level of India's development and the impact of the British conquest on that level. Indeed, if we start from "the basic features of a given epoch" at the turn of the 18th and 19th century nothing can be offered as a standard of historical progress apart from the Industrial Revolution, that is, the transition from the manual to the mechanised mode of production. At the same time, if, according to Lenin, we consider the global Industrial Revolution only as the foundation "for an understanding of the specific features" of the socio-economic processes in this or that country, our evaluation of the impact of British capitalism on India will become more complex and mediated.

The Capitalist Sector as an Element of the Multisectoral Structure.— Lenin emphasised that the main point in studying the genesis of capitalism was to find out where and how precisely it originated.[22] That is why in considering the pre-capitalist sectors of India, one should give thought to the kind of system of social relations they constituted.

According to Marx, even in the middle of the 19th century the eroding influence of the British commerce in India and China was countered by the internal stability and system of pre-capitalist national modes of production.[23] This proves the groundlessness of the assertions that Marx had absolute and unconditional preferences for the "Asiatic", feudal or any other single mode of production in India. Marx clearly formulated his understanding of the Indian socio-economic system as a multistructural one, which, of course, does not dispense with the problem of the emergence within it of a dominant, formation-moulding structure.

Similarly, those who study economically lagging countries in the modern and contemporary period should apply Lenin's methodological approach primarily to an analysis of capitalism as an element of multisectoral society. That is the only approach that helps to avoid the methodological error of studying capitalist sectors in the countries of the East as such, outside the context of their interaction with other sectors, something that inevitably results in a hyperbolisation of capitalist relations. The first thing that needs to be established is the nature of the interaction between the capitalist sector and the other sectors, beginning with the pre-capitalist sectors and the individual pockets of capitalism. Among the questions that need to be considered are these: did these pockets initially emerge in the course of a redistribution of feudal rent? Was it perhaps the receiver of rent, for whom luxuries and weapons were fashioned, that was the first consumer of the products of the emergent pockets of capitalist production?

Nor is it possible to avoid considering these questions: where were the capitalistically produced commodities exported to, and who were their consumers on the external markets? Apparently, even with the foreign-trade orientation it was the feudal lord, even if a foreign feudal lord, that was the chief consumer of such commodities. It is equally important to establish when capitalist production of consumer goods for the agricultural population was started on the basis of independent commodity-money relations with it, while the receiver of rent was eliminated as the intermediary between town and country. In India, such relations were not fully developed for a long time.

Then there arises the problem of the growth and extension of the ties between capitalist production, on the one hand, and reproduction in the other sectors, the peasant economy in the first place, on the other. Where, for instance, were the farming implements made? Without an answer to this question it is impossible to tackle the problem of nation-wide extended reproduction on a capitalist basis, specifically the technical reconstruction of agriculture. The second line of relations between the capitalist and the pre-capitalist sectors runs through the sphere of accumulation, which at the early stage of capitalism appears as a key problem of the emergent capitalist sector. Accumulation in the petty-capitalist and the manufactory industry through direct exchange with the peasant economy is possible only at a stage when capitalist production in industry is already ahead of agriculture in productivity. At this stage there already appears the problem of non-equivalent exchange, which is frequently regarded as being exclusively an aspect of external economic relations, whereas it must have originated as a problem of exchange between the sectors with different levels of labour productivity, as a contradiction between classes within the nation. The relationship between economic and extra-economic methods of accumulation as capitalism originates is of especial interest in the study of colonial and present-day countries in Africa and Asia, because it is not at all a matter of indifference for their labouring masses whether the capitalist way can provide other and more progressive and democratic methods of accumulating capital for industrialisation than taxes (for instance, free commercial commodity exchange).

That is probably the most concise enumeration of the questions of the genesis of capitalism, whose study involves perhaps most obviously a link-up of past and present problems. This kind of approximation of the objectives of research calls for a coherent set of methods based on an analysis of comparable facts and information, although the historian is, of course, far from always capable of obtaining from the sources of the past the material of the same volume, quality and authenticity that is at the disposal of the economist and the sociologist, who operate with contemporary statistical data, sample surveys and personal observations.

Nevertheless, in this work I have tried to consider the phenomena I intend to study, above all the individual pockets of capitalist production, chiefly depending on how they interact with each other through the system of the social division of labour. Many authors have taken for their principal criterion of historical progressiveness the organisation and scale of production instead of its role in the social division of labour. Here, I have set myself the task of collecting the greatest possible number of illustrations for every type of production. I have sought above all to bring out the role of each type in the social division of labour through the relations of product and commodity exchange, because these relations reveal the scale, conditions and dynamics of the ties between the sectors within the framework of industrial production itself and within the whole socio-economic structure. Accordingly, I regard the main consequences of colonial exploitation, specifically the competition of foreign capital, to consist not so much in their influence on the sphere of circulation as in their impact on the processes of reproduction through a disruption and deformation of the traditional social division of labour.

My impression is that this approach has become or is becoming the predominant one among Soviet students of the genesis of capitalism, especially when determining the beginnings of the process. There is need for the greatest circumspection here also because the advocates of capitalism are inclined to discern its sources at the very dawn of civilisation. That is why Soviet historical science sets itself as the main task a study of the genesis of capitalism as a complex process, whenever it has emerged as such, instead of discovering the various pockets of capitalism.[24]

In this book, I have given no more than a partial and preliminary answer to these questions. A wide range of problems, such as India's place in the world capitalist market and in the world capitalist economy, have remained outside the framework of this book. That is why my subject-matter and allied problems will require further sustained efforts by many students.

Of especial value in the study of this problem are Marx's ideas about the Indian village community, the redistribution of the agricultural product and the social division of labour in India. At one time it was suggested that the concrete material of research goes well beyond the framework outlined by Marx for these and other phenomena of India's socio-economic life. To this let me say the following: first, Marx's ideas about India did not remain static but were developed and specified (thus, he reviewed his evaluations of how fast British capital would establish control of the Indian market), and, second, Marx's propositions laid no claim to providing an exhaustive characteristic of India's socio-economic phenomena but merely brought out their specific features in the light of the general regularities of the historical process.

To see the truth of this, let us recall once again that in 1853 Marx characterised India's existing social system of particular features—the so-called village community system, "which gave to each of these small unions their independent organisation and distinct life.... Now, sickening as it must be to human feeling to witness those myriads of industrious patriarchal and inoffensive social organisations disorganised and dissolved into their units, thrown into a sea of woes, and their individual members losing at the same time their ancient form of civilisation and their hereditary means of subsistence, we must not forget that these idyllic village communities, inoffensive though they may appear, had always been the solid foundation of Oriental despotism, that they restrained the human mind within the smallest possible compass, making it the unresisting tool of superstition, enslaving it beneath traditional rules, depriving it of all grandeur and historical energies."[25]

Thus, according to Marx, from that traditional institution, the village community, emerges a whole beam of diverse and differently oriented but equally conserving impulses. Some, on the descendant, shaped the historically concrete individual who was deprived of creative potential; others, on the ascendant, propped up the macro-organism of the Oriental despotism. If we recall what Engels said about it being impossible for capitalist accumulation to occur under Oriental despotism, we shall have before us the starting complex approach of the founders of Marxism to the problem of stagnation and retardation in Asian society.

Translating Marx's passage from its medium, poetic in form and scientific in content, into the formalised propositions of present-day sociology, we obtain a model of a bilateral social structural organisation in which the aggregation of similar-type micro-structures (village communities) appears as a unity of elements underpinning the macro-system (Oriental despotism). The mechanism of this organisation operated through an interconnecting system of social division of labour within each micro-structure (agriculture—handicrafts) and on the scale of the macro-structure (through the withdrawal and redistribution of the rent-tax). The economic and social equilibrium of the system engendered stagnation, and this was subjectively expressed in the historical lack of initiative of human reason, its traditionalism and subservience to superstition.

Marx's general conception of the complex stability of Indian society's socio-economic structure is being steadily confirmed by evidence and substantiations shaping out into a system. There is no doubt that under national sovereignty this complex would have long since been broken up by that section of society which had come to realise the imperative need to move out of stagnation.

Survey of Sources and Studies on the Subject.—I have tried to give a critical analysis of the sources and studies when setting forth my views and interpreting the data in this book. In the Introduction, I shall confine myself to a short preliminary survey. There is no reason to complain, as is the custom, of a lack of sources. On the contrary, these are in abundance, which makes choice and systematisation all the more important. Given a fixed scheme for their selection and interpretation, one is actually in a position to provide fairly solid backing, with various evidence, of several ostensibly authentic versions of India's socio-economic development over the century under review.

One way of avoiding preconceived systematisations and interpretations of the sources is to carry out the most systematic analysis of every source that is initial in time and problem. That is why I have tried to avoid numerous references to sources which would appear to confirm this or that individual proposition. I have tried to extract authentic and—what is most important—complex and systematised information from one or several sources of similar origin and character. Hence my urge to set forth as fully as possible the whole complex of problems for a given region or period of time. It is true that I have not always succeeded in arriving at the desired complexity and comparability of the series in chronological order, something that is largely due to the differing quality of the sources.

In the first section of this book I have had to take for my information basis the various observations by European travellers, the materials of the East India Company and observations by its officials. This selection of sources has been largely forced upon me and is a vulnerable spot, for it implies the perception of India through the eyes of Europeans, whether it be wise old Frenchmen, like F. Bernier or J. Tavernier, whom Marx valued very highly, or F. Buchanan, B. Heyne, J. Grant, W. Chaplin and R. Orme, all of whom were schooled in the classical tradition of British political economy. The unwitting projection of their Indian observations onto the European standard of socio-economic structures has both its weak and strong aspects. Their approach to collecting and interpreting the data, while opening up possibilities for comparing the levels of India and Western Europe, also makes one reflect with especial circumspection about any possible gaps in their perception of various phenomena in India's life which were altogether incomparable with any processes in European history.

In addition, British researchers, especially those who were less connected with administrative duties, had a tendency in general to deny India's historical process all originality and ability for independent progress, and to present Indian society as a hopelessly retarded subject (rather, object) of world history, which had been long delayed at the early stages. This line was started by A. Dow (1768) and J. Mill (1817) and was continued, if not completed, outwardly with much evidence, by W. H. Moreland in his three monographs which were published from 1920 to 1923. Because the same level of West European capitalism was selected in advance as the indicator of progress, the level of feudalism achieved in India naturally appeared in the worst light.

That is why it is quite necessary for the sake of scientific objectivity to supplement British information and studies with information drawn from the works of Indian historians studying national archives. Unfortunately, the study of the national archives in India, to say nothing of participation in this effort by Soviet scientists, is still at the initial stage. But what has already been done by D. R. Gadgil, H. Sinha, I. Habib, N. K. Sinha, T. Raychaudhuri, B. Chandra, A. Guha, A. Tripathi and other Indian scientists in studying the archives has made it possible to present whole layers of the country's socioeconomic past in a totally different light. For the mid-19th century a study of the Indian press is becoming ever more important, since it gave its assessments of contemporary processes, even if the record is not always systematic.

A special group of sources consists of the discussions in Britain concerning her policies and interests in India. A large part of this material has been published in Blue Books, and this makes it possible to judge about the clash of opinion, say, between the supporters and the opponents of the East India Company. In the heat of the polemic, both sides frequently gave vent to some very bitter truths about the state of affairs in India.

There is an even greater need for a critical reappraisal of the relatively later official British surveys. Thus, while Buchanan did not feel any special guilt about the situation which took shape in Mysore or even in Bengal or Bihar in the early 19th century, W. W. Hunter, a pillar of British official information, tried very hard to ascribe the negative indicators of India's socio-economic life in the 1860s and 1870s to the phenomena inherent in its system, and the positive ones to beneficial intervention of the British rule. Accordingly, his subordinates who compiled "The Statistical Accounts of Bengal" produce some stereotype evidence on matters bearing on the problem.

Indeed, the type of the British official producing information itself tended to change. In place of the man who had sailed out to India not only for the purpose of making a fortune but also for investigating what was then largely terra incognita, came the bureaucratic official who was well aware of all the costs and even more of the benefits of the Indian Civil Service. This man no longer reflected on the economic features of the country or the district in his charge, but merely supplied the higher authority with the intormation required. He had either little or no politico-economic training. That is why, while statistical information did appear to be outwardly more perfect, it tended to exclude some key elements, especially those bearing on the sphere of reproduction and its conditions.

Furthermore, when compiling the gazetteer itself, its authors were aware that their information would be published (the early surveys were not intended for wide circulation) and would be the subject of discussion in India and elsewhere. However—and this is especially evident in the gazetteers of the Bombay Presidency—the participation of Indian officials was beginning to have an effect on the selection and interpretation of tax information, for apart from their wide knowledge, they tended to interpret the facts in a national light, and this was most pronounced when Indian officials were assigned to independent studies.

I do not at all imagine that this book marks the completion of my work on the economic history of India. A continuation of this work will require, among other things, an extension of the range of sources. Thus, no further study of social processes in the sphere of industrial life is possible without a deeper knowledge of India's population censuses. A study of India's economic ties with the rest of the world and her position in this sphere will entail consideration of a whole complex of new sources.

When substantiating my subject-matter, I have already tried to bring out the basic lines in the research by Soviet scientists who have dealt with the economic history of India in the recent period. Let me add that this study was initiated in the USSR by the prominent Orientalist I. M. Reusner in his work "Ocherki klassovoi borby v Indii" ("Essays on the Class Struggle in India"), which appeared in 1932 under the editorship of R. A. Ulyanovsky. Reusner's interpretation of some problems, like the relationship between the Indian bourgeoisie and the British Raj bears the mark of that period, but even then Reusner succeeded in providing some preliminary answers to a number of basic questions bearing on the genesis and development of capitalism in India (periodisation of this process, influx of British capital, its oppression of national enterprise). He stressed the connection between the movements of the accumulations of the propertied strata in India with the agrarian policies of the British, but gave only a cursory evaluation of the conditions of reproduction in agriculture and industry, and also of the economic ties between them.

It was a great achievement of A. M. Dyakov, a prominent Soviet student of India, that he brought to the fore the national-regional principle in the study of the subcontinent, including its economic life. While he himself did not give any detailed analysis of the economic structures of the individual regions, the method he suggested has proved to be fruitful, because it has turned the attention of researchers to a study of objects which were regionally limited, and for that reason allowed preliminary generalisation.

Virtually every one of the problems I have tackled was variously considered in Indian scientific writings in the late 19th and the early half of the 20th century, but, regrettably, the inter-connections between the individual phenomena and processes of economic life were studied in accordance with the most mediated, "short-cut" lines. Thus, causal ties like land-taxation—decline of the peasant economy, British competition —ruin of the handicrafts—growing pressure on the land, the drain of colonial tribute—disruption of internal accumulation, etc., were established and described long ago.

In the period under review, Indian students of economic history did not set up any special national school. Their theoretical views are marked by an eclectic mixture of various trends in bourgeois political economy. B. Chandra's studies confirm the evolution of Indian nationalist leaders from purely bourgeois attitudes, accepting the free-trade view of industrialisation, to a more complexified view of it as a contradictory interaction of various spheres and sectors of production—ranging from the rural handicrafts to modern heavy industry. In the recent period, this approach was supplemented by the state-capitalism conception and even by some elements of scientific planning.

The collapse of illusions about the beneficial nature of the free-trade doctrine for a dependent society with a lagging economy induced Indian economists to carry out a critical reappraisal of their evaluations of British classical political economy, especially that part of it which advanced the doctrine. The theoretical crisis which Indian economists were in a way going though from the early 20th century was due to the fact that, having abandoned the classical political economy, they were unable to find—through their own efforts or by borrowing—an economic theory suitable for their changing political views. B. Chandra says: "In spite of the use of adjectives like 'Indian' and 'national' before their economic thought, the Indian nationalist economists did not discover any new economic laws which would arise out of, and be applicable only to, the specific and peculiar conditions of India.... It might almost be said that Indian Political Economy was more an attitude of mind, an approach towards Indian economic problems, and a method of economic reasoning than a system of economic thought." [26]

In the early 20th century, leading Indian economists favoured the capitalist way of development. But while remaining ideologists of the middle class, they tended to outstrip the political ideology of that class in their conclusions and recommendations, and this was especially true of the ideological evolution and political position of D. Naoroji and B. G. Tilak, who sincerely sought to give expression to their people's national needs and aspirations. That is why, by the early 20th century, both came to repudiate British rule, even if they did this in different ways and forms. Naoroji "the Grand Old Man of India", who started out by calling British rule in India "un-British", ended in 1905 by issuing a call "to evolve the required revolution—whether it would be peaceful or violent. The character of the revolution will depend upon the wisdom or unwisdom of the British government and action of the British people."[27] Meanwhile, other national leaders and ideologists in India were evolving towards a compromise with "economic imperialism".

In formal terms, the approach of Naoroji, Tilak, R. Dutt and other economists and politicians at the turn of the century appeared to be a defence of India's overall position against the British Raj, but the fact that the aspects of British policy which they criticised were selective showed that their starting-point was a limited class conception. Thus, Naoroji selected as his main subject-matter an analysis of the drain of India's national resources through external-trade channels, Tilak attacked the foreign competition which tended to ruin national small-scale production, while Dutt criticised the excesses of the British administration in its land-tax policies.

Subsequent Indian studies of economic history deal with either separate regions or industries and are, as a rule, descriptive. In regional terms, most studies related to Bengal (especially in the 18th century) and, in sectoral terms, to the local credit system. Among the works dealing directly with my own subject-matter there is the book by D. R. Gadgil on India's industrial evolution in the modern period, even if it is cursory and descriptive.

I have made use of many other studies by Indian scientists on India's economy in the modern period. Unfortunately, some of them simply do not fit into my system of data collection, because they treat India in the most general terms. For instance, a very interesting work by Radhakamal Mukerji, "The Foundations of Indian Economy", does not apply to any definite region or period (although it clearly deals with Bengal in the early 20th century), a fact which makes it less valuable both as an immediate testament and as a piece of research. That is why I have preferred works in which the place and time of the study are clearly delineated, like the book by A. S. Raju on the economic condition of the Bombay Presidency in the first half of the 19th century.

In the recent period, there have appeared studies in which there is, under direct or indirect influence of Marxist methodology, a gradual adoption of the analytical approach to the history of India's industrial development as a complex of socio-economic phenomena. But this line has yet to produce major monographic studies and is, for the time being, confined to relatively short works, articles and papers. Outstanding among this group of studies are the works of D. R. Gadgil on the formation of the Indian bourgeoisie, of I. Habib on the potentialities of the genesis of capitalism in Mogul India, of S. Chandra on the reasons for which India was unprepared for the Industrial Revolution in the 18th century (rather, for transition to the manufactory stage of production), and of A. Guha on a similar situation in the early half of the 19th century.

In 1963, the US historian Morris D. Morris published an article urging a reinterpretation of India's economic history in the 19th century.[28] I. Habib said this was an effort to defend imperialism, while T. Raychaudhuri, Bipan Chandrà and the Japanese scientist Toru Matsui persented a series of wellargumented articles refuting most of Morris' contentions.[29] This is only one example of the ideological clashes over the question being considered.

Of course, the concrete range of problems being discussed tends to change with the stage of India's historical development. Among the Problems for the period of per-British India are not only the existence of pockets of capitalism, but also—and perhaps to an even greater extent—agrarian relations and the level of agricultural productivity. For the colonial period, the most important probelm continues to be the establishment of the potential, latent in the different variants of capitalist development. For independent India, the alternative way of socio-economic development that is different from a capitalism tends to gain in strength inexorably. But however that may be, this always implies independent historical creativity by the peoples of India, whether the researcher considers their past, present or future.

NOTES

1. An enlarged edition of this book was published in English: V.I. Pavlov, The Indian Capitalist Class. A Historical Study, Bombay, 1964.
2. See: V. I. Pavlov, *Economic Freedom Versus Imperialism*, New Delhi, 1963, p. 239; *"Asia and Africa: Fundamental Changes"*. Editors: V. 1. Pavlov, I. B. Redko, R. A. Ulyanovsky, Moscow, 1972, pp. 244-263; R. Ulyanovsky, V. Pavlov, *Asian Dilemma: A Soviet View and Myrdal's Concept*, Moscow, 1973, pp. 152-169.
3. For more detail, see: *"Asia and Africa: Fundamental Changes"*, pp. 124-128; V. Pavlov, V. Rastyannikov, G. Shirokov, *India: Social and Economic Development (18th-20th Centuries)*, Moscow, 1975, pp. 227-237.
4. V.L . Lenin, *Collected Works*, vol. 1, Moscow, 1963, p. 136.
5. K. Marx, F. Engels, *Selected Correspondence*, Moscow, 1956, p. 564.
6. K. Marx, F. Engels, *Selected Correspondence*, p. 563.
7. V.L. Lenin, *Collected Works*, vol. 3, 1964, p. 311.
8. K. Marx, *Capital*, vol. I, Moscow, 1965, p. 581.
9. *Ibid.*
10. *Ibid.*, p. 597.
11. K. Marx, *Capital*, vol. III, 1966, p. 792.

12. *Ibid.* p. 883.
13. *Ibid.*
14. K. Marx and F. Engels, *Selected Correspondence*, p. 496.
15. K. Marx, *Capital*, vol. III, p. 328.
16. *Ibid.*, pp. 330-331.
17. K. Marx, F. Engels, *Sochineniya* (2nd ed.), vol. 1, Moscow, 1955, p. 579.
18. K. Marx, *Capital*, vol. I, p. 77
19. *Ibid.*, p. 76.
20. See *ibid.*, p. 77.
21. V. L. Lenin, *Collected Works*, vol. 21, 1973, p. 45.
22. V. L. Lenin, *Collected Works*, vol. 3, p. 382.
23. See K. Marx, *Capital*, vol. III, p. 333.
24. See: "Teoreticheskiye i istoriograficheskiye problemy genezisa kapitalizma" (Proceedings of the scientific conference held in Moscow, May 11 to 13, 1966), Moscow, 1969.
25. K. Marx, F. Engels, *On Colonialism*, Moscow, 1963, pp. 27-28, 29.
26. Bipan Chandra, The Rise and Growth of Economic Nationalism in India. *Economic Policies of Indian National Leadership*, 1880-1905, New Delhi, 1966, p. 733.
27. Quoted from: R. P. Masani, *Dadabhai Naoroji: The Grand Old Man of India*, London, 1939, p. 441.
28. Morris D. Morris, "Towards a Reinterpretation of Nineteenth-Century Indian Economic History," *Journal of Economic History*, vol. XXIII, No. I, December 1963.
29. Toru Matsui, On the Nineteenth-Century Indian Economic History—A Review of a "Reinterpretation", *The Indian Economic and Social History Review* (further referred to as "IESHR"), vol. V, No. 1, March 1968, Bipan Chandra, *Reinterpretation of Nineteenth-Century Indian Economic History, ibid.*; T. Raychaudhuri, *A Reinterpretation of Nineteenth Century Indian Economic History?*, *ibid.*

SECTION ONE

INDIAN HANDICRAFTS AND TRADE BEFORE THE FALL OF MOGUL DESPOTISM

Production and Redistribution of the Agricultural Product in Feudal India

The mechanism for the extraction and redistribution of the land product, which in Indian traditional society constituted the bulk of the national product, had a decisive influence on the scale and conditions of exchange of products between agriculture and the handicrafts in India. On the specific features of this mechanism depended the balance between direct exchange of products between the handicrafts and farming (in natural or commodity form) and the exchange which was mediated by the redistribution of the agricultural product extracted from the cultivator through market channels. This complex of connections and interactions could be the subject of a special study. In this section, I intend to confine myself to a preliminary consideration of the problem on the basis of my study of various sources, mainly on North India. In terms of time, these bear on the decades immediately preceding the British conquest, which is why this will not be a study of the long-term social division of labour, but an attempt to determine the level it had reached by the said period.

A study of India's agrarian system is extremely complicated by the multiplicity of forms of land-holding and regional differences in the socio-economic level. That is why I shall note here only the general features which determined the three key elements of the socio-economic structure of agricultural production in India: the state property in land and some irrigation projects, the property of individual land-owners which either coexisted with state property or emerged under its sponsorship, and, finally, the highly heterogeneous forms of land-ownership and land-holding within the framework of the rural community or other micro-local units.

State property in land was the economic basis of India's last Oriental despotism of the Great Moguls. The product extracted from the holders of land on the strength of this property right took the form of rent-tax. The concentration by the state of vast material values, received in the form of rent-tax, was the chief material condition for the existence of this powerful centralised despotism. There is need for a special study of the formation characteristic of this complex super-structural organism to bring out, alongside the undoubted feudal components, also tribal and slave-holding relicts, and to establish their proportions and functional load in the state and other activity of the despotism. I shall here confine myself to some brief considerations concerning the production and redistribution of the aggregate product on the scale of the subcontinent, the agricultural product in the first place.

From the 13th to the 17th centuries, there must have been periods when the Delhi Sultanate, and then the State of the Great Moguls, ranked very high among the states of the world in the amount of tax revenue. Under the Moguls, the maximum appears to have been reached under the rule of Aurangzeb, when the declared amount of the land-tax was estimated at 332-387 million rupees, while about 60 per cent of this amount (up to 200 million rupees) was, in effect, collected.[1] According to the data obtained from the chronicles and decrees of that period, the land-tax fluctuated between one-third and one-half of the gross harvest.[2] However, these data require further analysis. On the one hand, the actual share of the land-tax was lower, because it was hard to determine the whole product of the taxed units (including the product from animal breeding, subsidiary crops and wild plants), and to take account of all the lands tilled, especially those newly tilled. Besides, among the official exemption from the tax were the padishah's grants to the priests, temples and mosques, and also lands subject to taxation but, in effect, exempted from it by local chiefs. On the other hand, apart from the land-tax, the state received from the holders other types of rent in kind, cash and labour, and also all manner of additional taxes, services, offerings, gifts and levies, which amounted to down-right plunder by the powers that be. That is why the total drain from the cultivators was, at any rate, not less than one-third to one-half of their total product.

Let us note that the prescriptions of the Sharia which said that no more than one-tenth of the crop from the lands of the Muslims was to be collected in the form of tax gave way to the prevailing land-tax rates in India and were, with several exceptions, abolished.[3] The successive waves of Afghan, Turkic, Mogul and Iranian conquerors were attracted to India not only by the prospect of making an easy sweep of her treasures. The surplus-product which their top sections extracted from Indian agriculture was many times greater than the material goods they could discover in the valleys of Afghanistan, and the deserts and relatively small oases of Central Asia. It is quite another matter that for this vast fund of articles of consumption and their own natural reproduction the conquerors had to pay the price of ethnic and social assimilation by the conquered.

To obtain a true picture of the rate at which the agricultural product was being extracted, one should start not so much from the decrees on state taxation as from the actual deductions from the tax-payers' crop. Some early information on the distribution of the product of various agricultural crops is contained in a survey by Benjamin Heyne of South India in the first decade of the 19th century. Thus, one khandi of raggi, a millet crop, grown on unirrigated lands in the kasba, of Darmaporam (Mysore), was allocated among the following persons[4] (in tums, equal to 1/20 of a khandi; it has proved impossible to establish the value of the local khandi; in the British period, the standard Bombay khandi was equal to 20 maunds, each of 80 English pounds, that is, 36.2 kg × 20 = 724 kg):

Sirkar	7
Sirkar's guards	1
Local guards	1
"Pariah" tilling the field	1 1/4
Sirkar's servants (including artisans)	1/2
Brahmans	3/8
Shanbog (account-keeper)	3/8
Gauda (chief rayat, i. e. elder)	1/8
Lingayat priest	3/16
Total deductions	12

Thus, the rayat was left 8 tums; consequently, the tax (the sirkar's share) took up 35 per cent of the crop, the share of the administration and the guards 12.5, the priests over 2.5, the servants (non-farming) and artisans 2.5 per cent. Altogether, the share of the toiling element of the village (the rayat himself, the "pariah", the servants and artisans) was about one-half of the product.

On black soils, one khandi of raggi and $8\frac{1}{4}$ tums of anuta, a subsidiary crop, were allocated as follows (in tums): [5]

Sirkar	10
"Village pariah"	1½
Village servants	1
Sirkar's servants	¾
Rayat	15
Total	28¼

In this case we do not find the share of the village administration and the priests, which is apparently due to the low productivity and low consumer quality of these crops, to which the village elite did not lay any claim. But on the lands watered from tanks one khandi of paddy rice was allocated as follows (in tums):[6]

Sirkar	10
"Village head"	¼
Shanbog	¼
Guard	¼
"Village pariahs"	¼
Barber	⅛
Carpenter	⅛
Temple and Brahmans	⅜
Sirkar's servants and guards	⅜
Rayat	8
Total	20

We find that where the fertility of the soil was higher because of irrigation, and the crop a more intensive one (rice), the share of the toiling sections of the village was reduced to 42.5 per cent of the product, while that of the administrativecoercive and ideological apparatus was increased accordingly. This tendency was also evident in other areas, but it should not be seen as operating everywhere.

Heyne shows the structure of the costs and deductions in the growing of cane (addachu) on a rather indefinite area on which one tum of seeds was sown. The total deductions and costs of fieldwork and preparation of juice for boiling came to 43 pagodas 7 fanams (10 fanams equal 1 pagoda), of which 10 pagodas went to the sirkar, 3 for religious services, 12 for the purchase of seeds, 1 pagoda 6 fanams to the carpenter, 3.5 pagodas for the sugar mill and fuel, and the rest (almost 15 pagodas) for various agricultural operations and carriage of heavy burdens (fertilisers and the cane itself). Another three maunds of the ready product went to the men who boiled the sugar (1/2 maund to the owner, as much to the carpenter, and for the boiler, a quarter to the master, and the rest to the boilermen). But here we find the retention of the system of internal community remuneration, because as much—three maunds—went to the elder, the account-keeper, the guard, the tanner, and to the "pariahs" who saw to the watering of the field (1/2 maund each), the potter and the barber (1/4 maund each).

The said 6 maunds of sugar were valued at three pagodas (at half a pagoda per maund) and this brought the total costs of producing the sugar to 50 pagodas 7 fanams. Considering that the total quantity of the sugar produced came to only 100 maunds, the results of the production would have even entailed a loss for the rayat, but for two factors: first, the seed was reproduced (12 pagodas), and, second, some of the agricultural operations were performed by the rayat himself and members of his family with the use of their own implements and draught animals.[7] At the same time, there is some doubt about the fixed character of the amount going to the sirkar. Other sources indicate that the switch to more intensive crops was accompanied by a formal increase in the rent payments or their actual increase by means of new levies and offerings to the landlord and his officials.

Finally, if we consider the share of the costs in the price of the relatively intensive production of sugar, the actual subjectmatter of this enquiry, these were on the whole represented by the following items: carpenter—1 pagoda $8\frac{1}{2}$ famous, owner of the mill—1 pagoda, owner of the boiler (who appears to be the same person)—1 pagoda $7\frac{1}{2}$ fanams, potter—$3\frac{3}{4}$ fanams, tanner—$2\frac{1}{2}$ fanams, that is, a total of 5 pagodas $2\frac{1}{4}$ fanams. Even if to this we add the remuneration in kind for the master and the boiler-men—$6\frac{1}{4}$ fanams (in cash terms), the total costs of production will not be in excess of 5 pagodas $8\frac{1}{2}$ fanams, that is, just over $\frac{1}{10}$ of the total value of the product, about one-third of its agricultural component and $\frac{2}{5}$ of the deductions in favour of the land-owner, the priests and officials. Consequently, the higher intensity of farming did not introduce any fundamental changes in the structure of the production costs of the agricultural product and, accordingly, in the scale of the production demand in the Indian countryside (to say nothing of the share of the individual groups in the surplus-product of farming.

Summing up his observations on the distribution of the agricultural product in Mysore, Heyne observed that quit-rent prevailed in the "highlands", and share-cropping in the low-lands or rice lands, with the share depending on how convenient the plot was for irrigation. Nominally, in most regions of Mysore the holder of the land received one-half of the product, but had only one-third left after fulfilling his obligations to the sirkar's servants in the village. That is why, Heyne remarked, the rayat was reluctant to till the sirkar's lands, but was eager to till the inams—the tax-free plots of the Brahmans. Here, he received his one-half of the crop without any deductions. This shows, by the way, that the extension of inam plots tended to upset the traditional system of remuneration in kind and deductions.

However, the deductions from the rayat's crop were not confined to the traditional payments and remunerations. The payments to the sirkar were divided into four parts (kists), of which only the last was paid by harvesting time. That is why the rayat usually applied to the usurer for loans, the interests on which came to 18 per cent of the rent, or an average of 9 per cent of the value of the crop. Thus, the rayat retained only a quarter of the fruits of his labour.

The rate of product-deduction among land-holders in Gujarat was just as high. In the early 1820s, there was the following system of dividing the agricultural system in the Gujarat villages belonging to the chief of the district: from a maund of rice of 40 pounds 1 pound went to the chief, $\frac{1}{4}$ to the weigher, 1 to the guard, $\frac{1}{2}$ to the courier, and $\frac{1}{2}$ to the village establishment. In addition, every cultivator gave away from his total crop: to the elder—5 pounds, to the temple— 20, to the Muslim divines—10, to the manager's cook—10, and to cover the chief's travelling expenses—5 pounds. After all these shares were paid, one-half of the remainder went to the chief, the landowner. Thus, 7 per cent of the crop went into services, and 48 per cent to the land-owner, so that the land-holder kept 45 per cent of the rice crop.[8] This share is duly reduced when the usurer's deductions are taken into account.

I shall subsequently return to the natural and production reasons for the high surplus-product rate in India's farming. For the time being, I shall confine myself to some general propositions, in particular, the very fruitful idea which I. M. Reusner expressed: "The balance between the necessary product, which went to reproduce the labour-power of the peasant, his family and his holding, and the surplus-product extracted by the feudal lords, was more favourable here for the exploiters than in the natural geographical environment of a temperate climate. There is no doubt at all that the higher rate of feudal exploitation was an additional source of strength and power for the feudal lords over the peasants (and the emergent bourgeois elements), a fact which helped to maintain the feudal exploitation and hampered the transition to relations of a capitalist order, a fact which fuelled the tendency to stagnation in the feudal societies of the East."[9]

When returning to this idea of Reusner's, one must, apparently, also specify one's attitude to the natural geographical environment as a factor underlying historical development. This problem has yet to be solved because it calls for deeper research involving a comparison of data on the most stable formation entities in similar natural geographic conditions. On the strength of India's material, I shall allow myself to make only two assumptions: first, the natural geographical environment tends to accelerate or, conversely, to slow down historical progress not in general but depending on the attainment by the population of a definite level of development which, in fact, produces this or that effect, as a response to that environment; second, the dynamic or, conversely, stagnant nature of this effect depends on the capability of the existing socio-economic structure to maintain its basic proportions in the given natural geographical environment under the given level of the productive forces. That is why in some natural geographical environments some local populations go through (or even by-pass) some stages of historical development at a relatively rapid pace, but then tend to slow down at other stages, which become, in a manner of speaking, inherent, adequate to the population, its environment and the given region. Besides, the volume of the surplus-product which the mode of production and distribution that has been achieved yields to the ruling classes under the given natural conditions tends to exert a vast influence on the stability of the whole structure.

I Habib points out the high surplus-product rate in Mogul India. He polemicises with the widespread notions in the West (notably, assertions by Morris D. Morris) that the per capita product in India was much too small to allow the formation of a surplus-product and capitalist accumulation on its basis. Habib says that, according to official sources, the area of cultivated land along the middle reaches of the Ganges and in Central India in the 17th century was only one-half of the area in the early 20th century. This shows that there was the possibility of cultivating the more fertile and higher-yield plots and setting aside vast areas of wasteland and meadows for the grazing of cattle. That is why, incidentally, the per capita animal husbandry product and the per capita draught cattle were higher than in the British period. But the most important thing was that the rayat holdings were close to optimal in area, and the higher quality of cultivated land made it possible to harvest two crops more frequently.

The Indian scientist believes that Prof. Morris takes a onesided view when he speaks about the low-crop yields of traditional Indian farming, and is quite right in pointing to the relatively high product per producer (which is not below the medieval European level); he insists that, for instance, the input of wheat seeds per crop-unit in Mogul India was not higher than it was in Western Europe in the corresponding period.[10]

But, Habib continues, the level of production is not the only indicator of the scale of the surplus-product. The formation of the latter is also influenced by the volume of the means of subsistence, which is smaller in tropical and subtropical countries than it is in countries with a more severe climate. Indeed, even in India it was lower in the southern part. That is why accumulation is determined not only by the level of agricultural production but also by the mode of appropriation and final redistribution of the surplus-product of agricultural.[11]

But the potential for accumulation does not yet signify that it was realised the capitalist way. I think that in Indian society by the middle of the 17th century the imperative for a formation leap into capitalism had not yet matured. The relatively high and absolutely vast scale of the rent appropriated and used by the ruling classes of India and the sections they maintained helped to keep stable and somewhat stagnant its socio-economic structure, which rested on an unusually large population feeding on the agricultural surplus-product. At the same time, the predominantly extensive, subsistence economy and the embryonic nature of the purely economic interaction and general economic interests of the rent-consuming classes and sections impeded the formation of a socially homogeneous apparatus of administration, ideology and coercion (however heterogeneous in the vertical, proprietary plane) capable of ensuring external security and internal political stability on the scale of the state of India as a whole.

Let us note that for centuries the Hindu ruling classes were incapable of setting up such a state (even if only on a part of the subcontinent's territory). This function was fulfilled by the Muslim conquerors, who brought with them their own system of social bonds and group interests. In the early period after the conquest, this existed side by side with the Hindu system, thereby ensuring political centralisation, but without an adequate socio-economic structure it gradually came to be swallowed up by the Hindu system of social bonds, that were centrifugal on a local scale and centripetal on the scale of the country as a whole. That is why there were two tendencies in medieval India which outwardly appeared to be different but were, in effect, interconnected: the stability of the socio-economic micro-system, and the instability of India's contralised macro-system, which tended to delay the formation of new social relations.

In certain historical conditions, chiefly in the early Middle Ages, the state form of property in the East constituted the economic basis for relative state centralisation, having a progressive role to play by resisting external invasions, domestic anarchy and internecine strife and promoting urbanisation. At the same time, the embryonic forms of private property in land were a serious obstacle blocking the emergence of new, more mature relations within the framework of feudal society.

Marx stressed that the historical inevitability of capitalist development in the specific form which is described in Volume One of his "Capital" was confined to the countries of Western Europe, so that wherever there was no transformation of one form of private property into another, as was the case in Western Europe, wherever, for instance, common property in the means of production prevailed in agriculture, the process of socio-economic development, he believed, could be different from the one in Western Europe,[12] and in effect had its own specific features. The dialectics of historical development consists, in particular, in the fact that at a certain stage state property in land in India began to slow down the deepening of the social division of labour and the consolidation of the elements of independent enterprise among the urban population, that is, further economic progress of society as a whole.

In the heyday of the Mogul Empire, the sovereignty of this powerful centralised despotism was expressed in state landed property most forcibly, even though private landed estates were still there. But as the Mogul Empire began to fall apart there was a highly indicative change in land relations. State property in land and water, up to then more or less a reflection of actual social relations, was increasingly alienated by individual chiefs, holders of jagir estates and the rural elite. There seems to be no doubt that the political decentralisation of the Mogul Empire and its disintegration were caused by social processes within Indian society, which had already worked out its potential for feudal development on the basis of state forms of landed property. What was a tragedy for the whole country is that at this period of inevitable feudal fragmentation came the intrusion of the

West European powers, which determined India's further development for a long time, but along the colonial path.

The class of rent-receivers in Mogul India may be divided into three main groups: the Mogul, mainly Muslim elite, with the biggest holdings (jagirs); the big and middle, mainly Hindu, land-owners, who largely retained their hereditary right to their lands; and the influential land-holders who had added to their official land plots various waste-lands and allotments of community members. The relations between these groups, and these groups and the central authority, were complicated Studies of India show that alongside the holding of land in fee (the predominant form of feudal land-tenure) private property in land was always maintained in Mogul India, that is, the Moguls had in effect been unable to convert all the land of the Empire into the full property of the state.

The contradiction between state property in land, on the one hand, and the land-holdings and land-cultivation of individual rent-receivers became one of the chief contradictions of Mogul society in the period of its disintegration. So long as the Mogul Empire carried on successful wars and spread its power to more and more areas of India, the feudal lords doing service to the Moguls received more and more land in fee in the newly conquered areas. That is why on the whole they were reconciled to the fact that a sizable part of the rent they collected had to go to the Treasury in the form of tax. But in the second half of the 17th century, when the Mogul Empire had almost everywhere (except in the South) reached India's natural boundaries, the Mogul èlite was no longer able to increase its revenues in the old way, by conquering new areas and incorporating them in the Empire. From then on, the Mogul rulers were able to increase their revenues only by intesifying the exploitation of the peasants and by modifying the principles on which the rent was distributed between the state and the individual feudal lords.

The attempts to increase the absolute volume of rent were resisted by the élite of the village communities and the land- holders (rayats) socially akin to them. The most powerful and organised movement was that of the Sikhs in the Punjab, where, supported by the urban artisans and merchants, it First undermined and then—in the second half of the 18th century—abolished Mogul rule in this very rich province. The Sikh uprising and other similar movements sounded a terrible warning to the upper sections of the rent-receivers, thus forcing them to cast about for other ways of increasing their revenues to supplement the more intense exploitation of the peasantry. Thus, the feudal lords, especially in the remoter areas, sought to increase their share of the total rent by cutting down on the state rent-tax. This struggle for a larger share of the rent was one of the motive forces behind the separatist anti-Mogul movements, which were led by local chiefs.

Such action was usually led by the élite of the community. Feudal exploitation was frequently ruinous not only for the mass of the peasant population, but also for the community élite. However, this could not interrupt the process of its feudalisation, which was taking place through the impoverishment and partial deprivation of the bulk of the community members of their land. From the 16th to the first half of the 18th century, under growing feudal exploitation, the community élite ruined and oppressed by the feudal lords in some instances, itself acted as a fierce feudal exploiter of the peasantry in other instences.[13] One should note, apparently that apart from the exploitation of agricultural servants, the community élite, for instance, among the Marathas and Sikhs, also consolidated their positions as they escaped from Mogul despotism and then as they mounted their own campaigns into neighbouring regions.

On the whole, however, the Mogul land-tax system, to the extent that its principles were practised, put the lower and middle sections of the land-owners and military and administrative personnel in a relatively oppressed condition, and the élite in a privileged condition. I. Habib has estimated that after deductions in favour of rural and local officials, soldiers and all manner of rural rent-receivers, including intellectuals and idlers, one-quarter, one-third or even one-half of the net product was drained from the rural locality.[14]

An official of the East India Company said that under the last nawabs of Bengal the principles of despotic legislation appeared to be highly effective because it had been initially designed to remedy the ills of the corrupt system of middlemen, which was, apparently, inseparable from any government not relying on national recognition of social dignity. He went on to say that the representative of the central authority had considerable power with respect to all financial operations in which the ruler was involved in one way or another. Thus, during his rule the Viceroy (Jaffar Khan) made a vast personal fortune, something that lesser officials were unable to do.[15] But even the highest officials of the Mogul Empire were in a precarious position because of the uncertainties of war, the whims of the rulers and the conspiracies of their own subjects.

Depending on a number of factors, with religious membership of the majority of the population and the local social élite being highly important, separatist movements either resulted in a gradual separation of various areas, while nominally remaining vassal (for instance, the Bengal subah) or burst into armed uprisings (in Maharashtra). But in both instances there was a tendency for land officially held in fee to be converted into hereditary holdings. In the mid-18th century, the institution of state property in land even in Bengal was in a state of far-gone disintegration. From the rent-tax was deducted the rent appropriated by the feudal lord, with the share of the surplus-product going to the individual land-owners already tending to exceed that part of it which the state extracted in the form of tax. All of this meant that the landed property of individual rent-receivers was, in effect, being shaped at the expense of the landed property of the state.

Recently, historians have increasingly come to focus their attention on the social strata who opposed Mogul despotism. Thus, according to M. N. Pearson's report, Satish Chandra,[16] Ashin Das Gupta,[17] A. M. Shah,[18] B. S. Cohn[19] and others find new men from outside the mansabdari (rank-holding) system entering the political arenas of the smaller regional states and participating fully and influentially in decision-making; A. M. Shah, for instance, finds the Gaekwad's officials engaging in political activity with Desais and revenue contractors, while Das Gupta's article brings out the important role of merchants in Surat politics.[20]

In Maharashtra,where feudal relations in the 17th century were not as mature as they were in Bengal, the withering away of state property and the formation of private property passed through several stages. The victory of the liberation movement of the Marathas, headed by Sivaji Bhonsla, naturally led to the abolition of the Mogul Empire's property in land. However, the continued intense struggle against the Moguls required the establishment of a strong centralised state, and the material basis of such a state could be only the selfsame state property in the basic means of production—the land. That is why Sivaji set up a vast fund of state lands from the possessions of expelled or killed Mogul chiefs. The separatist uprisings of hereditary Maratha chiefs were ruthlessly suppressed. The feudal circles, on which Sivaji depended, consisted of the military and civilian élite, whose members received their maintenance from the Treasury, and the holders of military fiefs (saranjams).

Still, the middle and small feudal lords of Maharashtra enlarged their own land-holdings. The farming out by the state of rent-tax collection also tended to undermine state property in land. The tax-farmers usually consisted of small land-owners from among the Patels (heads of village communities). Thus, in Maharashtra, state property in land was also giving way to individual landed property.

In the state of Bhonsla, the land-tax also prevailed among the other revenues of the state. Unfortunately, we have no generalised data, but the data available on the individual districs, as rearranged after the British conquest, show that the land-tax came to 85-95 per cent of all the tax revenues. Let us note that among the other taxes more than one-half consisted of receipts from taxes on the trade in grain, cotton and confectionery (including gur), and the taxes on the trade in cloths—about one-tenth of all the other taxes.[21] It is true that other taxes were collected in the city of Nagpur (city customs). These came to 15-20 per cent of the land-tax, but roughly onehalf of these consisted of import, export (insignificant and transit duties, among which revenues from grain absolutely prevailed; the duties on handicraft goods were insignificant (chiefly exported cloths). The principal tax among the city customs was the tax on the sale of alcoholic drinks followed by a levy on the minting of coins, and these together yielded up to two-thirds of all the city customs. They were followed by the tax on houses, shops and other real estate (10-15 per cent of the revenues).[22]

In the historical perspective, the establishment of individual property in land in the countries of the East opened up the possibility for transforming early feudal property, above all the property of the élite in the communities (and through their economic activity) into mature feudal property. But the intervention of the British left its mark on the incipient processes in India's feudal society. The development of feudal relations went hand in hand with some deepening of the social division of labour. A substantial obstacle in medieval India to the development of the division of labour and trade between town and country was the preservation and peculiar organisation of village communities.

The division of labour established within the community led to the formation of the institution of community handicraftsmen specialised along definite lines to cater for the needs of community members. For this they received a part of the crop grown by community land-holders and also a small tax-free plot of land, or either of these types of remuneration. Thus, the intra-communal division of labour rested on a subsistence basis and determined the existence of the community as a self-sufficient entity in which production "is independent of that division of labour brought about, in Indian society, as a whole by means of the exchange of commodities."[23] The economic self-sufficiency of the Indian community ruled out the development of the manufactory stage of the division of labour in the sphere of community handicrafts.

Recent studies have shown that conceptions and institutions like "village", "community" or other rural micro-localisations resting on the basis of a natural interconnection of farming and handicrafts, tend to differ fairly widely territorially, structurally and functionally. Without questioning the importance of independent studies of institutional connections within the framework of the community and similar entities, let us note that of crucial importance for an understanding of the general model of social division of labour in India in terms of political economy is the relationship between the rural micro-localisation (which may assume the form of a community, but not necessarily) and the spheres of society whose functioning has already been mediated by the exchange of goods.

The development of trade between town and country was hampered not only by the economic self-sufficiency of the rural community, but also by the fact that a large part of the surplus-product of agriculture was alienated and extracted on a subsistence basis in the form of rent-tax. The economic relations between town and country were dominated by a one-sided influx of the agricultural product to the cities, this being extracted from the holder of the land by the state and also by individual land-owners. Marx wrote that in India surplus alone became a commodity, and a portion of even that, not until it has reached the state, "into whose hands from time immemorial a certain quantity of these products has found its way in the shape of rent in kind."[24]

An interesting guess concerning the role of rent-tax in the redistribution of the national product in feudal India was made by R. Orme at the end of the 18th century. He wrote: "The king, by being proprietor of the lands, sells to his subjects their subsistence, instead of receiving supplies from them. Hence a resource exceeding that of all the taxes, imposts and customs of other governments; but still a resource incapable of producing gold or silver without the assistance of commerce."[25] It was this, Orme believed, that made India's rulers provide the merchant with some personal and property immunity. But I must specify one essential point: the ruler was able to sell subsistence (or make this available in the form of a salary) not to all his subjects but only to the non-agricultural population, while the other subjects—the cultivators—were in effect engaged in producing this subsistence. Besides, by saying that the subsistence was sold, Orme had in view the archaic practice of realising the tax which arrived in kind, whereas in the 18th century the Treasury most frequently received it through the tax-farmers in the form of cash. But the intrusion of the tax farmers merely tended to modify the process, and did not deprive the rent-tax of its decisive role in the redistribution of the national product.

How then was the subsistence basis of alienation combined with the abundance and diversity of commodities, especially those designed for consumption, flowing through the channels of India's domestic and foreign trade, the scale of operations and the wealth of its merchants and bankers, and the feudal lords' extensive involvement in commerce and even usury? This naturally makes it necessary to clarify where this mass of commodities was produced and what the economic and social results of their consumption were. In other words, what needs to be clarified is the structure of the national product, the balance between its subsistence and commodity elements, and the ways and means used to redistribute them among the various classes and groups of the population. These are the phenomena and processes which ultimately determined the social structure of Indian society at its lower echelons and on the regional and all-national scale.

There is not enough information, especially statistical data, to provide the answers in the available sources of the feudal pre-British or even the early British period. At present, it seems possible merely to outline the approach to their study and draw what might be called the hypothetical contours suggested by the content of these sources. The lack of completeness and precision, and frequently their biased approach could produce a priori and other unreliable elements in research. To reduce such a possibility to a minimum, one should refuse to succumb to the temptation of explaining the mechanism of redistribution and commercialisation of the agricultural products in simple terms, and insist on regarding these processes as being complex and as occurring on something like different tiers of India's socio-economic structure.

Indeed, at first sight the introduction of a cash land-tax appears to be convincing evidence of commercialisation of the peasant farms. Fragmentary information about the levying of such a tax dates from the period of the Delhi Sultanate.[26] But, as K. Z. Ashrafyan has noted, "there is great doubt about the possibility of cash rent in pure form having existed in the Delhi Sultanate from the 12th to the 14th centuries, considering the relatively embryonic development of the process of separation of the handicrafts from agriculture, and the absence of an established internal market."[27] This view must apparently be accepted, quite apart from the author's inexact reference concerning the separation of the handicrafts from agriculture, which had on the whole been complete, although, as I intend to show later, a sizable sphere of natural links between them was preserved within the village community.

At the same time, it is not to be denied that from the mid16th century, following the reforms of Sher Shah and Akbar, the land-tax receipts came into the Treasury, especially the Central Treasury, mainly the cash. But that is where the difficulties begin for the researcher who is not satisfied with this general statement but seeks to clarify for himself at which stage and by whom the rent-tax was converted from tax in kind to cash tax. This operation could have been performed by the land-holder himself, by the merchant's and usurer's capital at its various points—from the rural usurer to the big banker, by the rent-receivers and by the tax administration apparatus (again ranging from the community heads to regional chiefs and even the highest rulers themselves).

All these sections of the population appear to have usually taken part in one way or another in realising product-rent on the market, but the share of each of the sections in the marketing of agricultural produce tended to change with time and from one locality to another. Because the seller of produce on the market tended to appropriate for himself at least some part of the surplus-product, connections with the market largely determined the place and functions of the given section or group within the system of the consumption of the national product. Thus, the researcher cannot take some single line and hope to arrive at a general solution of the problem.

It was natural for the fisc itself and the big feudal lords to secure control of the distribution and marketing of that part of the product mass which arrived in the form of rent-tax in kind. Such information can be gleaned from the chronicles according to which there was a practice in the Delhi Sultanate of storing up the grain coming in as tax, subsequently to be sold by the sultan or the higher nobility to the population at fixed prices. According to Barani, under Ala-ud-din, the tax (haraj) in the Doab was paid exclusively in the form of grain, which was stored in the sultan's granaries in Delhi and used to keep prices low, especially in crop-failure years. Under Ibrahim Lodi the emirs and maliks were forbidden to collect taxes in cash, and this forced them to sell the grain themselves at low prices.

But this direct and apparently simple way of realising the rent-tax obviously no longer accorded either with the extensive and complex requirements of the state and its upper sections, or the existing system of commodity movement. There is no direct indication that the Treasury had set up within the limits of the state or even of some large region its own and permanently operating system for marketing the product coming in as tax. Let us note that Ala-ud-din had to resort to the services of middlemen (karavaniyan), whose duty it was to deliver the grain to the capital. Such difficulties naturally made the Treasury more interested in cash receipts. Indeed, the reforms of Sher Shah and Akbar sprang from the need to obtain a cash equivalent of the tax, ideally when it came in from the tax-payer himself and, at any rate, when the tax was being transferred from the lower to the central echelons of the Treasury.

The direct levying of the land-tax in cash was made more difficult because the rural tax-payer—whether the cultivator or the small and middle feudal-type land-owner—operated a subsistence economy and because there was not enough local paid-up demand for food and raw materials in some areas. Let us also note that Shershah and Akbar, having laid down a tax in cash terms, went on to exempt many important areas from direct levying of tax in cash, and the measure was interpreted by the chroniclers as an easement for the tax-payer in accord with usage.[28]

Instead of accepting the popular reading of the term "rayat" as a "land-tax paying peasant", I have here deliberately proposed a broader interpretation of the term, so as to include in the "rayat" category land-owners who were either engaged in economic activity on a feudal basis with the prevalence of indentured labour from the rural lower echelons or, at any rate, belonged to the upper sections of the community and its administration. This naturally leads to some doubt about its being legitimate to use the term "peasantry" with reference to the Indian rural population. If this conception is based on the labour attitude to the land, that is, personal participation in agricultural production, the category will have to include sections as incomparable in social and proprietary status as the untouchables among the servants of the community, and its upper sections which (as in Maharashtra, for instance) took part in cultivating the soil. But these did not in any sense unite in a single class-estate, even if only on the basis of their relation to the land and the volume and grounds for their claim to the faults thereof.

With a number of reservations, the conception of "peasantry" may include only the tillers of the soil from among the upper castes who held the land as rayats. But the small numbers of this category of the rural population in India contradict the accepted European notion of "peasantry" as the land-tilling majority of the countryside.

The Maratha synonym of rayat—"malguzar"—in general means "he who pays tax", and this goes to emphasise the more extensive meaning of this conception.That is why on the strength of the mere mention by a source of tax-payment, whether in cash or kind, by a rayat or similar category of the population, it is impossible to establish, without additional material, which concrete type of population is meant by the term: an ordinary holder of land, a feudal-type land-owner, or a rural headman. There is even less ground to assert which of these was engaged in marketing the product in order to obtain the amount necessary to pay the tax.

Besides, the extract from the "Ain-i-Akbari" ("Akbar's Code") frequently quoted to confirm the payment of cash tax by the peasant himself should apparently be interpreted in very narrow terms. The extract says that each year's tax receipts were paid in parts over a period of eight months. The rayats themselves brought mohurs and rupees to the spot designated for the receipt of taxes, because here (in Bengal) there was no practice of dividing the grain between the Treasury and the husbandman; crops were always abundant, there was no insistence on exact measure, and the tax amount was determined by an estimate of the harvest. This shows that the tax was not fixed but was established annually depending on the harvest. This practice would run counter to the duty of each province to contribute a strictly fixed amount of land-tax. That is why T. R. Raychaudhuri is right when he says that the described practice of fixing and levying the tax could apply only to the lands of the khalisa, who was under direct control of the Treasury (the Indian scientist bases his statement on the fact that the rayat and the tax authorities were in direct relationship).[29]

Indeed, it is hard to imagine that the land-tax in Bengal was paid by the peasant himself, without the zamindar's services. Finally, the rayats in this instance could include only the heads who paid in the tax for the whole village, because individual peasants paid a tax amounting to less than a gold mohur.[30] I intend to show, on the strength of later material, that the "rayat" was a conception including very different sections of the community in Bengal. At any rate, the above-mentioned extract from the "Ani-i-Akbari" does not in any sense provide solid evidence that Bengal's agriculture in the late 16th century had enough connections with the market to enable the rank-and-file land-holder to pay tax in cash. Indeed, even much later—two centuries later—we shall find many intermediate links between them and the tax machine.

In Maharashtra the village head (patel) had an especially big role to play in extracting and appropriating the agricultural surplus-product. In the state of Bhonsla the patel's participation in collecting the tax not only helped him to bind the rayats as a usurer and alienate their land plots; he also had the right to receive one-quarter or one-sixth (some say 15 per cent) of the total land-tax coming in from the fiscal unit in his charge. It is true that in some instances the tax authorities of some princely states deprived the patels of this right or reduced their share. But the patels found loopholes to collect additional levies for themselves from the rayats.[31] Fiscal and usurious operations led to the concentration of large tracts of land in the hands of the patels, and this is evident from the fact that some of them had from 10 to 20 sets of implements (called "plough"). In contrast to other areas of Maharashtra, there were no watandars (that is, persons with tax-free lands) among the patels or among the rayats. That is why the patel nominally paid the same tax on his lands as ordinary land-holders, that is, from 4 to 16.5 rupees per "plough".[32] But the patel also had the right to keep a definite part of the tax receipts from his own lands.

The sources say nothing about the various items of the patel's enrichment: deductions from tax, income from his own farm, and usurer's interest. That is why it is hard to decide when the patel acted mainly as an agent of the tax machine, as a land-owner or as a usurer. But the patel was undoubtedly a leading figure in the economic life of the community both as a land-owner with a fairly large-scale holding of his own, and as a lender regulating the economic activity of ordinary cultivators by means of loans for seed and cattle. That is why the condition of the community artisans was directly (when they worked for him) or indirectly (when they worked for ordinary cultivators) and to a large degree dependent on the patel.

Regardless of the level at which the agricultural product was commercialised, the level of ultimate commercialisation of the product on the scale of society as a whole under Oriental despotisms could, in a sense, be inversely proportional to the commercialisation of peasant production itself, while the vast rent payments to some extent hampered independent commercial relations between town and country. "The export or sale of produce helped in paying the dues owed to the state or landlord by the agriculturist but did not usually give him resources in exchange with which he could buy significant quantities of the products of urban industry."[33] Even in the 18th and early 19th centuries land-holders usually paid their tax directly to the tax-farmer in kind or in cash borrowed from the usurer, to whom they then gave a part of their crop in Gujarat, Mysore and Rajasthan, that is, areas with relatively developed commodity-money reastions.[34] In either case, the land-holder had no need to go to the market or to become an independent commodity producer to pay the cash tax.

An interesting observation confirming that the land-tax (paid in cash) and the labourers' wages in the cities of Mogul India were actually based on the tax in kind, was made by I. Habib, who insisted that in the 17th century the "price revolution" also spread to India, because of the influx of valuables from Europe (via the Middle East and along the sea route round the Cape). Such a complex phenomenon undoubtedly requires special study (and this was started by Aziz Hasan), but it may well be assumed that the rise in prices in the 17th century, especially in its second half, was also influenced by the wars, which undermined the economy and disrupted the supply of important areas like Gujarat, Maharashtra and the Punjab.

But to return to the problem in hand, the most remarkable thing is that both the cash tax and apparently the payment of wages in the cities followed in the wake of rising prices, above all the prices of food-stuffs. The Mogul authorities, says Habib, engaged in the practice of simply increasing the amount of cash tax and also calculating it in kind (subsequently converting it into cash at market prices). The rates paid to wage-labourers increased accordingly (it is true that there is only one example: the monthly remuneration of an unskilled worker in Surat increased from 2.4 rupees in 1616 to 4 rupees in 1690-1693).[35] The sliding scales for tax and wages suggest, apart from everything else, that neither the upper sections of the village community which engaged in economic activity nor the entrepreneurial elements in the urban handicrafts could obtain any substantial benefits from the price revolution (as their counterparts in the West did).

Finally, there is need to draw attention to this still frequent confusion between two essentially different categories: the commodity nature (commercialisation, to be more precise) of the product, and the commodity nature of production itself. Considering the relatively high surplusproduct rate in Indian agriculture and its extraction through the land-tax and other rent payments, a sizable part of the agricultural product could be converted into commodities in the hands of the nominal rent-receiver or tax-farmer, without it being marketed directly by the owner of the product himself.

Whenever the land-tax was collected by tax-farmers and their agents, the usurer's interest paid by the agriculturist tended to approximate the rent-tax and in a sense appeared as its converted form (having a tendency to stand out on its own, something that was finally established in the British period). The commercialisation of the agricultural product through the channels of rent and usurer's interest worked against the comercialisation of production in agriculture, because it deprived the producer of that part of the surplus-product which he could have exchanged, after marketing, for purchased means of production and could have applied to extended reproduction.

NOTES

1. K. A. Antonova, *Ocherki obshchestvennykh otnosheniy i politicheskogo stroya Mogolskoi Indii vremyon Akbara* (1556-1605 gg.), Moscow, 1952, p. 63.
2. See: ibid., pp. 241-242; K. Z. Ashrafyan, *Agrarny stroi Severnoi Indii* (XII seredina XVIII v.), Moscow, 1965, pp. 257-260.
3. K. Z. Ashrafyan, *Agrarny stroi Severnoi Indii...*, pp. 247-248
4. B. Heyne, Tracts, *Historical and Statistical, on India, with Journals of Several Tours through Various Parts of the Peninsula,* London, 1814; p. 69.
5. *Ibid.*, p 69.
6. *Ibid.*, p. 70.
7. *Ibid.*, pp. 71-73.
8. *Gazetteer of the Bombay Presidency* (further referred to as *GBP*), vol. IV (Ahmedabad), Bombay, 1879, p. 167.
9. I. M. Reusner, K. voprosu ob otstavanii stran zarubezhnogo Vostoka *Voprosy istorii*, 1951, No. 6, p. 78.
10. I. Habib. Potentialities of Capitalist Development in the Economy of Mughal India. An Enquiry, *International Economic History Congress. Section 4. The Extent of Capitalistic Development Outside Europe'* [s.l. s.a. , pp. 3-5.
11. *Ibid.*
12. See: K. Marx and F. Engels, *Selected Works in Three Volumes*, vol. III, Moscow, 1973, pp. 152-161.
13. See: K. Z. Ashrafyan, *Agrarny stroi Severnoi Indii...*, p. 287.
14. I. H a b i b, *Potentialities...*, p. 11.
15. "The Fifth Report from the Select. Committee of the House of Commons on the Affairs of the East India Company. Dated 28th July, 1812, vol. II.

Extracted from a Political Survey of the British Dominions and Tributary Dependencies in India", by Mr. James Grant, April 27, 1786. Introduction and Bengal Appendices, Calcutta, 1917, p. 214.
16. Satish Chandra, *Parties and Politics at the Mughal Court*, Aligarh 1959.
17. Ashin Das Gupta, "The Crisis at Surat, 1730-32", *Bengal Past and Present*, 1967.
18. A. M. Shah, *"Political System in Eighteenth Century in Gujarat, Enquiry*, New Series, I, 1, 1964.
19. B. S. Cohn, "Political Svstems in Eighteenth Century India: the Banaras Region", *Journal of the AOS*, vol. 82, No. 3, 1962.
20. M. N. Pearson "Political Participation in Moghul India", *IESHR* vol. IX, No. 2, June 1972.
21. R. Jenkins, *Report on the Territories of the Raja of Nagpur*, 1827, Nagpur, 1901, pp. 87-93.
22. *Ibid.*, pp. 102-108.
23. K. Marx, *Capital*, vol. 1, p. 357
24. Ibid.
25. R. Orme, *Historical Fragments of the Moghul Empire, of the Maratoes*, London [1805], p. 413.
26. W.H. Moreland also assumed that before Ala-ud-din's reform the rent in the Doab was levied in cash (W. H. Moreland, The Agrarian System of Moslem India, Cambridge, 1929, p. 37).
27. See: K. Z. Ashrafyan, *Agrarny stroi Severnoi Indii...*, p. 261.
28. See: *ibid.*, pp. 261, 263-265.
29. T. Raychaudhuri, *Bengal under Akbar and Jahangir*, Calcutta, 1953, p. 24.
30. K. A. Antonova, *Angliyskoye zavoyevaniye Indii* v XVIII veke, Moscow, 1958, pp. 75-76.
31. R. Jenkins, *Report on the Territories...*, pp. 75, 79.
32. *Ibid.*, pp. 92-93.
33. D.R. Gadgil, *Origins of the Modern Indian Business Class*, New York, 1959, p. 5.
34. A. K. Forbes, Ras Mala, *Hindoo Annals of the Provinces of Goozerat in Western India*, vol. II, London, 1856, p. 247; F. Buchanan, *A Journey from Madras through the Countries of Mysore, Canara and Malabar ... for the Express Purpose of Investigating the State of Agriculture, Arts and Commerce, History ... in Dominions of the Raja of Mysore, London*, 1807, vol. I, p. 265; J. Tod, *Antiquities and Annals of Rajasthan*, vol. II, London, 1832, p. 282.
35. I. Habib, *Potentialities...*, pp. 66-67.

CHAPTER ONE

THE SOCIAL DIVISION OF LABOUR BETWEEN AGRICULTURE AND THE HANDICRAFTS

The Bonds between the Village Handicrafts and Agriculture

The volume of commodity-money relations in the Indian countryside was influenced by the fact that weaving and oil-making had dropped out of the system of community handicrafts (by the period here being considered, at any rate). But their separation from the system of community production of the means of consumption did not have a direct effect on the subsistence basis of reproduction in agriculture, that is, on the natural relations between farming and the handicrafts providing it with implements.

The main reason for the formation of a section of community artisans in India and also for a converse lack of development of handicrafts of the peasant family was the intensification of farming as expressed in the virtual round-the-year cycle of field- work.[1] At the same time, the withdrawal of farmers from these handicrafts applied to women to a lesser extent, for they continued to engage in spinning and similar other handicrafts ancillary to agriculture. On the strength of what F. Buchanan said (something I shall consider later), L. B. Alayev reproduces some elements of remuneration for community artisans and servants.[2] However, he does not make a special study of the differences taking shape in relations between farming landholders and artisans depending on the consumer or productive purpose of the handicraft products.

Before considering this problem itself, let me give a reminder that the consolidation of proprietary rights to land among individual rent-receivers, including those who were appearing within the community and those who stood over and above it, did not change the subsistence basis of farming or its technical basis. In qualitative terms, the proprietary stratification among the sections engaged in farming affected only consumer demand for handicraft articles, without introducing any immediate correctives into the structure of productive demand. That is why, while showing interest in the role of private land-ownership in the destruction of earlier community forms and the incipient overcoming of its closed subsistence system, one should not exaggerate the scope and depth of these processes, which ran on the basis of the subsistence economy.

In particular, the formation of large landed estates did not in itself introduce any fundamental changes into the existing system of social division of labour. Whereas under the prevalence of state property in land and the community organisation the surplus-produce was converted into commodities mainly through the state's rent-tax, with the consolidation of land-owning rights a part of the farm surplus-product in the form of tribute or land rent was directly consumed in kind by the big feudal lords, another part was converted into articles of luxury and other means of consumption for them, the rest constituting the wages of the artisans. Thus, the growing share of the land rent going to the local land-owners did not in itself eliminate the subsistence basis of the economy.

That is understandable because for the time being development did not run beyond the framework of the feudal mode of production, which was characterised by the prevalence of the subsistence economy. At the same time, the growing share of the local land-owners in the rent tied its distribution and consumption to the locality where the farm surplus-product was produced and formed the fund of exchange with the surrounding handicrafts.

With the consolidation of private property rights to land the rights of the community to distributing not only a part of the surplus but also of the necessary product of farming were increasingly infringed. Interesting information about the impact of the consolidation of zamindari land-ownership on the mechanism of intra-community distribution of the product was given by James Forbes in his description of Gujarat's society. In 1765, at the age of 16, he arrived in Bombay, where he became an official of the East India Company. He spent about four years in Gujarat as a tax collector and was engaged in the cotton trade in Broach. He returned to Britain in 1784 and published a book based on his Indian notes, which will yield much interesting information under a critical review.[3]

Describing the land-tenure system in a village community he said that "some particular fields, called pysita and vajeesa lands, are set apart in each village for public purposes...; in most the produce of these lands is appropriated to the maintenance of the Brahmins, the cazee, washermen, smiths, barber and the lame, blind and helpless; and also to the support óf a few vertunnees, or armed men, who are kept for the defence of the village."[4] That is why, Forbes believed, the peasants were done much harm by the fact that the zamindars took over the crop from the pysita lands which was to go to the Brahmans and the artisans.[5]

When studying the connection between the changes in the sphere of land property and the division of the product within the community, one should not hasten to draw any conclusions about the scale of commodity-money relations between farming and the handicrafts. The intention to concentrate on new and progressive phenomena in the life of Indian society by some authors (including myself) has led to premature and one-sided conceptions and conclusions. Thus, at one point I produced an overs-implified formulation, according to which in India "the old manner in which the community remunerated the artisan in kind, that is by allotting him a share of the harvest or a plot of land, was beginning to give way to commodity-money relationships between the craftsman and the consumer or customer."[6]

Habib was quite right in criticising the notions expressed by L. Alayev and myself in some earlier writings concerning the influence allegedly exerted on the "destruction" of the community by the separation from it of weavers, and also, Habib added, oil-makers and cotton combers. So long as the relations between these artisans and the rural inhabitants, Habib said, were determined by traditional practices, it was hard to discover how the community could have disintegrated.[7] We find, therefore, that my present stand is in principle closer to Habib's.[8] At the same time, in each concrete case one should have a clear idea of these practices and the corresponding relations entailed.

The conclusions drawn by A. I. Chicherov on the basis of special studies mark an important step forward. In his work he has collected abundant material testifying that the artisans who catered mostly for the productive demands of the peasant economy (carpenters, blacksmiths, tanners and potters), as a rule, steadily maintained their status in the community and received from it the corresponding remuneration. Consumer orders were the subject of individual deals between the farming holder of the land and the artisans and were paid for in kind or in cash (here the payment for work goes beyond the limits of the community system of remuneration). One will find this to be so by looking at the evidence drawn from the sources collected by Chicherov.[9]

Much interest attaches to the information discovered by Chicherov about the making by urban and rural blacksmiths of farming implements, especially of the iron parts, for sale. But here one should try to establish the real balance between the making of farming implements for sale and for the traditional remuneration from community land-holders. Chicherov goes on correctly to stress that, before the iron reached the village, it had frequently been worked into special blanks for the making of ploughshares, hoes, hammers and other implements of labour. The blacksmiths worked close to the spots where ore was obtained and iron smelted, because according to Buchanan, the low-grade iron was never carried to distant Markets.[10] Let us add that the smelted iron contained so many additives that it required repeated treatment for purification. In the process of this work, the forging was usually given its initial working shape.

But the initial or even complete working of iron by non-community blacksmiths into parts for farming implements did not upset the essential intra-community bonds between farming and the handicrafts (in this case smithing). First of all, the iron part had yet to be fitted to the wooden elements of the implement. Furthermore—and this was even more important— the purchase by a land-holding husbandman of the iron part of the implement was effected once in 10-12 years,[11] whereas its repair (especially in view of the low quality of the iron) remained the day-to-day business of the village smith. Moreover, the widespread usage according to which the holder of the land had the duty to provide the carpenter and the blacksmith with the material or a semi-finished product tended to retard any possible tendencies among these artisans to establish independent commodity-money relations with the outer world, and kept them tied to the community framework. Let us note that the land-holders had no such duty with respect to the tanners and potters, who had to obtain their own materials within the village At the same time, one should bear in mind that the closed intra-community system of making farming implements did not apparently extend equally all over India (for instance, many areas of South India and Bengal). There is an obvious need to establish the regional distinctions in the relationship between agriculture and the handicrafts.

Forbes adds to the early descriptions we know of the system of remuneration of community artisans his own description of the system as it functioned in the Gujarat countryside in the 1770s. He says: "The cattle for the plough, and other services of husbandry, are sometimes the common stock of the village, oftener the property of the individuals. The patel provides seed and implements of agriculture...." We have noted above that some particular fields, called pysita and vajeesa lands, were set apart in each village for public purposes. While there is some difference in the way these lands are used in different districts, in most they are designated for the maintenance of Brahmans, kazis, washermen, barbers and smiths (the only artificer mentioned by Forbes). Because the barber has no time to "attend to husbandry or to provide for his family, it is but just he should be maintained at the public expense; this is also to be applied to the washerman and the smith, who work for the village, without any other emolument."[12]

The type of community described by Forbes (or, at any rate, one of these) contains features like the common ownership of a part of the cattle, the supply by the community (through the patel—the headman) of seeds and implements for the landholders through the establishment of a special land fund which must have been worked in common, and the division of the crop grown on this land between the officials, the servants and the artisans of the community. Among the latter, only the smith is mentioned who is paid for the making of farming implements. But Forbes' description does not explain how payment was made to those who produced only the articles of consumption (for instance, the weaver and the oil-maker) or those who made articles of consumption and the means of production (carpenter, tanner and potter). Nor does he give any information about the principle on which the smith was paid for fulfilling the consumer orders of community members.

A tax report from Broach, dated June 10, 1815 contains a clearer description of the pysita as a land allotment "for the maintenance of various descriptions of artificers" in each village. It was also made available to priests, community servants and district officials. In the district, the total area of such lands came to 36,563 bighas. Of these only 5,190 bighas were in the possession "of village artificers, such as carpenters, blacksmiths, potters, tailors, washermen, barbers, shoemakers and tanners". Much more—14,380 bighas—constituted the holdings of community servants (bhils, jeirs, etc.); the rest of the land of this category was in the possession of administrative personnel and priests, temples and mosques, that is, it was in effect feudal land property exempt from taxes.[13] We find, therefore, that the land-holdings of the artisans were an insignificant part even of that category of land-holdings.

Different Emoluments for Community Artisans Making the Means of Production and the Articles of Consumption

A study of this problem (as of some others) would be made more difficult but for F. Buchanan's studies providing material on the social division of labour. From 1801 to 1811, this official of the East India Company was ordered to tour Bengal, Bihar, Mysore and Karnatak, chiefly for the purpose of studying agricultural production, trade and the handicrafts. The Company required information about these branches of India's economy to regularise its exploitation of the Indian population not only with the use of extra-economic means (that is, taxes and military indemnities) but also by means of trade expansion. Buchanan's was one of the first attempts by an English official to produce a description of the occupied territories in India district by district. Apart from his personal observations, Buchanan made use of the material provided for him by local British personnel, notably, reports from the Company's commercial residents; he also interviewed landlords, merchants, artisans, etc. Buchanan's circumstantial approach and wide information, his industry and obvious interest in what he was learning, together with the systematic arrangement of his material make his writings a unique source for the study of India's economy at the close of the 18th and the beginning of the 19th century) Buchanan's line of reasoning and his terminology indicate that he was acquainted with classical political economy.

In that period, the political and to some extent economic condition of the districts he observed was not the same. While Bengal and Bihar were conquered by the British in the 1750s and 1760s, and were converted into the direct possessions of East India Company, Mysore was conquered only in 1799, that is, only two years before Buchanan's tour. The British maintained Mysore as a princely state, having curtailed its territory and reduced it to a vassal status. By the early 19th century, Bengal and Bihar, more than Mysore, had felt the fatal consequences of colonial plunder as expressed in the deformation of the socio-economic structure and incipient decline of the economy in these provinces. That is why the information on Bengal dating to the same period will be considered later, in the chapters dealing with the colonial period.

According to Buchanan, a system of remuneration of officials, artisans and servants of the community in kind was preserved in Mysore in the early 19th century. They were given a definite share (ayam, similar to the khak in Maharashtra, the awadi in Gujarat, etc.) of the crop grown by the community member. The ayagars (persons receiving ayam) also had the use of a small plot of land—when artisans and servants were involved—which was fully or partially exempt from tax[14] (the watan-type holding in Maharashtra or the pysita in Gujarat).

Buchanan's data also confirm that the remuneration of the artisan by the land-holder differed depending on the purpose of the latter's products. In the latter half of the 18th and early 19th century some village artisans in Mysore were provided with maintenance in kind. Thus, the blacksmith received 20 seers of grain per plough from each heap of grain (apparently an established measure of volume) of the community landholder.[15] The plough was the conventional designation of area worked by one set of implements, and near Seringapatam one poor holding had one plough, a middle holding two or three, and a rich holding four to seven ploughs. In another area, with apparently less fertile soils, the area of farmland for the groups of holdings was larger.[16]

Let us also note that Buchanan says nothing about weavers being provided with maintenance in kind. Even in the remoter parts of Gorakhpur district (eastern part of today's Uttar Pradesh) village weavers were provided not only with grain and yarn but also with cash. In Purnea district, the village weavers bought a large part of their yarn for cash and sold their products on the market each week.[17]

Information about the village weavers of Mysore helps to characterise them as artisans making cloths from the customer's yarn for a certain amount of cash. The weavers never cultivated the soil nor did seasonal work for rich peasants.

"The Toogotaru are a class of weavers (probably a caste.—V. P.) that make a coarse, thick, white cotton cloth with red borders, which among the poorer class of the inhabitants is used as the common waist-cloths of all ages and sexes.... The weavers of this class are poor and say that they cannot afford to make the cloth of their own account. They in general receive the thread from the women in the neighbourhood, and work it up into cloth for hire. For weaving a piece that is worth 8 fanams, or 5s. $4\frac{1}{2}$ d., they get $2\frac{1}{2}$ fanams, or 1 s. 8 d. This occupies a workman four or five days; so that his daily gains are from four to eight pence. They never cultivate the ground."[18] Weavers of the Walliaru caste, who produced coarse cloth for the poor, lived in the countryside and were often employed as day labourers by farmers and others prepared to hire them. These weavers bought yarn from women of all castes who spun it at home.[19]

Thus, cloth, the most common consumer product of the handicrafts, was made for cash from yarn obtained from peasant-women customers or purchased on the market. But even in the first instance, when production was not yet commercialised, it was still free from the intra-community bonds which regulated the making of implements.

A more solid judgment about the nature and mechanism of relations between the land-holder and the various categories of artisans can be made from British official studies of the Maharashtra countryside after its conquest. Here is what James Grant said in a report on June 17, 1822

"... The Sootar or carpenter. His duty is to make and repair all woodwork of the implements of husbandry, free of expense to the cultivators, for which he holds enam lands, and makes bullooty collections in kind; these are quite indefinite, depending on the custom of the village, which is extremely various. The collections are made twice on every crop, when the grain is cut and stacked, and again when it is threshed out. The carpenter likewise generally gets a small present of grain on finishing any job; and when employed on work not connected with the implements of husbandry he receives regular hire.

"... The Lohar or blacksmith makes and repairs the iron work and is recompensed in the same manner as the carpenter.

"... The Chambar or currier and shoemaker furnishes the villagers with shoes on payment, but keeps them in repair, as well as the moths or leather bags used in drawing water, free of expense. He also supplies leather thongs for bullock whips, and acts as village mushal (guide.—V.P.); for the performance of these duties he holds enam land and collects bullooty dues."[20]

This extract, I think, contains very important information: the productive requirements of farming were satisfied through the traditional system of community payments in kind (both in land allotments and a share of the crop), whereas the individual consumer requirements of the land-holder and his family were met by the artisan as an independent producer entering with the land-holder into relations independent of the community which involved exchange of products in kind or payment for commodities in cash.

That handicraft articles for consumer purposes were involved earlier than implements of labour in deals between the artisans and the consumer independent of the community will also be seen from the early separation from the community of weaving, the largest handicraft industry producing chiefly articles of consumption. It is interesting to note that jewellery-making was on the verge of separation from the system of community handicrafts. That is why the jeweller (sonar) was classed as an artisan with the third group of bullootydars, who received the smallest share of the crop. This is connected not only and not so much with the fact that the sonar performed the functions of the usurer and community treasurer (these functions were frequently usurped by the banias and the Brahmans), but also with the strictly individual scale of his orders. Thus, Grant says that the sonar was a maker of gold and silver ornaments for rich inhabitants, which is why the sonar obtained the bulk of his income from his direct deals with his customers.

The satisfaction of the land-holders' consumer requirements through individual deals with artisans is due, I think, to the fact that the distributive mechanism of the Indian village community was not based on any egalitarian principles. The very fact that it was profaned by the dependence of the socially lower castes deprived their members, especially those who had no farms, of the right to claim a share in the handicraft articles equal to that of land-holding husbandmen. The proprietary and economic stratification (above all, in the scale of land-holding among the fullfledged community members) produced a situation in which the depersonified recompense of the artisan with a fixed share of the crop of all the land-holders would be out of line with his actual relations with his customers who had strictly individual requirements concerning the volume, quality and range of consumer articles.

Things were different with the making of farming implements. The differences in the size of holding and land-tenure did not result in any qualitative changes in demand for farming implements, because the same implements were used to work the lands of the ordinary community members and the lands of the community élite. Of course, the larger the land area worked, the greater the demand for implements. That is why if the artisans were paid equally by each land-holder, their recompense would cease to accord with the actual volume of individual requirements in implements. However, the Maratha community, for example, had a system of recompense for making implements under which it made little difference to the maker whether he was fulfilling orders for a big or small land-holder, that is, the economic and proprietary differentiation of village community's land-holding members did not destroy the natural bonds between farming and the handicrafts turning out implements of labour.

We can obtain an idea of the mechanism of these ties from a report by R.N. Gooddine, Sub-Assistant Superintendent, Ahmadnagar Revenue Survey and Assessment (the report is dated October 10, 1845). He said that, in terms of recompense, village artisans and servants were divided into three oli or khas, according to the Muslim terminology In the first group were the sootar, lohar, chambhar and muhar; in the second the koombhar, nhawee, pureet and nuhar; in the third the bhat, goorow, moulana and moohar. The members of the first group were paid at 30 units of produce from a unit of farm land; of the second—25 units and of the third—20 units. This produce was issued "by the Patel from the farmer's stack, on the appeal of either party" (i.e., the artisan or the servant).[21]

Gooddine explained the duties and the right to recompense of the various artisans as follows: "Sootar. —The Carpenter is at the head of the artisans, his service being most in requisition; he makes up and mends all wooden implements for agricultural purposes, the owners finding the materials; but for any other work, as building a house, or making a cart for other than agricultural purposes, he is paid. His average remuneration is about 6 paeelees per paeen.

"Lohar.—The Smith makes and repairs the iron work for all agricultural instruments, the owner finding the material; but anything apart from these, such as a cart, etc., for other than agricultural purposes, he must be paid for. Remuneration $5\frac{1}{2}$ Paeelees per paeen.

"Chambhar.—The Shoe-maker makes all leathern halters, whips, ropes and bands for agricultural purposes, the owners finding the leather; but he must find the leather himself for all repairs.... He has also to furnish gratuitously the Deshmookh and Deshpandee of the disstrict, and the Patel and Coolkurnee of the village, with a new pair of shoes each annually. His average remuneration per paeen is $5\frac{1}{2}$ paeelees.

"The above are the three principal artisans of the village and they possess several perquisites above the others, among which may be mentioned the privilege of sowing in every farmer's field a strip of land each with ralla, each strip consisting of four furrows. The farmer tills the land, and these artisans merely bring each his basket of grain, which is sown by the farmer, and reaped by the recipient when ready."[22]

What was the remuneration received by the artisans, officials and community servants in the Maratha village in the 1840s? Table 1 gives British official data on individual remuneration (huk) in the village, which had farmland of 80 paeen.

TABLE 1

Size of Annual Remuneration of Heads, Servants and Handicraftsmen of the Village Community

Name of the Hukdars	*Annual remuneration*	
	in seers	*in kgs*
Patel (headman)	900	680
Coolkurnee (official)	2,840	2,160
Sootar (carpenter)	2,000	1,520
Lohar (smlth)	1,800	1,360
Chambhar (harness-maker)	1,800	1,360
Koombhar (potter)	1,340	1,020
Nhawee (barber)	1,340	1,020
Pureet (washerman)	1,500	1,140
Bhar (servant)	900	680
Goorow (temple servant)	1,040	780
Moulana (teacher)	900	680
Sonar (goldsmith)	740	560
Bheel (watchman)	900	680
Kolee (water-carrier)	1,040	780
Mang (servant)	740	560
Muhar (servant)	4,700	3,600

* See: "*Report on the Village Communities of the Deccan* (Government of Bombay Selections from Records)"

It is possible to estimate the share deducted by the rayats from their crop to the hukdars in general, and artisans, in particular (which, like any other estimate, is, of course, approximate). From Table 1, we find that all the hukdars annually received 17.5 tons of grain, of which 5.25 tons fell to the share of four artisans (the lohar, sootar, chambhar and koombhar). It may be assumed that the crop from this area (300 hectares, less the area under cotton, oil-bearing plants and vegetables) averaged about 250 tons. But after the deduction to the seed fund there remained 190-200 tons. Thus, all the hukdars received 7-8 per cent of the crop, and the artisans, about 3 per cent only for satisfying the productive needs of farming. Such were the inputs by the Indian farmer into the reproduction of his implements of labour.

Still this system of remuneration of the artisans provided them with means of modest subsistence and guaranteed a more secure position than that of the urban artisans in the mid-19th century. The outskirts of the village still safeguarded the village artisans from the invasion of the British machine-made commodities.

The inventory of the peasants' implements made by a British official, D. G. Graham, in 1852 in the state of Kolhapur (Southern Maharashtra) gives an idea of the size and principal material elements of agricultural reproduction. Having noted that carts (and certainly cattle) are omitted from the inventory, he gives the following list: a plough (3 rupees); and probably a harrow, which is not mentioned by him anywhere, for "levelling the ploughed ground" (1 rupee); a yoke (6 annas); "an implement used for land planing" (4 rupees 15 annas); "a kolpa, an implement for outrooting grass and weeds from fields", i.e., for weeding (6 annas); a tube with an endpiece, apparently a sort of manual seeder (3 annas); an implement (obviously, a harrow) which is used on the land after sowing (8 annas); another yoke (8 annas); a seed-drill with six tubes for seeds (2 rupees); a light plough (1 rupee); a ploughshare (1 rupee 8 annas); a weeding tool (1 anna); a cutting tool (4 annas); a hoe (8 annas); a chopping-knife (8 annas); a crowbar (1 rupee); a large well bucket (6 rupees 5 annas); a well rope (2 rupees 8 annas); another hoe (4 annas); reins (2 annas); two-yoke leather straps (5 annas); a whip (4 annas). The total cost of the implements listed was 28 rupees 11 annas.[23] These implements, however, do not account for the whole stock of peasants' equipment, as it also included a cart and earthenware for irrigation and storage purposes.

It is hard to imagine that one carpenter and one blacksmith were able to make and mend all this inventory for something like a hundred households. What is more, the implements and tools were made of wood and their working parts of soft iron, which increased the volume of work involving mending, sharpening and repairing. It will be easily understood why the carpenter and the blacksmith were the most respected figures among the village artisans. D.R. Gadgil reported that the carpenter and the blacksmith concentrated on the Making and mending of farm implements, and stressed that the village blacksmith was not highly skilled, as every report said, and that one of the obstacles to the use of improved implements was his inability to repair them.[24]

In the period under review and much later (up until the 1920s) the Indian countryside did not present any massive market demand for farm implements, so that reproduction in agriculture continued to be based mainly on the old technical foundation and on natural exchange between farming and the handicrafts producing implements for farming. This will be seen from the fact that in the first half of the 19th century and in subsequent decades as well, there is no mention of farm implements among the goods offered at fairs and bazaars in Maharashtra (in some sources these items are listed in fairly extensive detail).

I shall return to the mid-19th century sources later to consider their even more detailed description of the system of remuneration for rural artisans. But I think that what I have said is enough to form an idea of the basis on which the mechanisms of the division of labour between the farmer and the artisan operated. In this context Marx wrote: "The whole mechanism discloses a systematic division of labour; but a division like that in manufactures is impossible, since the smith, and the carpenter, etc., find an unchanging market, and, at the most there occur, according to the size of the villages, two or three of each, instead of one. The law that regulates the division of labour in the community acts with the irresistible authority of a law of Nature, at the same time that each individual artificer, the smith, the carpenter, and so on, conducts in his workshop all the operations of his handicraft in the traditional way, but independently, and without recognising any authority over him."[25]

Because this is a clear reference to community artisans, let us recall that the market (demand, to be more precise) was relatively unchanged only for finished implements. That is why one cannot quite agree with Habib when he says that it is hard to discover how an internal village market or capitalist elements could emerge from any internal development of the Indian rural community, despite the individual organisation of production and the economic stratification among the peasantry.[26]

Indeed, the demand for consumer articles was undoubtedly shaped under the influence of the customer's preferences and potentialities. The diversity of this demand will be seen from the list of household utensils and instruments of labour of a well-to-do Maratha peasant of the Kunbi caste, which was drawn up by an official called Coates in 1819: a stone hand- mill valued at 1 rupee; two wooden iron-tipped mortars—$\frac{1}{2}$ rupee, a large copper vessel for water—10 rupees; two or three copper vessels for drinking at 2 rupees each; two or three small copper bowls for eating at $1-1\frac{1}{2}$ rupees each, two iron fryingpans at $\frac{3}{4}$ and 1 rupee each; five glazed and from 20 to 30 unglazed pots—total value $2\frac{1}{3}-3$ rupees; a small wooden trough, several baskets, two iron lamps, two knives at 1 rupee each, a total of roughly 40 rupees.[27]

The value of these utensils exceeded the value of a set of implements even in Maharashtra, where they were more sophisticated and expensive than, say, in Bengal. But in contrast to the implements, the untensils were not in need of regular mending and repair, and this reduced the overall volume of constant artisan services in using them. It may be assumed that the fundamentally different ratio (as compared with Maharashtra) of the inputs for handicraft articles designed for productive and consumer purposes among land-holder sections engaged in farming (in the broadest sense, including cultivators) could result in a situation in which the system of intra-community remuneration of four artisan castes based on productive demands tended to become meaningless. For instance, this kind of ratio could take shape in Bengal and partially in Bihar, where the higher fertility of the soil and the facility of working it reduced the costs of farming implements and increased the mass and share of the agricultural product going not only to the rent-consuming but also to the rent-producing section of the rural population.

Let us look at Buchanan's evidence about Bihar: "In some parts of the district (Bhagalpur—V.P.) the professions of blacksmith and carpenter are united in the same persons. In other areas they are separated, and I have mentioned that those of both classes who are employed in making the implements of agriculture are usually paid for their labour in grain, and are often entitled to a certain share of the crop, forming a regular part of the establishment on each estate. From among those who labour at the anvil alone, I must notice two classes who do not belong to the manorial establishment; one of them in the forests forges the crude iron, as it comes from the smelters; the other in towns makes the finer kind of goods."[28]

It will be more appropriate to judge about the last two groups below. This fragment does not provide a clear picture to the rural artisans' position. The fact is that Buchanan used the word "estate" according to the existing British terminology, implying a whole multitude of villages and land comprising the zamindar estate. A mere statement that some rural artisans are part of the zamindar personnel adds little to the understanding of their position but for the information about their being kept within the rural population.

More detailed information was provided on the position of artisans belonging to the "manorial establishment". Buchanan gives the name "manor" to a lower administrative-tax unit called mauza, headed by a muqaddam (in Bihar it could apparently be a zamindar).[29] The usual meaning of this word is village", but in the fiscal terminology of the early 19th century mauza meant a village community with the function of a lower fiscal unit ("collection of farms", that is, a collection of rayat holdings constituting a given zamindar estate),[30] headed by a mandal (headman).

Buchanan often refers to the question of how different officials of rural communities are paid in Bengal and Eastern Bihar (Purnea and Bhagalkot), but he never mentions blacksmiths, carpenters or leather-dressers. The official personnel of a rural community were rewarded in different ways: with a share in the land revenue (in kind or in cash), a fixed monthly salary and tax-free land.[31] Among these bailiffs (gomastha), clerks (patwari), evaluators (bania), supervisors (diwani), guards (peyada), and suchlike big and small tax collectors, there is little mention of the potter who was drawing 1/320 or even a smaller share of the revenue.[32] The retention of the potter among those receiving rewards in traditional or modified form from the total tax revenue should apparently be explained by the fact that he still had some duties to perform in making ritual utensils, figurines of the gods, etc.

But on the whole, by the beginning of the 19th century or probably much earlier, the rural community of Bengal—and Bihar to a considerable extent as well—had lost its functions of regulating the exchange of products between agriculture and the handicrafts and had turned basically into a fiscal institution. In places where such relations prevailed (the blacksmith's reward with a harvest share), they were based on relations between the cultivator and the manufacturer of his implements independently of the rural administration. The purely individual character of these relations under the distinctly pronounced economic differentiation in agriculture inevitably changed the levelling of the artisan's reward, and was conducive to the transition to individual orders on definite operations paid for according to the quantity and the complexity of the work.

It is most likely that when moving to the north-west of the Ganges valley, the traditional links of agriculture and the handicrafts were encountered in their original form. In the Patna district, the blacksmith and the carpenter "usually belong to the manorial establishment, and the payment for the implements of agriculture arises from a share of the crop."[33] There is no mention of the payment of rural potters and leather-dressers. Still, according to Buchanan, in the Shahabad district

(Western Bihar) "the harvester, carpenter, blacksmith, shoemaker (most probably the harness-maker.—V.P.), village Brahman and weigher are paid from the heap before division. The amount of the crop is settled by a survey, and from this the allowances above mentioned having been deducted, the share due to the landlord is usually paid in kind, sometimes, however, in money."[34] On the strength of this extract one can draw the conclusion that under the traditional communal deductions the land cultivator and the rent-receiver shared in appropriate proportions only that part of the harvest which was left after the deduction, but not the whole of it.

My assumption that by "manor personnel" Buchanna meant the rural population of a definite fiscal unit is also borne out by his data on Shahabad. Thus, about the chamars he says that they mostly belonged to the "manorial establishment and are paid by a share of the crop for furnishing ropes, bags for drawing water and shoes for the ploughmen."[35]

The disruption of intra-community bonds and the socio-economic abasement of the majority of the toiling agricultural population in Bengal was also reflected in the status of the local artisans who provided services for that population. It is true that Buchanan claims that in Bengal the blacksmiths, carpenters, weavers and barbars "obtained the dignity that pure birth confers."[36] But later on, in a more detailed examination of the status of the individual artisan castes, he himself says that some sub-castes of carpenters and weavers and also oil-pressers (kalu) had the status of being "unclean".[37] Indeed, the status of the blacksmiths was apparently lower than it was in Western India, although they made the whole range of farming implements (the carpenters were excluded from this work and engaged in fashioning household utensils and making carts).[38]

Information about the prices of agricultural implements shows that they became articles of widespread purchase and sale. However, it is known that the purchase and sale of agricultural implements did not become common-place even in Bengal. For instance, in 1810 Buchanan wrote the following on the situation in the division of Purnea (it included Bengal's districts of Dinajpur and Rangpur) : "None of the balckmiths enjoys any popularity. Their customary business is manufacturing simple tools for agriculture and adjusting their wooden or metal parts. They are everywhere paid in cereals, are well rewarded and have permanent work."[39] This information is much too scant for any final conclusion. Yet it does draw attention to the situation of the communal artisans who received payment in kind. Separately mentioned are blacksmiths who manufactured household goods: "They made a better job of roughly worked knives, scissors, swords, lamps, spears, locks and other hardware that were highly in demand.

Everything that claimed good quality was importd."[40] That is why the following estimates of the agricultural implements do not in any sense prove that they were realised through the market.

Those are some of the data about the division of labour between farming and the handicrafts and their relationship, the volume of productive and consumer demand coming from the farm and the family of the land-holder. Alongside the information on agricultural production, these data help to obtain a rough idea of the structure of that part of the national product which went to form the mass of goods (including commodities) involved in the exchange between agriculture and the handicrafts.

On the Transformation of Farm Produce into Urban Handicraft Products

The division of labour on the scale of the community or other rural micro-region was, we find, the basis of the social division of labour in India. At the same time, when analysing the premises for the genesis of capitalism, special interest attaches to the movement and transformation of that part of the agricultural product which went to the cities. Considering this problem, Habib examined the assumption under which the surplus-product extracted from agriculture contained within itself the same share of food (cereals in particular) as the product remaining in the rural locality; that being so, the proportion of the population in the rural and non-rural sectors would be roughly in accord with the subdivision of the land product into the surplus (extracted, to be more precise) product, and the product remaining in the countryside; this would imply a very small urban population because the mass of raw materials remaining for the satisfaction of the needs of the rural population would be almost the same as that being extracted to satisfy the requirements of the urban population feeding on the surplus-product; under this assumption, a majority of the population in the non-agricultural sector would consist of persons engaged in non-productive labour and provision of personal services.[41]

But Habib goes on to consider another assumption under which the surplus-product would for the most part consist of cash crops with higher yields per unit of area in terms of value. In this case, the share of the non-agricultural population would be lower than the corresponding share of the surplus-product; on the other hand, this population would include a more numerous producing section of artisans, while the non-agricultural population would on the whole tend to be concentrated in the cities. The latter variant, according to Habib, creates certain premises for the development of capitalism, which cannot originate without a minimum concentration of non-agricultural manpower in the cities[42] (this is not quite true, because initially capitalism often preferred to base its industrial production in the rural localities).

A simple calculation on Habib's data shows that his approach is well justified. Indeed, it turns out that under the first variant the urban population would tend to grow but with a declining standard in its social and occupational composition; under the second variant the urban population would be reduced in absolute and relative terms, but then—and this is most important—a qualitative shift would take place within that population in favour of the productive element. The optimal ratio of urban inhabitants to the total population deserves to be specially considered. Let us recall that at the dawn of Russian absolutism under Peter I, the urban population came to 500,000, or 3.6 per cent (1721).[43] That appears to have been adequate for fulfilling its historical tasks.

Furthermore, Habib admits that he has no statistical data to prove which of these two assumptions was the historical reality in India, and accordingly opts for the indirect examination of the problem by studying the distribution of the excess product (say, rent) among its consumers. He recalls that from $\frac{1}{4}$ to $\frac{1}{2}$ of the agricultural product left the rural economy (after all the deductions in favour of the rural and local rent-receivers) to be distributed among the less numerous ruling sections. In 1647, only 445 mansabdars (out of 8,000) appropriated 61.5 per cent of the taxes of the Mogul Empire, which, however, were not included in the dynasty's land revenue. Habib has estimated that two-thirds of the income of the leading mansabdars went to provide maintenance for the troops, especially the cavalry. He believes that in Mogul India the outlays on the troops went to feed, alongside the soldiers themselves, members of their families, servants and the merchants and handicraftsmen catering to them, a total of up to 5 million persons. Thus, work was provided to the numerous and skilled artisans by the need to manufacture side-arms and especially fire-arms (at least 25,000 pieces).

Apart from these two-thirds, one-quarter of all the revenue was spent by the nobility on their personal requirements, and about one-tenth on the maintenance of clerical persons, scholars, physicians, poets, artists, musicians and dancers. The Mogul élite spent vast amounts on harems, countless idle servants (who were frequently kept underfed), "representation" according to rank, and gifts to the padishah and his entourage. Still, upon the death of various dignitaries the Treasury took over fortunes in which the cash alone ran to millions of rupees.

The military-administrative personnel of the Empire and the

population catering for their needs created a demand for consumer goods of diverse quality and purpose. Hence the contemporary testimonials about the great numbers of artisans and the diversity of their specialities. In addition, there was large-scale construction in Mogul India of religious and administrative buildings and military installations, and this consumed masses of manpower of different skills.[44]

In conclusion of his reasoning about the extent of the land revenue going to the maintenance and reproduction of the non-roductive manpower or the handicrafts, Habib admits that he does not have enough data to draw a final conclusion. He starts from the assumption that in reality both variants of distribution operated side by side. In particular, he notes that the number of artisans and unskilled workers was in excess of the den and for servicing the nobility, because the handicrafts had to meet the requirements, especially in clothing, of the whole mass of the toiling population, both productive and non-productive. Besides, although the per-head consumption of manufactured articles was not high, the artisan's productivity was also low.[45] That is why Habib assumes that although the first variant of distribution was quite strongly established in Indian society, it coexisted with the second to a certain extent. That is why the urban population did not constitute one-quarter or one-third of the total population (as they would have done if the structure of the extracted and the remaining product had coincided), but less than one-fifth.[46]

In the most general terms, Habib's approach to the problem of redistribution and structure of the surplus-product produced in agriculture appears to be highly fruitful and correct in principle. At the same time, he tends to reduce the mechanism of extraction and subsequent redistribution of this product to the tax apparatus and its connecting channels and ramifications among the urban producer and consumer. Actually, the formation of the subsequent necessary structure of the extracted product of agriculture was much more complicated if only because its non-food raw-material component was not produced in many parts of India (for instance, in Western Maharashtra and Bengal local cotton production was insignificant). Indeed, all the known descriptions of crop distribution speak of a sharing of the cereals and not of any industrial crop (which could have been a staple and annual crop among peasants only under favourable conditions).

That is why one should assume that industrial raw materials and food, such as milk and sugar products, reached the towns through market channels. It is another matter that the peasant could sell this produce to pay the land-tax, but in that case merchant's capital joined in the extraction and redistribution of the agricultural product at the very initial stage. Finally, the urban artisans processed not only agricultural raw materials, but also metals, precious stones, wood, chemicals, clay and other materials and semi-finished products of non-agricultural origin. Their transportation to the place where they were worked up required the participation of merchant's capital, so that in the process the surplus-product of agriculture underwent even more complicated and mediated transformations.

It goes without saying that we cannot establish the actual proportions of the gross product in the various spheres of production in India in the 17th and 18th centuries. The difficulties are just as great in determining the spheres where the surplus-product was produced, although the general prevalence of agriculture appears to be indisputable. By way of approximate illustration here are the considerations expressed by a British official concerning the structure of the gross product in Bengal in the early 1780s.

Balance of the National Product in Bengal in the Late 18th Century

In assessing the evidence quoted below one should start not only from the obviously biased approach by the British expert (J. Grant), but also from the specifics of Bengal itself. Besides, in projecting this information and the conclusions into the past or into the future one should bear in mind that the province had been under a foreign yoke for over two decades. It is true that British economic, above all land revenue, policy in that period was aimed at re-establishing the property of the state (in this instance of the East India Company) in land, which is why it did not make any substantial new changes in the social division of labour and its product. The only new element is that, in contrast to earlier rulers, the administration of the East India Company strove to allocate the maximum from the tax funds for the purchase of goods for export. Accordingly, the share of the national product that was exported increased, while the share of the product that went for the personal consumption of the ruling class, its servants, and the merchants and artisans decreased.

Grant's report said that in order to pay rent peasants were "forced to carry the surplus of their industry beyond a homely consumption, to interior markets, where it is then properly distributed into two branches of inland trade; the one, furnishing the necessaries of life to the rich, or class of idlers, soldiers, artificers, mendicant priests, the civil list of the government, with all such as are maintained for public service, or in the employment of the wealthy private dealers of every denomination: the other affording raw materials in silk, cotton, or such animal and vegetable productions for the use of that portion of the peasantry who are journeymen manufacturers, as well as labouring husbandmen, and work up those rare inimitable fabrics, or valuable commodities serving as the basis of foreign commerce."[47]

We must give this official of the East India Company his due. He has clearly reproduced the mechanism of exacting the peasants' produce and its consumption or processing. At the same time, it is evident that Grant took an interest in those artisans who were engaged in manufacturing goods for export (following the subjugation of Bengal, its export was entirely controlled by the British). He mentions that, as a rule, the same artisans, particularly the weavers, also produced goods for the needs of the Indian ruling class. That is why having partly got rid of the latter, the East India Company intensified the foreigntrade orientation of Bengal handicrafts. There is an interesting reference to "that portion of the peasantry" who engaged in the handicrafts for hire or independently. The export branches of the handicrafts were situated in the rural localities as well, and involved the population that had not lost its ties with agriculture.

But what is more essential is that Grant says nothing about the productive requirements among the peasants in handicraft products. He reduces all their needs to personal consumption,[48] which provided an opportunity for extracting from the rayats also that part of their produce which went for exchange—in kind or in cash—against the productive-purpose handicraft articles. That is why very little is said in this document about the exchange of peasant and handicraft products.

Grant subdivided the total market supply in the early 1780s, estimated by the colonial administration at 65 million sikka, rupees (sikka-rupee, a coin of the latest year mint, was the standard monetary unit), into three categories. The first category included staple food products with a total value of 20 million rupees, i.e., rice, beans, wheat, and other cereals and pulses, fruit, root-crops and greens; oil and butter, dairy products. All this was consumed locally with the exception of one-twentieth part of it supplied for boat provisioning or shipped to the Coromandel Coast. The second category comprised consumer goods worth 12 million rupees, such as salt, betel, saltpetre, liquor, hashish, ironwood, pottery, hemp (possibly jute), hides, wax, flax, indigo, spices, woollen blankets; these goods were assigned for home consumption except for one-fifth of their value which included salt, opium, indigo and saltpetre. The third group consisted of luxuries, i.e., cotton and silk articles, two-thirds of which were exported to Europe and the countries of the Indian Ocean (16 million rupees); home consumption goods amounted to only 11 million rupees; the overall turnover of this category of goods constituted 33 million rupees.[49]

Without considering for the time being the commodity nomenclature of these three groups, let us note only two circumstances:

the share of foreign trade increased in the marketing of the goods of each subsequent group; among the goods there was no direct mention of the articles of consumption of peasants or the implements of their labour. The products of local exchange between peasants and artisans were apparently not involved in taxation and were not, for that reason, listed in the data on product exchange.

James Grant goes on to estimate Bengal's agricultural production. He considers that all the cultivated area in the province came to 35 million bighas, and the gross value of the total agricultural output to 210 million rupees, assuming that the product's value per bigha was equal to 6 rupees; the rural population (including rural artisans) was estimated at 8 million persons. If one adds to this another 30 million rupees' worth of articles produced by manufacturers and artisans, including those breeding silk worms, the total value of the annual product of this country will come to no more than 240 million rupees, apart from small outlays on animal husbandry which in effect constituted the means of subsistence for the mass of the people engaged in productive occupations or depending on them (that is, members of the families of peasants and artisans).[50]

All these calculations were made by Grant in order to refute "the mistaken supposition of the existence of a great comparative stock of labour in agriculture or manufactures, requiring either a proportionate quantity of circulating species, or a large capital, necessary for annual production and capable of considerable increase by accumulation of the profits." Although from the end of the 16th century the amount of money in circulation increased, it "hath yet at all times been extremely small, comparatively to what might be necessary for any European state, resembling most in circumstances the situation of Bengal; and can bear no proportion to the whole annual produce of the country."[51]

Grant explains the limited commodity-money circulation by the fact that the "bulk of the people here, being husbandmen and manufacturers, provide independently of each other, perhaps fully for their family maintenance or wants; and as there is no occasion for interchanging the product of the respective industry of these two great orders of men, among themselves; and so neither can they have any need for the ordinary medium of circulation."[52] The arguments here are obviously based on British bourgeois notions: so long as there are no market relations there is, consequently, no exchange of products. However, such exchange was going on but in the form of direct, purely natural relations between the owners (who were usually the producers as well) of the agricultural and the handicraft products. It is quite another matter that the money circulation involved was minimal.

That is why the East India Company official is not very far out when he insists that the money circulation was necessary only for trade servicing the "homely consumption of all the other inhabitants or the less important demands of luxurious foreigners. The trade value comprises the surplus of the land and the manufacturers' labour carried annually for interior sale", and does not exceed 65 million rupees. "Of this, near 5.5 krore, exclusive of the amount of sayer and salt revenue, should be received yearly into the public exchequer." The government "thus absorbs five-sixths of the surplus product of the soil and labour."[53]

Therefore, the cost of commodities taxed by the customs is nearing the colonial profit. Estimating the value of Bengal's agricultural produce at 210 million rupees, Grant makes a note that it is "rather beyond the quadruple of our largest assigned rental to government",[54] that is, the land revenue exacted by the colonial authorities amounted to something like 52 million rupees. Considering that to pay revenues the peasants had to sell or make available for sale a corresponding part of their produce, one may conclude that the trade share of the peasants' produce was primarily determined by the volume of the land revenue, and the amount of marketed products was balanced by an adequate amount of money which was collected by the colonial exchequer as land revenues. Therefore the Company's administration, as well as the pre-British rulers of Bengal, were able to control the principal branches of Bengal's trade production and determine its development through systems of orders to artisans and peasants, who produced the raw materials. This product alienated from the peasantry and turned into commodities indirectly sustained the urban population that did not, possibly, receive payments from the British.

However, not only the part of the village produce exacted through taxes went into trade exchange. There is no doubt that another, lesser part of it, was turned into commodities and obtained by private rent-receivers, so unkindly called "idlers" (the attitude to them would subsequently change fundamentally for the better). By the end of the 1780s, according to the estimates of the Company's administration, the Company's share in Bengal's agricultural gross output constituted 45 per cent; the private rent-receivers' 15 per cent and the peasants' only 40 per cent.[55] The share of individual rent-receivers had obviously been larger in the pre-British period. However, another fact is more noteworthy just now, and it is the conversion into commodities of that surplus agricultural produce which remained with the zamindar landlords and was redistributed through them.

The structure of the expenditures of major and average zamindars in Bengal in the 1780s will be seen from the data cited by N. K. Sinha. A simplified and amalgamated view of these expenditures is as follows. The owner of the Moysadul zamindar estate, whose annual income amounted to 92,000 rupees, spent 28,000-29,000 rupees on religion and charity; 15,500 rupees on relatives and "dependants", that is, apparently the families of clients, receiving their maintenance directly from the zamindar patron; 4,800 rupees on maintenance; 24,000 on servants; 2,800 on house expenses; 2,900 on clothes; 1,500 on bronze ware; 1,500 on keeping elephants, horse stables and camels. The total expenditure on these, obviously unproductive items, exceeded 82,000 rupees, which makes up almost 90 per cent of the zamindar's total income.

The following expenses may be regarded as being productive: 3,800 rupees on the zamindar's "own farms"; 1,500 rupees on "repairing of boats"; 69 rupees 10 annas on maintenance of bridges; 154 rupees 7 annas on labourers, i.e., nearly 6 per cent of the total amount.

Accordingly, zamindari income was of a fiscal character: 29,700 rupees made an annual assignment of the Company; 8,500 rupees—salt tax, 2,500 rupees—land assessment assigned to cover religious expenses. Along with other profits (mainly various gifts) the zamindar estate received 48,300 rupees, out of which farms' incomes were only 3,200 rupees,[56] that is, the zamindar householding proper yielded little profit (a certain amount of the profit might have been consumed by the servants in kind). The deficit of 43,600 rupees between expenses and profits was covered by the owner, in her words, by selling her treasures.

The regrettable fact is that it is not always easy to imagine the structure of expenditures in its ultimate commodity form. For instance, religious expenses could be anything from a meagre meal for pilgrims and hermits to land appropriated by priests, who could not ignore mundane benefits. The keeping of relatives, "dependants" and others was mostly realised in the objects of their consumption, though it was possible that some of them could buy land or lend money on interest. Whatever the situation, it is clear that the system of exacting and redistributing the surplus agricultural product had nothing in common with capitalist accumulation for Bengal itself.

This will be seen from the relevant data on an even larger zamindar estate at Dinajpur. Here, the total annual expenditure of 566,700 rupees consisted of the following main items: religious ritual and the maintenance of priests, about 274,000 rupees, household expenses and clothes, 68,200 and 17,800 rupees, respectively; servants' pay, 68,800 rupees; repairs, 5,200 rupees; a total of 200,000 rupees. The third big item of expenditure was the "revenue of the village of Durgaram"—113,000 rupees (the zamindar may have exempted the village from the payment of tax for some reason, and was paying it himself). There is no mention of any item directly connected with productive needs, although on the revenue side the product of his "farm" is shown as a fairly large amount of 41,500 rupees.[57] The Dinajpur zamindar must have regarded the farm as being self-sufficient and for that reason did not deem it necessary to show the outlays on reproduction among the items of his own budget.

We find a roughly similar structure of expenditure among the small zamindars. Thus, the zamindar estate of Foota Sing had an annual expenditure of 6,900 rupees, and had the following basic outlays: 1,900 rupees for religious purposes; 3,500 rupees for personal and household requirements of the land-owner, and 1,260 rupees for "relatives".[58] We find that the basic items of expenditure and their rough ratios are maintained even when the size of the zamindar estate is reduced. Thus, 20 odd years after the establishment of the British regime, the expenditure side of the budget of a Bengali land-owner went to maintain numerous priests (in this case Hindu priests), the land-owner himself and his relatives, which must have included some very distant kin indeed.

Let us note that the Bengali zamindars acted as something like keepers of moral and ethical standards. Hunter refers to a 1815 document listing the levies exacted by the zamindar of Majnamuta in Midnapur district from the population in the form of payment for recognition of acts of civil status or for the absolution of sins. For instance, there was the marriage of a widow, the dissolution of an engagement, marriage to a girl from another zamindar estate, a brawl with a man from a lower caste and other similar cases (a total of 25) which entailed the payment of about 1 rupee to the zamindar. In addition, there were 32 other levies of the most diverse kinds, including a payment in connection with the zamindar's "bathing ceremony", payment for the use of special nets in fishing, the growing of improved kinds of rice, etc.[59] The latter levies indicate that the zamindar's status exerted a drag on the improvement of the implements of production.

One is left with the impression that the zamindari system in Bengal, to the extent to which it was in the hands of the privileged, usually Brahman castes of the Hindu community in the 1780s, served as an instrument for redistributing the agricultural surplus-product among the nobility. The zamindar himself undoubtedly enjoyed the leading status, and his duties in maintaining his caste entourage were exercised by him with sufficient responsibility. The maintenance of this partially ideological and partially parasitic élite ruled out the formation of any sizable fund of productive accumulation, even within the limits of feudal economic activity.

Up to now we have been considering the budget of Hindu zamindars. It is important to note that the budgets of Muslim zamindars had roughly the same structure. For instance, out of an annual expenditure of 43,600 rupees of the zamindar Mahomed Shayhy, total outlays for religious purposes and charities came to 17,500 rupees, or over 40 per cent of the total. Unfortunately, this item of expenditure in the Muslim zamindars' budget, as of the Hindu ones, does not show any break-down of the outlays for the Muslim or the Hindu cult. This would have been helpful in gaining a picture not only of the contemporary state of Hindu-Muslim relations but also, and this is now more important, of the system of maintenance for the priests of these two leading religions of Bengal. But one can assume that the maintenance of the priests of other creeds made up a part of the zamindar's expenditures, whatever his own religion. Thus, the zamindar Mahomed Shayhy listed a fairly large outlay—1,727 rupees (more than for the remembrance of the zamindar's own parents—1,412 rupees) on jaunes (string) given to the children of Brahmans.[60] Unfortunately, it is impossible to determine the needs of which religion were met (fully or in part) by the largest outlay for religious purposes (usually over one-half of the item), called the "Dewatur Poojah", which meant religious offerings.

Thus, the surplus-product of the peasant economy retained by the zamindars was converted, with a small exemption, into articles and products of consumption by the land-owners themselves, their followers, servants and the priests of the two leading religions in the country. The consumer claims of the rent-receivers and their clients, and this means the quality of the articles of products consumed, were duly modified according to the quantity of the resources appropriated. Accordingly, the lesser requirements were met by local artisans and the more refined tastes were catered for by imported goods. In either case, the demand was mainly for consumer goods, so that only a small part of the feudal rent was embodied in the implements of production.

To return to Grant's data, we find that on the strength of the expenditure items in zamindar budgets we must assume that a part of the handicraft mass-consumption product (let us recall that it was valued at 30 million rupees) was consumed by the zamindars and their entourage, while the rest was exchanged mainly for the rayat's produce. To the extent that this exchange was carried out via the market, there occurred additional commercialisation of the peasant produce, which is why apparently about one-third of the rayat's produce was converted into commodities, although as an independent owner of commodities he could realise them by exchanging them for handicraft products only within the limits of under 30 million rupees, that is, only one-seventh of the value of his produce. The question of whether this exchange involved only the rayat's articles of consumption or also his implements remains obscure because of lack of direct information.

However, Grant's report contains some consideration of expenditure on agricultural reproduction. "In agriculture instruments of husbandry, the seeds and wages of labour, absorb the requisite productive capital." Expenditure on cattle was not great, since it grazed freely on rich pastures throughout the year. "Ten yoke of oxen sufficient for the ordinary yearly three-fold cultivation of 100 begas of ground (the Bengali bigha $= \frac{1}{3}$ acre, so that this is a plot of about 13 hectares.— V.P) may be purchased generally throughout the country for 40 rupees, while less than a fifth of the same amount, will furnish ploughs with all the other implements required.... In like manner, the seed is supplied in a very unconsiderable portion safe from annual produce, and probably for all the lands of the soubah, doth not exceed a value of 20 lakhs. Then supposing 14 crore to be the aggregate wages of the labour for the whole year, at the rate of 17 to 18 rupees to each individual of all ages, male or female, furnished by 350,000 mokuddeman ryots, or chiefs of inferior farmers; yet as this sum is chiefly paid in provisions daily or proportionate to the returns of the triple annual harvest by monthly instalments, so the amount required in advance, never can exceed a twelfth of the total (annual.— V. P.) in money and kind. In a word, we are sure of being within bounds, in estimating the whole productive stock employed or necessary in agriculture, at less than amply compensated by the proprietory sovereign of the land entitled to rent, through the extraordinary profits (to the rayats.—V. P.) accruing from free unbounded pasturage."[61]

This account evidently reflects the British view of the subject, and therefore clearly needs a very critical examination. First of all, it estimates the value of the harness and implements for ten yoke of oxen necessary to work 13 hectares of land. This estimate is close to later data under which the standard "labour allotment" in Bengal came to 5 acres or 2 hectares, and was worked with two oxen and one set of implements. Thus, Grant's observations are based on a fairly large farm on which five sets of implements and the corresponding amount of manpower were used. In general, the fact that the British official operates (pending the introduction of the Permanent Settlement) with this kind of farm as being typical provides indirect evidence that the rural upper sections in Bengal in the 18th century engaged in cultivation themselves very widely and perhaps even generally (in terms of farmland). The estimate of the value of a set of implements (8 rupees for the harness and about 2 rupees for the farming implements) is also close to subsequent data, although the share of the harness, which was made by the leather-dresser appears to be exaggerated. However that may be, the general regularity—the insignificant share of the most active element (implements of labour) in the total value of the farming inventory (implements and oxen, at 8-10 rupees per head)—appears in these proportions quite clearly. It also becomes possible to estimate the share of handicraft articles and services in Bengal's overall national product.

Recalling that the value of agricultural produce in Bengal was estimated at 210 million rupees (at 6 rupees per bigha with the cultivated area totalling 35 million bighas), and with the implements necessary to cultivate 100 bighas valued at about 50 rupees, its total value for Bengal comes roughly to 17 million rupees. Let us add the value of carts and devices for irrigation and wells, and the volume of handicraft services will increase to 25-30 million rupees. This amount, like its commodity expression, was not listed in the earlier enumeration of the handicrafts whose commodities were taxed. But it is close to 30 million rupees of handicraft products which, together with the farm produce, constituted the "total value of the annual industry of the country".

These figures are not quite comparable: first, the 30 million rupees also include the value of the articles of peasant and other local consumption; second, the farming implements, whose total value we have estimated at 25-30 million rupees, were made for periods longer than one year (iron parts—for 10 to 12 years), which is why the value of the annual handicraft production can include only a part of that amount; third, the implements required repairs every year, and the value of this was fairly considerable, but the source does not reveal whether or not it was included in the annual handicraft production. One is left with the general impression that 30 million rupees roughly determine (perhaps slightly understating) the volume of goods and services provided by artisans for the rural population.

The rural population engaged on the farms of the village élite was, we find, paid in kind on the daily or monthly principle but in proportion to the size of the crop. These data do not suffice for one to judge about the nature of the use of these working people. But one may assume that these were the lower sections of the rural population, whose remuneration combined the principles of time payment and the traditional community deduction of a share of the crop.

As for the 140 million rupees which went to pay for agricultural labour in one form or another, this clearly implies not only payment to additional workers recruited for work on the farms of the village élite, but also the cost of maintenance of manpower of the tenants themselves and members of their families.

That being so, the total value of farm produce—210 million rupees—consisted of 140 million rupees' worth of labour and production costs (of this amount a part went for the maintenance of artisans servicing the village), 52.5 million in land-tax and the mass of rent which went to the land-owners. Clearly, this kind of break-down of the agricultural product is highly approximate and even more conditional because of the attempts to express in money terms a product which for the most part was distributed and consumed without being involved in commodity-money relations.

The information we have at our disposal is highly diverse in value and incomparable, and makes it possible to draw but the most preliminary conclusions on a number of aspects. However, it is apparently possible to assume, on the basis of the information quoted above and of subsequent material, that in pre-British India this type of rural community was highly widespread, with reproduction on the peasant farms being carried on mainly in the course of a natural unity with the artisans turning out farming implements, although trade in these implements did exist. At the same time, the data on economic life in Bengal and Bihar in the early 19th century warrant the conclusion that even in the pre-British period the system of intra-community relations had been seriously disrupted. These changes affected both relations between the artisans and the agricultural population, and the production ties within the latter.

The Status of the Various Sections of the Rural Population

In considering the information already set forth above and that which is to be considered later, I shall try to avoid the use both of the traditional English terminology and the notions introduced in Indian studies later and adapted to the former. Thus, the "mokuddeman rayats" cannot be classed as "farmers" (despite the area they cultivated), but must rather be classed among the lower sections of the land-cultivating and tax apparatus—but simultaneously among the upper section of the rural population itself which engaged in farming and recruited village serfs, but which also took a hand in the actual cultivation.

In Bengal there was a special term for the peasant cultivator—"chashi" or "chasha"—although, according to Colebrooke, the term "rayat" included, alongside the rural tax-payers, also tax-payers from among the merchants and artisans, while village serfs, naturally, were not regarded as rayats.[62] But because the British officials were interested specifically in the tax-paying population of the countryside, among whom cultivators prevailed, with that population being the chief tax-payer, the later documents of the British administration usually used the term "rayat" to designate cultivators in general. Subsequently, "rayat" became a virtual synonym for "peasant" even in Indian studies, although there were any number of reservations and specifications. The traditional generalisation of the term "rayat" hampers the analysis of the sources, beginning, as we have seen, with the "Ain-i-Akbari" and ending with present-day studies.

E. N. Komarov unwittingly paid tribute to this approach, for he did not carry the term "rayat" beyond the limits of the upper well-to-do sections of the peasantry, although his own work contains the conclusion that "the accumulation of cash property among some rich peasants led both to the feudal exploitation of share-croppers by these peasants and now and again to the farming of cash rent throughout the village or a part of it. As a result, the rich peasant could virtually become, and sometimes did indeed become, a petty feudal land-owner."[63] However, the leasing of a section of the land which could not be worked by members of the family recruiting the traditional number of servants from the community became commonplace even among the rural élite in Maharashtra (just as the appropriation of tax amounts).

The nature of economic activity among Bengali and, let me add, Bihari rural upper sections requires a major independent study. The intention on the part of some British surveyors to present them as entrepreneur-type farmers (and this was reflected in Grant's terminology), and the zamindars—as British landlords sprang in part from the unconscious Anglicised approach to the Indian countryside and partly from a conscious attempt to substantiate the principles of British land-taxation.

The information about the farms of the rural élite in Bengal and Bihar becomes something like systematic only in sources dating from the first decade of the 19th century, including the studies by Buchanan, Colebrooke and Varda. But even the earlier testimonials contain some mention of economic differentiation of the rural population. Thus, the poem "Shivayana" by the Bengali poet Rameshwar Bhattacharya (1750s) portrays the figure of a rural land-owner, who was not very typical of Western India and whose activity boiled down to vigilant supervision of those who cultivated his lands.[64] But that is undoubtedly no more than a hint at some social type.

The rural upper sections are described in more concrete terms in a study by N. K. Sinha, who draws on British official information and speaks of the privileged status of the "upper rayats" in the 1780s, that is, on the eve of the introduction of the Permanent Settlement. Because from their midst were appointed the village headmen—mandals ("mandal" is a term closely approximating in meaning "muqaddam"), the "upper rayats" had the opportunity to shift the burden of the land-tax onto the "lower rayats". Unfortunately, Sinha says nothing in detail about the economic activity of either.

The size of the holding among the various categories of rayats in Bengal varied as it did in Maharashtra. Some of the rayats had plots of 200 bighas (over 26 hectares) and three or four sets of implements. According to Sinha, the lands of these rayats were cultivated by hired workers, who received for this work an allotment, "chakaran", which is similar to the watan, that is, one may assume that they were essentially the section of the rural population which was feudally exploited and worked off the labour rent on the farms of the rural upper crust. Basing himself on Buchanan's data (as set forth by Montgomery Martin) about cultivators with allotments working two-thirds of the time for the land-owner, E.N. Komarov draws the conclusion that the form of exploitation was reminiscent of labour rent.[65] At the same time, the majority of rayat holdings had something like 16 bighas (2.1 hectares) of land under rice. It was assumed that these rayats were able to provide for their families after giving away one-half of their crop in the form of tax.[66]

Judging by Grant's estimates of the product cost being 6 rupees per bigha, "upper rayats" had up to 600 rupees left after revenue payments, and "lower rayats" had about 50 rupees. Because in Mogul times and even after the British conquest (until the introduction of the Permanent Settlement), the rich villagers had an opportunity considerably to evade payment of revenues, their gross income, no doubt, exceeded one-half of the harvest and provided sufficient opportunities to extend their farmland and enlarge their householding. The relationships between such landlords and rural artisans could not be based on exchange as a relationship between independent producers. We shall see later that in Bengal not only community servants but respected artisans like smiths were destined to belong to the lower castes.

The lower rayats' income—after revenues were paid and production expenditures covered—enabled them to maintain their family living standards at the rate of 3-4 rupees per month (provided there were some additional earnings), i.e., at a level typical of the average working Indian, which left no opportunity to acquire more land or enlarge the householding. It was obviously difficult for these rayats to maintain their implements and keep their cattle. That is why they often rented them from the "higher rayats" on the condition of compensation with work in their households.

For all the distinctions in the size of property, land-holding and farm, none of the main groups of the agricultural population in Bengal had outlays on implements that would constitute an important item on the expenditure side of their budget. With the surplus of manpower, there was virtually no incentive to improve techniques. Productive accumulation was insignificant or went almost exclusively into simple reproduction. All this intensified the tendencies towards stagnation in agriculture.

The material brought together in this chapter gives an idea of the mechanism behind the social division of labour only at the lower micro-unit: the direct relations between agriculture and the handicrafts. The more extensive ties of this mechanism were mediated by merchant's capital, and we shall now consider its functions below.

NOTES

1. L. B. Alayev, *Yuzhnaya India. Sotsialno-ekonomicheskaya istoriya* XIV-XVIII vekov, Moscow, 1964, p. 42.
2. *Ibid.*, p. 36.
3. J. Forbes, *Oriental Memoirs: A Narrative of Seventeen Years Residence in India*, vols I-II, London, 1834.
4. *Ibid.*, vol. II, pp. 41-42.
5. *Ibid.*, p. 45.
6. V.I. Pavlov, *The Indian Capitalist Class*, Bombay, 1964, p. 22.
7. I. Habib, *Potentialities...*, p. 6.
8. As a matter of fact, I reviewed my notions concerning these matters about ten years ago. This will be seen from an article published in 1966, which appeared also in English (see: V. I. Pavlov, Rural Handicrafts of India in the System of Social, Division of Labour, *Soviet Oriental Studies. Achievements and Problems. South and South-East Asia*, Calcutta, 1970, pp. 214-223).
9. A. I. Chicherov, Ekonomicheskoye razvitiye Indii pered angliyskim zavoyevaniyem (remeslo i torgovlya v XVI-XVIII vv.), Moscow, 1965, pp. 25, 31, 40, 45. The book is also available in a new, revised edition in English: *India: Economic Development in the 16th-18th Centuries (Outline History of Crafts and Trade)'*, Moscow, 1971.
10. In the sources from which A.I. Chicherov draws his information, both systems of remuneration for carpenters and smiths e described on the same pages (see: R. M. Martin, *The History, Antiquities, opography and Statistics of Eastern India*, London, 1838, vol. II, pp. 261-265).
11. The ploughshare, for instance, lasted for a similar period. See: *GBP*, vol. XXIV (Kolhapur), Bombay, 1886, p. 157.
12. J. Forbes, *Oriental Memoirs...*, vol. II, pp. 415-417.
13. *Selections of Papers from the Records at the East India House*, vol. III, London, 1826, pp. 649, 654.
14. F, Buchanan, *A Journey...*, vol. I, pp. 265, 268.
15. *Ibid.*, pp. 267, 337.
16. *Ibid.*, p. 41 vol. II, p. 108.
17. R. M. Martin, *The History...*, vol. I, pp. 324-328; see also vol. II, pp. 252, 261.
18. F. Buchanan, *A Journey...*, vol. I, p. 218.
19. *Ibid.*
20. *Selections of Papers at the East India House, Relating to the Revenue, Police, and Civil and Criminal Justice under the Company's Government in India*, vol. 4, London, 1828, pp. 661-662.

21. *Report on the Village Communities of the Deccan, Government of Bombay, Selections from Records*, p. 11.
22. *Ibid.*, p. 12.
23. D. Graham, *Statistical Report of Kolhapur*, Poona, 1854, p. 260.
24. D.R. Gadgil, *The Industrial Evolution of India in Recent Time*, Calcutta, 1954, p. 163.
25. K. Marx, *Capital*, vol. I, p. 358. Marx refers to: M. Wills, *Historical Sketches of the South of India*, London, 1810-1817, vol. I, pp. 118-20. Marx also notes the good comparison of the various forms of Indian communities in: G. Campbell, *Modern India*, London, 1852.
26. I. Habib, *Potentialities...*, pp. 6-7.
27. *GBP*, vol. XVIII, pt I (Poona), Bombay, 1885, p. 285.
28. F. Buchanan, *An Account of the District of Bhagalpur in 1810-1811*, Patna, 1939, p. 601.
29. *Ibid.*, p. 480.
30. F. Buchanan, *An Account of the District of Purnea in 1809-1810*, Patna, 1934, p. 474.
31. See, e.g.: F. Buchanan, *An Account of the District of Bhagalpur*...pp. 480-482.
32. *Ibid.*, pp. 490, 494, 503-504.
33. F. Buchanan, *An Account of the District of Bihar and Patna in 1811-1812*, Patna, [s.a.], vol. 2, p. 639.
34. F. Buchanan, *An Account of the District of Shahabad in 1812-1813*, Patna, 1834, p. 367.
35. *Ibid.*, p. 400.
36. F. Buchanan, *An Account of the District of Purnea...*, p. 221.
37. *Ibid.*, pp. 221-222, 236.
38. *Ibid.*, p. 530.
39. *Ibid.*, pp. 535-536.
40. *Ibid.*, p. 536.
41. I. Habib, *Potentialities...*, p. 27.
42. *Ibid.*, pp. 27-28.
43. B.Ts . Urlanis, *Rost naseleniya v SSSR*, Moscow, 1966, p . 23.
44. I. Habib, *Potentialities...*, pp. 29-39.
45. *Ibid.*, pp. 39-40.
46. *Ibid*, pp. 40-42.
47. *The Fifth Report from the Select Committee...*, vol. II, pp. 321-322.
48. *Ibid.*, p. 321.
49. *Ibid.*, p. 322.
50. *Ibid.*, pp. 276-277.
51. *Ibid.*
52. *Ibid.*, p. 271.
53. *Ibid.*, p. 277.
54. *Ibid.*, p. 275.
55. N.K. Sinha, *The Economic History of Bengal. From Plassey to the Permanent Settlement*, vol. II, Calcutta, 1962, p. 159.
56. *Ibid.*, p. 238.
57. *Ibid.*, p. 241.
58. *Ibid.*, p. 240.
59. W. W. Hunter, *Statistical Accounts of Bengal, District of Midnapur and Hugli* (including Howrah), London, 1878, pp. 111-112.
60. N.K. Sinha, *The Economic History...*, vol. II, pp. 244-245.

61. *The Fifth Report from the Select Committee...*, vol. II, p. 278.
62. E.N. Komarov, Bengalskaya derevnya i krestyanskoye khozyaist-vo vo vtoroi polovine XVIII v., *UZIVAN*, vol. XVIII, Moscow, 1957, pp. 35, 36, 71.
63. *Ibid.*, p. 67.
64. *Ibid.*, p. 58.
65. *Ibid.*, p., 60. This type of relations will subsequently be considered in detail.
66. See: N. K. Sinha, *The Economic History...*, vol. II, pp. 131-143, 196-198.

CHAPTER TWO

MERCHANT'S AND USURER'S CAPITAL IN FEUDAL INDIA

The structure and functions of merchant's and usurer's capital were determined by the scale and character of the social division of labour, the inter-connection between the individual spheres of production and consumption, the methods of extracting and redistributing the surplus-product and the specific features of the processes of reproduction. The caste and religious community system of feudal society in India left a deep imprint on the social organisation and personified representation of this capital. Even in Western Europe, where merchant's capital displayed a relatively greater transformative potential, the merchant, according to Engels, acted not "as a conscious revolutionary" in his world, but, on the contrary, "as flesh of its flesh, bone of its bone. The merchant of the Middle Ages was by no means an individualist, he was essentially an associate like all his contemporaries."[1]

Indeed, the merchant is represented in the sources dating from the 17th to the early 19th century as an element of the caste system of India. That is why it would be meaningful to start the exposition by considering the organisational structure of merchant's and usurer's capital. In medieval India, commerce and usury were largely concentrated in the hands of members of occupational castes and communities and were their traditional business activity. In the aggregate, merchant's and usurer's capital constituted a complete functional system through which commodity and money values moved in the socially required directions. Thus, if the vertical outflow of the product prevailed within the limits of the micro-region, upon reaching a definite middle, to say nothing of a higher tier of the system of redistribution, the product was involved in channels of horizontal connections, which ranged over large provinces and even the territory of vast state entities like the Mogul Empire. Accordingly, in the internal functional connections of merchant's and usurer's capital there prevailed: vertical ties (from the petty usurer-trader to the merchant banker) within the limits of the district, and horizontal ties between roughly equal partners within the macro-regions and between them.

The functional system of merchant's and usurer's capital is reflected in the organisational structure of Indian merchant's capital as a whole and in the hierarchical construction of the major castes and communities. The combination and interaction of dealers of different statures operating on different lines constituted the basis of the mechanism for the micro-region, and could be effected by the representatives of the caste or community of traders. But the more extensive the territory on which merchant's capital operated, the more inevitable it was for various castes and communities to be involved in the overall operations.

The castes among the trader-merchant group were not based on particular specialised economic activity. Hence, at all times trader-merchant groups in the larger centres would include members of more than one caste or community. The long distance over which trader-merchants often travelled and the existence of correspondents of branches of big indigenous financial houses in all the main trading centres made for a somewhat mixed caste composition of the merchant group in central locations. Thus, in the case of merchant-traders congregated in large centres of trade the problem of a group organisation for economic purposes would necessarily arise.[2]

In this interaction, the positions of the individual castes and communities were not similar. Some of them (for instance, Bengali) did not transcend the limits of the lower, local functions, while others operated along the whole range of vertical and horizontal interactions. That is why although the merchant and money-lending castes were to be found among almost all the peoples of India, they were most developed in Gujarat and Rajputana, through which ran the famous trade route from the Gujarat ports to the historical centre of the Mogul state. Influential castes of Gujarati—Marwari ("Marwari" was the name given to the inhabitants of the north-eastern part of Rajputana—Marwar or Jodhpur), and also merchant and money-lending castes originating from other districts of Rajputana, and castes of other merchants and money-lenders were tax-collectors (especially collectors of the land-tax); they supplied the feudal lords with goods and gave them credit, and acted as army purveyors and money-changers. Moreover, they exploited the peasants directly through commerce and usury.)

Direct Participation by Merchant's Capital in Alienation of the Agricultural Surplus-Product

The important role which the trading and money-lending castes played in the collection of the feudal rent-tax—the basic form of surplus-product in Mogul India—accounts, first and foremost, for the close ties linking the Marwari and Gujarati traders and money-lenders with the ruling class. For instance, the rent-tax in the Rajput princely states was paid in kind by the peasants and converted into money by the Marwari or Gujarati tax-collectors. Merchants who undertook to collect tax in a given area paid the Treasury a sum of money fixed in advance, collected the tax in kind from the agricultural population, and then sold the products for a profit in the towns and army camps. Tax-collecting and conversion of the land-tax which was paid in kind into money was, for example in Jaisalmer, in the hands of the Brahmans of the Palliwala subcaste that had become a trading and money-leding caste.[3]

The tax-farming activity of the Marwari money-lenders reached a particularly wide scope after the formation of the huge Mogul Empire in the middle of the 16th century. The great distances separating the centres of provinces from the capital and the frequent replacement of the jagirdars, who superintended the collection of taxes, were factors conducive to the development of the tax-farming system. The decay of the state ownership of land and of the central fiscal bodies, which began in the 17th and 18th centuries, provided the big tax-farmers with new opportunities to extend their activities in the various provinces of the disintegrating Mogul Empire.[4] "The Bania communities (such as Aggarwals, Oswals, Meshris, etc.) were all trading communities also of U.P. and Bihar. It is possible that the migration of these, especially into U.P. and Central India, took place at an early period. However, their migration to regions other than U.P. and Central India cannot have taken place much earlier than the 17th century, and most probably occurred in substantial numbers only in the 18th century. This migration took place, in the main, to the East and to the South. To the North and the West, there were predominantly Muslim areas in which important Hindu trading communities with capital resources and high skill already operated. To the South-West (in Gujarat and Saurashtra) also there already existed highly organised expert business communities."[5]

The positions of the trading and money-lending castes in the collection of taxes, the financing of rulers, army supplies, commerce, and also their personal business abilities helped many of their members to rise to high posts in the government, and primarily in the tax administration. Thus, members of the Marwari castes held high posts in the princely states of Rajputana; the ancestors of the biggest Marwari capitalist, Gopaldas Mohta, many times headed the administrative apparatus of Bikaner and were granted jagirs and various privileges for their military and administrative services.[6]

Tax-farming also helped many members of the trading and money-lending castes to advance to high posts in the administration of the Mogul state. Todar Mal, a member of Agarwal, a Marwari caste, organised and headed the financial department of Akbar at the end of the 16th century. Kharsukhrai, a Jain,[7] was treasurer of the Moguls and responsible for paying the troops. His successor, P. D. Ramchandar, was in charge of remitting revenue payments to Delhi.[8] At the beginning of the 18th century, the Gujarati shroff, Anandrai Mashraf, was minister of the last Mogul Viceroy in Gujarat.[9]

The big merchant's and usurer's capital of the tax-farmers acquired especially strong influence in the early 18th century, when the fiscal functions of the Mogul state were largely concentrated in their hands. In that period, the activity of big merchant's and money-lending capital is illustrated by the operations of the great banking house of the Jagat Seths. An ancestor of the Jagat Seths, Hiranand Saho, appeared in Bihar in the late 17th century as a banker and purveyor for the Mogul military chief Man Singh, the maharaja of the Rajputana state of Jaipur. Hiranand Saho was a banker from Amber, the capital of Jaipur, and belonged to the Oswals, a Marwari mercantile and money-lending caste.[10] His son, Manik Chand, was at the beginning of the 18th century the banker of Murshid Kuli Khan, the virtually independent Nawab of Bengal, and his right-hand man regarding financial matters in Bengal, Bihar and Orissa. Manik Chand enjoyed also great influence at the Delhi court. Using his influence and money, Manik Chand helped Murshid to retain his position as nawab and secure his independence in the administration of Bengal. In return for his services, Murshid Kuli Khan fully supported Manik Chand when the latter solicited the title of Jagat Seth (world banker), a title which was granted by the Mogul Shah Farrukhshiar in 1715.[11] This became the proper name of Manik Chand and his heirs Fathi Chand and Maktab Rai, who enjoyed an enormous influence with the court of the Bengal nawabs during the first half of the 18th century.[12]

It was no mere chance that Bengal and Bihar became the principal field for the activities of the Jagat Seths. Huge revenues were collected every year in these rich provinces of the Mogul Empire and sent to Delhi. Bengal was one of the most important centres of the handicrafts (especially weaving) and commerce not only in India but in the whole of Southern Asia. The tax returns of Bengal were remitted to Delhi by means of the banking house of the Jagat Seths, who had their branches and gomashthas (agents) for the collection of taxes and the transmission of the money raised in all the important commercial towns of the country.[13] They also converted into money the tax levied in kind from the population.[14] The Jagat Seths extended credits to the hereditary land-owners, the zamindars, who needed money to pay the land-tax and then, taking advantage of the zamindars' liabilities, seized many of their estates.

W. Bolts says: "The zamindars, who . . . generally are in want of large sums of ready cash, as well as of security to be given for the payment of their rents according to agreement, have been usually necessitated to call in the shroffs, or bankers or money-changers, to their assistance. Juggut Seat, the head of a Gentoo family of the weaver tribe or caste (Bolts was probably mistaken.—V.P.), in the time of the Nabob Jaffer Khan, availed himself of this circumstance, which the succeeding times of confusion in the empire enabled him to improve, to the introduction of new customs at the Durbar, in the department of the revenues, and to the raising and enriching of himself and his family."[15]

The Jagat Seths conducted an extensive trade, especially in Bengal cloth, and carried out big financial operations in the commercial centres of Bengal with merchants from various Asian and European countries. During the first half of the 18th century, the English and other European trading companies in Bengal were given credits by the Jagat Seths.[16] The well-known historian of India's economy, T. Raychaudhuri, made an interesting assumption, which, as he stresses, needs to be studied, namely, that the emergence in the first half of the 18th century of wealthy bankers, like the Jagat Seths, who specialised in money-lending, testifies to the fact that the monopoly of the British East India Company to the sea trade, by ousting Indian merchants from that sphere of activity, forced them to switch to money-lending.[17] It is hard to assert that but for the British the Jagat Sehts would have engaged in the sea trade to which they were unused. Whatever the circumstances, one should assume they would not have refused to engage in tax-farming. But on the whole, the British had undoubtedly forced Bengal's merchants to extend their activities on the land by forcing them off the sea routes.

Currency speculations were an important source of the riches amassed by the Jagat Seths, who also controlled the mint in Murshidabad. Using their position in the Treasury of Bengal, the Seths fixed a compulsory rate of exchange for the sikka rupee (i.e., the rupee of the latest issue) in terms of rupees coined earlier. Transactions involving the exchange of sikkas were, according to Bolts, "a fund of infinite wealth to the family of the Seths."[18] The "Sair-ul-Mutaharin" relates that the wealth of the Jagat Seths was so great that no banker could compare with them, either in Hindustan or the Deccan. It is quite obvious that at that time all bankers in Bengal were either associates of the Jagat Seths or members of their family. The following incident gives an idea of the size of their fortune: during the first Maratha invasion, when Murshidabad was not yet surrounded by walls, Mir Habib with a detachment of his best cavalry managed to take the city before Aliverdi was able to come to its aid, and removed 20 million Arcot rupees alone from the house of the Jagat Seths. The loss of so huge a sum seems to have affected the brothers no more than might have the loss of two sheaves of straw. They continued to draw bills amounting to 10 million rupees for the government.[19]

Relying on their economic strength, the Jagat Seths were able to exert considerable political influence in Bengal. Bolts asserts that the Jagat Seths "acquired an influence at the Durbar little inferior to that of the Nabob himself."[20] Although the most important, the Jagat Seths were not the only Marwari bankers in Bengal. During the reign of the last Moguls there were seven rich bankers, called kothiwalla (the owner of the firm), in Murshidabad who had their own agents in important towns. All of them were members of the Oswal caste from Western India who had settled in Bengal. They imported European woollen cloth, cotton and cotton goods, as well as pepper and other spices, and exported ginger; their main business, however, was the provision of bills of exchange. Taxes collected in various localities were, during the Muslim rule, remitted by these bankers to Murshidabad.[21] The close relations usually maintained within their caste helped the Marwari moneylenders and bankers in Bengal to consolidate their position. In 1748 for instance, the Jagat Seths dismissed a number of employees who were not members of their caste.[22]

The structure of the mass of products was determined by the vast scale of the operations in collecting and remitting the land-tax, which initially was paid in kind (that is, in grain). Habib lists grain first among the items of merchant trade in Mogul India, connecting this circumstance with the fact that the system of agrarian exploitation under the Mogul Empire was based on the great movement of grain and other farm produce from the countryside to the towns. According to the Persian terminology accepted in India, the merchant-bania was also designated as bakkal, which meant "trader in grain". Habib observes that regardless of whether the peasant sold his grain in the village, at the nearest fair or at the urban market-place, the merchant took part in this trade. The capital involved in the grain trade was large because, unlike the artisans who frequently worked directly on orders, the peasant very rarely established commodity relations with the consumers of his produce.[23] That is why the participation of urban capital in the marketing of agricultural produce was relatively more intense than in the marketing of mass-consumption manufactured articles.

Retail trade in farm produce was commonplace. For instance, travelling from Surat to Agra, Tavernier counted in one of the small towns on his route "five or six shops belonging to Banias which sell butter, rice, straw and vegetables." In describing one of them, Tavernier remarked that "by its side stood a large warehouse filled with sacks of rice and grain."[24] Unfortunately, we have no information to enable us to judge how the farm produce reached the retail trade, whether through purchases from the peasants or in the form of the natural component of money-lending interest, rent and taxes.

The question of the direct exploitation by money-lending capital of small land-holders through cash loans has been virtually not studied at all. K. A. Antonova remarks on the role which the introduction by Akbar of a cash tax played in intensifying the exploitation of the peasants by the money-lenders, because it sharply increased their rayats' cash requirements.[25] Information on the conversion of tax in kind into cash by tax-farmers shows that the rayats did not pay the tax in cash themselves everywhere or at any time in Mogul India.

In Gujarat, the village money-lender was sufficiently important in the village community to lay claim to a share of the crop of the community land-holder. It was the money-lender who weighed the harvested crop and set aside the part due to officials and artisans in the community, sharing out the rest equally between the rent-receiver and the rayat himself. Nominally, he received his share of the crop for his "labours" in sharing it out.[26] But it is much more convincing to connect this fact with the role which money-lending had to play in the Indian countryside in the pre-British period.

Let us note that the organisation of land-holding castes prevented the transfer of the peasant debtor's land into the hands of the money-lender.[27] Members of the trading and money-lending castes owned hardly any land on the rayatwari basis when India was conquered by the British. However, the difficulties faced by the rayats in having to pay their taxes and rents were used by the money-lender as a means of enslaving them. Thus, Buchanan says that the village officers and senior farmers "informed me, that the merchants of Bangalore frequently advance them money to pay their rents, and are afterwards contented to take one-half of the crop for the advance and for interest. These advances are sometimes made six months before the crop is reaped."[28] This fragment shows, incidentally, that the tax itself was somewhat smaller than onehalf of the crop, but together with the interest the rayat had to give up one-half of his crop.

The money-lenders frequently converted the rayat's payments in kind into cash tax in the Peshwa state, at any rate in the final period of its existence. According to studies by British officials just after the conquest of Maharashtra (1821), "the money rent, when paid, is stated to have been founded on the grain rent, and the conversion is said to have been made at one-seventh of the prices of the present day."[29] We find that the amount of the money-lender's reward provided sufficient opportunities for his enrichment. But the money-lender did not stop there. In one way or another he was usually connected with the "farmer (tax-farmer.—V.P.) or Mamlutdar of the district, who had always the means, after the demands of the latter were satisfied, of compelling the cultivator to pay to the utmost of his ability. In many instances, the money-lender paid the cash direct into the hands of the Mamlutdar and took bonds of from fifty to one hundred per cent from the cultivator, to be paid in kind at the harvest season. These lenders usually managed all the money concerns of the Ryots, keeping an account of grain against cash; and it not infrequently happened that the Ryot got back at the end of the year, or received at an advanced rate, the same grain he had previously paid for at a depreciated rate to the Sahookar (money-lender.—V.P.), in liquidation of the last year's demand."[30] There is also other evidence of the deep indebtedness of the Maratha rayats caused by the coercion of the Naib tax-farmers. The old debts, at compound interest, reached amounts which the rayat was unable to pay.[31]

The British officials may have somewhat overstated the case, in order to whitewash their own tax oppression. But one thing is quite clear: the collection of cash tax in Maharashtra was also realised without any breach in the natural closed cycle of reproduction in agriculture, which was fenced off from direct and free relations with the market by merchant's and usurer's capital. The rayat usually gave the money-lender his bond, and the former paid the patel (the headman) the tax due from the rayat. When remitting the taxes to the district fiscal establishments, the patel himself issued a bond (hawalla) to a bigger money-lender, who then paid the amount of the tax in cash. This "mode was most prevalent, so much so that it is estimated that scarcely 25 per cent of the revenue was paid directly in money."[32]

The marketing of grain coming in as tax required a vertical credit and trading system in Maharashtra as well. The cash tax itself was either remitted by bills drawn from the districts upon the Poona banks, or was paid in cash and passed through the hands of bankers "who profited by the exchange of coins before the collections reached the public Treasury. Bankers had, in consequence, their agents in the districts, and the ramification of the money trade, in loans to the Ryots, to the renters of villages and districts extending to every quarter, created a wide circulation of specie which returned to their coffers with an abundant accumulation of interest."[33] Tax-farming was also practised with regard to the collection of customs duties. A rich merchant engaging in tax-farming would pay to the Treasury a sum ranging from 50,000 to 150,000 rupees and thereupon resell parts of his contract to the local landlords. The tax-farmer himself retained the right to collect duties in strategic localities, which were carefully selected by him to allow the merchants using them to bypass the usual customs posts. The merchants also stood to gain by paying the lower duties, and the tax-farmer himself, like the merchant, gained from such duties, forcing the other merchants to take a circuit road.[34]

Merchant's and money-lending capital was also closely interwoven with the tax apparatus in the state of Bhonsla (Eastern Maharashtra). The patel made the tax-payments in the kasba (the centre of the pargana) in cash or in bills drawn on the sahukar. If the patel did not enjoy sufficient confidence among the money-lenders, the chief of the pargana vouched for him, and then the sahukar paid the amount due under the chief's bond. For this the patel transferred to the sahukar the right to collect the whole tax or a part of it corresponding to the loan. The sahukar sent his agent to the big villages to make copies of the rayat bonds or to verify, in their presence, the tax records kept by the community accountant (pande). Where the rayat did not have any cash, he took a loan from the patel or sahukar; in the latter instance, he issued a bond under the security of the patel, who kept the debtor's property in restraint until the debt was paid off. These operations frequently ruined the rayats, who, once in debt, were unable to clear them off.[35]

The rayats resorted to two types of loans : in one case, they pledged with the creditor (the patel-warrantor, as we shall see later) the standing crop on the basis of prices which were much lower than market prices; in the second instance, the rayat undertook (usually before the sahukar) to pay the debt and the interest (2 per cent a month) after the crop was harvested and sold. If a rayat failed to pay off his debt in due time and was forced to apply to the creditor again, his cattle and implements, to say nothing of the crop, were than pledged. When a rayat was unable to pay off his debt, the patel (the source makes no mention of the sahukar) took over all the property of the rayat, formalising his actions as an act of voluntary sale.[36]

Thus, the information contained in the source warrants the assumption that the conversion of the surplus-product into cash paid as tax could be performed by any of these three persons: rayat, patel or sahukar. The existence of two types of taxes confirms the possibility of the patel or the rayat participating in the sale of the grain, while the credits issued by the sahukars to the patels with grain as the security, and the speculations by the former in grain (of which more later) show that at this or that stage the bulk of this chief farm produce fell into the hands of the money-lenders. Finally, one is left with the impression that the expropriation of the lands and the inventory of indebted rayats was carried out exclusively or mainly by the patels and not the sahukars, who were hindered by the caste principle of land-holding and the system of economic activity based on it. This principle would be later breached by British legislation, but even then the force of tradition would restrain the judicial formalisation of the rights acquired by the money-lender to the land.

At the same time, as the money-lenders realised the rayats' debts, they must have created friction with the village rich and the local land-owners. To the extent that the money-lender acted as an agent of the tax-farm system, he was also a representative of the rent claims of the state's landed property. That is why clashes between the landlords, the village upper crust and the money-lenders in securing a role in tax-collection directly from the labouring rayat frequently became very acute.

For instance, in Gujarat the local land-owners limited the tax-farming activity of the shroffs in an effort to increase their own share of the rent. Moreover, the zamindars began to intrude into the money-lending sphere, crowding the money-lenders and the bankers. Forbes says that in the 1770s corrupt men, called zamindars, stood between the patel and the government- nominated tax-farmer, obtaining benefits from both sides.[37] On the eve of the sowing, the zamindars provided the patels and the peasants with loans at $3\frac{3}{4}$ per cent a month (45 per cent a year) for the purchase of cattle, seeds, etc. Their future crop was handed over to the zamindars as security which is why at the time the tax had been paid they were called minutedars. By rights this title belonged only to the shroffs and the moneyed men of the district, who undertook by agreement and upon thorough examination to pay the amounts fixed by the government tax-collector.[38] We find that the East India Company official is highly hostile to the Gujarat zamindars, but we are interested in something else, namely, the clear urge on the part of the big land-owner to oust the tax-farming banker as the government's middleman in exploiting the peasantry. He did not always manage to do this. For instance, in Bengal the zamindars themselves became dependent on the banking house of the Jagat Seths.

The steady intrusion of money-lending capital into the fiscal system was quite natural because it opened up direct access to the bulk of the surplus-product. But what has been said shows that tax-farming was not the only form of activity among Indian merchants and bankers, although certain other operations were in one way or another adapted to the alienation of the agricultural products. At the same time, the foreign-trade activity of some groups of urban merchants and bankers, especially in the coastal and frontier areas, could constitute a fairly independent sphere.

Participation by Merchant's Capital in the Mediated Redistribution of the Agricultural Surplus-Product and other Operations

In medieval India war always entailed a redistribution of the surplus-product of agriculture and also of other branches, and the redistribution was either short-term or long-term, depending on how lasting the military success was. Actually, the inclusion of merchant's capital in such redistribution amounted to providing services for the military-administrative apparatus, which had become highly inclined, as it always did in war-time, to resort to arbitrary methods. When it came to war, merchant's capital naturally made money on supplies to the troops and resale of the booty plundered in the campaigns. In Mogul India, the bankers enriched themselves by acting as "modi"[39] or suppliers of the Mogul army.[40]

The banker-purveyors had agents in various centres of the country along the roads used by the military forces, whose job it was to supply the military on the march. "The prevalence of general self-sufficiency in products of agriculture did not mean that there were no specialised products and that sometimes these were not traded over long distances. Even the carriage of grain for large distances overland in considerable volume was absolutely essential for all military operations of the time. As a result, we see growing in importance the special business of big pack-animal carriers, who satisfied the needs of the military on the march. Apart from the carriage of produce for the military, there were also specialised products in which long-distance trade took place."[41]

At the end of the 17th century Tavernier wrote: "A great part of the money belonging to the state is always in the hands of the shroffs, who derive from it considerable profits. According to the rules of the country, the troops are paid monthly, but the majority of soldiers as well as many captains and other officers do not wait till the end of the month but borrow money from the shroffs who take 18-20 per cent interest per annum."[42]

The Marathas employed a similar system to finance and provision the troops on the march. For the Maratha states predatory raids were one of the principal sources of revenue, but the organisation of such a raid largely depended on whether the local bankers were prepared to advance the money necessary for the maintenance of the military personnel. "It is no exaggeration to say," wrote I. M. Reusner, "that merchant's and money-lending capital had a considerable role to play in financing the plunderous military campaigns of the Maratha feudal lords and secured for itself a sizable share of the booty. It should not be forgotten that these wars were carried on by mercenary troops, that they constantly required money, while the Maratha Peshwas were chronically short of money to pay their mercenaries."[43]

Beginning with Peshwa Baji Rao I, the government at Poona constantly resorted to loans from local bankers. After his death Baji Rao left an outstanding debt of 1,450,000 rupees. These had been taken from 30 money-lenders at 12-30 per cent per annum. The biggest of them were Ragunath Patwarjan (a loan of 300,000 rupees), Gorakh Mandravami (105,000 rupees) and Balaji Joshi (36,000 rupees).[44]

In 1736, Baji Rao had large debts and all his attempts to obtain fresh loans were refused by the money-lenders of Poona, who believed the Peshwa was not credit-worthy. According to S. Sen, the Peshwa was unable to finance military campaigns, and the feudal chiefs had to find the money themselves. It turns out that only a few of the Maratha chiefs had surplus or reserve funds which could be used for the purpose, and in such instances they applied to the money-lenders. That is why rich bankers, like J. Parekh, could rise to the status of Chief Minister under Daulat Rao Sindhia.[45]

When the Marathas marched north for the decisive fight against the Afghans in 1760, the Peshwa was able to give only 200,000 rupees in cash to Sadasheo Bhau, who commanded the troops, while the expenses of the campaign exceeded 500,000-600,000 rupees per month.[46] One of the chief functions of the big money-lenders and bankers charged with supplying the Maratha troops during campaigns was to advance money to the so-called banjaras, with which the latter were to purchase grain and bring it to the camp. Accounts of British eye-witnesses confirm that big money-lenders and merchants helped to provision the Maratha troops.[47]

The bankers were instrumental in plundering by means of taxation the regions seized by the Maratha chiefs, for whom the phrases "to wage war" and "to collect taxes" were synonymous.[48] But it was seldom possible to collect the taxes in cash over a short period. The Marathas, therefore, sought the help of the local banker, who gave them a bill of exchange (apparently, the local authorities undertook to repay with interest the sum for which the bill was drawn).

The conqueror could present the bill for payment in any part of India.[49] The highly developed system of bills of exchange was thus used by the Marathas during their forays to obtain the greatest possible amount of tribute in the shortest time. "Banking houses might be authorised to receive payments made either by local officials or functionaries and remit them to headquarters. Even where they were not so directly authorised, exchange business would arise out of needs of remittance."[50]

Finally, the trading and money-lending castes were engaged in supplying their nobility with luxury articles, weapons, horses and other imported goods. Information on trade in handicraft articles will be given below. Let me note at this point only that trade in these goods helped to extend the business ties of Indian merchants well beyond the borders of the country.

Apart from trade with the countries of the Middle East and South-East Asia, let me point to the fact that Indian merchants, including Marwari traders, made their way through Central Asia, Iran and the Transcaucasus, to Astrakhan, where they established permanent colonies. N. M. Goldberg ascertained that a Muslim merchant from Bengal sent three ships with a cargo of silk to Russia as early as the middle of the 16th century; they were, however, shipwrecked in the Persian Gulf. Indian merchants played an active role in trade along the Volga and were frequent visitors not only to Nizhny Novgorod and Yaroslavl, but also to Moscow during the 17th and early 18th centuries.[51]

The exchange of money was an important source of income for the castes of traders and money-lenders. Indeed, the name for Indian banker—shroff—is a distortion of the Arab word "sarraf" (money-changer). The fact that coins from a variety of mints circulated in the country provided the shroffs with many opportunities to enrich themselves by changing coins and assessing their value in terms of the legal tender.[52] According to Tavernier, the shroff would, after having evaluated a certain quantity of coins, sew them up in a bag, indicate their value on it and affix his personal seal. When the bag passed from hand to hand, the shroff confirmed the value of its contents and received for this a fixed interest.[53]

Under the peshwas in Maharashtra there was "so large a number of siccas, with such variation in their value when they were brought for exchange to the market, that the suraffs, sawkars and merchants defrauded the public at will."[54] The bankers extensively resorted to the falsification and counterfeiting of coins. "Coining was not highly centralised and there were large numbers of local mints. The variety of coins put into circulation was thus large. Moreover, coins were liable to deteriorate and new issues of even the same mint were usually at a premium. Large transactions, therefore, involved operations with a variety of coins and the fixing of their mutual value in exchange. This led to the creation of agencies ready to accept payment in a variety of coins or ready to exchange one type of coinage into another. Sometimes the money-changers were specialised as such, but usually money-changing was combined with other financial or banking business."[55]

The great volume and territorial scope of the commercial and financial operations required of the Indian merchants and bankers the establishment of a complex and smoothly working system of credit and information. Here is Jawaharlal Nehru's characteristic of the system: India's banking system "was efficient and well organised throughout the country, and the hundis or bills of exchange issued by the great business or financial houses were honoured everywhere in India, as well as in Iran and Kabul and Herat and Tashkent and other places in Central Asia ... there was an elaborate network of agents, jobbers, brokers and middlemen ... a very rapid and ingenious system of communicating news and market prices had been evolved."[56]

D.R. Gadgil, an outstanding associate of Nehru, adds: "Transactions connected with the issuing and discounting of bills of exchange were an important source of the bankers' wealth. One 'function' of the bankers ... was that of providing bills of exchange. These usually arose out of commodity trade and were the means by which trade was financed or money remitted for purposes of trading. These operations depended on the existence of a system of banking houses with either branches or correspondents all over the trading area. Such a system was in fully developed operation in India before the beginning of the 18th century. The system obviated the need for carriage of large amounts of coins over long distances, which in view of contemporary transport and political conditions would have been both risky and costly. Highly developed forms of bills of exchange had been evolved with elaborate security practices and a number of banking houses in important centres of trade in India were in a position to provide bills drawn on branches or correspondents throughout the country. The resources of the largest among these banking houses were very large and some of them maintained independent courier services of their own."[57]

Trading and Money-Lending Communities and Their Social Status. Conditions for Accumulation and Investment of Money

It will be easily seen that the organisation and spread of trading and money-lending castes and communities in a sense followed upon the operations of merchant's capital and the remittance of tax revenues. This regularity was personified: as soon as some area was involved in the sphere of intensive trading or tax-farming activity, money-lenders and bankers made their way into it.

Thus, the rapid extension of trading and credit activity caused merchants and bankers from the outlying areas to move into the cities of Maharashtra. While the bulk of the urban artisans were Marathas, the situation among the merchants was different. By the time the Maratha states were founded, the village community had not yet overcome its economic isolation, while the social division of labour between town and country lagged markedly behind the division of labour in the advanced areas of India. That is why no such powerful trading and money-lending castes were formed in Maharashtra as, for instance, in Gujarat, Rajputana or the Doab.

In the Peshwa state, most of the big local merchants and tax-farmers belonged to the Brahman caste. J. Malcolm wrote: "A very small proportion (of the Deccan Brahmans.—V. P.) are devoted to religious duties." Most of them "constitute that active and abstemious body of men of business who carry on all the duties of the Mahratta governments, and are the most industrious and intelligent, both of the higher and lower classes of merchants and clerks."[58]

An entry relating to the year 1797-1798 in the "Selections from the Peshwa's Diaries" gives the names of nearly 175 persons (all apparently Brahmans from Konkan) employed in the administrative offices of Poona, who were exempted from payment of transit excise when crossing over the passes of the Ghats, on the imports made by them of rice and other products from Konkan. "The imports would mostly represent bulk purchases made in Konkan but might also partly represent receipts of rent. They point to streams of internal trade set up by important migration movements."[59]

But the leading positions in large-scale commerce and banking continued to be occupied, as previously, by Gujarati and Marwari Banias, who had begun to immigrate into the country when it was still under Mogul rule.[60] "In Poona, the earliest migrant elements appear to have been Gujarati, Banias and Bohras, and it is likely that both of these came to Poona through Burhanpur and Aurangabad. In Nagpur, on the other hand, the trading immigrants were Bania castes from Rajasthan, which had spread into Central and North India. With the rise of cotton exports from the Berar-Nagpur tract, it was these elements that came to control this trade."[61]

In the 1820s, J. Malcolm met "princely bankers" of Gujarati descent in the states of Central India ruled by the Marathas. Some of these bankers' families had already settled in this region at the time when independent Rajput states existed there. For instance, the ancestor of the principal banker in Ujjain, who hailed from Gujarat, had come there 300 years ago.[62] Many of them occupied high positions in the Maratha administration. The dispatches, for example, of the English residents at the Sindhia court, written between 1811 and 1818, contain references to the great influence exerted upon state affairs by the banker Gopal Parekh, who headed the financial administration of Gwalior. The banker's nationality was not indicated, but from his typically Gujarati name and especially his surname, which is the same as that of the biggest millowner in Gujarat at the end of the 19th century, we can safely assume that Gopal Parekh was a shroff from Gujarat.

Gopal Parekh made his way up by granting a loan to the ruler's

Treasury, which was about to go bankrupt, for the taxes had been collected for several years in advance.[63] Out of gratitude, the rajah entrusted Parekh with the Treasury. Later on, however, Parekh's position bacame rather shaky. It was quite natural that the Banias always headed the fiscal administrations in the small states of Gujarat, their native country. Evidence of this will be found even in late 18th-century sources.[64] Malcolm asserted that in the 1820s "almost the whole of the Soucars and Shroffs (bankers and money-brokers) and a great proportion of Banias (or retail dealers), in Central India are either from Gujarat or Marwar, and generally not very old settlers.... The number from Marwar is greater than from Gujarat, but this is only since the Mahrattas governed Central India."[65] Up to the British conquest, bankers in Western Hindustan served the Maratha chiefs, their main occupation being tax-farming in the Maratha dominions.

Having got hold of tax-collecting, the Marwaris began to exert an influence on the administration of the princely states. Malcolm wrote: "As many of the renters are business bankers, or men supported by that class, they have acquired, and maintained an influence both in the councils of the state and the local administration of the provinces, that gives them great power, which they solely direct to the object of accumulation. The richest bankers mix in the petty revenue details of the smallest village."[66] Taking advantage of the heavy tax burden the starving rayats had to shoulder, the usurer or tax-collector would "help" the peasants by granting them a loan in kind for which he charged interest at a rate of 50 per cent per annum.[67] Under the conditions of the subsistent peasant husbandry, tax-farming, therefore, was a means employed by money-lending capital to enslave the rayats. Not only did the Marwari emigrants in the first half of the 19th century remain in touch with Marwar, their native land, but they usually returned there in their old age, "handing over the share they held in the small shops to their young compatriots who were arriving every year from Marwar to scrape up a fortune in Central India or the Deccan."[68]

Thus, merchant's and money-lending capital in India in the 17th-18th centuries amassed great accumulations, taking part in the tax drain of the land-holders and enslaving the artisans. But the development towards the following, historically higher stage of feudal society, was to a considerable extent hampered by the despotic Oriental structure, because Oriental rule was incompatible with pre-capitalist society. The appropriated surplus-value was not safe from the hands of rapacious satraps and pashas; the first fundamental condition of profitable trading was wanting—security for the person and property of the merchant.[69]

This remark of Engels', bearing directly on the Ottoman Empire, helps to understand the position of merchants and money-lenders in Mogul India as well. J. A. de Mandelslo wrote about the merchants of Gujarat: "Merchants are infinitely more happy than tradesmen; but they also have this inconvenience, that as soon as they have gotten any wealth together, they are exposed to the envy of the Grandees, who find out ways to fleece them, as soon as they make any show of it. And whereas they cannot do it with justice, they many times make use of such pretences as cost those their lives who had acquired excessive riches."[70] Mandelslo also remarked upon the low social position occupied by Hindu and Jain castes of merchants and money-lenders in Indian society: "The men (Banias.—V.P.) are very civilly apparell'd, and live without any scandal among the Mahomedans, who being imperious and insolent (this is, undoubtedly, a reference to Muslim chiefs.—V.P.), treat the Banias as if they were their slaves, with great contempt, much after the manner the Jews are treated in Europe, in those places where they are permitted to live."[71]

To get hold of the wealth accumulated by the merchants and money-lenders, the rulers did not hesitate to use the most savage tortures. James Forbes speaks of the cruelty exhibited by the Muslim ruler of Sind, at whose court in Tatta only Hindus—members of the trading and money-lending castes—were employed in the revenue administration. The vizier and his retinue subjected a rich Bania, who was a customs collector, to the most brutal tortures for two days. But only the threat to kill his only son forced the man to disclose where his treasures were hidden.[72] In 1798, the wealthiest shroffs of Poona were tortured to death. One of them, the richest and most influential one, died on the scorching hot muzzle of a cannon.[73]

Such atrocities conflicted with the ethical declarations of the Peshwa state. Here is a free translation of an extract (devoted to traders and bankers) from the "Āgnyapatra", an ancient Maratha treatise on statecraft: "The saukars are ornaments or royalty and of the kingdom. They make the realm prosperous. Unobtainable commodities enter the territory. The kingdom becomes wealthy. When contingencies arise they provide loans. By their aid, calamities are averted. There is much profit in extending protection to them. For this they should be accorded status. They should be protected from arbitrary acts and insults. Shops and markets should be established in various localities of the city for elephants, horses, silk clothes, cloth of gold, wool, jewellery, weapons, etc., so that they can conduct trade. Leading merchants should be encouraged to reside in the aristocratic quarters."[74] The fact, incidentally, that such principles are advanced is in itself significant, for, as every historian realises, laws in a way represent the reverse side of reality.

But even the awe-inspiring Maratha warriors were not all-powerful with respect to the defenceless bankers. In general, as this frequently happens, the defects of the laws and their observance were made up for traditional Indian society by customs. One of these, known as the tukkaza, was used by creditors to extract repayment of debt from powerful debtors. In the Peshwa state, the military sections of the people were almost always in debt, and often depending on their saucar or modi for their day's subsistence. It was naturally neither a safe nor an easy task to extract debts from these fighters. That is why the creditor, following futile reminders, hired one or several persons, who practised tukkaza as a full-time job; they would take up their place at the door of the debtor and "by the invariable rule of the country" the debtor was bound to provide maintenance for them as a matter of honour. "They followed the debtor wherever he went, they salaamed to him, fell at his feet, and sometimes insolently demanded payment for their employers, at times when the debtor was most anxious to be rid of them.... A rich man was generally very careful not to strike a tukkaza, because the government had then the right of exacting a very heavy penalty, which the debtor knew they only sought an opportunity to enforce." When the debtor was prepared to talk about repaying his debt, the creditor appeared on the scene with the terms of his agreement.

If the creditor was not rich enough to hire special tukkaza men, he would himself sit by the debtor's door. He could call upon his debtor when he knew that he was asleep, sometimes, the creditor would get the whole of his caste to make common cause, and press the demand upon the debtor. The tukkaza was even more effective because the local administration had the right to heavily fine the debtor for causing a public disturbance. But where the creditor was a representative of the authority or a relative of such a man, a more effective means was used: the debtor was thrown into prison.[75]

The position of the rich Muslim merchants was not adequately safeguarded either. A. Hamilton, an Englishman who traded with India and the countries of the Middle East from 1688 to 1723, wrote about a merchant he knew in Surat, Abdul Gafour, who "drove a trade equal to the English East India Company, for I have known him fit out in a year, above 20 sail of ships ... and none of them had less of his own stock than 10,000 pounds, and some of them had 25,000.... When he died, he left his estate to two grandsons, his own son, who was his only child, dying before him. But the Court had a fling at them, and got above a million sterling of their estate."[76] The famous French traveller, F. Bernier, asserted that both Hindu and Muslim merchants were often even afraid to make too great advances in commerce, because they were under the apprehension that people might consider them rich and think up a way of ruining them.[77]

It appears that the position of the rich Muslim merchants was nevertheless better than that of the Hindu merchants. J. Fryer, in any case, notes: "There are some great merchants among them (the Muslims.—V.P.) that are buoy'd up more by the authority of their religion and cast, than cunning, the Banias being forced to flee to them for patronage."[78] The Muslim trader's greater personal security also showed itself in his outward appearance and his habits; in contrast to the Hindu or Jain Bania, who dressed like an ascetic, the Muslim merchant wore rich garments. The comparatively privileged position which the Muslim merchants held in Mogul India undoubtedly slowed down their defection to the side of the British invaders.

Incidentally, the restraint with regard to the satisfaction of their requirements, which was a distinguishing feature of the Hindu trading and money-lending castes, was due to the necessity to conceal their wealth from the grasping emirs and rajas. Thus, Ovington relates that the constant fear of expropriation caused the rich merchants in Surat, brokers of the East India Company, who owned from one and a half to three million rupees, to spend as little as 3,000—4,000 rupees per annum on their personal requirements.[79]

It is obvious that wealth in the form of money, bills of exchange and jewellery can be more easily preserved (or rather hidden) than land, buildings and other real estate. "It is not surprising that bullion and jewellery should play a very important part in the economic life of these centuries. They had advantages of easy concealment (which was important in times of political insecurity), of comparatively little risk of depreciation of value, and of being easy to transport. In the absence of avenues of capital investment for productive or development activities accumulation of resources in these times logically became tantamount to hoards of bullion and jewellery."[80] That is why the fact that the merchants' property was constantly threatened by the despot's functionaries did not simply slow down the accumulation of capital but also—and this is very important—hampered the conversion of capital from the money form into the productive form, that is, its materialisation as the means of production.

D. R. Gadgil mentions the fact that buyers-up financed handicraft production, but stresses that "they would provide loan capital and not risk capital. Therefore, accumulation of capital in the hands of trader-merchants did not augment in any way resources invested in capital equipment for industrial production. The unit of industrial artisan production was the small individual workshop."[81] This is undoubtedly a correct reflection of the prevailing state of affairs, but it is also extremely absolutised, because, as I will show below, the sources note the merchant's participation in production. There is a similar defect in the following basically correct conclusion: "Apart from commercial and financial capital, investment by the merchanttraders would be chiefly in houses and gardens, etc., and other real estate or property round the city. Thus, mercantile accumulation did not affect productive activity either in agriculture or in handicraft industry. The growing fortunes of city merchants would be exhibited outwardly, where such outward exhibition was not considered unsafe, in such features as the rich carved frontages of merchants' houses as in Gujarat cities; or they would be exhibited in acts of religion or charity by way of building temples, tanks, dharmashalas, etc."[82]

Gadgil does not specify when, in effect, the Gujarati merchants displayed their riches. At any rate, it is hard to imagine that this was done in the late 17th century, at a time when Gujarat was alternately occupied by the Moguls and the Marathas. That is the period to which the following observations of Ovington's about the Surat Banias apply: "Their wealth consists only in cash and jewels, the distinction of personal and real estate is not heard in India and that they preserve as close and private as they can, lest the Mogul's Exchequer should be made their treasury. This curbs them in their expenses, and awes them in their great secrecy in their commerce, especially in their receiving, or payments of money, for which they either make use of the darkness of the night, or of the obscurity of the morning, in conveying it to the place of payment."[83]

It is not right to use one colour in depicting the legal and actual status of merchants in India before the British conquest. It varied from state to state, and within those boundaries varied from one period to another, depending on the needs and whims of the rulers. Thus, Aurangzeb, who pursued a policy of religious intolerance and spent much money on futile wars, introduced a special tax, the jizia, on Hindus and other non-Muslims. The jizia and other levies infringed the interests of the merchants and artisans, most of whom belonged to the Hindu, Jain and Sikh communities.

Quite naturally, the states of the Sikhs and Marathas, which emerged on the ruins of the Mogul Empire, tried to pursue a policy of encouraging local merchants and artisans, especially since the long wars had taken a heavy toll of the cities of the Punjab and Maharashtra, and had laid waste many of these, especially on the territory of the latter. That is why local non-Muslim merchants in the states of the Marathas and the Sikhs, and also in Mysore, escaped the discrimination and harassment to which their fellow non-Muslims were subjected under the Mogul Empire. Or course, when the rulers of these states were most acutely in need of money, and this happened frequently, they could resort to similar violence or, like Tippoo Sultan during Mysore's intense struggle against the British, set up their own monopoly on trade in the most profitable goods.[84] Still, the more lasting interests of the new states required that their governments should encourages trade and the crafts by easements in the sphere of taxation. For instance, in the Peshwa state money-lenders were frequently exempt from the payment of mohturfa (a tax on the merchant and artisan population). House property in Ahmednagar, including that owned by shroffs and saukars, was exempt from taxes.[85]

It is true that in some cities the putee tax, that is, levies for the repair of the city walls and aqueducts was still maintained. According to a British official (1823), these levies in Ahmednagar came to: 300 rupees for 73 Marwaris, 555 rupees for 142 Banias (apparently, Gujarati), and 200 rupees for 66 shroffs (apparently, from among the Marathi Brahmans). Because these figures have been rounded out, the tax must have been levied on the community as a whole, with the headmen apportioning the amount among the members at 2.3 rupees per head. The levies from the artisan population were relatively higher (with respect to income), but were not burdensome either, for instance, 68 oil-pressers paid 100 rupees, and 10 smiths only 5 rupees. The total amount paid by 88 groups of the urban population came to 3,012 rupees.[86]

In other cities of the Peshwa state, respected traders in cloths paid from 2 to 50-60 rupees, and artisans from 1 to 10-15 rupees a year.[87] Even if the highest tax rates fell on the well-to-do artisans who resorted to hired labour, the privileged position of merchant's and especially of usurer's capital in the sphere of taxation was obvious.

The mohturfa taxes in the Peshwa capital were equally low. These were also paid from each caste by a specially authorised agent, with the maximum annual payment by saukars coming to 40 rupees, shroffs 39 rupees, the richest grocer 50 rupees, and a grain merchant from 3 to 30 rupees. By contrast, the petty peddling traders paid a pice a day, which was very hard relative to their income.[88] This state of affairs was due to the fact that, because a considerable part of the operations involving traders and money-lenders was connected with catering to various requirements of rent-receivers and the state, direct taxes on merchant's and usurer's capital would have, in effect, amounted to an indirect tax on the latter. Besides, direct taxation was made difficult by the small share of real estate in the fortunes of Indian merchants and bankers.

It is interesting to note that in the Peshwa state tax assessment was based on personal observations by the tax-farmer and his agents or the evidence of neighbours. The only objective indicator was the customs records of export and import transactions by some merchants. In the absence of precise data about income and the principles of levying taxes on it, opportunities arose for abuse and extortion by tax-farmers and officials. Some limits to this kind of thing were apparently laid down by the practice of levying taxes wholesale on all the members of a given caste resident in a given place. The community heads re-allotted the tax within the caste.[89]

Whereas in some states of India merchant's capital and handicraft production bore a relatively light burden in direct taxes, this advantage was offset by the levying of excessively high duties when goods crossed the numerous borders of the Indian states or even the domains of individual rulers.[90] The burden of customs levies was felt less keenly by the big merchants who traded in luxuries for the élite, and had a detrimental effect on trade in cheap articles for mass consumption.

For instance, in Mogul Bengal, apart from the land-tax, there were levies designated by the general term of "sayer duties", which included taxes on the construction of boats (at $\frac{1}{4}$ rupees each), on all goods sold in the market-place, on the sellers of hay in the town—from 2 to 6 rupees a year, on the sellers of wood, bamboo and straw for roofing in the town, on artisans making shields and equestrian equipment from leather, on urban trade in betel and vegetables (in the latter instance, from 1 to 5 rupees depending on the volume of trade), on the sellers of paper—36 rupees a year per stall, on all urban traders—from 1 to $2\frac{1}{2}$ rupees, and as much on the various urban craftsmen including those making gold and silver thread, jewellery, flowered muslins and fireworks. Apart from the urban taxes, similar taxes were levied by local zamindars at all village market-places. We find, therefore, that the amount of the taxes was such that they were keenly felt by the small traders and artisans. But for the big merchants and bankers these taxes were purely symbolic. That is why it is hardly right to regard the system and principle of taxation as a serious obstacle for the accumulation and concentration of merchant's capital and its subsequent influx into industrial production. Such obstacles are rather to be found in the traditional caste limitations and regulations and also in the legal status of the merchant and his capital in pre-British India.

At a seminar of Indian scientists on the problems of social and economic history, held in Aligarh in 1968, Surendra Gopal read a paper on the social status of the three main trading communities—of North India—the Jains, the Vaishyas and the Kshatriyas—in the 17th century. His aim was to consider the changes in their condition and also the notions of social values among these communities, and to establish the reasons why they lacked "the spirit of scientific inquiry". He said that it was not the possession of wealth in itself, but the donations for the construction of temples and for religious ceremonies that gave one the right to claim a leading position in the community. The building of a temple with the money donated by a merchant or a banker, and not, let us add, the capital handed down to his heirs to be increased by them, was seen as the most fitting culmination of a man's lifetime efforts.

Surendra Gopal noted the religious conservatism of the Jains, which reduced their schooling to a penetration into the metaphysical mysticism of their religion and ruled out any knowledge of the material world. That is why neither their contacts with Europeans nor the new developments in social life resulted in the emergence of a rationalistic approach to reality among the Jains. The social ideals among the Vaishyas were roughly similar, and despite their wealth, their condition in the caste hierarchy of Hinduism remained fairly modest. No changes in their traditions resulted from the support by the Vaishyas of the Vallabhachary a movement against caste limitations under Akbar.

There appears to have been somewhat less rigidity in the outlook of the Kshatriyas, who first inhabited the Punjab and Sind and then spread to the whole of North India. They were prepared for embracing Sikhism, with its denial of castes and the rules of desecration, by their constant stay among Muslims, and their travels on commercial affairs to neighbouring countries and even to distant Russia. Their service in the Mogul administration induced them to study Persian, which also broadened their cultural horizons. But the invasions and the chaos into which the areas of their activity were plunged hampered their opportunities as vehicles of capitalist transformation.

Surendra Gopal's general conclusion was that the unification of the economic efforts of the members of these three communities was hampered by the ideal of personal spiritual salvation as the goal of life. They were unable to establish an institution like the joint-stock company, which is why the accumulation of capital—a necessary condition for the industrial revolution—lacked the appropriate organisational basis.

In point of fact, India did have associations of the joint-stock company type, as witnessed, for example, by the following conclusion:

"The concept of the joint-stock must certainly have been prevalent in some form in the merchant guilds that flourished under the Vijayanagar Empire (14-16 centuries). With the decline of this empire, these ancient institutions seem to have suffered destruction, leaving individual merchant families operating on their own in relations with the Arabs, the Portuguese and the later European companies.

"Under the conditions existing in the second half of the 17th century the European companies found it advantageous to foster the formation of such associations.... By 1700 supply through these Indian joint-stock partnerships had become the norm.....

"...The share-holders were carefully selected not only from the point of view of their reliability and wealth but also on the basis of their caste and family relationships to ensure that they could work effectively as a team. There were two categories of membership—the head merchants and the ordinary merchants. The former provided the bulk of the capital and controlled the organisation of the company. A cashier was responsible for the subscribed money and kept accounts. The ordinary merchants did most of the physical work of travelling to the weavers' and painters' villages in the interior of the country, placing orders with them and transporting the goods to the factory.

"...The total capital accumulated by these joint-stocks varies between 150,000 pagodas (1 pagoda = 12 shillings) at the highest and about 10,000 pagodas at the lowest. The value of a share was 100 or 500 or 1000 pagodas.

"...As the eighteenth century advances, one does get the impression that these partnerships are getting less numerous and less effective. It would be interesting to know why this European initiative did not lead to the extension of the partnership idea among Indian merchants. One factor certainly seems to be that the merchant class was drawn from a number of caste groups. There were Chettiars, Komaties, Mudaliyars and Brahmins...."[91]

One would think that this conclusion correctly brings out another, but only one more, of the reasons which prevented Indian merchant's capital from flowing into industrial production.

In the first half of the 18th century, in the period when the Mogul Empire was disintegrating and when everyone was at war with everyone, the condition of the merchants and the money-lenders in many parts of the country became even more precarious. The person of the merchant and his property were under constant threat not only from the external enemy (J. Thevenot says that after the invasion of Surat in 1666, Shivaji carried away valuables to the tune of 30 million, apparently, livres' worth; in the house of one Bania alone he seized 22 pounds of pearls; these figures are, of course, approximate, but they go once again to confirm the information about the great wealth of the merchants in India).[92] He was also threatened by his "own" ruler, who was always in need of money for internecine wars. It was, indeed, the need to safeguard their property and person from the arbitrary acts of the powers that be that impelled a part of the big Indian merchants to commune with the European invaders. This was also largely promoted by the discrimination against non-Muslim merchants as a part of the overall policy of religious intolerance and persecution of the non-Muslim population under Aurangzeb.

Finally, the rapprochement between the local merchant and artisan sections and the foreign companies was promoted by economic interests, among others, especially in the coastal areas. The establishment by the Europeans of their own monopoly on foreign trade placed under their control the production and marketing of many traditional Indian exports. However, the collaboration of local merchants with foreigners will be dealt with in a separate chapter. One can hardly accept A.I. Chicherov's assertion that "in the 17th-18th centuries there proceeded an intensive coalescence of the merchants and money-lenders with the feudal class, which led to the greater participation of the merchants in the feudal exploitation of the people."[93] Chicherov holds that evidence of this coalescence lay, on the one hand, in the tax-farming operations of the merchants, in their financing of the wars of feudal rulers, and the purchase of land and irrigation installations, and, on the other, in participation by the feudal lords, especially of their upper sections, in domestic and foreign trade.

On this score one can remark, first, that these phenomena had been in evidence in India even at an earlier period, and were also to be found in medieval Europe, but that they merely resulted in personal "swings" by individual merchants and bankers into the ruling camp and did not result in a feudalisation of merchant's capital. Second, the periodical incursions by the powers that be into the sphere of trade usually went hand in hand with proclamations of their monopoly rights to the purchase and marketing of the most profitable goods, which did not mean any coalescence with merchant's capital, but its deprivation of profitable sources of gain.

I. Habib, remarking on the occasional investments by Mogul nobles of their accumulations into trade (like Mir Jumla), says that this kind of activity was combined with the establishment of a monopoly resting on the use of force, which is why such investments can hardly be regarded as additions to merchant's capital. In general, he adds, the nobility made very small investments in trade as compared with its vast resources.[94] I think that the Indian rulers' inclination to engage in trade sprang from the concentration in their hands—through feudal rent—of vast masses of the surplus-product, and their ability to secure their trade operations by force of arms. This is perhaps evidence of the archaic nature of feudal relations, while the actual coalescence of merchant's capital and the feudal lord's accumulations starts only at a later stage of feudalism, when in the course of its disintegration both come to be connected with capitalist production. The fact is, however, that in pre-British India this process was observed only in sporadic and occasional instances.

NOTES

1. F. Engels, Supplement to Vol. III of K. Marx' *Capital*, p. 900.

2. D.R. Gadgil, *Origin . . .*, p. 26.
3. J. Tod, *Antiquities and Annals of Rajasthan*, vol. II, London, 1882, p. 282.
4. D.R. Gadgil, *Origins...*, p. 18.
5. *Ibid.*
6. *The Rajputana Gazetteer*, vol. III (Simla), 1880, p. 27; *Indian Year-book 1947*, Calcutta, 1947, p. 1449
7. The religious community of the Jains in the north-east of India consisted mainly of Marwari traders and money-lenders.
8. B. Bhargava, *Indigenous Banking in Ancient and Medieval India*, Bombay, 1934, pp. 29-32.
9. B. Bhargava says in *Indigenous Banking* that among the outstanding Marwari banking houses, that had the honour of serving many rulers, were such well-known firms as those of Tarachand Ghanshiamdas and Bansilal Abirchand (p. 31).
10. B. Bhargava, *Indigenous Banking....*, p. 29.
11. H. Sinha, *Early European Banking in India*, London, 1927, p. 1.
12. W.W. Hunter, *Statistical Accounts of Bengal*, vol. IX. District of Murshidabad and Pabna, London, 1878, pp. 258, 259.
13. W. Bolts, *Considerations on Indian Affairs; Particularly Respecting the Present State of Bengal and Its Dependencies*, London, 1772, p. 157.
14. R. Mukerji, *The Foundations of Indian Economics*, London, 1916, p. 276.
15. W. Bolts, Considerations..., p. 15.
16. *Ibid.*
17. *Readings in Indian Economic History*, Bombay, 1964, p. 76.
18. W. Bolts, *Considerations.....*, pp. 157-158.
19. See: *Murshidabad (Eastern Bengal District Gazetteers)*, Calcutta, 1914, pp. 60-61.
20. W. Bolts, *Considerations.....*, p. 158.
21. *Report of Bengal Provincial Banking Enquiry Committee*, vol. 1, Calcutta, 1930, p. 183.
22. *Selections from Unpublished Records of Government for the Years 1748 to 1767 Inclusive Relating Mainly to the Social Conditions of Bengal*, Calcutta, 1869, vol. I, p. 9.
23. I. Habib, *Potentialities...*, p. 39.
24. [J.B. Tavernier], Les six voyages de Jean-Baptiste Tavernier...Seconde partie, ou il est parle des Indes, et des Isles voisines, Paris, 1681, p. 34.
25. K.A. Antonova, Ocherki obshchestvennykh othosheniy..., p. 125.
26. A.K. Forbes, *Ras Mala...*, vol. II, London, 1856, p. 247.
27. A. Sarada Raju, *Economic Conditions in the Madras Presidency 1800-1850*, 1941, p. 134.
28. F. Buchanan, *A Journey...*, vol. I, p. 265.
29. *Selections of Papers from the Records at the East-India House*, vol. IV, p. 318.
30. *Ibid.*, p. 328.
31. *Ibid.*, p. 514.
32. D.R. Choksey, *Economic History of the Bombay Deccan and Carnatak* (1818-1868), Poona, 1945, p. 8.
33. *Selection of Papers from Records at the East-India House*. vol. IV, pp. 516-517.
34. *Selections from the Deccan Commissioner's Files (Peshwa Daftar). Period of Transition (1818-1826)*, Poona, 1965, p. 65.
35. *Ibid.*, p. 78.
36. *Ibid.*
37. J. Forbes, *Oriental Memoirs...*, vol. II, p. 44.

38. *Ibid.*, p. 75.
39. Many big capitalists in India had the name of Modi, which shows that they originated from the army purveyors.
40. B. Bhargava, *Indgenous Banking...*, p. 29.
41. D.R. Gadgil, *Origins....*, p. 6.
42. [J.B. Tavernier], Les six voyages..., p. 12.
43. I.M. Reusner, Narodniye dvizheniya v Indii v XVII-XVIII vv., Mascow, 1961, p. 302.
44. V.A. Kincaid and D.B. Parasnis, *A History of the Maratha People*, London, 1918, vol. II, p. 272.
45. S. Sen, *Administrative System of the Marathas*, Calcutta, 1925, p. 469.
46. See : J. Sarkar, *Fall of the Mughal Empire*, Calcutta, 1949, vol. II, p. 243.
47. T. Broughton, *Letters Written in a Mahratta Camp during the Year 1809*, London, 1813, p. 54; J. Sarkar, *Fall of the Mughal Empire*, vol. II, pp. 293-294.
48. A.K. Forbes, *Râs Mâlâ....*, vol. II, London, 1856, p. 50.
49. Ibid.
50. D.R. Gadgil, *Origins....*, pp. 31-42.
51. See the documents at the Central State Archives of Ancient Acts, and also the works of A. F. Malinovsky ("Trudy i letopisi Imp. obshchestva istorii i drevnostei rossiyskikh", pt VII, 1837), V.A. Ulyanitsky ("Chteniya v Imp. obshchestve istorii i drevnostei rossiyskikh", Book 3, 1888) and N.M. Goldberg ("Ucheniye zapiski Tikhookeanskogoinstituta," vol. II, "Indiysky sbornik," Moscow, 1949).
52. [N. Downton], *The Voyage of Nicholas Downton to the East Indies* 1614-1615, ed. by W. Foster, London, 1939, pp. 146-147.
53. [J.B. Tavernier]. Les six voyages...., p. 11.
54. D.R. Choksey, *Economic History of the Bombay Deccan and Carnatak*, p. 53.
55. D.R. Gadgil, Origins...., p. 32.
56. Jawaharlal Nehru, *The Discovery of India*, London, 1951, p. 262.
57. D.R. Gadgil, *Origins...*, pp. 30-31.
58. J. Malcolm, *A Memoir of Central India including Malwa and Adjoining Provinces*, vol. 2. London, 1832, pp. 115-116.
59. D.R. Gadgil, *Origins...*, p. 4.
60. *Imperial Gazetteer of India* (in fourteen vols), vol. I, London, 1885, p. 104.
61. D.R. Gadgil, *Origins...*, pp. 19-20.
62. J. Malcolm, *A Memoir of Central India...*, vol. 2, pp. 115-116.
63. *Daulat Rao Sindhia and North Indian Affairs* (*English Records of Maratha History, Poona Residency Correspondence*, vol. XIV), Bombay, 1951, pp. 70, 106.
64. A.K. Forbes, *Râs Mâlâ...*, vol. II, pp. 113, 208.
65. J. Malcolm, *A Memoir of Central India....*, vol. II, pp. 159, 162.
66. *Ibid.*, p. 38.
67. *Ibid.*
68. *Ibid.*, pp. 162-163.
69. K. Marx, F. Engles, *Sochineniya*, vol. 22, 1962, p. 38.
70. J.A. de Mandelslo, *The Voyages and Travels into the East Indies* (1638-1640), London, 1669, p. 65.
71. *Ibid.*, p. 51.
72. J. Forbes, *Oriental Memoirs....*, vol. II, p. 54.
73. J. Douglas, *Bombay and Western India*, London, 1893, vol. I, p. 107.
74. See : D. R. Gadgil, *Origins....*, p. 22.
75. *Selections of Papers from the Records at the East-India House*, vol. IV, pp. 228, 912.

76. A. Hamilton, *A New Account of the East Indies....*, vol. I, pp. 147-148.
77. F. Bernier, *Histoire de la dernière révolution des états du Grand Mogol.....*, vols. I-IV, Paris, 1671-1672, pp. 309-310.
78. J. Fryer, *A New Account of East India and Persia being Nine Years' Travels 1672-1681*, vol. II, London, 1912, p. 112.
79. J. Ovington, *A Voyage to Surat in the Year 1689*, Oxford, 1929,] . 118.
80. D.R. Gadgil, *Origins....*, p. 35.
81. *Ibid.*, pp. 34-35.
82. *Ibid.*
83. J. Ovington, *A Voyage to Surat...*, p. 187.
84. F. Buchnan, *A Journey....*, vol. I, p. 69.
85. *Selections of Papers from the Records at the East-India House*, vol. III, London, 1826, p. 810.
86. *Selections from the Deccan Commissioner's Files (Pechwa Daftar). Period of Transition (1818-1826)*, ed. D.R. Choksey, Poona, 1945, p. 61.
87. *Selections of Papers from the Records at the East-India House*, vol. IV, p. 709.
88. *Ibid.*, vol. III, p. 810.
89. *Ibid.*, vol. IV, p. 709.
90. For more details on taxes, see : A.I. Chicherov, India: Economic Development..., pp. 154-155.
91. S. Arasaratham, Indian Merchants and Their Trading Methods (circa 1700), *JESHR*, vol. III, No. 1 March 1996, pp. 86, 87, 90.
92. [J. Thevenot], Les voyages de Mr. de Thevenot aux Indes Orientales, contenant la relation de l'Indostan des nouveaux Mogols, et des autres peuples et pays des Indes, paris, 1684, p. 84.
93. A.I. Chicherov, *India, Economic Development....*, p. 148.
94. I. Habib, *Potentialities....*, p. 61.

CHAPTER THREE

NON-COMMUNITY HANDICRAFTS WITHIN THE TRADITIONAL SYSTEM OF INDIA'S SOCIAL DIVISION OF LABOUR

Criteria for Assessing Handicraft Production

The conventional division of the handicrafts in feudal society into village and urban does not quite fit India. As I have already shown, the artisans living in the countryside had two fundamentally different types of relations with the farming population, primarily with the land-holders. If one takes the artisan's involvement in the system of intra-communal division of labour as the criterion for assessing his place in the whole social division of labour, the village artisans who had separated from this division were closer to the urban artisans than to their neighbours working within the framework of the community. Besides, in India there were no socio-juridical or economic distinctions, as there were in Europe, between the urban and the rural artisans, because in India the urban artisan did not have such obvious political advantages over his rural fellow in the form of special rights and guild privileges. Conversely, the rural artisan in India did not have any marked economic advantages over the urban artisan such as freedom from production regulations, because the caste system, their vehicle, equally applied to both (in Europe, the bulk of the village crafts had escaped guild regulations).

These considerations induce one to divide India's traditional industry above all into community and non-community production, but this should not be seen as static or immobile. As I have said, some rural crafts (chiefly leatherdressing and pottery) were located at the junction of these two spheres of production as regards the type of their relations with consumers, and even in the traditional community crafts (smithing and carpentry) had individual relations with customers, especially in Bengal.

In his very interesting survey, I. Habib has unfortunately not made any special analysis of the potentialities in the genesis of capitalism which were latent in the crafts catering directly for the peasants and the village communities. He held that it was possible to exclude these from the sphere which generated capitalist relations because there was no real commodity production in these industries: the artisan was rewarded either with a fixed remuneration or, as he proceeded from one village to another, he purchased materials and sold his articles at prices possibly fixed in kind.[1]

One can hardly accept this separation from commodity production (which also means from potentially capitalist production) crafts like weaving, oil-pressing, sugar production and even the traditional intra-communal crafts, because they, too, showed signs of incipient transition to commodity-money relations with urban consumers. The main thing is that only the development of such relations with agriculture and the population employed in it gave the crafts a sound historical prospect for the genesis and subsequent development of capitalist relations on the basis of the social division of labour on a regional and all-national scale.

The scale on which the closed intra-communal character of the crafts was being eroded determined the deepening of the social division of labour and the growth of new forms of relations of production in industry. While the status of the crafts within the framework of the village community ruled out the origination of new relations within it, the crafts acquired a definite historical activity only by breaking out of this framework, including the capacity of engendering stable petty- commodity and then early capitalist relations.

These new relations, which were progressive for feudal India, necessarily attracted the attention of Soviet scientists. The first attempt to describe these pockets of capitalist relations and to establish their connection with the social division of labour was an article written by E.N. Komarov and myself[2] in 1955. The authors proceeded from Marx's proposition about the dependence of the national social division of labour and the emergence of manufactory-type enterprises on the disintegration of the economically closed community. However, these propositions were not backed up by relevant research data, while concrete information on the organisation of the crafts was drawn mainly from F. Buchanan's studies (incidentally, he continues to be the key source for subsequent studies).[3] Besides, the analysis of the material was limited by the size of the article.

In my 1958 book, "The Formation of the Indian Bourgeoisie", I gave some new data on the organisation of the handicrafts in feudal India, their economic links, technical facilities and labour productivity. The next stage in the study of Indian crafts in the 17th-18th centuries by Soviet Indologists was A.I. Chicherov's monograph on India's economic development before the British Conquest (1965), containing an array and analysis of vast factual material about the different types of handicraft production: from the household village crafts to capitalist manufactories. The fundamental nature of the study[4] makes it superfluous to add anything considerable to the information about the types of Indian handicrafts.

But the purpose of this book is not so much to provide additional evidence of the existence in pre-British India of scattered pockets of capitalist relations as to try to determine their importance in the overall socio-economic structure, and to establish the nature and the conditions of their relations with the various sectors of the national economy and spheres of consumption.

The social and economic status of the various categories of community craftsmen was determined, as I have said, by their place and importance within the system of the intra-communal division of labour and reproduction. Accordingly, the status of the non-communal craftsmen was determined by the place and importance of their production and products in the local, regional or even all-India social division of labour and redistribution of the national product. But the virtual absence of any social division of labour on an all-India scale and its immaturity within the framework of the separate regions was determined by the fact that the non-communal crafts (excluding, perhaps, the production of metals) had tenuous connections with the process of reproduction in agriculture. A part of the consumer demand in the countryside was met by the artisans who had not broken with the community (potters, leather-dressers and jewellers). Weavers were the only large group of non-communal artisans on whom the population of the community markedly depended (this fact largely determined their relatively privileged condition).

Because the weavers and other artisans made some of their own labour implements, the communal artisans who could have made such implements had only very limited participation in the process of reproduction not only of the rural but also of the urban industries. Accordingly, the division of labour between different branches within industrial production itself was reduced. Boats and carts were the most important output turned out by non-communal artisans for the purposes of production, or rather, of transport.

The evidence of the sources on the artisan's specialisation (for instance, in Bengal) in making reeds, shuttles and other key parts on looms are not numerous but are still very valuable.[5] Nevertheless, according to the aggregate of the evidence discovered so far, a majority of urban carpenters and smiths confined themselves to building houses, making household utensils and also weapons. There is no doubt that some evidence by European observers, which is quoted below, contains a much too categorical denial of production of implements by the artisans who could have been engaged in such work according to the character of their specialisation. It is just as certain that the differentiation and specialisation of implements in pre-British India fell far short of that which was the premise and condition for the manufactory division of labour in Europe.

Technology and Production Skills in the Crafts

The state of the productive forces in the handicrafts in the period under consideration was characterised not only by simple and even primitive tools but also by a fairly high degree of productive experience and craftsmanship among individual producers and the benefit of millennia of production secrets. Marx wrote about the Indian weaver: "It is only the special skill accumulated from generation to generation, and transmitted from father to son, that gives to the Hindu ... this proficiency."[6]

As an example of such proficiency one may refer to the enthusiastic account which was given by an eyewitness after observing the skill of the Bengali silk-winders in the 18th century. Although the yarn was classified according to its fineness into 20 assortments and the thread ran through the fingers of the women winders so swiftly that the eye was unable to discern it, their sense of touch was so perfectly developed that they managed to break the thread "exactly as the assortments changed."[7] Describing the extremely simple tools of the Gujarati artisans, Forbes relates that jewellers using nothing but an iron nail were able to produce the most magnificent articles.[8] According to J. Dubois, a Frenchman who visited India early in the 19th century, the carpenter's only instruments were one or two axes, a few saws and planes, "all of them so rudely fashioned that a European workman would be able to do nothing with them."[9]

Like other European observers, R. Orme admired the unusual skill of the Indian weavers and spinners who used very simple implements by European standards. "The rigid, clumsy fingers of an European would scarcely be able to make a piece of canvas with the instruments which are all that an Indian employs in making a piece of cambric." Orme goes on to make a highly valuable observation about the hereditary specialisation of weavers in a given area: "It is farther remarkable that every distinct kind of cloth is the produce of a particular district, in which the fabric has been transmitted, perhaps for centuries, from father to son—a custom which must have conduced to the perfection of the manufacturer." This local specialisation of production, combined with differentiation in demand, led to very extensive trade in consumer articles. "The numerous productions of Hindustan, and the difference of wants in different parts of it, afford a large scope for an extensive trade within itself."[10]

Considering the reasons for the relatively slow improvement of handicraft implements in India, Habib has ventured the opinion that this happened because the making of the same articles was effected by inefficient implements with the use of cheap but skilled labour-power. At the same time, he rejects as an over-simplification the notion that there was no need to improve handicraft implements in India, where professional skills, he says, were the only progressive element of production and were said fully to compensate for the stagnant character of its technical equipment. While accepting that the role of professional experience and implements of labour may differ in the progress of production in different societies and under different circumstances, Habib maintains that no amount of skill can substitute for definite implements in the making of definite articles.[11]

Continuing this line of thought, one would have to admit that technical progress was undoubtedly contained by the poor remuneration of Indian artisans, especially high-skilled craftsmen, whose incomes differed little from those of rankand-file artisans, because it depreciated the outlays on more sophisticated and costly equipment. On the other hand, the cheapness of the artisan's labour-power was predetermined by the low prices of the produce they consumed (especially food-stuffs, because of the relatively high level of productivity in agriculture), and the limited volume of vital requirements in clothes and housing (which sprang from natural conditions and historically rooted moral and ethical standards).

It is hard to make a direct comparison between the labour productivity of an Indian and a European producer. In most cases, the very different assortment of articles and the traditional ornamentation and finishing makes it impossible to compare the labour inputs into articles designed for similar purposes. But there is no doubt that by the mid-18th century, European industry, British industry at any rate, had a higher level of productivity than Indian industry. Apart from its technical superiority and detailed division of labour, this was due to the physical strength of the more solidly built and taller Englishman and his correspondingly higher intensity of labour, especially in arduous operations.

Some interest attaches in this context to the consideration expressed by an English army engineer on the recruitment of men to the engineering corps of the East India Company's army in the 1770s. He claimed that an English carpenter, naturally using different tools, had a productivity that was three times as high as that of an Indian carpenter. Besides, the Indian carpenter used the services of a mate, the begari, who brought up, held and turned the wood as it was worked. The engineer assumed that on the march an English carpenter was worth six Indian carpenters. He also claimed that the Indian smith, who used a lighter hammer, had to heat up the metal he was working much oftener and so had to expend more metal and coal.[12]

A more general explanation for the slow change in the implements and methods of labour lay, I think, in the fact that in some lines of production they constituted, as in agriculture, a complete set. The improvement of one of the tools of this set led to the disproportions, and upset the whole technological process; and this had an effect on the quality of the product. That was the case in iron-smelting, tanning, and in preparing and using dyes. It is also clear that a purely empirical notion of the sequence and importance of the parts and components of the process could result, however gradually, in a general optimal transformation. But the skills of the Indian artisans handed down from generation to generation were scarcely subjected to conscious experimental improvement (to say nothing of any complex scientific modifications). That is why the technology which had once taken shape and which had been tested by ages of experience was usually converted into a kind of production ritual which was sacrosanct in every detail.

Thus, the technology of the dying of yarn had been worked out over the centuries and millennia. Heyne described this process in great detail, although the artisans may have concealed from him some of their secrets (Heyne complains of their unwillingness to share their production secrets with foreigners). Even the simplest method of dyeing took 24 days, on each of which one or several processes were performed. There was great thoroughness in using the necessary ingredients. Much depended "on the goodness of the yarn to be subjected to this process. The success of the colour, however, is to be chiefly ascribed to a proper regulation of the proportions of the substances employed, and of the time during which the yarn is subjected to each particular process."[13]

As in the description by other English authors of the technology in Indian metallurgy, Heyne studied the dyeing of yarn for a definite utilitarian purpose. He said that "though the methods of the Indian dyers are exceedingly tedious and complicated and though they are utterly unable to explain the rationale of their processes, yet the beauty of their colours cannot fail to be admired, and must inspire us with the opinion that a knowledge of their methods might improve the processes of European dyers, and might enable them to make some advantageous changes" in their art. At the same time, the "application of the light of chemistry to explain the nature of the Indian processes, to enable the enlightened artist to throw out all the useless steps, might contribute more to the improvement of this beautiful art than even the most sanguine is at present aware of."[14] Let us note that this was said by a man who represented a society that had already carried out its Industrial Revolution on the strength of a scientific understanding of production processes and their inter-connections.

Certain other lines of industrial production in India had technologies that were highly complicated and tested over the millennia. They also involved strict observance in the use of components and the time for introducing them into the process. That is why, despite the simple and primitive nature of their equipment, Indian artisans frequently had results that surpassed similar achievements in European industry.

Heyne gives an interesting description of how the dyes were prepared and the methods used in applying them to the walls of the palaces of the rulers of Mysore—Hyder Ali and Tippoo Sultan. The "brilliancy of the colours" was achieved above all by means of thorough preparation of the dyes. The initial mass consisted of five components mixed in the corresponding weight proportions. Then, as the mass was being heated, two other components and then a third (linseed-oil brought to boiling-point) were added, the mass so obtained was boiled for two hours on a low flame, in order to give the dye the necessary colour, more ingredients were added, etc. Finally, before painting, the wall was covered with a special substance and painted only after it was thoroughly puttied.

In a village near Marihar (Mysore), goat-skins were subjected to similarly complicated tanning processes before being turned into "a very pretty kind of red morocco". One day the skins were dried in the sun, then for two days they were soaked in a river, and then placed for four days in a vat in which, to a definite amount of water, were added half the same amount of the "milk of wild cotton" and a handful of salt; for four more days the skins were soaked in water and scraped clean of hair. Over the next two or three days the skins were dried in a cool place, whitened by means of a special clay, soaked twice again in solutions, and only then subjected to dyeing. For this purpose a dye consisting of three components added in the right proportion was prepared under an appropriate regime of heating. The dye was rubbed into the skin, which was then placed in another solution for five or six days, with the skin taken out of the vat every morning and washed thoroughly. The skin was finally ready only after another period of drying, when it assumed a dark-red colour and became soft.[15]

We find that these processes resulted in a very high quality of product. But because there was no science-grounded knowledge of the empirical operations, it was impossible to step up the processes which were drawn out over long periods and undoubtedly led to long interruptions in the use of manpower and to unavoidable idling. All this necessarily had a negative effect on the productivity of labour, increased the cost of the product and, conversely, reduced the earnings of the producers.

The usually very limited detailed division of labour within the production process itself is the most important indication that in general a low development level of the productive force prevailed in the handicrafts of medieval India. The producer often carried through the whole production process, from beginning to end, without any assistance. "Sub-division of labour" was, according to Buchanan, "very unusual in India".[16] H. Colebrooke has given the following description of the framework of Indian handicraft production at the close of the 18th century: "The want of capital in manufactures and agriculture prevents the division of labour. Every manufacturer, every artisan working for his own account, conducts the whole process of his art, from the formation of his tools to the sale of his production."[17] Orme says that the arbitrary acts of the authorities prevented the concentration of several workers in one workshop, thereby making any detailed division of labour on European lines impossible. He said that weaving was an exception in which the division of labour was effected by the weaver involving his wife and children in ancillary operations.[18]

The above evidence is much too categorical. Signs of a detailed division of labour appeared in a number of Indian handicrafts, and not only in weaving, in the 17th and 18th centuries, indicating that certain progress had been made in the development of the productive forces. Lenin pointed out that "on the basis of hand production no other progress in technique was possible except by division of labour."[19]

Even in the 1630s, Mandelslo noticed that "a piece of work must pass through three or four hands before it is finished."[20] Although Mandelslo wrote about the handicraft industries of Surat in general, without giving any further details, one can hardly doubt that he had specific instances in mind, which he had observed himself. We shall subsequently discover on many occasions that in India there was detailed division of labour within the framework of the workshop.

Labour Productivity in Agriculture and the Handicrafts and Exchange Relations Between Them

We find that it is impossible to accept statements about the low productivity of Indian handicrafts without essential reservations and correctives. Still, in considering the factors preventing a deepening of the social division of labour in India on the basis of comprehensive commodity exchange through the market between the cultivators and non-communal artisans, one must turn his attention to the lag of the handicrafts behind agriculture in labour productivity. In this sense, India was no exception, because pre-capitalist society in general has a higher productivity in agriculture than in manufactures.

In this context, Marx wrote: "On the whole it can be assumed that under the cruder, pre-capitalist mode of production, agriculture is more productive than industry, because nature assists here as a machine and an organism, whereas in industry the powers of nature are still almost entirely replaced by human action (as in the craft type of industry, etc.). In the period of the stormy growth of capitalist production, productivity in industry develops rapidly as compared with agriculture, although its development pre-supposes that a significant change as between constant and variable capital has already taken place in agriculture, that is, a large number of people have been driven off the land."[21]

The second half of Marx's proposition cannot, certainly, be applied to India, either in the period under consideration or in the subsequent British period, because up to the mid-20th century there was neither any sign of tempestuous development of capitalist production nor any considerable change in the proportion between variable and constant capital in agriculture. The superiority of industry in labour productivity was brought about in a different way, namely, by the introduction of machinery from outside.

At the same time it appears that in pre-British India the gap in productivity in favour of agriculture was greater than it was in medieval Europe. I intend to return again and again to the description of the sets of Indian farming implements which differed greatly from one area to another, depending on the soil, the crops grown, the irrigation, and so on.

One of the first descriptions of such implements is contained in Heyne's book (early 19th century); apart from the description itself, he gives a drawing of three types of ploughs (two for inter-row tillage), heavy harrows pulled by two bullocks, two types of seeders (with one having an attachment for sowing an additional crop), and two implements for evening out the soil before and after sowing. Let us note that the cutting parts of two types of ploughs, one seeder and one planing implement were made entirely of iron.[22] This list does not include any manual implements (sickle, hoe, etc.).

Apart from his superiority in the implements of labour, the cultivator in India was not inferior, at any rate, in professional skill and craftsmanship, to the artisan who made the ordinary articles of consumption and implements. In the recent period, Indian and Soviet scientists have shown very well the groundlessness of the myth about the primitive state of Indian agriculture. Thus, L. B. Alayev concludes his study of the relevant sources with these words: "A study of the data from the late 18th and early 19th centuries shows that agriculture in India was at a fairly high level of development. Despite the relatively primitive nature (but, let me add, profound diversification.—V.P.) of the implements of labour, they were well adapted to the peculiar systems of agriculture. These systems were highly intricate and had several features which approximated them to the most advanced contemporary systems."[23]

Apart from its technical superiority, agricultural production was relatively more concentrated. The use of several "proughs" (actually, sets of implements) and of a corresponding number of "outside" labourers was clearly more common-place on the estates of the rural élite than even simple cooperation of hired labourers in industrial production. At any rate, it is fairly safe to assert this with respect to the industries which had product or commodity-exchange relations with agriculture, especially that part of it which was included in the rural élite sector. That is why one must assume that that sector surpassed the corresponding handicrafts in labour productivity even though the latter did sporadically switch to early capitalist forms of organisation.

To this should be added the highly favourable climatic conditions in the main agricultural areas of India and also the possibility of harvesting two or three crops a year, involving more labour-intensive and intensively farmed crops (rice, sugarcane, ground-nuts, cotton) than in Europe, which increased the peasant's employment and raised his productivity in annual terms. The superiority of India's agriculture over its handicrafts will become even more obvious if we add irrigation, under which nature takes a most immediate part in human labour "as a machine and an organism". In such conditions, direct exchange between agriculture and the handicrafts in accordance with the quantity of labour expended by each meant that the former gave away a part of the product it produced without getting any equivalent in return.

Had such relations persisted for a long time without the interference of external regulators, a situation could have arisen at a definite level of development under which capitalism could have originated in agriculture, which in India had more favourable conditions for accumulation. Let us recall that in the later stages of feudalism in Europe, with the handicrafts having the advantage in productivity, these favourable conditions proved to be on their side (exploitation of the countryside by the town). A third situation is also possible: roughly similar levels of productivity would have led to the production in the same periods of time of equal values exchanged for each other. Indeed, says Engels, the medieval peasant had a fairly precise knowledge of the quantity of labour-time necessary to make the articles which he received in exchange from the village blacksmith, the carter, the shoe-maker or the tailor. That is why the articles turned out by these producers were exchanged in proportion to the labour expended, according to the quantity of labour they embodied. But with the penetration of money the tendency to conform with the law of value was disrupted in consequence of interference by money-lending capital and the fiscal system.[24]

This condition for disruption is very essential for the Indian version we have been considering. Leaving aside money-lending capital, which could exert pressure equally on the cultivator and the artisan, let us consider the influence of the Indian fiscal system, which clearly gave preference to agriculture. Let us consider the example of a man engaged in agriculture producing 10 kilogrammes of grain a day, and a weaver producing a metre of cloth in the same time. Given the cultivator's two-fold superiority in productivity, his product would embody twice as much labour as the artisan's article, so that, in direct exchange between them in accordance with labour inputs, the weaver appropriating the whole of the agricultural products produced in the same time as he produced his cloth would be receiving a two-fold gain in value. But with the intervention of the Treasury (or another rent-receiver), that extracted from the cultivator, say, one-half of his product, the latter would have kept only a part (in our example 5 kilogrammes) of the product, which was comparable in value to the handicraft article (in our example a metre of cloth) produced during the same time as the whole agricultural product (including the part extracted by the rent-receiver). Thus, the levying of rent in a sense tended to re-establish the tendency for correspondence with the law of value in the exchange between the cultivator and the artisan in conditions where labour productivity was higher in agriculture.

Apparently, with the traditionally regulated remuneration of the community artisans and the feudal lords' payment (directly or through a buyer-up) to the urban artisan, there was a redistribution of a part of the value produced in the peasant economy so that the aggregate value of the handicraft article (both that created by the producer's labour and that added in the redistribution) ensured the maintenance of the artisan and his family on the level of a rank-and-file land-holder, and also reproduction, even if only in its primary form. This state of affairs, originating from the relatively low productivity of handicraft labour, made extended reproduction in industry dependent on the traditional system of redistribution and rendered impossible the process of sufficiently extensive genesis of capitalism in it, which, Marx says, required a rapid development of the productivity in industry as compared with agriculture.[25] Indeed, without a marked superiority in labour productivity over agriculture, industry was not able to ensure for itself in the course of direct commodity exchange with it the accumulation capital necessary for extended reproduction on the basis of improved technology and capitalist relations.

The weavers who were engaged in direct exchange with the peasant population or used the services of merchant's capital were in a special position, with merchant's capital realising its profit in the price of the cloth to the extent to which it participated in such an exchange. The formation of prices for cloth in mass consumption undoubtedly requires special study. Let me note here only the specific feature that the bulk of the value of the cloth was produced by the agricultural population (in the production of cotton by the cultivator and the preparation of yarn by his women folk). The weaver handled only the final and not the most labour-intensive process in fabricating the cloth. As a result, according to Buchanan, the remuneration of the weaver's labour constituted less than 30 per cent ($3\frac{1}{2}$ rupees out of 12) in the price of production of cheap cloth. Let us note that no other product of the handicrafts consumed by the peasants embodied as much of their own labour as the cheap cloth. To it, however, can be added (the relevant calculation will be given later) sugarcane products and vegetable oil, but this does not invalidate the assumption because in these products the share of the value produced by the peasants was also very large.

It is interesting to note that the structure of the price of costly cloths used by the social élite was quite different from that of the low-cost cloths. According to Grant's data, which I have already cited, only the labour of mainly urban women spinners increased the price of the raw material (cotton worked into yarn) sixteen-fold, with the weaver adding to it at least another half. The landlord alone (to consider only the domestic consumer) could cover such vast costs of manufacture out of the rent which he exacted from agriculture.

N.K. Sinha reports fairly complete data on productivity and remuneration for spinners and weavers and also on the structure of the price of yarn and cloths in Bengal in the second half of the 18th century. Although these data refer to the start of the British period, they help to continue the study of price formation in Indian handicrafts. Thus, according to a resident of the Company in Santipur, the monthly output of spinners of different skills was made up of the fallowing value components (in rupees, annas and pices):[26]

Kind of thread	*Cost of finished Product*	*Price of cotton used*	*Earnings of spinners*
Superfine	1-8-0	0-1-8	1-6-4
Fine	1-6-0	0-2-0	1-4-0
Middling	1-2-3	0-2-0	1-0-3
Ordinary....................................	1-3-0	0-2-3	1-0-4

Thus, in terms of value, the agricultural component (cotton) constituted about 7 per cent of the price of the best grades, the rest of the value being created by the professional urban spinners. For the lower grades, cotton constituted over 14 per cent of the price, and considering that these were usually made by women from the peasant families, the low-grade yarn was obviously a peasant product. The making of the lower grades of yarn inevitably became an ancillary trade also because the remuneration here barely covered the cost of the spinner's food.

Incidentally, in 1800 the average monthly wages among spinners of the lower-grade yarn come to 12-14 annas, while spinners of medium and high grades of yarn earned up to 2 and 3 rupees a month, respectively, that is, their wages approximated those of the artisans who were the family's bread-winners. These distinctions in payment also had a social basis : while the lower grades of yarn were spun by the wives of ordinary rayats, the making of high-grade yarn was frequently the sad privilege of widows from the upper castes, because only the sensitive fingers of women who had not done any rough work were capable of turning out this miracle of skill and patience. Quite obviously, no category of spinners was capable of producing entrepreneurial elements from its midst.

The sharp distinctions in the value of the yarn predetermined the differences in prices for the various grades of cloths. Furthermore, the price of cloths took shape under the impact of the weaver's productivity and remuneration in terms of units of length, and not of units of time in production. An experienced weaver could produce up to 60 pieces of low-grade cloth a year, but the output dropped to 6-12 pieces a year for the higher grades. These figures reflect only the general tendency towards a reduction in the quantity of products with the rise in the quality of cloths and the complexity of their fabrication. It is impossible to cite any accurate calculations because the size of a piece differed from a few metres to 15 and was determined by agreement between the middleman and the weaver.

Information on the average price of a piece of cloth for the various weaving centres helps to gain an idea of the type of product in which they specialised. Thus, in 1783 the East India Company purchased in Dacca 40,500 pieces for 829,200 rupees, i.e. at $20\frac{1}{2}$ rupees per piece, and in Patna, 96,800 pieces for 414,200 rupees, i.e. at $4\frac{1}{3}$ rupees per piece; the prices at the other weaving centres of Eastern India fluctuated between these two extremes. Let us note that these purchases were made by the East India Company, which never bought any coarse or cheap cloths. Actually, the prices fluctuated between 1-2 rupees per piece of coarse cloth to 200 and even 450 rupees per piece of artistically finished muslin.[27] However, the condition of the weavers of various skills and specialisation did not differ so sharply. What is more, the need to make large outlays in purchasing yarn and the length of the production cycle in turning out one article still made the especially skilled craftsmen dependent on credits from buyers-up, whose profits came to a quarter of the wholesale price.

This general reasoning about the place of the individual non-community handicrafts in the processes of reproduction and distribution suggests the need for further subdividing them into two sub-groups: handicrafts which engaged in exchange with the countryside (for instance, some weavers and metal-makers) and those which either had no such exchange or had very little of it. In other words, in contrast to the farming and handicrafts circumscribed in subsistence relations within the framework of the community, there was, on the other pole, the economic isolation (full or partial) of some non-community, especially urban, handicrafts from the economic and consumer requirements of the rural localities and their population.

Conversion of the Agricultural Surplus-Product into Handicraft Articles. The Producer's Social Status

The following question arises: which was the product that ultimately served as compensation for the handicraft articles? Marx gave us the political-economy model in which the alienated (mainly surplus) product of agriculture was transformed into articles for the branches which catered for the consumers of rent. Even in the mid-19th century, he observed, archaic forms of relations between big rent-receivers and artisans were preserved in the backward provinces of British India: "The non-agricultural labourers ... are directly employed by the magnates, to whom a portion of the agricultural surplus-product is rendered in the shape of tribute or rent." A part of this surplus-product, Marx said, was consumed by the magnates in kind, another part was converted by the labourers into luxuries and other articles of consumption for them, while the rest made up the wages of the labourers who owned the implements of their labour.[28]

Indeed, in the 1840s artisans were still directly dependent on their feudal rulers in the heartland areas of India. In 1841 an official of the British administration in Bundelkhand described the condition of local Muslim weavers who made the famous chanderi cloth (so named after the district). In order to protect from dust this extra-fine yarn, which was worth its weight in silver, they worked in dimly lit and damp cellars deep underground. The weavers were employed on a permanent basis and were unable to produce for the free market, because the princely courts of Gwalior and Indore, and also the local chiefs maintained their agent (kothi) on the spot, who made advance payments to the weavers. The coarser cloths were sold on the market, while the best ones were a monopoly of the rulers. Duties were levied on every bale of cloth by the Gwalior authorities.[29] By the mid-19th century, such relations were undoubtedly a relic of earlier times.

The socio-eccnomic aspect of a mechanism under which the rent-consuming sections were the main customers and consumers of urban handicraft articles, while merchant's capital acted as their agent, was not only political but also economic subjugation of the Indian town to the feudal chiefs. To this should be added the important fact that, in India, state feudal property in land also applied to urban lands. Merchants, artisans and other inhabitants of towns paid rent to the landlord on the land where their houses and shops stood. That is why neither the land nor the air of the Indian towns made their inhabitants free from the arbitrary acts of the feudal lords, as they did the West European towns-people.

Quite naturally, the heads of the local communities of merchants and artisans were frequently appointed by the feudal chiefs ruling a given town. An interesting extract from the "Ain-i-Akbari" shows that the Mogul governor of the town had the right to appoint the headmen of the artisans' castes and persons supervising the artisans' commercial affairs and submitting daily report to the urban authorities about all transactions. The very possibility of such control by the despotic state over commercial operations by artisans shows their profound economic dependence on the good will of the local administration. Such control would naturally have been impossible with respect to the European guilds, which had strong market connections with their burgher, plebeian-peasant customers and acted as the exploiters of the countryside.

In Gujarat, the heads of local artisans' communities collected taxes from the members of their caste and paid the amounts into the Treasury themselves or through the headman of the merchants, who was responsible for the payment of taxes by all the merchants and artisans in the town. An influential official of the local administration had the right to order the head of the artisans' community to make for his own use one article or another at the expense of the community. In exchange, this official acted as the community's patron. In other words, the artisans were forced to pay for their political impotence in their own town.[30]

But the communities of merchants and artisans were themselves monopolising the given type of trade or craft. They were open only to persons of a definite caste, and every newcomer to the town had to pay a large initiation fee (in Ahmadabad from 20 to 500 rupees). The caste monopoly of employment in a given occupation made superfluous the institution of apprentices, which had existed in Western Europe. The young artisan was trained in his father's workshop and upon the completion of his training period gave a dinner for the members of the community. The chief of the artisans saw to it that the traditional method of work and standards of manufacture were observed.[31] Thus, the organisations of merchants and artisans had the basic conservative features of the West European guilds, but lacked their main progressive feature, the capacity to stand up for their rights against feudal arbitrariness. However, some castes put up passive resistance to the authoritarian attitudes of the rulers. One example is cited by the Indian scholar Ishvar Prakash: the weavers refused to reduce the prices of cloths, as the governor of Baroda suggested, and were imprisoned. They subsequently left the town and went to Ahmadabad. The governor had to retract and asked them to return.[32]

The weak ties between a number of occupations and the local market demand and also the insufficient coalescence of the handicraft castes with the urban system were conducive to their mobility and easy "take-offs". And this served as a kind of self-defence against the excessive oppression by local rulers or military exigencies. This is how K. N. Chaudhuri describes the situation that took shape in Gujarat in the early 18th century:

"The political insecurity which had been increasing in the decaying empire since the early years of the century had suddenly escalated and become a positive threat to the established centres of trade. In Gujarat, for example, as early as 1712 the Company's broker was complaining that marauding bands of Marathas were continually disturbing the chintzprinters in the neighbouring villages of Broach. In 1725 the printers fled from village to village carrying with them unfinished pieces of cloth in order to avoid the invading troops. By 1734 the Surat Council was noting the exodus of weavers from

Ahmedabad in the direction of Surat, and three years later the Factory was able to recruit 48 families for Bombay. Towards the close of our period Surat which had little weaving industry of its own in the seventeenth century had become a considerable manufacturing town. It is evident that the alleged attachment of the Indian workers to homesteads applied only to times of prosperity".[33]

Polemicising with the established Western notions of insuperable obstacles erected in Mogul India by the caste and its regulations in the way of economic progress, I. Habib points to the following facts: first, working men from castes of other occupations (in this case from peasants and community servants) were recruited for work in other trades, for instance, the mining of diamonds in Karnatak ; second, the castes could change their specialisation (in the 18th century, the caste of tailors in Maharashtra took up the dyeing of cloth); third, the Mogul authorities frequently prohibited any restrictions on the pursuit of definite occupation (Aurangzeb ordered the authorities of Ahmadabad to allow any person wishing to engage in weaving, embroidering or knitting to pursue these trades).

While the latter example may also be interpreted conversely as an attempt by the Muslim rulers to eliminate caste restrictions among Hindus, one has to agree with Habib, who says that we have no knowledge of any instance where manpower was short for any line of production and that, on the contrary, the sources testify to an abundance of handicraft manpower everywhere, which is an indication of its sufficient mobility. The only obstacle to the free supply of handicraft labour, says Habib, was the extortion and the setting of understated prices practised by the nobility.[34]

B. G. Tilak, who spoke at the Second Industrial Conference at Poona in September 1892, must have had in mind this capacity of European guilds to provide protection for their members, when he said: "The history of ancient European guilds further shows that the institutions of guilds and castes, if they cannot be actually traced to the same origin, have many features in common." He noted that the development of European institutions sufficiently indicated "the lines on which we must reform and modify our caste system, if we really mean to improve the condition of the working classes in the country."[35]

One of the most interesting descriptions of the artisan's general status in feudal India will be found in R. Orme's "Historical Fragments of the Moghul Empire." Orme was born in India and spent most of his life in that country, so that he is undoubtedly a great authority on mid-18th century India, but his economic passages are somewhat abstracted from the concrete circumstances of the artisans' activity in the various regions or towns. First of all, Orme observes that the artisan was not personlly free, which is why he had extremely limited opportunities for accumulating capital and extending production. "The mechanic or artificer," Orme insisted, "will work only to the measure of his necessities. He dreads to be distinguished. If he becomes too noted for having acquired a little more money than others of his craft, that will be taken from him. If conspicuous for the excellence of his skill, he is seized upon by some person in authority, and obliged to work for him night and day, on much harder terms than his usual labour acquired when at liberty. Hence all emulation is destroyed; and all the luxury of an Asiatic Empire has not been able to counteract by its propensity to magnificence and splendour, the dispiriting effects of that fear which reigns throughout, and without which a despotic power would reign no more. If any improvements have been made in the few years of a milder administration, they are utterly lost again when the common methods of government succeed."[36]

The data on commercial connections between manufactures in the various towns suggest that even in the second half of the 18th century in some towns artisans still continued to work for the court, the military and the nobility, and also for the external market (mainly in the major military-administrative centres). Such, for instance, was the market orientation of Bangalore, where the weavers, having been deprived of orders from the court of the Mysore Sultan, were able to live only by producing for the external market. Buchanan said that there was little hope that the manufactures of Bangalore would ever reach the level achieved under Hydar, unless some external marketing outlets were found.[37]

A good example of the formation of an urban economy catering to the needs of the court, the officialdom and the military was the development and diversification of the handicrafts in Maharashtra, especially in its capital, Poona, in the 17th and 18th centuries. The great wealth plundered by the Maratha military chiefs in the conquered regions and the intensified exploitation of the local peasantry helped to expand the orders coming from local chiefs and the state, which expended vast amounts of money on the maintenance of the troops, the officials and the court. The urban handicrafts of Maharashtra flourished as a result of the growing state and even private orders from the Maratha feudal chiefs in the 18th century. Their dependence on the state was expressed, in particular, in the state regulation of manufactures through a system of orders and the granting to individuals of a monopoly on the manufacture of some goods. Thus, back in the early 18th century, Radho Naik granted Shamdas Balji, a Gujarati Bania, a monopoly on the production of silk in Yeola.[38]

The local artisans were unable to satisfy fully all the requirements of the growing towns, and skilled weavers and other craftsmen from Hindustan, Bihar and Andhra Desh settled in Maharashtra, notably

Poona. The immigrating craftsmen preserved their religious, communal and caste isolation, forming separate groups within the artisan population of Maharashtra. The urban castes of both Maratha and newly arrived artisans were a kind of guild organisation.

In one of his studies, D.R. Gadgil cites data from the Daftar (chancellery) of the Peshwas, to emphasise that in the 18th century there was no evidence of any sectoral specialisation in the Poona industries, whereas in the town these were so diversified as to meet its requirements as the militaryadministrative centre.[39] "In Poona during the latter half of the 18th century there was considerable immigration of artisans, like cobblers, potters, carpenters, etc., from regions outside Maharashtra. The local artisans in these occupations continued also to ply their crafts. The immigrants came and established themselves chiefly because they either specialised in certain products which members of the indigenous castes did not ordinarily produce or because they brought in greater skill. There is no evidence, contemporary or later, to indicate that the two caste groups engaged in the same craft were brought under one craft or trade association."[40]

There were also many crafts in Dacca, a major centre of Bengali manufacture, with pride of place going to the manufacture of the famous Dacca muslins, which were sold almost all over the world. In 1753, the export of cloths from Dacca came to 2,650,000-2,850,000 Arcot rupees (at that time 8 Arcot rupees = one pound sterling). The British, French and Dutch East India Companies and individual European merchants carried away from Dacca cloths worth 950,000 rupees. Armenian merchants purchased goods worth 500,000 rupees for Iran and the Arab countries; and Persian merchants, goods worth 100,000 rupees. That year merchants trading on markets in North India purchased in Dacca cloths worth 550,000 rupees. In addition, the value of cloths earmarked for Delhi, the capital of the Great Moguls, and to Murshidabad, the capital of the Nawab of Bengal, came to 100,000 and 300,000 rupees, respectively; Indian merchants trading in Bengal took away cloths worth 200,000-300,000 rupees, and the Jagat Seth House ordered cloths worth 150,000 rupees.[41]

The condition of the Dacca weavers provides yet another graphic example of the dependence of artisans, even the most skilled ones (and, perhaps, these especially), on the orders of the authorities. "The annual investments for the imperial wardrobe at Delhi and for the vice-regal court of the province monopolised the whole of the finer muslins. The manufacturers were not allowed to sell cloths exceeding a stated value to native or foreign merchants, and, to superintend the provision of these state investments, a special agent resided on the spot, who exercised an authority, independently of magistrates and government officers, over all brokers, weavers and embroiderers engaged in the business."[42] An official from Delhi got the weavers together in an institution, which was reminiscent of the Mogul karkhanas, where they worked under the supervision of guards.[43]

This state of affairs existed despite the fact, as Orme admits, that weaving, which yielded a considerable part of the tax revenue, was given a special treatment by the authorities and was usually free from their extortions. But for this patronage, the most skilled weavers had to confine themselves to working exclusively for the Treasury. That is why the most magnificent cloths for the court and harem cost ten times more in Dacca than the best of the cloths reaching the market.[44] Thus, the weaver had to pay the price of losing his independent market connections for the high privilege of supplying his manufactures to the courts of the local and higher-placed despots.

The growth of enterprise among the weavers of Dacca was contained by the absence of free market ties and by rigid supervision on the part of the authorities. Even the most skilled has to be content with a very modest level of welfare. John Taylor, the Company's commercial resident in Dacca, said in his report for 1800 that a weaver with two assistants worked for a year to produce a piece of the best muslin worth 250 rupees for the Mogul court. The cost of the yarn was 100 rupees. Thus, if the weavers were not cheated, they earned 150 rupees a year, or 8 rupees a month for the master-weaver, and 2 rupees a month each for his assistants.[45] However, this fails to take account of the fact that the purchases of the yarn and the maintenance of the weavers themselves could hardly have been made possible without loans. Taking account of the interest on loans and also the abuses in settling such loans (of which we have direct testimony), the earnings of weavers, especially of the master-weaver, will appear to be much more modest. Meanwhile, rice in the 18th century in Dacca cost 1 rupee for three maunds. A modern researcher has drawn the conclusion that a working man earning 2 rupees a month was barely able to feed a family of five.[46] Indeed, the master-weaver's earnings could not provide a basis for entrepreneurial accumulation.

The articles made of iron in Monghyr, the famous centre of metal-working in the early 19th century, were also meant for the military and the rich rent-receivers. Buchanan, listing these manufactures, mentions fire-arms and sidearms: "double-barrel guns, rifles, single-barrel pistols, fowling-pieces, muskets and blunder-busses, ordinary and carved match-locks, pistols, swords, spears and ramrods." Next came household utensils for well-to-do families: saucepans, frying-pans, snuffers, chafing irons, chamber stoves or grates, kitchen stoves, various locks, ladles, tongs, knives and forks, scissors, etc. Then followed pieces of equestrian equipment: horseshoes, stirrup irons, spurs, curry-combs, etc., and even palanquins. All these equipments were used by the nobility or the privileged mounted troops. Of the farming implements, there was mention only of "sickles without teeth", spuds and large sickles for cutting grass, and also wheel spindles which could be used for the carriages of rich people; among the other articles were razors, nails of every kind, including cobbler's nails, needles and knitting-needles.[47]

Buchanan also gives the prices of these articles. Fire-arms cost from 10 to 32 rupees, swords from 1 to 3, kitchen ranges 15 rupees, a fire-place 125 rupees, a dozen table knives and forks from 4 to 6 rupees. Peasant sickles were worth much less—from 1 to 4 annas, a hundred nails 3 annas, etc. Thus, in range and value weapons and household articles for the richer sections prevailed among the manufactures of Monghyr. Of course, one could assume that in listing the articles the source gave preference to weapons and articles of artistic design because they attracted the attention of the foreign observer by the high standard of craftsmanship. But the decline of Monghyr, which followed upon a reduction of demand for articles of this kind, serves to confirm that they predominated in the total volume of production. Goods meant for the plebeian—peasants' and craftsmen'—demand could not compensate for the reduction in aristocratic consumption. Indeed, Buchanan says explicitly that "the chief articles are the different kinds of firearms mostly sold to passengers, and carried towards the west; and tea-kettles and chafing-dishes sent to Calcutta."[48]

The following data help to gain an idea of the organisation and scale of manufacture in Monghyr. It had 40 blacksmith shops, with two or three men working in each, these being usually partners or members of the same family. Whenever anyone received a large order, he shared it with his neighbours. Depending on skill, a workman received 2-3 annas a day, that is, 3-4 rupees a month (provided he was fully employed throughout the month, which is doubtful). We find that in this well-known metal-working centre there remained slightly more than 100 artisans, who led a very modest existence, offering no opportunities at all for accumulation. The number of workmen may have been somewhat larger, because apart from balcksmith, chasers, jewellers, tinsmiths and others also took part in the working of metal, but however that may be, early 19th-century Monghyr could no longer vie with similar European centres even in the size of its labour-force to say nothing of technical equipment and scale of production.

Petty-Commodity Production and Pockets of Enterprise in the Handicrafts

Apart from the artisans directly or indirectly living off transformed rent, there were also non-communal artisans who worked as independent producers on the basis of product or commodity exchange. These were usually grouped by occupation and caste. But there were, apparently, exceptions to this rule as well. Thus, J. Hough reports about an interesting mountain community of artisans, the kothurs.[49] This is the only known community which engaged in several crafts: the production and working of iron and steel, the manufacture of gold, silver and wooden articles, pottery and tanning. It also engaged in agriculture. An attempt by a district collector to study their methods of iron production from local ores was firmly rejected by the kothur headmen, who objected "that it was impossible for strangers, who had been so very short a time on the hills, to obtain from them (kothurs.—V. P.) an article which neither they nor their fathers had ever been able to discover."[50] This kind of artisan tribe was undoubtedly historical relict.

Some towns in the 18th century had crafts catering mainly for the mass consumer demand in the neighbouring countryside. There is evidence of urban artisans making coarse cloths for a fairly lively domestic trade in Bengal and Bihar. In the towns and artisans' settlements in the Dacca region in the 18th century cloths were made in a very wide range, from the finest muslins worn by the inhabitants of the local chiefs' zenana (the female part of the house) to coarse cloths which went to make the garments of the poor rayat.[51] Taylor names 5 towns in various regions of Eastern Bengal which were known for the manufacture of coarse cheap cloth. The Dutch merchant, S. Master, who was in India from 1675 to 1680, said that a factory of the East India Company dispatched cloths worth 300,000 rupees from Malda to Dacca, and included not only coloured silks (which were used in India for female garments), but also the coarser grades. Goods worth roughly the same amount were also purchased by petty traders from Rajmahan, Murshidabad and other places down the Ganges,[52] that is, in Bengal proper. The town of Patna, the largest artisan centre in Bihar, was known for its production of woollen blankets, a mass consumption article in demand in Bengal. However, in the early 19th century the export of blankets from Patna was markedly reduced.

In Bellary, a relatively large town in Mysore, where the leading line was the manufacture of cotton cloth, the weavers worked to meet local needs and for export. Coarse cloth was sold at weekly fairs, and the following fact is highly indicative of the solid trade relations between Bellary and the neighbouring regions: when during the Anglo-Mysore war the ruler of Mysore, Tippoo Sultan, banned trade with South Karnatak, which had been occupied by the British, cheap cloth was smuggled there from Bellary.[53] Mass consumption cloth was also manufactured in other Mysore towns, like Sinjapur, a small manufacturing centre, which was oriented to Bangalore and which produced both costly and cheap cloths, part of which was supplied to Bangalore.

The extent to which trade was developed even between distant regions in South India will be seen from the fact that merchants from Bellary, Adoni, Hubli, Guti and other places situated hundreds of kilometres away from Bangalore, maintained permanent agents in that city. Among the goods sold by these agents were cotton, coarse yarn, blankets and wheat. In exchange, Bangalore supplied dyed cotton cloth. Altogether, 1,500 cartloads of cotton, 50 of cotton yarn and 230 of raw silk arrived at Bangalore every year.[54] Some data showing a deepening of the processes of separation between town and country, and the development of trade between them are also available for Bengal and Bihar.

It may be assumed that in the 18th century there were signs of small local markets merging into a general market of consumer goods for one large region, say, Bengal or Mysore. Although trade in 18th-century India was largely confined to meeting the requirements of the major rent-consumer and those who catered for his needs, the establishment of markets for some mass consumer goods reflected the level achieved in the division of labour between town and country.

What has been said and also subsequent data about the structure of the commodity masses involved in wholesale trade make it possible to assess this level as being inadequate for any extensive genesis of capitalism. The absence of constant demand frequently led to lengthy interruptions in the professional occupations of artisans. In his "Remarks on the Husbandry and Internal Commerce of Bengal" Colebrooke said that the Indian artisan in the late 18th century, incapable of waiting for a market or anticipating its demand, was only capable of following "his regular occupation as immediately called to it by the wants of his neighbours. In the intervals, he must apply to some other employment which is in present request."[55]

In order to understand the specifics of the economic organisation of the urban handicrafts, much importance attaches to the study of the activity of merchant's capital in the manufactures and identification of the initial signs of industrial-capital formation. Having noted the existence in Mogul India of phenomena like the large urban market for non-agricultural products, a division of labour based on occupational specialisation and an abundance rather than a shortage of skilled manpower, I. Habib sought to clarify the extent to which under these circumstances the organisation of production had gone in the origination of capitalist or semi-capitalist forms. As I have said, he had, regrettably, failed to consider the manufactures which catered for the countryside and farming.

Habib subdivided the urban artisans into two groups: the first included those who remained owners of their product until it was sold on the market; and the second those who carried on production by receiving advance payments from merchants, especially when their products were sold in distant areas. Whenever the raw material was costly, it was supplied by the merchant in kind, while cash credits were made available for the purchase of cheap raw materials.

Apart from the organisation of production in forms which corresponded to the distribution system, there were forms which corresponded to the manufactory, among which Habib classes large-scale construction, ship-building, the mining of diamonds and the production of potash. But he adds that these cannot be classified as capitalist manufacture units proper because, although the merchants did act as major entrepreneurs, there were no specialised occupations or systems of implements in these lines of production.

Concerning the state-owned karkhanas in Delhi, Habib makes the assumption that while the artisans did work there as wage labourers, they continued to own their tools; besides, there is no definite information about the detailed division of labour within the karkhana, for the products (luxuries) did not go to the market but directly for the use of the padishah and his entourage. This fact, Habib assumes, naturally tended to reduce the economic importance of the karkhanas and, let me add, does not make it possible to qualify these as capitalist units.

As for the undertakings which belonged to individual merchants, judging by the fact that hardly any mention of them is made in the sources, one could conclude that they were small. Despite the existence of small establishments with wage labour, the system of distributing raw materials among the workingmen, Habib believes, was the characteristic form of handicraft commodity production in Mogul India, for it had the advantage of making it possible to involve in exploitation not only the artisan himself, but also members of his family. Only where the material was too costly to be distributed among the artisans, or where the production process was of short duration, was it advantageous to set up karkhanas.[56]

Let us supplement these general considerations with evidence from other sources. The Dutch merchant W. Bolts, who stayed in Bengal in the 1760s, wrote that "in the time of the Mogul government, and even in that of the Nabob Allaverdy Khawn (the Nawab of Bengal in 1740-1756.—V. P.) the weavers manufactured their goods freely, and without oppression; ... it was then a common practice for reputable families of the Tanty, or weaver caste, to employ their own capitals, in manufacturing goods, which they sold freely on their own accounts." Bolts followed this up with an example showing that during the reign of the Nawab a certain English merchant bought on his own doorstep in Dacca 800 pieces of muslin from the weavers who brought them there.[57]

Side by side with this there are a number of facts which indicate that merchant's capital penetrated industry to a very considerable extent. The simplest primary form in which merchant's capital manifested itself in small industries—the purchase of wares by the merchant from the independent, small commodity producers—was wide spread in the weaving industry of so large a weaving centre as Dacca. S. Master, who described the methods used by the Company to acquire cloth in Dacca, related as early as the 1670s that comparatively big merchant-brokers (dallals), who had experience in the cloth trade, received loans from the Company. They then distributed the money among their paikars (retail dealers), who travelled from town to town making advances to weavers.[58] It will be shown later that a similar practice evolved in Bombay at the beginning of the 18th century. During the first decade a resident of the East India Company at Salem ordered cloth from the weavers of Coimbatore and advanced money to them, which they took eagerly in spite of the fact that they were often cheated when accounts were settled.[59]

It is hardly likely that the factories of the European East India companies could have acquired cloth in the way described if it had not already been customary for Indian buyers-up to advance money to artisans. In fact, an examination of the economic structure of various Indian regions reveals that, in a number of cases, artisans were held in bondage by local merchant's capital. Buchanan's investigation of the economy of Mysore contains the most detailed information with regard to the methods employed by money-lenders to enslave artisans.

For instance, he relates, that in the town of Nalarayana-palliyam, near Coimbatore, "native merchants frequently make advances for the cloth intended for country use. These persons endeavour to keep the weavers constantly in their debts; for so long as that is the case, they can work for no other merchant, and must give their goods at a low rate. When a merchant wishes to engage a new weaver, he must advance the sum owing to the former employer. With this the weaver buys goods to fulfil his own contract; but then he becomes equally bound to the person who has advanced the money. A few weavers are rich enough to be able to make cloth on their own account, and in consequence settle it to the best advantage.... Those who once get into the debt of a native merchant are ever afterwards little better than slaves, and must work for him at a very low rate."[60] This example illustrates vividly the combination of merchant's and usurer's capital, where the relations between the creditor and the debtor inevitably lead to the personal dependence of the latter, to bondage.[61]

Dealers in Nalarayanapalliyam advanced money against the

manufacture not only of cloth earmarked for distant markets, but also of cloth for local use, which indicates that merchant's capital strengthened its domination over the handicraft industries. It was, however, usual for traders to make advances to artisans against manufactures intended for distant markets. Merchants from the Nagarit caste, questioned by Buchanan, said that, as a rule, advances were not made upon the production of the common types of cloth unless the demand originated in a very remote locality. In that case, and also when ordering more expensive cloths, it was usual to advance half the value of the commodity so that the producer could buy raw material. The loan was made for three months and no interest was paid during this period, but if the order was not fulfilled on time, 0.75 per cent was charged for every additional month beyond the contracted date.[62]

One consequence of the extremely extensive development of money-lending was that the creditor of the artisan—especially when the latter worked for the local market—frequently was a professional money-lender and not the buyerup or merchant. Describing the whole organisation of the weaving industry, Buchanan writes: "When the goods are in much demand, it is customary for the merchant to advance one-half, or even the whole, of the price of the goods which he commissioned; when the demand is small the manufacturers borrow money from the bankers at 2 per cent a month, and make goods, which they sell to the merchant of the place. They never carry them to the public market."[63] If the weaver manufactured cloth for his own account, he sold a part of his product to dealers and a part at the weekly bazaar, but having received an advance, the weaver could not sell any cloth until he had fulfilled his contract. Buchanan's descriptions of various districts of Bihar and Bengal contain similar information with regard to the development of merchant's and usurer's capital in the weaving industry.

Buchanan's detailed report contains, however, no indication that the dealer handed out raw materials to the weavers. There is, indeed, evidence that peasant women received cotton from traders, spun it into yarn and, for a payment, returned it to the trader. But one cannot regard these spinners as home workers because for them spinning was only a subsidiary occupation. It is not known on what terms the traders sold the yarn to the weavers.[64]

Information relating to the same period indicates that raw materials were distributed by the buyer-up in other industries as well. On the basis of the data gathered by Buchanan, it is safe to say that handing out raw materials to certain artisans, such as shoe-makers, jewellers, smiths and oil-pressers, was widely practiced in Bengal and Bihar at the beginning of the 19th century.[65] These and other data indicate that at the end of the 18th century and the beginning of the 19th century almost all the principal forms of merchant's capital existed in the small industries of India, which is a characteristic feature of the handicrafts in the advanced stages of feudalism. An examination of economic relations in India's handicrafts leads to the conclusion that the form of merchant's capital prevalent in the handicraft industries of Bengal, Bihar and Mysore was that in which combination with usurer's capital was typical. In the manufacture of costly cloths, the artisan frequently purchased raw materials exclusively for the cash advanced to him by the dealer. This form of merchant's capital in the handicraft industries approximated the highest form under which the raw materials are handed out to the artisans to be processed for a definite payment.

For all that, merchant's capital was still not connected with handicraft production on any noticeable scale. Merchant's capital functioned outside handicraft production, without assuming the productive form, and exploiting the artisan through the sphere of circulation. Besides, the practices of hiring labour in the handicrafts were even less developed than in agriculture, where the seasonal nature of production required periodical recruitment of additional manpower. According to Grant, in the manufactures of late 18th-century Bengal the capital necessary to employ in industry a million and a half people was even less than the capital needed to employ the same number of people in agriculture.[66] This should apparently be seen as evidence that the relative volume of the manpower recruited from outside was even smaller in the local industries than it was in agriculture.

The purchases of raw silk are cited as an example of the small amount of capital required. "All the raw silk produced in the country, and chiefly for foreign exportation, may be valued at prime cost at 50 lacs; but of this sum scarcely a thirtieth part can be laid out in the purchase of cocoons, or rude materials in their original merchantable state." This was due to the fact that the cocoons were collected three to six times a year and each operation was separately financed, with the dealer having probably sold this stock before employing his capital again for the next collection of cocoons, which obviates the need for new capital. Throughout the whole of Bengal, the total value of equipment and premises (excluding the silk-winding factories of the East India Company) did not exceed 100,000 rupees. "So that, perhaps, the trading stock constantly employed in the whole of this species of manufactures, until it falls into the hands of the great foreign exporter ... may reasonably be estimated under 10 lacs of rupees."[67] We find that Grant, having first clearly understated the volume of merchant's capital in the purchase of raw silk, having determined it as a thirtieth part of the value of the product, gives the figure of 10 lacs (1 million) rupees, or a fifth of the value, which is undoubtedly closer to the actual volume of capital.

Merchant's capital was also similarly engaged essentially in purchasing the products, instead of organising their production, in the cotton industry. In late 18th-century Bengal, 400,000 maunds of cotton were picked annually, and after ginning this left 100,000 to 130,000 maunds of cotton fibre valued at 1.2 million rupees. (It is remarkable that the chief commercial crop yielded only 0.5 per cent of the value of the total agricultural product.) Another 600,000 rupees' worth of cotton was imported from distant Surat and Mirzapur. This mass of cotton was distributed among the spinners in lots which kept them busy for a month. Their labour "at once so laborious and cheap" enhanced the value of the raw material 16 times. But the wages they earned amounted to scarcely 9 annas (or 18 pence) a month.

Having remarked on the unique skill of the Indian spinners, Grant says: "A fact indeed which might appear altogether wonderful, if it were not at the same time observed that the greater part of this body of people is composed of women belonging to the families of the husbandmen or manufacturers and who could not otherwise be more usefully employed, at least during the hot and rainy seasons of the year." 300,000 weavers, "masters and journeymen", produced 3 million pieces of cloth a year, which cost 28 million rupees, including 1.5 million rupees worth of silk cloth; the price of the yarn needed was not more than half that of the piece goods, and the capital laid out had only to be large enough to provide sufficient raw material for two months' work. Grant concludes, accordingly, that "the whole productive stock at any time required or actually in use, for completing all those beautiful fabrics, so much the object of our admiration, after allowing a loom of 6 rupees to be renewed once in 20 years for every woman, will not exceed 25 lacs of rupees, being rather less than the eleventh part of the full advances, made by the great interior or foreign merchant."[68] In other words, according to Grant, the working capital and the annual expenditure on new looms came to less than one-eleventh of the wholesale price of the cloth produced annually. Although this figure, just as some of his other calculations regarding the requisite amount of money in circulation, may perhaps be too low, it undoubtedly indicates some of the features peculiar to the handicrafts in 18th-century India: if one takes each branch of production as a whole, the relatively very large outlays on living labour, the extremely low wages paid to highly skilled workers, the trifling cost of the artisan's tools, and the rapid turnover of the merchant's capital operating in the sphere of small-scale production.

Thus, the specific features of the social division of labour in India determined the dealers' scale and sphere of activity. Their capital was, naturally, not strong enough to "split" the direct subsistence bonds between agriculture and the handicrafts within the framework of the community. The mediation of merchant's capital in the exchange of goods between the weaver, the oil-presser and other non-communal artisans and the farming population was limited because from this exchange were excluded the fairly extensive direct connections of the artisan with a manufacturer of raw material and semi-finished products, on the one hand, and with the local consumers of the finished products. Only in manufacture for the élite sections, their servants, the troops and for distant markets was the domination of the dealers unchallenged.

Incidentally, the domination of dealers in such industries will be seen from a description of the self-administration bodies (panchayats) of jeweller artisans and merchants in Cambay (Gujarat), who engaged in the purchase and sale of agates. Each operation in the working of agates was performed by members of one of the artisan panchayats, but only the dealers' panchayat engaged in the buying of unpolished stones and the sale of the finished products.[69] Thus, in Gujarat the caste self-administration of the artisans was controlled not only by the administration of the despotism but also by the merchant's capital. There is some connection between the two, because in the industries where the agates were worked, the dealer catered for the needs of the authorities when selling the product. That is why the dealers' control over the industry was ultimately an expression of the general domination of Indian urban life by the despotic rule. Apart from this information, the description is also of interest because it shows that in this peculiarly diffused manufacture there was, on the one hand, something of an aggregate buyer-up, and on the other, an aggregate artisan, each represented by his caste panchayat. We find, therefore, that the emergent capitalist relations were still tightly enveloped by the caste integument.

Analysing the transition from the feudal to the capitalist mode of production, Marx pointed to the historical importance, as a transition stage, of the way along which the "merchant established direct sway over production". But Marx also said that it "cannot by itself contribute to the overthrow of the old mode of production, but tends rather to preserve and retain it as its precondition.... This system presents everywhere an obstacle to the real capitalist mode of production and goes under with its development."[70] In application to India there is especial importance in the indication that merchant's capital tended to conserve the old mode of production as a pre-requisite of its own activity because the old relations did not die off in any sense either in the period under consideration or later, in the epoch when colonial capitalism developed.

K. N. Chaudhuri, an authority on the Indian crafts, has come out against one of the routine attempts to "disclaim" Marx's statement by arguing[71] that the pre-capitalist "producer" worked solely for the market and could not have existed without buying and selling:

"To attempt to characterise a craftsman as one kind of specialised trader is to ignore all historical reality. A situation in which the industrial producer sells directly to the consumer is likely to be a limiting case of an extreme kind....

"Even in twentieth-century India a survey of the handloom industry revealed that in almost every major weaving centre, where the weavers were wholly dependent on their trade for a year-round livelihood, the output of cloth became too great to be disposed of locally, and the weavers were faced with the choice of either selling their products to the village dealer at disadvantageous prices or wasting much time and effort trudging from one local market to another with their goods trying to find better terms. The close interconnection between commerce and industrial development is too well recorded in pre-modern Europe and Asia to need much emphasis. In the pre-capitalist society, as Marx observed with some force, commerce rules industry which is the reverse of modern society."[72]

While accepting Marx's conception of the two ways of the origin of capitalist production in 16th and 17th-century Europe, that is, during the genesis of capitalism, K. N. Chaudhuri has also noted that in the same period the Indian method of textile production relied heavilly on the system of commercial advances. It was not the same as the "putting out" system. The merchants almost always advanced cash sums and not raw materials under the traditional contractual relationship. From the second half of the seventeenth century onwards, as we shall see, a system similar to it did develop in some places, but it happened invariably under the influence of European trading. It was striking that perceptive European servants of the trading companies were fully aware of Marx's first road and the contrast between the Indian system of production and that prevalent at home. In 1676, for example, Sir William Langhorn in the course of a spirited defence of the system of advances reflected: "In Europe industry is favoured and prosperity secured, and particularly weavers of all sorts like our clothyers and Italian fabriequers raise themselves vast estates; now with such the greater your dealings the easier your terms, it being sure gains in the makers' own hands. But here ... they dare not hoard nor increase their estates to any bulk. It's meat for Harpys. The merchants who are in some way of getting, spend it in a manner all in good works and plentiful living, where they dare; reserving little else but credit and a bare stock to carry on business. But the poor weavers between their inbred way of feeding Bramenys and the extortions of their Avaldars, live merely from hand to mouth ... and seldom able to put a piece upon the loom without the money beforehand." [73]

Langhorn's account, supported by numerous other instances, highlights several significant points on the nature of the Indian textile production. It is unquestionably true that the weavers needed working capital both to buy raw materials and to support themselves during the time the cloth was being woven. But even more important was the indispensable role of the advance system in securing the cloth in large enough quantities. It was a contract that imposed definite obligations on both sides. Just as the merchant was assured of receiving his supplies on time with a reasonable degree of certainty, the weaver on his part regarded the advance as a deposit on orders.[74]

In the key manufactures in India, including weaving, the highest form of merchant's capital in the small-scale industries did not as a rule become fully developed, while the exploitation of the artisans was excessively burdened by the bondage of money-lending. The accumulation of capital, innovation, etc., were much more possible and appeared to have occurred among trading and financial groups, but not among the petty and relatively poor artisans who were fettered with traditions.[75] This tended to enhance the conservative role of merchant's capital in the Indian handicrafts, slowed down extended reproduction and worsened the condition of the immediate producers.

There is indeed a good deal of evidence showing the poverty and cruel exploitation of the artisans in the late Middle Ages. For example, J. A. de Mandelslo, a Holstein diplomat, who visited India as early as 1638, wrote about the artisans of Surat (Gujarat): "All they can do is to get five or six pence a day. They must accordingly fare very poorly, their ordinary diet being only kitsery, which they make of beans pounded, and rice, which they boil together in the water till the water be consumed. Then they put thereto a little butter melted, and this is their supper, for all day they eat only rice and wheat in the grain."[76] The Englishman John Fryer relates at the close of the 17th century that the Indian artisan "can hardly live for those, who will grind their faces to fill their own hoards as much as the Desies do."[77]

The great skill of the Indian artisans, as well as their exceedingly low living standard, was also stressed in the work of the English mercantilist school published towards the end of the 17th century. The author of the work stated that the countries usually called the East Indies abounded in valuable commodities, good and cheap industrial raw materials and that the people inhabiting them were skilled artisans accustomed to processing these materials and who, in some places, worked for a penny a day. There were, continued the author, spices in large quantities, for many species were harvested twice a year and others even four times; a variety of diamonds and other precious stones; several kinds of medicines, and diverse useful and costly articles that attracted the eyes and hearts of all merchant nations of Europe.[78] In general, one can say that the Golden Age of the handicrafts, if this term is to imply the prosperity of the artisans, never existed in feudal India, but they did at any rate have work and food, although they were deprived of any opportunities for adequate productive accumulation.

Let us now consider some of the evidence of the sources about the existence in India of capitalist-type workshops. Let us note, first of all, the need for the greatest circumspection in classifying any establishment under this head. As I noted in my preface, the founders of scientific socialism urged the need to consider every concrete category, say, petty-commodity production, in a similarly concrete historical environment, and to draw the conclusions on the real substance of the category in question by comparing their interaction. This requirement of the scientific methodology should also be applied to the given concrete historical situation in interaction with which the individual categories (just as concrete in themselves) acquired definite historical substance.

The general truth of this will be seen, for instance, from a study of the approach to the mining of diamonds, which even the very circumspect Habib has classified as a capitalist manufactory—with some reservations, it is true. When the East India Company occupied the territory of the Northern Sirkars, it could not ignore the local mining of diamonds. In order to study the possibility of the Company's joining these operations, Heyne, whom I have quoted above, went to the mining area of Eluru in 1795. He gives the traditional history of the discovery and start of the mining of diamonds. One day, a shepherd discovered some stones on a mountain slope which he thought were flints, and used these to light his pipe. Unfortunately, he used the flints to light his pipe when visiting the estate of a big local zamindar, one of whose servants spied the stones, winkled the story out of the shepherd and brought the discoverer before the zamindar. When the latter arrived on the spot and found more diamonds, he sacrificed the ill starred shepherd to Lakshmi in gratitude for his own sudden enrichment.

Legend has it that the zamindar had managed to extract and conceal the biggest diamonds before the nizam heard of the discovery and established direct control of the place (Heyne says that this happened 80 years before his visit, that is, in 1715). He adds that since then only persons authorised by the nizam have the right to prospect for diamonds in the place.[79] Unfortunately, the status of these persons is not quite obvious were they officials of the nizam or independent contractors who farmed or leased the right to work the fields on definite terms?

Apart from Eluru, Heyne also inspected the diamond fields at

Kaddapa, which had been in operation for centuries. This was an open mine which had been dug until the diamond bearing layer (at a depth of 5 to 7 metres) was reached. The layer was determined by the presence of certain layers of rock (of which Heyne lists the nine main ones). First the big stones were removed, then the rock was washed and the diamonds were then sought in the mass of small stones. Depending on the colour, the diamonds were divided into four groups, each bearing the name of the four varnas and priced accordingly.

Heyne tells the story of a headman who had leased from the Company ten mines for 130 pagodas (about 400 rupees) a year. He worked three or four of these himself, subleasing the rest for 9 rupees a month per mine, which meant that he recouped the cost of the lease of all his mines. Sixteen men and women, each paid a pagoda (about 3 rupees a month), were employed at each mine. They belonged to the lower, shudra, castes from the neighbouring villages, worked in the mines from childhood and took pride in their honesty with respect to their employer.

Heyne estimated that the lessee earned up to 5,000 pagodas per mine, of which his expenditures came to 2,000. These figures appear to be highly exaggerated, because, for instance, the two main items of his expenditures—rent (13 pagodas a year) and wages (192 pagodas a year)—together came to just over onetenth of the amount of expenditure Heyne indicates. There is also the question of why the Company should have fixed such a low rent from such big earnings. That is why Heyne's figures should apparently be applied to all the ten-mines. A well-paid supervisor was in charge of each mine, the lessee himself never, or very rarely, putting in an appearance at the mines. This entrepreneur should perhaps be classified as a land-holder and merchant rather than as an industrialist.

In 1808, Heyne made a third visit to the diamond fields, this time in the Banganapalla area, where the diamond-bearing layer was at a depth of 3 to 6 metres. According to Heyne, the workers made deep holes down to the layer, and when they reached the rock, hacked at it with picks as they squatted; the workers belonged to the chambhars' caste, and their employers to more prominent men. The field was not a rich one and the supervision over the workers was indifferent.[80] The employers apparently made do with the earnings they obtained from the purchase and resale of diamonds. There again we have the ordinary type of merchant's capital, which showed no inclination of tying itself up with production.

There is no doubt about the property differentiation among some weavers and also about the existence of simple capitalist cooperation and the embryos of manufacture in the weaving industry. In the weaving industry of Mysore, for instance, the use of hired labour was commonplace. The employer-weavers, kept from two to five assistants, who were paid on a piece-rate basis. We have information about daily average earnings among weavers: these came to from 6 to 8 pence, depending on the skill and the complexity of the work. The arrangement under which one owner had several looms was so widespread that it was reflected in Mysore's tax legistation. Thus, the owner of one loom paid a tax of 3.75 fanams (2s. 6.25 pence), the owner of two looms 5 fanams, of three and more—2 fanams per loom.[81] Thus, Mysore's tax policy encouraged the enlargement of weaving workshops. In Mysore, small master-weavers who employed workers received credit from merchants and bankers at 2 per cent a month.[82] This type of relations also existed in Bengal's weaving industry. The well-to-do weavers who employed hired labour frequently acted only as middlemen between them and the merchant. Such relations delayed the development of the higher forms of capitalist production.

Types of Establishments in Ferrous Metallurgy

For all the main handicrafts in India, we find several types of establishments which are determined chiefly by the purpose of the products and the nature of the demand. In ferrous metallurgy, to these factors were added as the crucial conditions the extraction and the quality of the ore, and also the burning of charcoal. One is left with a definite impression that favourable natural conditions rather tended to conserve the primitive forms and methods of production than to promote their improvement. The absence of any extensive market did not apparently allow any comparison of production costs in the course of competition and stimulation of faster development of establishments which operated in a more favourable situation. It is, indeed, the worsening of the natural conditions that led to a complexification of the production process and to a concomitant improvement of the socio-economic organisation of production. Let us note that the price of the product was lower at the relatively primitive establishments which tended to delay the formation of incentives for their improvement. In other words, natural advantages were levelled out by social regulation.

In the late 18th and early 19th centuries, Heyne observed a very simple mode of iron extraction at a village near Satghurd (about 180 kilometres to the west of the city of Madras, on the border with present-day Andhra Pradesh). There were only three workers and they came from different families, belonging to the lowest sections of the village, because their main duty was to transport the cargoes of persons who travelled across the village territory. They were engaged in the smelting of iron only in the dry season—from early January to the end of March, but they started on putting up the ores much earlier, either during the rainy season or just after it ended. The ore consisted of the black sands which silted on the bottom of the mountain streams. These had an exceptionally high iron content, if we are to believe what Heyne says: nine seers (two pounds or just over 0.9 kilogrammes) of sand yielded seven seers of crude unpurified iron and five seers of forged iron fit for use.

The high content of metal and its structure undoubtedly facilitated the process of smelting. The furnace was an asymmetrical half-cone over 1 metre long and up to 70 centimetres high. When the furnace was loaded with coal it was fed with five portions of ore and coal at intervals of about a quarter-hour, with the third portion consisting of $2\frac{1}{2}$ seers of ore and the rest of one seer. The quantity of coal was always the same. Thus, the smelting process took about two hours and could be repeated three times a day. When the smelting was completed, the mass so obtained was cooled down with water, heated up again and then subjected to forging, losing $\frac{2}{7}$ of its weight in the process. The finished iron was sold in one-seer ingots at a quarter rupee each or 3.6 kilogrammes of iron for one rupee. Altogether, 360 ingots, or roughly 320 kilogrammes of finished iron, were produced by the men in one season.

Heyne's subsequent calculations are not clear. He assumes that these 360 ingots were sold for 40 rupees.[83] But if we go on his own prices (a quarter rupee per ingot), the receipts should come to 90 rupees. Heyne may have meant the net earnings, because the iron-makers may have had to pay for the extraction of the ore and the burning of the coal, to pay taxes and make other outlays.

In June 1794, the inhabitants of a village situated 14 miles from Rajahmandri (in present-day Andhra Pradesh) willingly told Heyne their iron-smelting secrets. They were poor and during the rainy period of the year engaged in agriculture, taking up metallurgy only in the dry season. Between seasons, they cut wood and burned charcoal (usually contracting malaria when in the jungle, and so having to spend some time on the sick-bed upon their return home). Heyne says that the low productivity of the local iron-makers was due to their ailments and the need to engage in farming. "Yet the iron which they produce is considered as the finest in every respect for tools, razors, etc."[84] Heyne says there was a great demand for the iron because the miners, smelters, wood-cutters and other workers altogether totalled no more than eight or nine men.

The ores were located near the village at a depth of 11-14 metres. Local miners were not aware of any horizontal workings, which is why the mines (or rather, pits with a diameter of just over a metre) were sunk 4 or 5 metres away from each other. The coal was burnt from a definite kind of trees, which grew only some 24-30 miles away from the village. The transportation of the coal was costly, which, says Heyne, together with other circumstances made the production of iron an unreliable occupation (in terms of profitability), but he adds that despite the small-scale production it attracted the attention of any curious observer by its simplicity and the high quality of the iron produced.

The furnace was made of clay and looked like half an egg 4.5 feet in length and up to 3 feet 9 inches in width. It had several openings through which the ore and coal were loaded (at a ratio of one to two), the metal was let out, the slag removed and the air pumped in during the smelting process itself. The smelting began at 5.00 a.m. and continued all day. The air was supplied by two pairs of bellows, worked by two men. The yield was about 112 pounds, that is, slightly over 50 kilogrammes of iron mass, one-half of it slag. This mass, which required further treatment, was sold for one rupee. But after forging "it acquires the properties of steel, and may then be usefully employed in the making of instruments."[85] Unfortunately, Heyne says nothing either about the smelting itself, or the final value of the iron, or of the price for the finished product.

Heyne completes his description of iron-making production near Rajahmandri by setting forth his considerations about the possibility of it being run by the East India Company. He believed that a substitution of the primitive bellows by powerful air-blowing machines, however complicated that may have been, would have rid the Company of the need to import steel from Britain. But very perspicaciously Heyne said: "I have strong doubts whether the establishment of extensive iron manufactures, in countries destitute of pit coal, be a prudent measure. Indeed, I think it probable that the iron manufactories of England are in possession of such advantage that no other country is in a capacity to compete with them."[86] The latter assumption held true for about 50 years.

Heyne's next description of Indian metallurgy was from a village situated near Nuzwid, to the north of Masulipatam. Prior to the famine which had hit the village shortly before Heyne's visit, it had 40 operating furnaces, of which only 10 were working when Heyne inspected them. The technology and the furnaces themselves were similar to those already described, but the organisation of production was different, because special groups of men, and not the iron-makers themselves, were engaged in the procurement of ore and coal, and supplied them to the furnaces and then sold them by the basket. Each smelting yielded roughly I maund (40 seers = 80 pounds = 36 kilogrammes) of iron mass, which was sold at 2 rupees, that is, three times the price at neighbouring Rajahmandri. Such price differentials are hard to explain by value categories, because here the ore was for all practical purposes deposited on the surface, close to the village, while the charcoal was burnt in the vicinity. It could be that the famine which had reduced the iron-makers had raised the prices of their product, that is, had made the local supply and demand balance decisive.

Heyne also mentions six surrounding villages, where the population also engaged in the smelting of iron.[87] We find, therefore, that there was some specialisation of whole regions in iron-making. There were dozens of furnaces in the area and the daily output came to several tons of metal.

Finally, Heyne also has a description of steel-making in Mysore, which allows the comparison with Buchanan's information. Steel was made in a small village lying among the hills near Chitradung, while the iron came from a neighbouring village (all in all, iron was smelted in 15 villages in the district of Salem). The smelting of iron was conventional: at intervals of one hour the furnace was loaded, four times altogether, with one basket (33 pounds or 14 kilogrammes) of ore with the appropriate quantity of coal. The smelting process continued for five or six hours, and then the iron mass was heated white-hot and forged several times. This local iron, fit for use in farming, was sold at 2 rupees per local maund (27 pounds or 12.2 kilogrammes) or a rupee per 6.1 kilogramme. Heyne says nothing about the organisation of labour among the iron-makers, but notes their sickly, emaciated looks.

For the iron to be worked into steel it was divided into 52 small ingots of 300 grammes each and then placed in a crucible. For six hours, the iron was smelted into steel, with the weight of the latter being one-fifth less than the iron placed in the crucible (that is, roughly 12.4 instead of 15.6 kilogrammes). The steel was sold at 15 gold fanams (10s. 8d or $5\frac{1}{3}$ rupees) per 27 pounds, that is, at one rupee for 2.3 kilogrammes.[88]

There was evidence of a peculiar type of cooperation among petty producers in the iron foundry in iron-making production of Mysore. Metallurgical establishments had from 13 to 22 workers. The receipts from the sale of the product were divided into a definite number of parts (42 in this case). The share of each producer depended on his place in the process of production and the expenditures on equipment. The owner received a quarter of the value of the product, and sometimes even more. At one metallurgical establishment in the north of Mysore, the product was allocated as follows: the owner received 11 shares, the blacksmith 3.5, the carrier of ore 2.5, four hammermen

7, six bellows workers 8, nine coalmen and one miner 10 shares.[89]

The larger share of the blacksmith and the ore carrier is due to the fact that the former owned the tools, and the latter the cart and the bullocks. Thus, even in this share-income (rather share-product) principle and in the multiplicity of the property in the means of production there were signs of pre-capitalist cooperation among petty producers. The workers themselves were villagers and during the seasonal breaks in the work of the establishment hired out to rich land-holders. These embryonic pre-capitalist relations were interlaced with bondage: the master loaned the workers from 70 to 100 fanams to help them subsist until they sold the iron they were given for their work. When the workers failed to pay off their debt, they had to continue working for the old master.

At the same time, some establishments in India, while remaining primitive in the level of detailed division of labour, were already much freer from these pre-capitalist relations. Buchanan describes some iron-making establishments in Mysore with a highly developed division of labour and payment in cash for work, which was differentiated depending on the worker's speciality (from 6 to 12 fanams per season). Thus, one of these establishments employed 20 workers, of whom four collected the ore, six prepared the charcoal, four worked by the furnace, and six in the smithy. For the season (8 months) the total wages came to 1,200 fanams. Besides, the owner paid taxes and rent which came to 100 fanams. Buchanan gives data on other such smithies employing from 11 to 22 men.[90]

While Buchanan confines himself mainly to a description of metallurgical production itself and the relations within it, Forbes, who inspected the iron-making establishments in Gwalior two decades earlier, has left information which makes it possible to draw much broader conclusions. Thus, his notes give some idea of the price of iron produced in the Gwalior area in the 1780s. Thus, he obtained information concerning the conditions of production both from a blacksmith engaged in the smelting of iron, and directly from men mining ore. Because these differ substantially, I here give both in full for subsequent comparison.

According to the blacksmith, "this iron-earth was sold at the mines for two pice, or one penny, for a bullock-load, and was delivered to the smiths at Baroy, seven miles from the spot, at the rate of two rupees and a half for a hundred maunds, or about six shillings for nearly three thousand pounds weight of earth. Each bullock-load of earth, purchased at the mines for two pice, produced on an average twenty-five seers of iron, certainly above twenty pounds English weight. This very low price of earth, and the great proportion of metal it contains, renders the value of the iron extremely cheap; yet not so much so, as from these circumstances might be expected: this is accounted for from the great scarcity of the charcoal, without which nothing can be done; none can be procured nearer than twelve miles, and there it sells for half a rupee the bullockload." [91]

Forbes obtained somewhat different information from his conversations with the miners. The ore, they said, was so abundant that contrary to the information given by the smiths it was "sold on the spot at two pice, or one penny, for eight maunds of twenty-eight pounds each. The loading of each bullock was one pice. About twelve seers of iron was extracted from a maund of earth... There are seven mines, and about fifty bullocks on an average are daily loaded."[92] On the strength of these calculations it may be established that, with the exception of outlays on labour, the production of a maund of crude iron cost roughly 3 rupees. A hundred maunds of iron ore with delivery to the furnaces cost 2 rupees, and charcoal 60 rupees per hundred maunds, with 2 units of coal being required to process a unit weight of ore.

Considering that Forbes's calculations included only the value of the ore and the coal per unit of smelted iron, they can serve only as the start for establishing the production expenditures and the market price of iron. Major D. C. Graham believed that among the iron-makers of Kolhapur in the mid-19th century the costs came to 0.7 and the "profits" (including wages) to 0.3 of the production costs.[93] Applying this coefficient to Forbes's data, the costs of producing a kilogramme of unworked iron (unforged iron or iron with heavy admixtures) in Gwalior came to $\frac{1}{3}$ rupee, and the selling price, including the cost of transportation and trading profit, should have been in excess of 500 rupees, or 50 pounds sterling per ton.

On the basis of Forbes's data one could also estimate the general volume of metallurgical production in Gwalior. The daily output of ore by seven mines came to 5 bullock-loads, each load containing ore for the smelting of 20 pounds of iron, that is, a total of 1,000 pounds or 450 kilogrammes of iron. Considering the seasonal nature of the work and the breaks during religious ceremonies, it may be assumed that the annual output came to about 100 tons of iron with a total value of 50,000 rupees.

The methods used in extracting the ore, whose deposits lay virtually on the surface, were very-simple. If the ore was not discovered at a depth of up to 20 feet (6 metres), the shaft was sunk elsewhere. There was no roofing, or this was imperfect. At any rate, Forbes quotes the miners as saying that "a mine seldom stood longer than three months; and numbers were destroyed by their falling in sooner."[94] Remarking on the high quality of the ore, Forbes says that the needle of his compass moved three points. Only the high iron content could explain the fact that with the primitive process of smelting, the yield came to at least one-third of the weight of the ore.

The mines were apparently the property of the Treasury because there was a special person appointed by the government "to receive the price of the earth from the merchants". Furthermore, "the workmen are not regularly in the pay of government, but are hired at the mines, and are paid for loading bullocks by the merchants."[95] If an average of 50 bullock-loads was sent out daily, with the price of loading ore per one bullock at one pice, the daily receipts from the seven mines came to only 50 pice (1 rupee = 64 pice) , and the annual receipts fluctuated between 150 and 200 rupees. With receipts on that level there was no hope of any serious entrepreneurial turnover, even if the mines had been in private hands. It is true that the smiths smelting the iron claimed that two pice was paid for loading per one bullock at the mines, while the merchants sold them the ore at just over 3 pice ($2\frac{1}{2}$ rupees per 100 maunds), but even then the annual receipts of the seven mines did not exceed 300-400 rupees.

Forbes has no description of establishments engaged in the smelting of iron, but considering the volume of production and the great number of these establishments (Forbes says that ore was worked in five towns) it is obvious that the size of each establishment was not large. However, the metal worked by the smiths was "for sale far and near, at least as far as the want of an inland navigation would admit of."[96] Apart from evidence of a fairly extensive market for the Gwalior metallurgy, the extract also contains indirect evidence that local demand for iron was very limited (if, of course, the seven mines ensuring the smelting of about 100 tons of iron a year were the only suppliers of ore in this princely state).

Ten years after his visit to the Mysore iron-making establishments, Buchanan inspected similar establishments in the Bihar district of Bhagalpur. He wrote about the very rich deposits of iron ore, which provided the raw material base for local metallurgy. Going over to a description of the production process, he remarks on its low technological level: poor preparation of the ore mass, lack of knowledge of the ore and the charcoal proportions by the local metal-makers, whom he characterised as totally ignorant and timid beings (they may have belonged to the "unclean" tribesmen).

The smelting furnaces in Bhagalpur were smaller than those in Mysore (3.5 feet high, that is, just over one metre, whereas the height of furnaces in Mysore came to 2.5-3 metres). The burning was maintained by bellows pumping air into the furnace. Two smeltings a day were carried out. The primitive nature of the process enabled one family to handle the furnace, turning out 9.25 pounds (4 kilogrammes) of crude iron a day, which it could exchange for 4.5-7 kilogrammes of rice. Because the iron-makers were interrupted by farming their own plots and had no orders for two months, each family produced up to 30 mans (about 1,100 kilogrammes) of unpurified iron a year, and, if we are to believe Buchanan, could exchange this for 1,200-1,500 kilogrammes of rice. In cash terms, this quantity of iron was worth 30-45 rupees, because buyers-up paid $1 - 1\frac{1}{2}$ rupees per man. Thus, the annual earnings of an iron-maker's family came to $2\frac{1}{2} - 3\frac{3}{4}$ rupees (Buchanan gives an average of $2\frac{3}{4}$ rupees). Besides, the family worked 4 or 5 bighas (0.5-0.65 hectares) of non-irrigated land. But they also had these outlays: $1 - 1\frac{1}{4}$ rupees paid for the right to use the ore and charcoal, and 12 annas as lease for the plot of land.

Still, the sum of direct earnings among iron-makers, as reported by Buchanan, appears to be overstated, because he estimates the annual output of iron on the strength of two daily smeltings over a period of roughly 300 days, although he himself says earlier that iron was smelted from 150 to 240 days a year, the rest of the time being spent on farming, the gathering of wild fruit, or idling during the two-month wedding season. Besides, it is hard to imagine that the burning of charcoal and the delivery of ore did not distract the head of the family from the smelting furnace. That is why one would assume that the annual output of iron and the corresponding earnings from its sale have been greatly exaggerated, perhaps doubled. Consequently, the farming was an absolutely necessary ancillary occupation for the iron-makers, who, according to Buchanan himself, were very poor and were, in addition, drunkards.

In view of Buchanan's obvious over-statement of the volume of iron production per furnace, one must take a more critical view of his estimates of the total annual output of crude iron in Bhagalpur district as coming to 9,600 mans (330 tons). The point is that this figure has been obtained by a simple multiplication of the 30 mans by 320 (the number of families of iron-makers in the three places where they were concentrated). However, for one of these places Buchanan was given a more modest figure for smelting per family—12 mans, but he did not accept this. All these considerations make us assume that the actual smelting of crude iron in the district was closer to 200 tons.

The smelted crude iron was subjected to forging, which was done by special blacksmiths. In this operation, the original weight of the iron was reduced, according to the smiths, at a ratio of 30 to 8 or 20 to 7; but Buchanan held that they tended somewhat to overstate the losses, and gave his own ratio—9 to 4. Thus, 90 seers of crude iron worth 3 rupees yielded 40 seers (one man) of forged iron worth 4.5 rupees, or about 8.6 kilogrammes per rupee, that is, a ton of worked iron cost roughly 120 rupees (12 pounds). With my correction for the smelting of crude iron, the annual output of forged iron in Bhagalpur fluctuated at a level of 100 tons worth 12,000 rupees. Such was the scale of metallurgical production in this district of Bihar, which was rich in ore and cheap charcoal.

The best-quality iron was sold in Monghyr at 13 pounds (about 6 kilogrammes a rupee), and was used to tip ploughs. It was prepared for adaptation to the plough and was sold in the vicinity. Iron for hoes and other implements was cheaper: at $17\frac{1}{4}$ pounds, or 8 kilogrammes a rupee. We find therefore, that a higher quality of iron was used for farming implements than for other articles.

Several opinions have been expressed about the quality of Indian steel. Thus, upon his return to Britain (unfortunately, the date can be only very approximate, but is apparently somewhere at the end of the first decade of the 19th century), Heyne sent some specimens of Indian steel for expert analysis by the well-known tool-maker Stoddard, who suggested that Indian steel is "not perfectly adopted for the purpose of fine cutlery. The mass of metal is unequal, and the cause of inequality is evidently imperfect fusion." [97] Stoddard resmelted the Indian steel, to make it homogeneous, and obtained a steel that was up to the contemporary British standard and that could be used even for the making of surgical instruments. The British expert said that, 30 or 40 years earlier, British steel had been worse than the Indian steel submitted to him He concluded: "I have at this time a liberal supply of wootz, and I intend to use it for many purposes. If a better steel be offered me, I will gladly attend to it; but the steel of India is decidedly the best I have yet met with."[98]

In 1839, a well-known iron manufacturer described the Indian technology of iron-smelting and the subsequent making of steel. He drew special attention to the strict succession of operations and the composition of the components involved. He quoted some British experts who admitted that Indian steel was superior to the best standards in Western Europe: "It has always appeared to me one of the most astonishing facts in the history of the arts, that the Hindus should be in possession of a process the theory of which is extremely recondite, and in the discovery of which, there seems so little room for the agency of chance. It is impossible to suppose, however, that the process was discovered by any scientific induction, for the theory of it can only be explained by the lights of modern chemistry."[99] The manufacturer insisted that the Indian method of steel-making in effect made use of technological principles which were patented in Britain by two inventors only in 1800 and 1825.

In 1840, Captain L. Jacob submitted a report on iron-making in Kathiawar and its cost relative to that of British iron. He managed to inspect two establishments out of six operating on the Peninsula, but he claimed that all the establishments were similar in size and techniques. The ore, with a high iron content, was obtained on the spot at a depth of from 5 to 30 feet. Just over 7 Bombay maunds of ore was loaded into the furnace and this was subjected to smelting for 6 to 8 hours. Two smeltings a day were carried out. The crude iron so obtained was transferred to a second furnace, where it was smelted once again to clear away the slag. The second furnace yielded about 40 per cent of the weight of the ore, which appears to be somewhat exaggerated. After the second smelting the iron was sold; depending on the quality, at 5 or 8 cowrie (1 cowrie = 1/3 rupee) per maund or about one rupee per 10-15 kilogrammes of mass.

The daily balance of the enterprise consisted of the following elements (in cowrie):

Item	Cowrie
Wages	10
Ore, 15 maundsor 8 baskets	8
Tax	12
Charcoal, 12 baskets	12
Cost of materials	1
Total expenditures	43
Cost of daily product	48
Daily profit	5

The master was paid $1\frac{1}{2}$ – 2 cowrie a day, or 8-10 annas, which was roughly equal to 1 shilling. The British official remarked on the arduous and noxious nature of the iron-makers' labour as they toiled from sunrise to sunset. The annual output per furnace was about 65 Bombay khandi or 14-15 tons. Depending on the length of the season, the Kathiawar Peninsula produced 100-150 tons of iron.[100]

I have allowed myself to transcend the chronological framework of the chapter in order to present a more visual picture of the difference between even the most advanced metallurgical establishments in India and the contemporary metallurgy of Britain. This comparison also helps to gain a better idea of some of the internal regularities of iron and steel production in India. For all the apparent abundance of information about it, its various items are, as a rule, hardly comparable, with the exception of two key ones: remuneration for the producer and the petty owner (where one exists) and the price of the end product. In two of Heyne's descriptions the worker's hire coincides: 2 annas per day (that is, about 4 rupees a month, but in fact less because of the seasonal nature of production); Jacob gives a much higher figure—about 5 annas a day, but in Gujarat wages were higher in general. That is why it may be concluded that a metal-worker's wages came to roughly the average for the industry.

Prices for the unworked iron mass fluctuated much more markedly, because the outlays on ore and charcoal depended on local conditions, and the quality of the ore was far from being up to any standard. Besides, the sources do not divide the outlays on the production of the mass and its selling price (where the mass was sold before treatment). However, the prices for the end product—iron or steel—were in every case within the limits of one rupee for 3-6 kilogrammes. This can also be confirmed by a reference to market prices. For instance, in Bahalkot in the early 19th century, half of a local maund of iron or 15 pounds (about 7 kilogrammes) cost 2 rupees. In 1818, a maund of steel was sold in the city markets of Khandesh for 18-25 rupees.[101] Unfortunately, the source does not specify the size of the local maund, but if it is accepted as the usual one for Maharashtra (40 pounds), the price of a kilogramme of steel came to only 1 – $1\frac{1}{2}$ rupees.

But at this point we come up against a new factor, which is British competition. In the mid-18th century, British steel already appeared to be cheaper and better than Indian steel and was used for making weapons. In periods of open hostility between the East India Company and the Maratha chiefs steel was regarded as a strategic material and its export to Maharashtra was not allowed. For instance, in the 1770s, the Company's Bombay Council banned the export of iron, which the Bohra and other merchants carried away across the Bombay harbour for the use of the Marathas.[102]

In the early 1840s, up to 150,000 tons of British iron was already being imported to India, its production in Britain having risen from 68,000 tons in 1788 to 703,000 tons in 1828, with the average furnace capacity going up from 800 tons to 2,529 tons, respectively. That is why, even in the areas of local metal production, European iron, usually of a higher grade, was sold at lower prices.[103]

In the first half of the 19th century, even the most advanced Indian iron-making production of the early capitalist type was still less capable of comparison with British metallurgy either in the volume of production or its economic indicators. It was bound to disappear, together with the other Indian industries of the capitalist or pre-capitalist type, among which ship-building was undoubtedly in the fore.

Pockets of Capitalist Production

The information given above shows that workshops with a detailed division of labour were fairly widespread in some industries in pre-British India. However, as the metallurgical and dyeing industries have shown, the division of labour was not always accompanied by the establishment of capitalist relations between the worker, who was free to sell his labour-power, and the employer, who personified capital. That is why it is not right unconditionally to class every workshop with a detailed division of labour as an establishment of the capitalist manufactory type. The truth of this will once again be seen from the later descriptions of establishments turning out sugar products and vegetable oil.

Studies of India, including those by Soviet authors, contain very extensive material about the use of wage-labour in industrial production in pre-British India.[104] Apart from the examples of early capitalist enterprise listed above, we find these in the silk-winding industry of Bengal in the mid-18th century, in the silk-weaving industry of Kashmir, and in indigo production at the end of the 18th century. On the strength of later dața, it is safe to say that large workshops with a division of labour existed in paper-making production.

In the famous shipyards of Gujarat, the production process was, apparently, organised on capitalist lines with a highly developed division of labour. Indeed, what kind of production could have coped with the technical problems that the Gujarat ship-building industry was able to take in its stride? One circumspect British observer wrote: "The very ship-carpenters at Surat will take the model of any English vessel, in all the curiosity of its building, and the most artificial instances of workmanship about it, whether they are proper for convenience of burthen, or of quick sailing, as exactly as if they had been the first contrivers. The wood with which they build their ships would be very proper for our men of war in Europe; for it has this excellence, that it never splinters by the force of a bullet...."[105] The Surat shipyards built vessels with a displacement of up to 500-1,000 tons, which were able to sail to China and Europe.

Apart from ship-building and paper-making, no other industries were to be found in India with the capitalist workshop prevailing. In other industries, which were more important in volume of production and employment, like weaving and iron-and-steel making, such workshops took shape only on the upper tier, and these did not constitute any special sector of the social division of labour either within the framework of one line of production or within an aggregation of industries. Commodity circulation of the products of workshops organised on capitalist lines did not yet constitute a system of constant market relations either between the workshops themselves or between them and agriculture (even that part of it which was designed for the market).

One is left with a definite impression that the manufactory in India on the eve of the colonial conquest had not yet been widespread, so that the manufactory period never arrived. That is why the existence of separate pockets of capitalist relations in pre-British India did not yet constitute a capitalist sector. In his book "The Discovery of India", Jawaharlal Nehru gave a brilliant sketch of the state of the productive forces in India on the eve of her colonial enslavement. With patriotic pride he referred to the skill of the Indian craftsmen and the magnificent articles they manufactured, the highly developed organisation of commerce and finance. Nehru was fully justified in stressing that foreign political rule "led to a rapid destruction of the economy India had built up, without anything positive or constructive taking its place."[106] But one cannot possibly agree with his assertion that at the time of the British conquest "the economy of India had thus advanced to as high a stage as it could reach prior to the industrial revolution."[107]

A 1968 symposium of Indian scientists met to consider problems of social and economic history and discussed why no industrial revolution had occurred in India. The discussion showed that Indian scientists used the term to mean not transition from the stage of the capitalist workshop with a division of labour (manufactory) to the stage of factory production, but rather the formation of such workshops on the basis of small-scale commodity producers, that is, the genesis of capitalism in industry. In the extract from Nehru's book, which I have quoted, he may have used the term "industrial revolution" in the same sense.

The thesis submitted by Satish Chandra sets out these problems, which he considered to be basic: relations between town and country; the nature and volume of domestic and foreign trade; the organisation of industry; the state of science and technology. He assumed that although the condition of the countryside did limit the influx of goods from the towns, the assertion that the Indian countryside had been completely self-sufficient was a myth, especially with respect to the developed areas. He did not see any basis for supporting Bernier's definition of the Indian town as a military headquarters and said that towns were in themselves extensive markets which in the fullness of time became centres of production. Let us note that this statement does not yet answer the question of the place such towns had within the system of all-national or regional division of labour, especially in view of the fact, noted by Satish Chandra himself, that towns tended to grow above all along the Gujarat, Koromandel and Malabar coasts and in Bengal, on the narrow strip along the Ganges, under the impact of foreign and coastal trade, and also in the Doab as a result of the influence exerted by political factors (the levying of tribute) and the growth of internal trade.

S. Chandra was right in assuming that with India's sub-continental proportions it would be unrealistic to expect a similar level of development across the whole country. As in Europe, industrial production tended to concentrate in definite areas: Gujarat, Koromandel and Malabar, and to a lesser extent in Bengal. He noted the penetration of merchant's capital into the textile, metallurgical, mining and other industries, but admitted that the merchants were not interested in developing new technology in production. The status of the master artisan was not clear either.

While recognising that India's lag in science and technology had become most pronounced by the 18th century, S. Chandra connected this with the influence of a mystical irrationalism, the caste system, and hostility for all foreign ideas. At the same time, he added, the requirements of the army brought about the growth of metallurgy, the casting of artillery pieces, the improvement of muskets and also of ship-building. He put forward the hypothesis that Gujarat and perhaps also the Koromandel and Malabar coasts had reached what he called the "first stage of the capitalist stage"—a hypothesis which appears to have remained a hypothesis for the time being. The British conquest of the coastal areas, S. Chandra says, not only disrupted internal trade, but also gradually reduced external trade and destroyed industrial production. In these circumstances, local capital turned to the acquisition of land, making use of British colonial law allowing its free alienation.

Let me stress in conclusion that in India no basic premise had taken shape for transition to factory production (which is what Marxists take to mean "industrial revolution")—a developed capitalist workshop with a detailed division of labour, above all in the making of the implements of labour. Independent commodity exchange between town and country covered a very small range of products, which were mainly designed for consumption. Commodity production, which existed in non-communal handicrafts and in the peasant economy in the form of separate elements, had not yet matured as such, because the sale of the agricultural products was effected for the purpose of acquiring mainly consumer goods or obtaining the means to pay off tributes.

The husbandman bought goods to ensure reproduction only as an exception, while the artisans confined themselves to purchasing semi-finished products and materials (yarn, dyes, metals, wood, etc.). In other words, petty-commodity production in India did not, after all, mature to the extent of providing an extensive basis for the Genesis of capitalist relations. Wherever pockets of such relations did take shape in industry, they were fed (foreign trade apart) by rent, while merchant's capital was just in the process of securing control of the existing forms of economy, without modifying the process of reproduction itself or its technology. Small-scale capitalist-type production in India was oriented on the traditional rentreceiver and the overseas consumer, or (in metallurgy, for instance) upon the making of goods which subsequently were the first to fall victim to the competitive clash with British factory products, and this was an expression of historically rooted doom.

India's propertied strata, the merchants above all, were far too late, in terms of history, to feel and comprehend the imperative need for equipment and technology that were fundamentally different. On the eve of the British conquest—and throughout the 100 years of the British raj—this imperative need was never vested in any real efforts. K. N. Chaudhuri has the following to say on this problem as regards the textile industry:

"Historians have traditionally sought an explanation for the occurrence of technological progress in one place and time as opposed to its non-occurrence elsewhere. However, was there any compelling economic and social reason why India should have embarked on a search for new techniques and production methods at this particular stage of her history? Was the Indian weaving technique inferior and backward to those of other countries? And what foreign threat was there to her existing supremacy in cotton textiles? When the threat did materialise in the nineteenth century, the necessary technology was imported from abroad by Indian businessmen themselves. Once again, it can be said that the emergence of the factory method in the production of cotton goods in the Indian context was no mere historical accident. The object of these remarks is not to deny the existence of economic backwardness and its causal relationship with the differential rate of technological progress, but to emphasise the importance of human motivation for change before one begins the search for more impersonal, fundamental reasons. It is the difference between the logic of 'necessary' and 'sufficient' conditions."[108] And so, it took another 100 years for the idea of the imperative need for the nation-wide technological transformation both of industry and agriculture to gain national recognition—already after Independence.

An important indicator of the level of India's socio-economic development, even if it is a negative one, is the absence of developed forms of urban self-administration, to say nothing of the independence of towns and their capacity for independent political acts. This problem has already been mentioned in dealing with the system of the castes and communities of traders, money-lenders and artisans, and the principles of taxation. But the specific features of Indian towns are ultimately explained by the structure of its population and the relations between its individual sections, on the one hand, and the state and the class of rent-receivers, on the other.

N.K. Sinha claims that "before British administration began in Bengal cities did not possess a common civic life. Even very big cities were little more than overgrown villages. Very few of those who stayed in them thought of a permanent residence there. They sojourned in cities. There was no urban patriciate—no class of rich merchants permanently residing in these cities. There were no corporate towns, no industrial nurseries. There was also no urban middle class."[109] This is true on the whole, but appears to be somewhat too emphatic. Thus, in the towns of Bengal there was undoubtedly a permanent labouring population, the artisans in the first place. They also had rich merchant and banking families (e.g. the Seths, who had long settled in Murshidabad). Sinha's remark about the mobility of the urban population applies perhaps to the nobility, especially to the military men, their retainers and servants. It is quite another matter that the welfare and, accordingly, numerical size of the population depended in many towns of Bengal, as in the whole of India, on the ups-and-downs of military campaigns and the prosperity of local rulers and grandees.

Nevertheless, alongside traditional relations new phenomena emerged in India's socio-economic structure. Evidence contained in the sources suggests the conclusion that by the 18th century the forms of land property and land tenure, the social division of labour and relations of production in the handicrafts in India's advanced regions had reached a level characteristic of developed feudal society.

NOTES

1. I. Habib, *Potentialities...*, p. 49-50.
2. See : Nekotoriye danniye ob obschchestvennom razdelenii truda i ekonomicheskoi organizatsii remesla v Indii na rubezhe XVIII i XIX vekov, *Kratkiye soobshcheniya Instituta vostokovedeniya*, XV, Moscow, 1955.
3. K.A. Antonova set forth her interpretation of Buchnan's material, which boiled down to a denial of any elements of capitalism in the handicraft industries of Mysore, See : K.A. Antonova, Otchyot Buchanana o Mysore 1800-1801 gg. kak istorichesky istochnik, *Uchoniye zapiski Instituta vostokovedeniya*, vol. XVIII, Moscow, 1957.
4. See : A.I. Chicherov, *India, Economic Development....*
5. See : R.M. Martin, *The History...*, vol. II, p. 973; J.A. Taylor, *A Descriptive and Historical Account of the Cotton Manufacturers of Dacca in Bangal*, London, 1851, pp. 75-79; T. Marshall, *Statistical Reports....*, p. 53.
6. K. Marx, *Capital*, vol. I, p. 340.
7. J. Forbes, *Oriental Memoires....*, vol. II, pp. 95-96.

8. Ibid., vol. I, p. 465.
9. Quoted from : *A. Sarada Raju, Economic Conditions in the Madras Presidency,* p. 148.
10. R. Orme, *Historical Fragments...,* pp. 405-406.
11. I. Habib, *Potentialities...,* pp. 44, 45.
12. *GBP,* vol. 26 (Materials Towards a Statistical Account of the Town and Island of Bombay), pt II, Bombay, 1894, pp. 425, 428.
13. B. Heyne, *Tracts...,* p. 212.
14. *Ibid.,* p. 204.
15. *Ibid.,* pp. 88-89, 90.
16. See : M. Martin, *The History....,* vol. III, p. 320.
17. H. Colebrooke, Remarks on the Husbandry and Internal Commerce of Bengal, London, 1804, p. 48.
18. See : R. Orme, *Historical Fragments....,* p. 410.
19. V.I. Lenin, *Collected Works,* vol. 3, p. 368.
20. [J.A. de Mandelslo], *the Voyage...,* p. 64.
21. K. Marx, *The Theories of Surplus-Value,* pt II, Moscow, 1968, p. 109.
22. B. Heyne, *Tracts...,* pp. 74-75.
23. L.B. Alayev, O sistemakh zemledeliya v Yuzhnoi Indii v kontse XVIII-nachale XIX v., *Genezis kapitalizma,* Moscow, 1965, p. 421.
24. See : F. Engels, Supplement to Vol. III of Marx' *Capital,* p. 897.
25. K. Marx, *The Theories of Surplus-Value,* pt II, p. 109.
26. See : N.K. Sinha, *The Economic History...,* vol. I, p. 186.
27. Ibid., pp. 176, 178, 181.
28. See : K. Marx, *Capital,* vol. I, p. 598.
29. *Return : Cotton (India),* London, 1847, p. 123.
30. "The greatest part of the sellers are the workmen themselves, so that the merchants buy at the first hand. These workmen, before they expose anything to sale, must go to him that has the stamp, to have the King's seal set upon their linen and silks, otherwise they would be fined and lambasted with a good cudgel" (Tavernier's *Travels in India,* Book I, Ch. 8, 11th December, 1665).
31. *GBP,* vol. IV (Ahmedabad), pp. 106-109.
32. *Readings in Indian Economic History,* p. 51.
33. K.N. Chaudhuri, The Structure of Indian Textile in the Seventeenth and Eighteenth Centuries, *IESHER,* vol. XI, Nos. 2-3 pp. 143-144.
34. I. Habib, *Potentialities...,* pp. 46-49.
35. *The Second Industrial Conference,* Poona, 1892, pp. VI-VII.
36. R. Orme, *Historical Fragments...,* pp. 405-406.
37. F. Buchanan, *A Journey....,* vol. I, p. 221.
38. *GBP,* vol. 16 (Nasik), Bombay, 1883, p. 155.
39. D.R. Gadgil (Assisted by the Staff of the Institute, Poona), A Socio-Economic Survey, pt II. Gokhle Institute of Politics and Economics, Poona, 1952, pp. 11, 15-16.
40. D.R. Gadgil, *Origins...,* p. 25.
41. J.A. Taylor, *A Descriptive and Historical Account....,* pp. 130-131.
42. J. Taylor, *A Sketch of the Topography and Statistics of Dacca in Bengal,* London, 1851, pp. 189-190.
43. A. Karim, *Dacca the Mughal Capital, Dacca,* 1964, pp. 84-95.
44. R. Orme, *Historical Fragments...,* pp. 410-411.
45. A. Karim, *Dacca...,* pp. 103-104.
46. *Ibid.,* p. 105.
47. F. Buchanan, *An Account of the Disctrict of Bhagalpur....,* pp. 605-606.

48. *Ibid.*, p. 607.
49. J. Hough, *Letters on the Climate, Inhabitants, Production etc., etc., of Neilgherries or Blue Mountains of Coimbatoor, South India*, London, 1829, pp. 101-108.
50. *Ibid.*, p. 105.
51. K. Datta, *Studies in the History of Bengal Subah*, pt I, Social and Economic, Calcutta, 1936, p. 425.
52. [S. Master], *The Diaries of Streinsham Master, 1675-1680*, ed. by R. Temple, London, 1911, vol. I, p. 40.
53. F. Buchanna, *A Journey...*, vol. I, p. 40.
54. *Ibid.*, pp. 185, 207.
55. H. Colebrooks, Remarks on the Husbandry and Internal Commerce of Bengal, London, 1806, p. 48. This work, as the author says in his preface, was written in 1794, prepared for the press in 1803, and first published in Calcutta in 1804.
56. I. Habib, *Potentialities...*, pp. 49-56.
57. W. Bolts, *Considerations on the India Affairs*, p. 194.
58. [S. Master], *The Diaries...*, vol. II, London, 1911, p. 14.
59. F. Buchanan, *A. Journey...*, vol. II, p. 265.
60. *Ibid.*, pp. 239-240.
61. See : V.I. Lenin, *Collected Works*, vol. 3, p. 368.
62. F. Buchanna, *A Journey...*, vol. I, p. 218.
63. *Ibid.*
64. *Ibid.*, vol. III, pp. 317-318.
65. See : R.M. Martin, *The History...*, vol., I, p. 337; vol. II, pp. 265, 958.
66. *The Fifth Report from the Select Committee*, p. 279.
67. *Ibid.*, p. 278.
68. *Ibid.*, p. 279.
69. *Gazetteer of Bombay Presidency. Statistical Account of Bombay*, Bombay, 1877, pp. 30-32.
70. K. Marx, *Capital*, vol. III, p. 334.
71. K.N. Chaudhuri polemicises with John Hicks, the British author of *A theory of Economic History*, Oxford, 1969, p. 29.
72. *IESHR*, vol. XI, Nos. 2-3, June-Sept. 1974, pp. 149-150.
73. *Ibid.*, pp. 151-152.
74. *Ibid.*, p. 152.
75. D.R. Gadgil, *Origins....*, p. 16.
76. [J.A. de Mandelslo], The Voyages and Travels of J. Albert de Mandelslo into the East Indies, London, 1669, p. 64.
77. J. Fryer, *A New Account of East India and Persia being Nine Years' Travels 1672-1681*, vol. II, p. 168.
78. *A Discourse of Trade, Corn and Paper Credit and of Ways and Means of Gain, to Retain Riches*, London, 1679, p. 96.
79. B. Heyne, *Tracts...*, pp. 92-93.
80. *Ibid.*, pp. 96-98, 101, 102, 106-107.
81. F. Buchanan, *A Journey...*, vol. I, pp. 121, 218, 222, vol. II, p. 264.
82. R.M. Martin, *The History...*, vol. II, p. 973.
83. B. Heyne, *Tracts....*, pp. 189-191.
84. *Ibid.*, p. 218.
85. *Ibid.*, p. 223.
86. *Ibid.*
87. *Ibid.*, pp. 224-226.
88. *Ibid.*, pp. 258-259.

89. F. Buchanan, *A Journey...*, vol. I, pp. 17-18, 35-36; vol. II, pp. 19, 21, 26-38; vol. III, p. 362.
90. *Ibid.*, vol. I, p. 175; vol. II, pp. 439-440.
91. J. Forbes, *Oriental Memoirs...*, vol. IV, p. 256.
92. Ibid., pp. 28-29.
93. D. Graham, *Statistical Report of Kolhapoor*, Poona, 1854, p. 243.
94. J. Forbes, *Oriental Memoirs...*, vol. IV, pp. 25-26.
95. *Ibid.*, p. 28.
96. *Ibid.*, pp. 25-26.
97. B. Heyne, *Tracts...*, p. 363.
98. *Ibid.*, p. 364.
99. *Journal of the Royal Asiatic Society of Great Britain and Ireland (JRASGBI)*, vol. V, London, 1839, p. 394.
100. *JRASGBI*, vol. VII, London, 1843, pp. 98-104.
101. T. Marshall, Statistical Reports on the Pergunnahs of Pedshapoor, Belgam, Kalaniddee and Chandgurh, Khanapoor, Bagulkot and Badamy in the Southern Mahratta Country, Bombay, 1822, p. 147.
102. *Selections from the Deccan Commissioner's Files, Period of Transition*, p. 4.
103. S.M. Edwardes, *The Rise of Bombay. A Retrospect (Vol. X of the Census of India Series)*, Bombay, 1902, p. 194.
104. As early as the 17th century, the hire of labour was commonplace in the big Indian cities, Ovington, for instance, notes that the low prices for food in surat encouraged "the daily labourers to work for very low wages" (J. Ovington, A Voyage to Surat in the Year 1689, Oxford, 1929, p. 189).
105. *Ibid.*, p. 166.
106. Jawaharlal Nahru, *The Discovery of India*, p. 263.
107. *Ibid.*, p. 262.
108. *IESHR*, vol. XI, Nos. 2-3, June-September 1974, p. 180.
109. N.K. Sinha, *The Economic History...*, vol. II, p. 219.

SECTION TWO

PRIMITIVE ACCUMULATION OF BRITISH CAPITAL AND ITS IMPACT ON INDIA'S SOCIO-ECONOMIC SYSTEM

British Merchant's Capital and Pre-Capitalist Modes of Production in India

By the early 19th century the basic consequences of the epoch of primitive accumulation were determined both for the countries in which the process took place and also for those which served as objectives for the accumulation of capital by other states and their ruling classes. However, an analysis of these consequences is made difficult by the fact that far from every European country can be classed, without the necessary reservations, under this or that head. The difficulties also arise from the fact that by the period in question Britain alone had the process of primitive accumulation completed in the main, whereas in the other countries of Europe it had either not started at all or had run in a curtailed or incomplete form. As for the countries of Asia and Africa, there were essential distinctions in the intensity and methods of their colonial exploitation. In some countries and areas lying in the heart of these great continents, colonial expansion had not yet manifested itself in economic terms, while in others it had a marked effect only on the coastal areas. Thus, in the epoch of primitive accumulation colonialism, having become global in the sphere of military and political conquest, had not yet become such in the economic sphere.

In the 17th and 18th centuries, only British and Dutch colonial policy was bourgeois in terms of subjective purpose and capitalist in terms of objective consequence, but even here some reservations have to be entered. That is why colonial plunder became an important element of the national processes of primitive accumulation only in Britain and the Netherlands (although in the scope and depth of this process Britain had far outstripped its rival). The consequences of colonial expansion for absolutist France were highly contradictory in their effects on her internal social and economic processes. In feudal Spain and Portugal, colonial plunder flowed into the royal treasuries, helping to strengthen the feudal and clerical reaction and, conversely, to weaken the bourgeois plebeian opposition. The mechanism of the "price revolution" and the anti-national policy of the feudal regimes led to the drain from Spain and Portugal of the wealth plundered overseas, which had promoted primitive accumulation in other countries, the Netherlands and Britain in the first place.

Nevertheless, although colonial policies pursued by some powers were not an element of the national process of primitive accumulation, it is quite right to define the colonialism of the 16th-18th centuries as the colonialism of the epoch of primitive accumulation. After all, the main historical result of colonial expansion in that period consisted in that the material values which flowed into Europe from other parts of the world ran directly or indirectly into the sphere of capitalist production in the most advanced countries, Britain in the first place. Besides, Britain's own colonial policy, especially with respect to India, and the ultimate, even if not always direct, subordination of this policy to the national needs of the primitive accumulation of capital is quite obvious.

However, this variant of relations should not be over-simplified either. The point is that the English East India Company represented not Britain's industrial but her merchant's capital, and this gave rise to some friction between the industrial bourgeoisie and the oligarchy of the East India Company, with a prevalence of multi-stage methods in channelling the Company's profits into capitalist production. Even with the formation of the capitalist sector, merchant's capital continued to be somewhat indifferent to the conditions under which production was carried on of the products entering circulation as commodities, whether the economy was organised on the lines of the primitive community, the slave-holding society or capital society. "The extremes between which merchant's capital acts as mediator exist for it as given, just as they are given for money and for its movements. The only necessary thing is ... these extremes should be on hand as commodities, regardless of whether production is wholly a production of commodities, or whether only the surplus of the independent producers' immediate needs, satisfied by their own production, is thrown on the market."[1]

It is indeed the indifference of merchant's capital to the socio-economic environment (and its individual components) in which it operates that helps one better to understand how vast was the geographical area over which Italian, Armenian, Arab, Indian, Chinese and other merchant's capital operated in the Middle Ages, to say nothing of British and Dutch merchant's capital in more recent times. But this indifference had not only an external but also an internal aspect, namely, the absence or embryonic development of objective interest in the socio-economic transformation of one's own country. The economic "voracity" of merchant's capital most patently revealed its social conservatism in stagnant structures in the Asian countries where European merchant's capital established its political power or at least indirect control.

However, this conservatism is two-pronged. Marx noted the obstacles which in India and China the internal solidity and "organization of pre-capitalistic, national modes of production" raised in the way of the corrosive influence of commerce.[2] The words quoted by us show that there was no ground at all for the discussion about his allegedly absolute and un-conditional preference for the "Asiatic", feudal or any other isolated mode of production in India. We find that in this work he quite clearly formulates his view of the Indian (and Chinese) socio-economic structure as a multi-sectoral structure (which further goes to emphasise the problem of bringing out the sector determining the essence of the given formation).

This formulation of Marx's deals with the impacts of British merchant's capital on the pre-capitalist modes of production, from which he brings out only the mode of production which had for its broad basis "the unity of small-scale agriculture and home industry", which in India was supplemented by the form of village communities resting on communal property in land.[3] Marx had apparently assumed that this mode of production in effect prevailed in the whole structure of the modes of production and gave it a general stability. In this extract Marx says nothing about the other modes of production and, consequently, about the concrete consequences of their contact with foreign merchant's capital. But judging by his well-known statement about the tragic lot of the Dacca weavers, who were ruined by British competition, we may infer that he took a different and less favourable view of the stability of this mainly petty-commodity production than of the basic mode of production. Marx also makes mention of the influence exerted by the British rule on the local pockets of capitalist relations, albeit in a later historical context.

Thus, if we consider Marx's various statements about the impact of Britisl. expansion on the various spheres of India's economy as an aggregate, it will become clear that he saw this impact in concrete terms in every case, depending on the objectives of expansion. Let us bear in mind that British merchant's capital and the East India Company—its militaryadministrative embodiment resorted to different methods of eroding and subjecting India's socio-economic structure in various sectors of that structure.

British merchant's capital being unable to destroy the natural unity of agriculture and the handicrafts through the market, started to take over the fiscal apparatus—primarily in the collection of the land-tax. It subjected the petty-commodity producer (artisan) to police regulation, and imposed on the cultivator the duty of growing export crops. In other words, British merchant's capital turned a whole system of extraeconomic, coercive methods of product appropriation, partially borrowed from the Oriental despotism and partially invented on the spot, against the internal solidity of the structure which rested on subsistence and traditional social relations.

By means of a complex of militry-police and administrative measures, Britain's capitalist society intervened in the system of relatively more backward, pre-capitalist sectors. The British were the first conquerors of India representing a society with obviously higher socio-economic and other historical characteristics. That is why the wars they carried on in India brought about, even if in an unusually savage form, a confrontation of the technico-economic achievements (in military-organisational terms) of the one mode of production and the other.

In this sense, the war carried on in a country whose economy was circumscribed by subsistence and self-sufficiency relations, on which Indian society rested, provided a very convincing means for demonstrating advantages of the capitalist forms of production, distribution and social organisation.

NOTES

1. K. Marx, *Capital,* vol. III, p. 333.
2. *Ibid.*
3. *Ibid.*

CHAPTER FOUR

PRE-CAPITALIST MODES OF PRODUCTION IN INDIA IN THE WORLD EPOCH OF PRIMITIVE ACCUMULATION

When considering information taken from the sources about the conditions of production, remuneration of labour and the way of life of the toiling and consuming classes and sections, about economic relations with the outer world and other information concerning socio-economic relations in India's vast pre-capitalist complex, the data for Bengal at the end of the first decade and for Maharashtra at the beginning of the third decade of the 19th century may be used. The incomparability of this information springs not so much from the chronological difference of 10 or 15 years as from the fact that the Bengal material describes a society that had been labouring under direct colonial oppression for a half-century, while the Maharashtra material, by contrast, describes a society that had been putting up armed resistance for a similar period, which means that we have two extreme variants (within the subcontinent's framework), each demonstrating in its own way the extent to which traditional structures resisted foreign merchant's capital. These two extremes apparently cover the overall regularity of the influence exerted by the British conquest on Indian society.

Despite the fact that the information for Maharashtra refers to a later period than the Bengal material, it should be considered in the first instance, because the historically rooted relations in recently conquered Maharashtra had been transformed to a lesser extent than they had been in Bengal. At the same time, there is ground for bringing together the material on Maharashtra and Bengal within the framework of the same chapter even if only because the sources take the same approach to the collection of information within the limits of a district—a large administrative unit, a locality with a population of 0.5 to 2 million. But the comparison of the data for Maharashtra and Bengal, including Bihar, is made considerably more difficult by the fact that F. Buchanan, making a study of the two latter provinces, did more work in consolidating the much more voluminous data under the various heads than his colleagues did (even if they, too, did collect unique data).

Socio-Economic Relations in Maharashtra in the Early 19th Century. Social Structure, the Status of the Producer in Agriculture and the Handicrafts, Trade and Credit in Nagpur

Some information about social and economic life in Eastern Maharashtra in the 1830s is contained in a report by the British official, R. Jenkins, about Nagpur, recently the capital of the state of Bhonsla, and the district of the same name. According to a census taken in 1820-1821 on orders of the British resident, the district of Nagpur had 249,800 males (only adults having apparently been reckoned), of whom the nine sub-castes of Brahmans included 12,100, the 13 agricultural castes 111,400, while another 19,000 persons belonging to other castes lived off agriculture (in various capacities, from zamindars and patels to peasants and day labourers). On the other hand, 6,400 members of the agricultural castes were not engaged in their traditional occupation; there were manufacturers, mechanics and craftsmen totalling 77,700, but among these are mentioned the usually very numerous mahars, who cannot in any sense be classed as manufacturers (but rather as servants or farmers). Traders and money-lenders belonged to 14 castes, numbering 4,900. Apart from them, many Brahmans, Muslims and persons from the agricultural castes also engaged in trade and credit. Finally, the district had 21,300 "coolies", but among these were 18,600 men from the Gonda tribe, who in the main did field work as agricultural labourers.[1] We find that these data make it impossible precisely to calculate the occupational structure of employment. But on the whole one is left with the impression that the agricultural population came to just over one-half of the inhabitants of the district, while the artisans numbered about a quarter.

Concentrated in the city of Nagpur were 10,900 artisans, about one-fifth of the artisans in the district (if we subtract the number of mahars). The urban handicraft population had the following structure: cotton weavers—4,162; female spinners (apparently professional)—

1,008, dyers—367; tailors—286; cobblers and tanners—284, saddle-makers and tanners—108; oil-pressers—1,594, makers of alcoholic drinks and sweet-meats—351 and 78, respectively; jewellers—356; copper-smiths—294; metal-polishers—74; potters—271; blacksmiths—265; carpenters—223; stonemasons—429; stonecutters—79, the other occupations were represented by smaller groups.[2] Here again we find a diversification of handicraft branches without any overall specialisation, which was common for a typical urban centre in India.

Considering the amount of profit in agriculture in Nagpur, Jenkins remarked that, on the one hand, the money used in agriculture (it is not clear whether for the purchase of land or the improvement of production, the first being more likely) is borrowed at an interest of 25 per cent and still apparently brings a profit to the borrower, and on the other, the rayats are very willing to give up their plots when taxes are raised, that is why only a small part of the actual rent possibly remained in the hands of the land-holders.[3] When reflecting on this contradiction, one should bear in mind these two circumstances: first, the reduction of prices for land plots itself made their acquisition after the establishment of the colonial land-tax highly promising, even where this entailed borrowing money; second, the source makes mention of the fact that the patels frequently kept here from 10 to 20 ploughs, that is, that there was some economic concentration of land, under which the mass of the surplus-product increased.

Day labourers in agriculture were often paid in cash in the course of eight months during a year. When there was a shortage of labour-power, a strong man was paid up to $2\frac{1}{2}$ pice a day, but the usual labourer's rate was 2 pice, both for men and women. When hiring labour for a month or a year, payment was almost always in grain, except in periods when the latter was very expensive. The labourer received, a month, 5 kuru, or 40 paeelees of grain, and also 2 rupees for a blanket and a pair of shoes (this amount must have been paid in annual terms). Adult day labourers employed in agricultural work received 2 paeelees of grain a day, and a child—one paeelee. The source does not mention the equivalent of these weights. The size of the payment may be judged by the fact that the toilers had two meals a day, at noon and at night, only in the period of fieldwork, having to make do on other days with one meal, after sunset.[4]

The data on the remuneration of agricultural labourers are vague and distorted in terms of the social essence of the relationship between the employer and the producer, as such data in British sources usually are. Still, it may be assumed that remuneration in kind for a given time period was the standard one; the length or even the constancy with which the labourer was employed by a given farm was evidence of long-standing relations of his subordination to the master. This is borne out by the mention of the deprived "coolies" and other lower categories of agricultural population. Cash payment was practised only when there was a shortage of manpower, and when workers were recruited from outside, that is, men who were not a part of the micro-local master-servant systems.

The maintenance of this system is also borne out by the status of the artisans. When they had employment, they worked from 9 a.m. to sunset. But village artisans did not always have work in their own line, and so they eked out a living by doing farm work. In Eastern Maharashtra, there also remained the intra-communal system of remunerating artisans for the making and repair of implements. This is directly indicated by Jenkins, who notes that peasants paid artisans a remuneration that was fixed once and for all. Apart from orders for the making of implements, the demand for the artisans' labour was small because the peasants built their own houses and furniture.

Jenkins' report also gives details about the remuneration of the village establishment, artisans and servants of the community, who were called afkari. Six officials were called servants of the government, and they were remunerated on a complex principle: the patel received a share of the tax revenue and exacted levies from the rayats; the pandia (village scribe) received a salary and an inam—a tax-free land plot; the joshi received an inam, a kuru of grain from each peasant, cash deductions and offerings; the kotwar (guard) received an inam and a kuru of grain from each plough, finally, the garpagari, a kind of "guardian" of the community who provided protection with the aid of magical charms, received a quarter of a kuru from each land-holder. Three artisans and two servants of the community were called gaon samandi (servants of the village) and received no rewards from the authorities. The carpenter and the blacksmith had the duty to repair the agricultural implements, for which they had 4-5 kuru of grain a year per plough. But new implements were paid for separately. The chamar, who repaired the leather implements for the wells, etc., received an insignificant award in grain. The barber and the laundryman received their offerings. It is quite possible that the preservation of the community goes to explain the dignity with which the Maratha peasants and artisans bore themselves, to the British official's surprise, when standing up for their interests before the high and mighty.[5]

Evidence of the stability of pre-capitalist relations also comes from the fact that establishments for boiling sugar-cane into gur belonged to the owners of the sugar-cane plantations, that is, wealthy land-holders, thereby in a sense completing the cycle from the growing of the cane to its processing. Judging by the description, the mill and the organisation of labour there were not complicated: the cane was run between two wooden cylinders, which were set in motion by two bullocks, with the juice dripping into iron vats, where it was boiled, cooled and refined. Each mill had three vats, which could turn out 27 maunds of gur a day. Judging by other, more detailed descriptions, several workers were recruited from the village servants and were rewarded by a share of the product, apart from members of the owner's family, who also took part in the work.

In two parganas of the Waingang district, where sugar-cane was grown, 4,000 maund of gur were produced. Unfortunately, the source says nothing about the size of the local maund, but if we accept it as the usual one, production here was just over 100 tons, hardly outside the limit of local demand.[6] Thus, both the relations of production and the market orientation in the making of gur remained pre-capitalist.

The organisation of vegetable oil-pressing in Nagpur is technologically reminiscent of the production of gur. Here there was also a press set in motion by one or two pairs of bullocks. The oil-seed was bought and the oil sold by the oil-presser's wife, while the husband supervised the establishment.[7] Quite possibly, when the family was a small one, the oil-presser hired assistants. We do not know whether he was a land-holder or whether he bought the raw material.

The weavers were undoubtedly the most numerous group of artisans. The growing of cotton and the spinning of yarn everywhere made it easier to acquire it, while the relative cheapness and simplicity of the local cloths reduced the need for credits to buy yarn. At the same time, the district had a surplus of cloths and these were sold outside its limits. The cloths were bought for export mainly by traders from the Jain caste of Parwars, who regularly sold them to Poona and Pandharpur.

When a weaver did not succeed in selling his goods right away, he pawned his cloth at a shroff's who gave him a loan, which came to about two-thirds of the price. Jenkins observed that the artisans received credits on the harshest terms: 3, 4 and more per cent a month, while the rayats, patels or persons offering security in goods received money at 2 per cent.[8] Thus in Nagpur, where the raw material (cotton) and the semifinished product (yarn) were made on the spot, the weaver's dependence on the money-lender was established not during the delivery of the yarn (as in Bengal), but at the sale of the cloth.

In his report for Nagpur, Jenkins gives the prices of the various textile goods, and does so in measures which make it possible to calculate them into metres. The value of this information is enhanced by the fact that it relates to the period (1827) just before the one in which British factory-made textiles were first imported. The bleached cotton cloths of ordinary quality cost from 6 rupees 10 annas to 10 rupees a piece—from 22 cubits (10 metres) to 32 cubits (14.5 metres) in length and from one and a quarter cubits (56 centimetres) to 2 cubits (90 centimetres) in width. Thus, the average price fluctuated between 1 rupee per 2 metres, that is, a rank-and-file workman could earn the cost of 4-8 metres of simple cloth a month. The price of sari cloth fluctuated, depending on the quality and the finishing, from 5 to 40 rupees per piece from 14 to 18 cubits long (6.3-8.1 metres) and 2.25 to 3 cubits wide (1-1.35 metres). Finally, there was great demand for the khadi, a piece of which was from 13 to 22 cubits long (5-9 metres) and from $1\frac{1}{4}$ to 2 cubits wide (55-90 centimetres) and cost from 12 annas to 3 rupees.[9]

Jenkins determined the local trade in the district of Nagpur as being insignificant. The prime necessities, above all grain, were imported into the city of Nagpur to a value of at least 700,000 rupees a year, and also various cloths, partly for the use of the towns-folk and partly for export. The rural areas received from the city the prime necessities imported from other areas (salt, metals, potash, coconuts and spices), and also imported and local cloths. The latter were the only important item produced in the city for rural consumption. But there is no ground to assert that cloths made in the rural areas did not flow into the city in equal quantities. These data, like the ratio of urban to rural artisans (1 to 4), suggest that an urban centre like Nagpur was mainly not a producer but a redistributor of handicraft products, with an overall balance between production and consumption being perhaps negative for the town itself.

Nagpur's external trade was carried on mainly with the neighbouring regions: from Dacca, Mirzapur and Bundelkhand came cloths and sugar, from Poona and Aurangabad precious metals in coins and bullion for the local mint, crockery, sandalwood and ferrous and non-ferrous metals (unfortunately, no mention is made of their origin). The district exported cloths, cotton, gur and grain. Considering that local cloths were of a lower quality than imported ones, the agricultural character of the exports (in cash terms) becomes even more obvious.

There are no complete data on the scale of Nagpur's trade turnover. I have already mentioned the volume of grain imports to the city of Nagpur. The export of local cloths came to 725,000 rupees (1826). It is interesting to note that a large part of this went to the west, to Western Maharashtra (500,000 rupees' worth) and Indore (50,000), that is, against the tide of the incipient imports of British factory-made textiles. We shall see later that within two or three decades, British imports would hit the weavers of Central India, but in 1826 Nagpur received only 700 pieces of British cloth, and also a small quantity of imported knives, glassware, small mirrors, etc.[10] For the time being, the economic effect of British competition was undoubtedly insignificant.

One is left with the impression that in the 1820s Eastern Maharashtra still retained its traditional trade ties and had the same commodity pattern of its domestic and external trade, but there were already signs of decline: for instance, the export of cloths to Poona, once worth 1,200,000-1,500,000 rupees a year, had fallen to 300,000 rupees by 1826.[11] It is hard to establish the volume of trade even of the wholesale sector, but it must have run to millions of rupees.

In the 1820s, Marwari traders and money-lenders had not yet filled up all the links of trade and credit in Eastern Maharashtra as they succeeded in doing over the next few decades. Jenkins remarks that internal trade in the rural localities was carried on mainly by the local Maratha traders from various castes. But the constant mention of patels among persons having recourse to credit is an indication of the growing dependence of the land-holders on the money-lenders. Indeed, at the higher echelons of trade and especially of the credit business, non-Marathas were already clearly in control. The district's external trade was usually in the hands of merchants from the areas with which it was carried on.[12]

Most sahukars in the district belonged to the Marwari community. In the period under consideration they were still engaged in money-changing because rupees of various denominations were current in the district, while the smaller denominations consisted of a great diversity of coins. As the local coins were replaced by the British-minted rupee, the money-changers lost their income, but then the sphere of trade and money-lending extended. In the 1820s, the money-lenders already made large purchases of grain at low prices, kept the grain in store, and issued it on loan for 8 months at 25 per cent, speculating in crop-failure years. Jenkins says that they traded in produce and articles made in the rural localities and loaned money to artisans.[13] Unfortunately, nothing is known about this line of credit activities except the high interest rate.

Earlier on, operations involving promissory notes had been carried on in Nagpur by two or three firms which had been spared the rajah's devastating attentions. The rest were afraid to keep large sums of cash at home. Jenkins says that with the establishment of the British order promissory notes were discounted by all bankers and sahukars enjoying respect, although the resultant competition did make the business less profitable and was handled almost solely by the Marwaris. The rise of the Marwaris was perhaps due to the fact that with the fall of Bhonsla the Maratha bankers had lost their erstwhile positions in the tax apparatus, and also in the supply line.

At any rate, apart from two banking houses owned by Maratha Brahmans, the other 15 were Marwari. Jenkins writes with admiration about the business qualities and acumen of their owners, which, however, were combined with cunningness and a readiness to derive profit at every opportunity. Other trading communities in Nagpur (Bohras, Pawars) were not involved in banking operations. In the very first decade of British rule, four or five new Marwari houses were set up in Nagpur, having been attracted by fresh opportunities and security for business activity.[14]

According to the bankers' own estimates, the annual transfer of bills of exchange came to roughly 5 million rupees, half of which fell to Benares, a quarter to Poona and the rest to Calcutta, Bombay, Jaipur, Hyderabad and other cities. Trade ties had a great part to play in determining the direction of discount operations, but other circumstances also had an effect. For instance, about one-half (1.2-1.5 million rupees) of the transfers to Benares covered commercial operations, 100,000 covered expenses of pilgrims, and the rest went for monetary speculations. All the transfers to Poona were, it was claimed, connected with monetary speculations.[15] (This appears to be somewhat oversimplified; the point is that the balance of payments with Poona, from which much coin and bullion came in, was clearly active for Nagpur, and this is what caused the return issue of bills.)

The designation and especially the directions of the bills of exchange circulation in Nagpur undoubtedly still retained their traditional features, and in this sense the data about these operations are of great interest. The direct economic relations of this city, which lay in the heart of India, appeared to be circumscribed within a radius of 600-700 kilometres, which is also confirmed by the data on trade. Direct contacts with Bombay and Calcutta were still insignificant.

Such are some of the facts about economic life in Eastern Maharashtra in the 1820s and the early consequences of the British conquest (earlier on I used some of the indicators on Maharashtra bearing directly on its sovereign past). We have more systematic data on the Kolhapur principality in the southwestern part of Maharashtra. But before considering this material, which dates to the mid-19th century, let us look at T. Marshall's study in the early 1820s of the so-called South Maratha country, which was adjacent to Kolhapur.

Land-holding, Agriculture and Urban Life in the South Maratha Country

As the early British students of the newly conquered territories were wont to do, Marshall concentrated on the tax potentialities in the area, but this, incidentally, helps to reproduce the amount of the alienated agricultural product. He claimed that some local persons, making use of the earlier upheavals and weakening of the central authority, had illegally extended their landed estates and had placed them outside the taxation system. Marshall complained about what he believed to be the very small amount of the land-tax; for instance, only 14,000-15,000 rupees of tax was collected from the Padshapoor taluq, which had a population of over 10,000:

"In fact, the appropriations of the local officers (known under the general but indefinite name of zamindars) are so enormous as to leave the Sirkar scarcely any land from which to make further donations." Still, Marshall himself classed among the "zamindars proper" the following four officials: the desai, "the general superintendent of a subdivision", who had, however, lost his former influence; the deshpande, "the keeper of the records in a similar subdivision"; the nargounda, "the police master of the subdivision"; and the kanunge, whose duties were roughly the same as those of the deshpande. Meanwhile, the patels had largely lost their erstwhile position.[16] Thus, in the Padshapoor taluq, the intermediate echelon of local land-owners and officials had seized the initiative in shaping individual landed estates.

It is perhaps the fact that non-communal officials prevailed among the land-owners, which resulted in the gap between the size of landed estates and the organisation of farming, conducted mainly on the middle and smaller plots. The size of holdings in the taluq, the zamindars apart, did not exceed 8 to 10 acres, for which 70-80 rupees were paid. But some holdings had only one-half to one-quarter of the area. The cultivators were usually short of animals for deep ploughing and took turns in tilling their plots, pooling the animals of small holdings (something that should be borne in mind in giving a sociological assessment to British data on the remuneration of farm servants, especially those engaged in ploughing). Only a few zamindars had their own bullocks for two ploughs, and leased out the lands they were unable to cultivate in their own husbandry either to relatives or to others on the above-mentioned terms. In one or two instances only did the zamindar farms exceed their possessions in the area, that is, they did lease land for farming purposes.

Roughly the same situation existed in the Khanapoor zillah, where the countryside had been ruined. Here, Marshall found no farming on any large scale. The zamindar estates from 30 to 40 acres, were leased out in part, while the plots of the patels, up to 20 acres, were partly tilled by their relatives. One did not find any ordinary rayats paying tax from a plot of over 10 acres.[17]

Farming implements and tilling techniques (especially deep four- or five-time tillage) appeared to Marshall, as it did to most other British observers, to be imperfect. When he told this to the cultivators, they replied that they would simply raise no crop in any other way. He observed: "To introduce a plough of a better construction would, I fear, be a vain attempt, as it would require more capital and more skill, both in the artisans and in the ploughmen, than there is any chance of finding."[18]

However, his own subsequent information refutes his assertion about the imperfections of the farming implements. Thus, the harrows were, like the ploughs, of two types: the first harrow was made of wood with six "stout iron tines", while the second was made entirely of wood. The seeder, which was pulled by two bullocks, was made of the simplest and most available materials, mainly of bamboo, and performed as effectively as if it "were of the most finished and expensive British workmanship". Another implement, also pulled by two bullocks, in principle resembled the English horse hoe.[19]

Alongside payment in cash, there remained payment in kind, and this prevailed in the countryside. Carpenters and blacksmiths were always paid in grain in accordance with the amount established for each cultivator. Hired men in Khanapoor were paid 3 or 4 pice a day (a rupee consisted of 38 pice); in the villages they were usually paid in grain (ragi) at 1.5-3 seers a day, and in the high season up to 3 seers a day. Prices on the Khanapoor bazaar were on a level of 1 rupee for 20, 12 and 10 seers of ragi, rice and wheat, respectively, i.e., in cash terms a day's earnings came to $\frac{1}{14}-\frac{1}{7}$ rupees or from 2 to 4 rupees a month.

The prices were somewhat higher in Padshapoor: 1 rupee went to buy 9 seers of jowar and 8 seers of wheat or rice. But the earnings here were also higher: a strong man was paid $\frac{1}{8}$ rupees a day, and a woman $\frac{1}{2}$ or $\frac{3}{4}$ of the amount. An unmarried man permanently employed received 1 seer of jowar a day, which in cash terms came to $\frac{1}{9}$ of a rupee. During harvest time, the worker was paid 46 seers of grain a day. Carpenters and bricklayers received $\frac{1}{4}$ of a rupee, which was much more than other workers.[20] Considering that the local seer was equal to 3.25 pounds, or roughly 1.4 kilogrammes, some calculations can be made. It turns out that a farm worker received, in terms of millet, from 1.5 to 3 kilogrammes, and in season from 4.2 to 10 kilogrammes a day. Meanwhile, the carpenter or the bricklayer could buy for his 1/4 of a rupee over 3 kilogrammes of jowar and somewhat less wheat and rice. As for carpenters and blacksmiths, who were paid a share of the crop, their precise reward is unknown. One would think that it was close to that of the hired carpenter. In general, a worker engaged 200 to 250 days a year was able to maintain his family, however meagrely.

As I have already said, the cultivator paid a rent of 6 rupees per acre. In order to obtain this amount, he had to sell on the market 160, 96 or 80 seers (224, 134.5 or 112 kilogrammes) of ragi, rice or wheat, respectively. On non-irrigated lands, the tax consumed the whole ragi crop. That is why where the cultivator grew rice and ragi, he used all the fertilisers for the former; indeed, rice was the crop, according to Marshall, on which the rayat pinned his hopes for paying the taxes. The best, irrigated lands were set aside for rice.

Because the farming and the consumption of the rural population were on strictly subsistence lines, the commodity exchange operations both within the individual taluqs and between them and the outer world was small, unstable and involved a short range of items. For instance, there were two bazaar villages in the Padshapoor taluq, where grain, vegetables, fruit, yarn and the simplest cloth were sold. People brought to the market the quantity of goods they needed to sell to buy the thing they required, and, Marshall observes, cash was only a medium in the transfer of goods. On the whole, the taluq manufactures were extremely insignificant, and tur and jowar were exported only when the crop was good, rice, wheat, salt, iron, copper and cloth being purchased in exchange.[21] The iron parts of farm implements were made by non-village artisans and were bought by the rayats. The same men who made the iron, forged it into hoes and other simple implements which were either sold on the spot to the farmers who came to buy them or were taken to the market at Khanapoor.[22]

In the zillah of Khanapoor, which had a population of 10,829, there was one town with a bazaar (population 2,648) and about 120 villages. Three-quarters of the zillah's rural population and three-fifths of that town consisted of Maratha farmers, or, as Marshall calls them, koolumbee. From the same caste came the desai and nearly all the patels. The Brahmans rarely lived in the villages, but in the town there were nearly 120 families of them. Apart from their religious functions, some of them also performed the duties of deshpande. The Muslims served in the police and in the tax offices. Marshall mentions among the other small communities and tribes "the common village artisans", but says nothing about the urban craftsmen.[23]

One is left with the impression that Khanapoor was a countryside administrative centre (kasba) of the usual kind for pre-British Maharashtra, being the seat of the administration, the priests, and their retainers and guards, rather than the centre of trade, let alone the handicrafts. The lands and the towns were almost entirely in the category of inam (tax-free) lands, and were owned either by temples or by the zamindars and persons connected with them. It may be assumed that the periphery of the Mogul despotism and its Maratha successors, which had infertile soil, enjoyed some kind of easement as regards land-taxation.

From among the land-owners were appointed the town heads, who, together with "the trading orders", made up the well-to-do part of the urban population. The poor were mainly the servants and dependents of the richer strata. As for the very poor, who had no permanent means of subsistence, they were the "gleaners in the great field of labour. Neither of these are at all below their natural level, and on the whole Khanapoor presents a respectable example of a well-organised Indian country town."[24]

Marshall's information shows that the East India Company officials had managed to secure control of a large number of villages, ousting the local land-owners. In the zillah of Khanapoor, 74 villages were under the administration of the Company's tax official, 12 villages were at the disposal of the Bhimgurh garrison, 17 made up the jagir of one desai and another 15-18 belonged to the zamindars and the temples. The town of Khanapoor paid a great many small taxes, a total of 22,000 rupees, among them mohturifs (house tax)—663 rupees; alcoholic drinks—557 rupees, salt—125, mango trees—116, and betel—116. But there were, in effect, no taxes on land.[25]

The small scale of Khanapoor's trade and handicrafts and the corresponding composition of its population were partially due to the fact that the old ruler had decided to set up a new trading centre at Nandgar, near his fortress, where he settled the merchants and the artisans. Khanapoor retained only the making of pots; the smelting of iron (6 miles from the town) had stopped, and none remained of the 30-40 looms.[26] But we find that the withdrawal of the merchants and the artisans did not result in any serious disruptions in the life of the town, which did not show any signs of decline. Indeed, the number of looms confirms the assumption that the handicrafts served mainly the urban population itself and could not have been a source of its prosperity in the exchange of goods with the countryside. The town lived and fed on rent.

Thus, the overall pressure on the socio-economic complex of Maharashtra in the early 19th century did not imply their split-up, let alone transformation. The system of traditional inter-onnections remained unchanged, with one but very essential exception: the upper echelon of distribution, the land-taxation system, turned out to be under the control of the administration of foreign merchant's capital. This produced the premise—but no more—for upsetting the whole balanced system of predominantly subsistence relations, including its separate commodity-and-money components.

Social Hierarchy, Land Relations, Structure of Production and Consumption in Bengal

The fact that the traditional ties were little disrupted was also seen from the results of the East India Company's half-century of control of Bengal's tax apparatus. To use the modern terminology of Western sociology, the dynamic potential of the British administration tended to bog down and peter out in the thickness of the local administrative and tax apparatus, which it would not, and indeed could not, replace by a bourgeois bureaucracy (which was possible under two equally unacceptable and unrealistic variants: with a massive substitution of British officials for the Indian personnel, or with an equally massive transformation of that personnel into a bourgeois-colonial machine of the "white dominion" type).

The Bengal material shows very well the three-tier system: the British colonial administration on top; the same kind of tax apparatus on the district level, which interlocked with the zamindari "native" personnel; and the lower echelon of the "upper rayats" and other purely local tax-collectors, partially well-to-do Bengali tax-payers. While each of these three tiers constituted an inter-connected system, each had its national and social incompatibility (disintegration aspect, one might say), because its aggregate personnel was classified not only according to the service and proprietary indicators (which is inevitable under any bureaucratic hierarchy), but also according to their social origin and the class to which they belonged. Still, however paradoxical this may appear at first sight, the extra-economic methods used by the merchant administration of the East India Company were more adequate to the functions of its subordinate Indian personnel than the subsequent, mainly economic methods of colonial exploitation were to the traditional claims laid by the native personnel (their descendants, to be more precise) to their share of the redistributed product.

In her comprehensive study, Ratna Ray has graphically shown that the tax apparatus of an individual zamindar estate was part and parcel of its general-functional social structure; hence all attempts to single out the tax-collection function in the overall system of the hierarchic relations within a zamindar estate are, as a rule, futile. Here is one example cited by R. Ray: "The outcome of the public sales in Bishnupur seems to suggest that in organised Zamindaris possessing the characteristics of a 'kingdom' (Raj), outside adventurers—in this case native capitalists from Calcutta—were not in the best position to convert auction purchases into effective rights. Families of standing, wealth and influence, like the house of Burdwan, stood a much better chance of making their auction purchases effective. Jaynatayan Ghoshal, a big capitalist of Calcutta, who had lent money to Damodar Singh, tried to take over the Bhitarjote mahals in satisfaction of his claims, but without success (in 1787.—V.P.). Other outsiders, such as Durgachatian Pakrasi of Calcutta and Kashinath and Biswanath Banerjee, purchased Bishnupur mahals at public auctions but could not take effective possesion. This failure was due to the stiff resistance of the Bishnupur family, which made it impossible for them to collect revenue."[27]

Ratna Ray further cites the complaints of the zamindari newcomers of the East India Company, who said that the fomer landlords, gathering as many as 2,000 followers, raided their estates, burnt down villages, dispossessed and drove away the rayats, and seized the tax money. As a result, zamindar estates were redeemed by their traditional rulers for a mere trifle.[28] Incidentally, even the first decade of the 19th century saw smallscale feudal wars between the rajahs of Bengal and their taluqdars for possession of some estates.[29] R. Ray believes that, in the final analysis, the Permanent Settlement was to the advantage of the "smaller local gentry" (at least in the Hindu districts of Burdwan and Bishnupur, which she studied) because they were able to affirm its putnee land-holding rights. "The Permanent Settlement laid the basis for the independence and consolidation of the smaller local gentry who had formerly existed as a subservient class to the big rajas and zamindars. With the creation of a vastly increased number of small landed properties carved out of the regional rajas, it was the local gentry rather than the merchant class of Calcutta who were in the most favourable position for acquiring the permanently leased-out revenue-collecting rights. Beneath these high-caste petty revenue-paying proprietors, there continued in occupation of the land dominant groups of village landlords who commanded the labour of poor and landless villagers for their fields. By putting these village landlords in the category of 'tenants', the Permanent Settlement created a perpetual tension between legal fiction (i.e., the pronouncement that the zamindars and taluqdars were the 'landlords') and economic reality (i.e., the fact that jotedars and mandals actually controlled the most profitable agricultural lands in their villages) which provided much of the driving power behind the processes of change in Bengali rural society down to the abolition of zamindari in the 1950s."[30]

The kind of economic organism on which this bureaucratic tax system was imposed will be seen from Buchanan's data. When he inspected the districts of Bengal and Bihar from 1807 to 1811, his ambit was defined by his instructions, which contained a list of the points to be studied: natural conditions, population and the condition of its sections, religious communities, natural resources, the state of the "farms" and their husbandry, the amount and forms of rent, remuneration, possibilities for extending and improving agriculture, landed property and its impact on agriculture, the handicrafts and their equipment with tools, the list of the goods produced, the provision of raw and other materials, the size of capital and the condition of the producers, the state of trade, and communications. In 1808, Buchanan inspected two north-eastern districts of Bengal—Dinajpur and Rangpur. For the first I used a separate edition published in 1833: and for the second, the relevant section of R.M. Martin's book.

Buchanan's description of socio-economic relations in Rangpur lacks many essential aspects, apparently because he believed them to be similar to those in Dinajpur and did not deem it necessary to repeat himself. The fact that these two districts were selected for study is a source of regret for the investigators of Indian history both because they were of about the same type and also because this leaves out from the sphere of study the important southern districts, where urban life was more developed. Besides, the prevalence of the Muslim population in Dinajpur and Rangpur makes it impossible to establish the socio-occupational structure in accordance with the caste indicator. However, there are also some advantages in the selection of Dinajpur and Rangpur for a survey because there the socio-economic relations of pre-British Bengal were much better preserved than in the southern part of the subah.

In estimating the population in the district of Dinajpur, Buchanan proceeded from the fact that it had 480,000 ploughs, which required about a half-million adult men. Assuming that the family averaged five people, Buchanan reached the conclusion that the agricultural population totalled roughly 2,400,000. Because the handicrafts were embryonic, the rest of the population did not exceed a quarter of this figure, that is, the total was about 3 million.

He backs up this estimate as follows: after the formation of the seed fund in the district, there remained 27.6 million maunds (the Calcutta maund equalled 84 pounds, or about 38 kilogrammes) of hulled rice, of which 4.4 million (worth 3.2 million rupees) was exported, and 23.2 million went for local consumption. With a daily ration of $\frac{1}{2}$ seer (slightly less than $1\frac{1}{4}$ pounds or 570 grammes) per head, this quantity of rice would go to feed as many as 4 million people. But a part of the grain was used as feed for cattle, for distillation, etc.[31] I shall return to the analysis of these figures later, accepting, for the time being, Buchanan's estimate of the population of Dinajpur.

Within the framework of the Bengal-Bihar region, surveyed by Buchanan, there was evidence of a change in the socio-economic relations in the countryside as one advanced to the north-west along the Ganges valley. In particular, there was something of a re-establishment of the traditional village community on the basis of a unity of farming and the handicrafts. It is true that at the same time there was a reduction in the share of the Muslim population, whose prevalence in the villages of Northern and Eastern Bengal inevitably upset the system, based on the caste hierarchy, of the artisan's remuneration by the owner of the implement.

Paradoxically, the subsistence relations between the land- holder and the artisan went hand in hand with a complexification and a corresponding increase in the cost of the farming implements. The implements used on the light soils of Bengal were relatively simpler and cheaper. Buchanan mentions the wooden plough (sometimes with an iron tip) worth 12 annas, a bamboo attachment for rolling the soil—1 anna, an iron hoe—14 annas, an iron cutter—8 annas, and other manual implements worth a total of 3 rupees 4 annas. The list of implements does not include a heavy plough, a seeder and a harrow (although there is mention of a rake pulled by two bullocks; being fitted with iron teeth it was used as a harrow). Where the husbandman had several sets of implements, some of these could be incomplete, and so the average price of each fell to $2\frac{3}{4}$ rupees.[32] Thus, one set in Bengal cost a fraction of the price in Maharashtra.

When one set of implements was used to till a plot of 15 bighas (5 acres or 2 hectares), which was considered to be the standard plot with which an average peasant family could cope, it had to have the following fund: $2\frac{3}{8}$ rupees for implements, 9 rupees for cattle, $3\frac{3}{8}$ rupees for seeds, 5 rupees for the house, $3\frac{1}{4}$ rupees for utensils and furniture, 4 rupees for clothes and ornaments, 15 rupees for food for six months until the harvest, and 4 rupees 11 annas for six months' rent, at 10 annas per bigha a year; a total of 47 rupees 1 anna. Of course, these items are incommensurate, because some were spent as a lump sum, while others, like the value of the cattle, the implements and the utensils, could be used for more than 6 months. All these outlays were inevitable only when a young peasant family started a separate husbandry or when new-comers settled in a village (in which case the cost of ornaments and utensils could be omitted).

The list of expenditures does not contain debt repayments. The point is, however, that lease of land usually entailed indebtedness, above all to the rayat from whom the plot was leased. Indeed, the advances in grain were also made mainly by the "senior rayats", and also by merchants from Murshidabad and Calcutta, who bought up the rice in the district for 4 million rupees a year. These expenditures and payments show that the establishment of new farming units on leased land at once turned the tenant into a debtor. In the district of Dinajpur, where Buchanan discovered vast areas of untilled land, he ventured the opinion that poor cultivators did not start to till them because they were unable to wait until these lands yielded a crop and rewarded their labours; those who had money, however, preferred to loan it out at high interest to needy neighbours instead of investing it in land improvement.[33]

I shall try to present a structure of these peasant-family expenditures as shares in annual terms. Let us assume that the lump-sum outlays on implements, the house, utensils, furniture, clothing and ornaments were made roughly for three years, that is, about 8 rupees was spent every year out of the 24 rupees for these items; in that case, the outlays on cattle in annual terms came to 2-3 rupees; seeds 6 rupees; food 30; rent 9 rupees 6 annas plus 8 rupees of the outlays on handicraft products (the house was built mainly by the peasant family itself, which is why the latter item may be reduced to $6\frac{1}{2}$ rupees), while the total annual outlays (without interest on debt) came close to 55 rupees, that is, the personal expenditures of the family equalled 63-64 per cent, outlays on the production about 20 per cent, and rent 17-18 per cent of the cultivator's budget. The share of the handicraft products used by the family itself came to roughly 10 per cent, and of the implements to less than 2 per cent of the budget. All these calculations have been made without taking into account debt repayments, whose introduction would effect a corresponding reduction in the share of each of the items and would increase the total expenditure.

Buchanan gives a somewhat different break-down of the agricultural product in another estimate. In Dinajpur, the fertile lowlands yielded 2 rupees' worth of grain per bigha (one-third of an acre); one rupee covered the household expenses, onehalf of a rupee the rent, and another half-rupee remained as "net profit" for the cultivator. Applying these figures to the 15-bigha plot we have been considering, we obtain: 15 rupees for production outlays, $7\frac{1}{2}$ rupees for rent, and $7\frac{1}{2}$ rupees for "net profit". For further comparison let us note that we have assumed one crop, whereas now and again two were harvested; but even with this assumption the total income from a plot barely approximated 35-40 rupees.

Where does the "net profit" come from? Apparently, under small-scale land-holding this item should be referred not to the surplus-product but, together with the labour inputs in the "production expenditures", to the consumption fund of the cultivator's own family. "Net profit" can be seen as surplus-product only in the income of the bigger "farmowners" who sub-leased land on a share-cropping basis, and sometimes tilled them with the use of serfs. For instance, the cost of working a one-acre (3-bigha) plot consisted of the following components: ploughing (11 ploughs per average day)—1 rupee, 10 men for planting rice—1/2 rupee, seeds—$\frac{1}{4}$ rupee, harvesting of rice (12 men)—9 annas, rent—1 rupee 6 annas, sundries—5 annas; a total of 4 rupees. The value of the product came to 6 rupees.[34] In this case, the surplus-product approximated one-half of the crop. In order to specify just how much, we must have information about the personal participation of the "farm-owner's" family in the labour operations, and the outlays on cattle, implements and seeds.

The "farm-owners" were not averse to entrepreneurial interest, which was most pronounced in the growing and processing of sugar-cane. The yield of sugar-cane per bigha came to 20-21 rupees, which was ten times the value of the rice yield on the same area. But, first, its growing and processing required considerably greater expenditures; second, it grew only on the most fertile lands, and its vegetation period ranged over about three seasons; third, either the land-owners openly raised their rent on a plot under sugar-cane (5 rupees instead of 1) or there occurred a general rise of rent on land which was fit for growing sugar-cane. Accordingly, this left the land-holder to decide which crop was more profitable. In these circumstances, only the biggest farmers had an acre under sugar-cane.

It took 24 days to process the sugar-cane crop grown on one acre, and involved the use of 8 workers and 12 bullocks. That is why the owner of the sugar-cane installation, usually a well-to-do man, let it out alternately to his neighbours, who operated the installation on their own. In the production of gur, the juice was funnelled into a boiling installation consisting of several vats, where it was brought to the required consistency. Working round the clock and involving 16 workers and 20 bullocks, the establishment produced 476 pounds of product. It is true, says Buchanan, that the working period was usually confined to the daylight hours (in which case the number of workers and bullocks was apparently halved).[35]

What, then, was the size of the land-holding and the use of the land that could be combined with the above-mentioned types of farming operations? Buchanan gives the following differentiation of land-holders for the Dinajpur district: 6,600 "chief farmers" with an average of 165 bighas each, or a total of 1,083,000 bighas; 8,800 "big farmers" with 75 bighas each, a total of 650,000 bighas; 11,000 well-to-do farmers with 60 bighas, a total of 660,000 bighas; 19,800 self-sufficient-farmers at 45 bighas, a total of 891,000 bighas; 55,000 poor farmers at 30 bighas, a total of 1,650,000 bighas; 110,000 needy farmers at 15 bighas, a total of 1,650,000 bighas. The total area of taxed land in the district came to 6.6 million bighas (apparently the Calcutta bigha, in which case the area came to 2.2 million acres or nearly 900,000 hectares). The total area of cultivated land equalled 7.2 million bighas, which meant that over 90 per cent of it was subject to land-tax.

Thus, at the one pole there were 15,400 big land-holders with 1,740,000 bighas; and at the other, 110,000 small holders with 1,650,000 bighas. But land-tenure was, as a rule, much more fragmented, because a sizable part of the land of the big rayats was leased out. It was the big rayats with poor lands yielding only one crop who resorted mostly to the leasing of land, giving up their own husbandry. These also prevailed among the richest local merchants and money-lenders handling amounts ranging from 5,000 to 20,000 rupees.[36]

These "farmers", that is, rayats, totalled 211,200. Let us recall that the ploughing of land required about a half-million adult men, usually heads of families, which meant that at least three-fifths of the agricultural population were excluded from the category of rayats. These were the people who toiled on the lands of the rayats whose land was in excess of the "labour norm" of 15 bighas. The 100,000 rayats who had 30 bighas and more each held a total of 3,940,000 bighas. Even if all these rayats tilled 15 "labour" bighas each, something like 2.5 million bighas still remained for them to lease out or cultivate by serfs.

Besides, all the categories of rayats held only 5.6 million bighas, while the taxed area came to 6.6 million bighas, and all the cultivated area to 7.2 million bighas, which meant that it was 1.6 million bighas larger than the area held by the rayats. In other words, the non-rayats and also the rayats with under 15 bighas tilled over 4 million bighas (2.5 million and 1.6 million), i.e., over one-half of all the land in Dinajpur. It is safe to assume that persons in these categories made up the 300,000 of the agricultural population in the district who were not included among the said rayats with 15 and more bighas of land.

Of course, these data and estimates provide no more than a general idea of the proprietary and especially the household stratification in the countryside of this Bengal district in the early 19th century. At any rate, it is obvious that the continuation of the community as a unity of farming and the handicrafts on a subsistence basis was highly complicated under the extreme inequality of proprietary and social status among the agricultural population in the Bengal countryside. This may be one of the reasons why Buchanan makes no mention at all of the bullooty type system in the two Bengal districts which he described.

At the same time, on the strength of information concerning the two neighbouring districts with a Muslim majority, it is impossible to anticipate that a similar system existed in other Bengal districts, especially in the western part, where Hindus predominated. Even sources dating from the second half of the 19th and early 20th centuries contain mention of continued remuneration in kind for rural artisans as a share of the crop. But in order to decide which factors—the adoption of Islam, especially by the land-holders, or natural and other conditions—determined the socio-economic structure of the countryside in the Muslim areas of Bengal, there is need for a special study. I shall confine myself to a statement of the situation which had taken shape in Dinajpur and Rangpur.

Buchanan's data on the lower tier of the tax and police apparatus confirm that the relatively small number of British military and other personnel was more than compensated by the preservation of a ramified network of local "guardians of the law". Besides, a look at the rewards going to this category of persons helps, I believe, to enlarge our notion of the distribution of the surplus-product of Bengal's agriculture and the use of tax-free lands.

Buchanan's data on the zamindar estate under the Rajah of Dinajpur gives an idea of the structure of the tax apparatus set up by the Bengal zamindars and the rewards going to those who served on it. At the head of the establishment was the diwani, whose annual reward was 1,200 rupees, then came 8 of his assistants (tahsildars), who had 300 rupees each, 8 scribes at 96 rupees, 24 sirdars (chiefs of the guard), who had tax-free plots of 50 bighas each (18.25 acres or 7.3 hectares), 16 junior chiefs of the guard with 30 bighas each (11 acres or 4.5 hectares), the rest of the guard being paid in cash: 8 seniors at 48 rupees, and 24 soldiers at 36 rupees a year; 16 account-keepers with 12 bighas (4.4 acres or 1.8 hectares), and 200 couriers with 10 bighas (3.7 acres or 1.5 hectares). The total cash reward came to 8,688 rupees, and the land made available for use by zamindar personnel equalled 7,872 bighas (2,873 acres or 1,150 hectares), which in practical terms, and at a tax of 10 annas per bigha, came to another 4,924 rupees in cash terms, which meant that the tax and police apparatus cost 13,600 rupees (bribes and other types of extortion apart). Besides, revenue collectors received 4 per cent of the 110,000 rupees, which actually came in the form of the revenue payments, i.e:, 4,400 rupees. Total rent revenues from the zamindar area, including the amount due (but not received from the tax-free land of the zamindar personnel), came to 114,924 rupees, of which 79,000 went as land-tax, 18,012 to the tax and police personnel, and 17,912 rupees to the zamindar.

On the strength of the amount of tax receipts and the rate per bigha it is possible to calculate the area of the zamindar estate, which was roughly 122,000 bighas (40,800 acres or 16,300 hectares). To till this land, it would take 8,000 ploughmen, and we find that only within the limits of the area of the zamindar estate there were over 500 administrative and police personnel for this number of ploughmen—one guardian of the law for 245 bighas (32.6 hectares) and for 16 ploughmen.

The principles of remuneration in the other zamindar estate, which was close in size to the former, were roughly the same. With total rent receipts of 99,674 rupees, 81,591 rupees went as land-tax, 7,978 rupees went into various personal rewards, and 10,105 rupees was left for the zamindar. In a smaller zamindar estate with rent receipts totalling 6,300 rupees, the tax came to 4,500 rupees, maintenance of personnel to 679.5 rupees, and the zamindar (a merchant who had bought the zamindar estate shortly before the survey) retained 1,120.5 rupees.[37]

We have not enough information to judge on the strength of these amounts about the actual receipts from the land received by the British authorities, the zamindars and their personnel. The amount of tax paid by the zamindars was more or less precise. As for their expenditures, these must have been indicated by the zamindars themselves and so were undoubtedly understated even in that part which was made up of direct rent receipts (let us recall the instances of the manyfold increase of rent of lands fit for sugar-cane growing). Besides, there also remained the system of indirect rent payments to the zamindar in the form of offerings, donations, services, etc. However, in these examples the share of the zamindars, even according to their own information, constituted over 50 per cent more than the one-tenth of the tax that was due.

In Dinajpur, as in the whole of Bengal, the Permanent Settlement, having increased the legitimate and illegitimate incomes of the zamindars, attracted capital to land property. Most of the zamindars in the district were men who had acquired their estates in the course of the preceding few years, and had earlier been merchants, "manufacturers", zamindar agents or government officials. However, the latter were not numerous.[38] It may be assumed that their share was higher in the districts around Calcutta.

The sharp increase in zamindar incomes after the introduction of the Permanent Settlement is a fact that is generally accepted in scientific writings. N. K. Sinha, remarking that the price of land, or to be more precise, of the property of the zamindars, increased in one generation after the introduction of the Permanent Settlement ten-fold or, sometimes, even twenty-fold, says this was due to the growing pressure on the land as a result of the general growth of the population, an influx of ruined artisans into agriculture, and neglect by the British administration of the proprietary rights of the rayats. All of this enabled the zamindars sharply to increase the rent, which actually doubled between 1800 and 1810.[39]

We have no data on the structure of Bengal's national product in the early 19th century, but we have an opportunity to consider the make-up of the agricultural product in the districts and their foreign trade. For Dinajpur, Buchanan gives information about the sown area for the main crops and the crop yields in cash terms. It is hard to analyse these data for two reasons: first, some of the crops were winter crops, with rice prevailing (11 million of the 19 million rupees of the total value of the product), some were summer crops, and others crops of both seasons. More detailed information is available on the structure of the agricultural products in the district of Rangpur. With a total value of 21,100,000 rupees, this was as follows: rice 28,120,000 maunds (after the formation of the seed fund—26,600,000) worth 9.3 million rupees (from these figures, incidentally, follows the fact that 115 kilogrammes of unhulled rice in the countryside cost 1 rupee, and, let us recall, 50 kilogrammes of hulled rice—1 rupee; this great gap may be due to the cost of hulling, which involved considerable waste, and also to the "addition" in the price introduced by the participation of merchant's capital); millet 784,000 maunds (after the formation of the seed fund—768,000) worth 213,300 rupees; wheat and barley 268,000 maunds (250,200) worth 108,500 rupees; pulses 516,500 maunds (467,200) worth 217,000 rupees, oil-seeds 1,212,700 maunds (1,151,600) worth 1,069,000 rupees; sugar-cane 285,000 maunds worth 445,000 rupees; jute 187,800; cotton 3,800, betel leaf 179,700; betel nut 469,300; tobacco 253,300; opium 53,000; and indigo 127,800 rupees.[40]

These figures clearly show the prevalence of cereals and pulses (9,750,000 rupees) in cropping. (The total value of the product of all the above-listed crops came to roughly 12,500,000 rupees.) It may be assumed that the remaining 8,600,000 rupees refer only or chiefly to the main harvest, in which rice characteristically prevails among the cereals. This does not, of course, rule out that the 8,600,000 rupees could include, apart from a second crop, also the products of animal husbandry, forestry and fishery. Industrial and subsidiary crops (betel, tobacco) accounted for an insignificant share, and even bearing in mind the high proportion of market products among them, they could not make up the bulk of all agricultural commodities.

Information about the handicrafts is scarce, because local artisans did not, in effect, work for export or take part in sharing the peasant product; thus, two of the main factors causing special interest among British investigations with regard to Indian artisans were lacking. Their numbers can be no more than estimated within the limits of the 600,000—Buchanan's estimate of the non-agricultural population of Dinajpur. In neighbouring Rangpur, artisans made up roughly 12 per cent of the population; and with the same percentage in Dinajpur they would have numbered about 360,000.

As a rule, their social status was low. Thirteen castes of merchants and artisans were "impure": money-changers (Buchanan calls them Subornabanik), jewellers, carpenters, traders in grain and salt (sungri), one caste of potters, oilpressers, four castes of fishermen, makers of ornaments, sellers of boiled rice and confectioneries, and distillers. These numbered 150,000, or one-sixth of the Hindu population of the district. To a special group of "impure" ones (a total of 225,000) belonged seven castes: laundrymen, jute-weavers, one caste of fishermen, basket-makers, gardeners, dustmen and leather dressers.[41] Only 90,000 Hindus out of 900,000 were regarded as pure in origin.[42] Thus, of the major handicraft castes only the cotton-weavers and blacksmiths did not find themselves at the bottom of the Bengal caste hierarchy. No mention was made of Muslim artisans, although one could assume that some of the weavers were Muslims.

In Dinajpur, the sub-castes of carpenters included not only carpenters proper but also joiners, cabinet-makers, and carvers. The members of these sub-castes occupied 600-700 houses. Most of them were engaged in making "miserable instruments of agriculture" or crude chairs and tables for peasants, and belonged to the poorest section of the artisans. In the towns, where the carpenters had to make frames, doors, posts, beams and also palanquins, their earnings rose to 4-8 rupees. Earnings of about 8 rupees required a capital of 40-50 rupees and the hire of several workers. Buchanan gives the price of some articles: a palanquin from 10 to 20 rupees, a bed from 2 to 4 rupees; but implements of labour were much cheaper: a spinning-wheel 2 annas, a plough (without an iron tip) from 4 to 6 annas. There is also mention of equipment for pressing sugar-cane and oil-seeds. In Dinajpur, boats were made but in small numbers, because there was small demand for these among local traders. Boat-making was organised there by a merchant, who hired carpenters at 7 rupees a month for the master-craftsman and 3-6 rupees a month for the others.

Carpenter's tools included a hatchet, a good adze, diverse chisels, a very imperfect plane, a small saw, a drill, and a wooden mallet. Buchanan did not discover any rules, squares, benches or compasses. Incidentally, the absence of benches required the participation of another worker in various operations, like the smoothing and levelling of wood. In the town of Dinajpur alone, European tools like planes of every kind, compasses, rules and squares were in use.

Buchanan heard that Dinajpur had seven turner's workshops, each employing two men: one pulled a rope alternately with one hand and then with the other to turn the lathe, while the other applied the chisel. The turners fashioned a part of the spinning-wheel, wooden plates and cups, rollingpins, various items for smoking, and legs for beds.[43] This detailed description makes it possible not only to gain a more precise idea of the extent of the technical backwardness in the Indian handicrafts, but also to avoid any exaggerations of that backwardness which, undoubtedly, were made in some of the above-cited descriptions.

Specialisation in some handicrafts had apparently gone farther in Bengal and Bihar than in Maharashtra. Thus, in the district of Purnea, blacksmiths had, as a rule, taken over from carpenters in making farming implements. The carpenters were left to make the simple household furniture, boats and carts. Buchanan notes that most of the carpenters were also turners, which enabled them to make spinning-wheels and beds, the most widespread products of the turner's lathe.[44] Thus, having been deprived of orders for farming implements, local carpenters switched to the making of consumer goods, means of transport and also—and this is especially important—tools for spinners and perhaps other artisans as well. Buchanan also mentions that in the district of Dinajpur local carpenters engaged in turner's work. However, the removal of farming implements from their sphere of production led to the decline of the social status of the castes of carpenters in Bengal and Bihar, and some of these were considered to be "impure".[45]

About the potters—1,400 houses in Dinajpur—Buchanan claims that they enjoyed complete welfare, because in pottery there was no need for much capital, since the equipment (the potter's wheel and the furnace) was cheap and lasted long, while the products were sold to the consumer directly and without delay. One family (which may have been joint, because it consisted of four men and two women) turned out products worth 20 rupees a month, of which 5 rupees went for fuel, 3 rupees 2 annas for clay and 11 or 12 rupees for the maintenance of the artisans and members of their families. However, because there were six people employed in the work, their earnings per head were very modest.

Buchanan gives a detailed description of the technology of pottery, but his illustrated list of the main items produced is more interesting, for it testifies to their diversity and to the fine taste of the craftsmen.[46] One is left with the impression that in Dinajpur petty-commodity handicrafts prevailed, being designed for local consumption, while community handicrafts and early capitalist branches were either an exception or did not exist at all.

The fact that most manufactures in Dinajpur and Rangpur were excluded from the overall Bengali social division of labour is also confirmed by the information about the structure of the district's external trade. Dinajpur district exported goods worth 4,819,400 rupees and imported 1,285,900 rupees' worth. The main items of exports were: rice 3,179,000 rupees; ghee 40,500; pepper 81,400, sackcloth, and bags of the same; 124,600; raw silk 62,600; cotton cloths 145,000; gur 35,500; sugar 300,000; molasses and treacle 72,000; and indigo 262,500. The main items of imports were: salt 825,000 rupees; cotton (mainly from Central India) 105,500; sackloth, and bags of the same, 51,000. The other items of external trade were much more modest, these being the most notable: tin 2,200 rupees (at 32 rupees for 40 seers), lead 1,500 (at 12 rupees), zinc 7,000 (at 26 rupees), country iron 29,800 (at 4-7 rupees), steel 2,200 (at 20 rupees), copper 18,900 (at 55 rupees), bronze- and copper-ware 20,000, cotton cloths 39,000, British woollens. 10,000 rupees.

The result was a vast surplus—3,533,500 rupees, an amount almost equalling the export of rice, the main taxed crop in the district. Bearing in mind that the land-tax was somewhat in excess of 4 million rupees, one is tempted to draw the categorical conclusion that the trade surplus consisted of the land-tax less the cost of local administration and garrisoning. Under this assumption, the funnelling of wealth from Bengal could be roughly presented as the difference between the trade surpluses of the districts and the expenditures of the authorities in the Presidency.

Such an assumption could be correct, but only in the most general terms, because it ignores the mechanism of merchant's and usurer's capital. However, one must bear in mind that the merchants of Calcutta and Murshidabad purchased rice worth 4 million rupees a year, and also that the extraction of tribute from Bengal was not in the form of rice but of handicraft articles, indigo and raw silk. The transformation of rice, a product extracted from the rayats (land-holders) by means of the forcible instruments of tax and rent, into export goods once again required the services of merchant's capital, but we have no information about picturing its activity on the scale of Bengal even in the most general terms.

The data on the export of rice make it possible to judge about the level of commodity component in this crop. Considering the production of rice on all the lands (including the taxed lands), we find that the amount of commodity rice going outside the district in itself came to a quarter of the crop. Moreover, at least the same share of the rice remaining in the district was consumed by the non-agricultural population, whose numbers Buchanan had estimated at 600,000, or onefifth of the whole population. Thus, over 40 per cent of the rice grown in the district was transformed into commodity form, and this is a figure which corresponds to our earlier calculations.

One's attention is drawn to the very small, even insignificant, quantities of handicraft articles (jute products cannot be included because at the time they were mainly made by the peasants themselves) moving across the boundaries of the district. The annual consumption of metals in the district, which had a population of 3 million, can be roughly estimated on the strength of metal imports, because there is no mention of any local metallurgy. What I mean is not the total amount of metal that was being worked (for this also included scrap metal), but rather the volume of the annual wear of metal and its restoration. According to my estimates, the figures for tin were 10.9 tons (at 0.85 rupee per kilogramme); lead 4.75 tons (about 0.3 rupee per kilogramme); zink 10.25 tons (about 0.7 rupee per kilogramme); country iron 170-280 tons (0.1-0.18 rupee per kilogramme); steel 4.2 tons (over 0.5 rupee per kilogramme), and copper 13 tons (over 1.4 rupees per kilogramme). As for the finished handicraft articles, we find that their production and consumption were virtually confined to the limits of the district and perhaps even smaller localities.

The structure of neighbouring Rangpur's external trade was roughly similar. Its exports (3,648,500 rupees' worth with imports of 1,450,000 rupees' worth) consisted of the following main items: hulled rice 1,177,500 rupees; unhulled rice 106,800; betel 44,100; tobacco 168,400, opium 32,000; paper 3,000; indigo 644,000; salt 332,000 (with imports at 692,000 rupees, which meant that exports were, in effect, transit), sackcloth and packaging 113,000; raw silk 252,000; cottons 63,500 (with imports at 64,700, which meant that the cloth trade was virtually balanced out); British woollens 14,000 (with imports at 17,000); sugar 67,000, molasses and treacle 81,600, wood 27,000; and spinning-wheels 200 rupees. Of the above-unmentioned import items let us note: salt 691,700 rupees' worth, medicines and herbs 36,400; copper 9,000 (with exports at 4,800); tin 1,600; iron 27,000; copper- and bronze-ware 17,300 (exports 4,000); and cotton 231,000.[47] Thus, the only essential distinction from Dinajpur was the large-scale export of indigo (which, in effect, fetched five times the value of its production in agriculture, something that may be explained by the very low prices of the raw material paid to the cultivator, and the high cost of its subsequent processing), with a lower export of rice, both relatively and absolutely. This, together with the total volume of agricultural exports, which were lower than those of Dinajpur, may be due to the greater fertility of the soil in the latter district,[48] which also implies a greater mass of the surplus product.

What, then, was the social structure that had taken shape on the basis of the described mode of production of agricultural and handicraft produce, and their distribution? The prevalence of Muslims in Dinajpur and Rangpur, especially among the cultivators, makes it impossible to judge about this structure only on the strength of the caste make-up, but I have already allowed myself to make several general judgments about Dinajpur's social-class structure. For Rangpur's population the data are more precise: there were 1,536,000 Muslims and 1,194,000 Hindus—a total of 2,730,000 of these 2,056,000 were ciltivators, 331,000 artisans and 343,000 "idlers or sukhvas".[49]

Thus, the cultivators made up from 75 to 80 per cent of the population in the district, undoubtedly maximum figures for Bengal, because Dinajpur and Rangpur were both country areas with small towns. The data on the export of rice from Dinajpur show that in Murshidabad, Calcutta and other places outside the district, a population roughly equal to the number of persons in the district engaged in non-agricultural pursuits, lived on the produce of the district's agriculture.

Unfortunately, the other two categories of the population are described in much too general terms. For instance, it is not clear how the merchants are listed. The general trend of contemporaneous British materials was to include all the categories of rent-receivers among the "idlers". That is why one is led to believe that the merchants are listed, as they are in various other extracts of the text, together with the artisans (just as are those who work in the services, which is more obvious). Because the biggest zamindars together with their retainers preferred to live in the large towns outside the district, the share of the rent-receiving "idlers" (about 12 per cent of the population) should be regarded as being lower than the average for Bengal (it being possible to reason on the same lines as in estimating the non-agricultural population). Besides, the upper strata of the rayats ("farmers"), who lived on rent, must have been classed by British statistics, on the strength of formal indications, among the cultivators, thereby understating the number of rent-receivers. But, however that may be, even the percentage of rent-receivers given above is very high.

Buchanan gives a description of the proprietary hierarchy of the Dinajpur population and information on the budgets of Hindu families in various walks of life in the administrative centre of the district. These data help to fill out our picture of the social structure of the inland regions of Bengal and also of the scale and make-up of the vital claims among the various sections of the population.

For the district of Dinajpur, Buchanan proposed a proprietary hierarchy consisting of six groups (big landlords or zamindars, who did not deign to reside permanently in the district, were placed by Buchanan outside his classification). Group one—the upper officials, representing the big zamindar land-owners, as well as the small and middle zamindars and the principal merchants and "manufacturers"; unfortunately, he says nothing as to who the latter were, for they may have been the owners of indigo plantations and establishments. Group two—officials and zamindars' agents with a status below those listed above, small zamindars and also a considerable number of merchants, among whom those in the sugar industry, virtually alone in this group, were "natives", that is, local inhabitants instead of new-comers from other parts of India. Group three—lower officials and agents of landlords and merchants, small shopkeepers and "manufacturers", rich "farmers", that is, the upper rayats. Group four—"farmers" with three or four ploughs and well-to-do artisans. Group five—cultivators with one or two ploughs, petty shopkeepers and artisans in moderate conditions, like an oil-presser with two presses or a weaver with one or two looms. Finally, group six—cultivators working a field on a share-cropping basis, day labourers and the lower strata of artisans, like basket-makers, laundrymen, carpenters, etc.[50]

The obscurity with respect to the upper sections of the "manufacturers", which I noted above, does much to reduce the value of this classification, but the inclusion of owners of sugar-cane installations in the same group as the small zamindars shows that the living standards of the upper rayats (with cash capitals ranging from 5,000 to 20,000 rupees) was close to that of the lower zamindar sections. There is no explanation at all of the well-to-do artisans' category, who are classed in the same (fourth) group with the rayats who engaged in farming with three or four sets of implements, that is, on 6 to 8 hectares of land. These artisans could perhaps be classed among the small entrepreneurs. Group five includes artisans not mentioned among the "impure". Their condition was similar to or somewhat better than that of our old friend, the owner of one plough. Finally, the bulk of the artisans were in a similar condition to that of the underprivileged lower sections of the countryside. In short, this proprietary hierarchy gives no ground for judging about the opportunities for enterprise among the artisans, but makes it possible to assume that in the early 19th century these opportunities were still open to weavers, oil-pressers and, perhaps, men of other occupations as well.

Buchanan must have had good reason for classifying the Hindu families of the town of Dinajpur in six groups according to their budgets and consumption, thereby illustrating the actual condition of the said groups in terms of consumption. But let us bear in mind that these data are applicable directly only to the urban population. They were collected by a Hindu clerk who was appointed to assist Buchanan, and who claimed that the expenditures of the Muslim families differed little from those of their Hindu counterparts with the same social status.

It would require a special digression to list all the house-hold utensils and ritual articles, ornaments and clothing, especially among the rich families, and to describe their diet in detail. One is struck by an unusual diversity of their personal belongings, which went hand in hand with a clearly traditional standard in individual vital claims. A high-ranking Hindu family in the town of Dinajpur (husband, wife, child and seven servants) had: a house with outhouses (worth 440 rupees, rent for the plot 6 rupees, expenses for repair and maintenance of the house 158 rupees a year); 19 ritual utensils—36 rupees; over 100 copper, iron and ceramic articles of household use—238 rupees (total outlays on all utensils 66 rupees a year); perishable furniture, that is, carpets, coverlets, curtains, bed-clothes, etc.—144 rupees (with annual outlays on this at about 54 rupees); ornaments for the wife, the husband and the child 675 rupees (with annual outlays at $162\frac{1}{2}$ rupees), clothes for the masters—$166\frac{1}{2}$ rupees, for the servants—$43\frac{1}{2}$ rupees (Buchanan refers the whole cost of the clothing to annual outlays, but these should, apparently, be reckoned at roughly one-half of the amount). The expenses were: food—about 335 rupees a year; payment for servants, barber, laundryman, horse and carriage—about 217 rupees a year; and, finally, outlays for religious purposes—300 rupees, and education for the child—about 6 rupees a year.[51] Total annual expenses of the family and servants: 1,414 rupees (with my correction for the outlays on clothing).

In order to establish how much land a Bengal peasant had to till to allow a high-ranking family to afford such expenses, let us consider, say, the information already given above about the small zamindar estate (receipts—6,300 rupees, of them land tax 4,500, maintenance of police and administrative personnel $679\frac{1}{2}$ rupees, and the little that remained for the zamindars $1{,}120\frac{1}{2}$ rupees). Despite the fact that the last figure is absolutely precise, let us assume that, together with unwilling offerings, the zamindar's income came close to the expenses of the highranking Hindu family in Dinajpur. Under this assumption we find that the tax of 4,500 rupees, with the average rate of 10 annas per bigha, came from an area of 7,200 bighas. With the "labour" norm at 15 bighas, this meant that 480 farming families had to work for the zamindar family and its servants.

Let us consider this budget in material terms. The biggest item, outlays on the repair of the house, utensils, ornaments and clothing (545 rupees), was met by the handicraft population: carpenters, jewellers, coppersmiths, potters and weavers. Compare with this item the outlays on food (335 rupees), which entailed the direct consumption of the agricultural product. Then came the outlays on personal and everyday services (217 rupees) and religious ritual (306 rupees). Materialisation of these amounts (in particular, the share of the agricultural product in these) depended on the needs and potentialities of those who rendered these services. But however that may be, in urban conditions the rich rent-receiver obviously converted it mainly into products and services that were of a non-agricultural origin.

Next came a family whose head, according to the above-mentioned proprietary hierarchy, could be either an official or a small zamindar. The property and expenses of this "family of some consideration", consisting of the husband, the wife and two children and also four servants, comprised the following items: a house with servants' quarters—150 rupees, maintenance expenses—54 rupees; lease of land plot (0.5 acres)—2 rupees; ritual utensils (13 items or units) and everyday utensils (32 items, 65 units)—18 and approximately 81 rupees, respectively, with annual expenses 23 rupees 11 annas; bedding, carpets, curtains, etc.—$76\frac{1}{2}$ rupees, with annual expenses at 27 rupees; ornaments—262 rupees, annual expenses—62 rupees (together with interest); clothing for the masters—62 rupees, for the servants—10 rupees, food—174 rupees; services—60 rupees a year; religious rituals and offerings—80 rupees; and education of children—4 rupees a year. Thus, reckoned per head, this came to 522 rupees, of which 202 rupees went to pay for the work of artisans, 174 for food, 50 and 84 rupees for everyday services and religious duties. We find that the several items of the budget were in roughly the same proportion as those of the preceding budget.

The expenses of a family "in easy circumstance", consisting of the husband, the wife, two children and two servants, whose head could be either a petty clerk, the agent of a zamindar or a merchant, a petty shopkeeper or a "manufacturer", and in the village roughly an upper rayat (that is, something like a member of the lower section of the then middle classes), came to the following: housing—60 rupees; annual expenses—24 rupees; ritual utensils (5 items or units) and everyday utensils (30 items and 43 units)—$2\frac{3}{8}$ and 36 rupees, respectively; annual expenses—9 rupees 5 annas; bedding, carpets, etc.—$18\frac{1}{4}$ rupees; annual expenses—6 rupees 9 annas; ornaments— 53 rupees 6 annas; annual expenses—12 rupees 12 annas; clothing—$37\frac{1}{2}$ rupees; food—120 rupees a year; services—16 rupees; and religious expenses—48 rupees. Here the proportion of the items is different: of the 262 rupees, nearly one-half was spent on food, while the outlays on the work of artisans (71 rupees 5 annas) were almost one-half of the earlier figure. On the other hand, the outlays for religious purposes were relatively higher.

The expenses of an artisan's family in easy circumstances, consisting of the husband, the wife, two children and one relative, were: cost of premises—24 rupees and outlays on them—9 rupees 10 annas; household utensils—8 rupees 11 annas, annual expenses—2 rupees 1 anna; bedding—6 rupees 3 annas, annual expenses—3 rupees $1\frac{1}{2}$ annas; ornaments—11 rupees 1 anna, annual expenses—2 rupees 10 annas; clothing—17 rupees 12 annas; food—$5\frac{1}{2}$ rupees a month or 66 rupees a year, the monthly diet consisting of 2 maunds (76 kilogrammes) of rice (1 rupee 12 annas), 10 seers of pulses (3 annas), 4 seers of salt (7 annas), 5 seers of vegetable oil (half a rupee), fish and vegetables (1 rupee), tobacco and betel (half a rupee); barber's fee—12 annas; religious ceremonies—15 rupees a year. We find a further increase in the share of the outlays on food: 66 out of 90 rupees, and the outlays on the work of artisans only 18 rupees $6\frac{1}{2}$ annas. At the same time, there is a sharp drop also in the outlays for religious purposes, which could have been due to the low social and caste status of this group of the population.

The expenses of the family of an ordinary artisan, who had a wife and two children, were made up of the following items: cost of housing—5 rupees and maintenance expenses $2\frac{1}{4}$ rupees; utensils—2 rupees 11 annas and annual expenses 10 annas; bedding—9 annas a year; ornaments—1 rupee 3 annas and annual expenses 4 annas 6 pice; clothing (cost and annual expenses)—3 rupees 6 annas; food—$2\frac{1}{2}$ rupees a month (1.5 maunds of rice costing 1 rupee 5 annas, 12 seers of pulses costing 4 annas, 2 seers of oil costing 4 annas, 2 seers of salt costing 4 annas); barber once a month—half a rupee (clearly for one year); and religious ceremonies—2.6 rupees a year. According to the source, total annual expenses were $36\frac{1}{2}$ rupees. But our recalculation shows a larger amount: 44 rupees 13 annas, which is only one-half of that of the artisan in easy circumstances. Although the proportion of the items is roughly the same, their halving meant privation with malnutrition.

Finally, the property and expenses of a common labourer with a wife and two children came to the following: repair of hut—3 annas; payment for land plot—4 annas a year; utensils—3 annas; bedding—10 annas; ornaments—$1\frac{1}{2}$ annas a year; clothing—2 rupees 6 annas (the husband's dhoti—5 annas, shirt—4 annas, the wife's sari—8 annas, three wrappers—8 annas, four waists and two shirts for the children—12 annas; this poor Indian family's wardrobe was too small not to have been renewed every year); the food consisted of 1.5 seers of rice a day ($10\frac{1}{4}$ rupees a year), 1 seer of oil a month ($1\frac{1}{2}$ rupees a year), 6 seers of pulses a month ($1\frac{1}{2}$ rupees a year), salt $1\frac{1}{2}$ rupees a year, but many had to do with ash, tobacco and betel $1\frac{1}{2}$ rupees a year, all the food costing 16 rupees 10 annas a year; then came the outlays on the priests—2 rupees, and on the barber—half a rupee. The total annual expenses of these poorest families were estimated by Buchanan at 22 rupees 10 annas a year, that is, less than 2 rupees a month.[52]

Thus, as the Bengal consumer of material and spiritual goods descended the ladder of the proprietary and social hierarchy, he was forced to lower not only the quantity but also the quality of the goods he consumed, which was expressed in the reduction of the share of handicraft articles and their assortment, and a drop in their quality. That is why the poorest sections were best prepared for the consumption of the low-cost mass-produced British goods. But at the same time, their purchasing power was insignificant. Taking as the basis the landless population of the countryside (about 300,000 families) and adding to these the urban poor (at least 50,000 families), we find that these two-thirds of the population of Dinajpur could buy (with about 3 rupees per family a year) manufactured goods worth less than 1 million rupees. That is why it was possible to extend the market to any considerable degree only by catering for the better-off sections, where British products had to complete with handicraft articles, which were manufactured up to the traditional and high standard, which in some cases was quite refined.

Thus, after Bengal's first half-century under the yoke of foreign merchant's capital its main socio-economic indicators may have changed but not towards any qualitatively new formational shift. The British invaders, having established themselves on the upper tier of the social hierarchy of Bengal society, exerted a backwash effect on many aspects of economic life. But on the whole, the social mechanism continued to function in all its principal internal inter-connections. The inclusion of the British merchants in this mechanism through commodity-money channels was slowed down by the British administrative and tax system itself, for it extracted a large part of the product of agriculture and the handicrafts, which could have become an object of free alienation through the market and the basis of growing effective demand—and, what is most important, of relatively standard demand—among broad masses of the producing population.

Bihar: Use of Land and Its Cultivation; National Product, Conditions of Handicraft Production, Trade and Credit

The transformation of traditional socio-economic relations in Bihar in the early 19th century was, one would think, even less profound than it was in contemporaneous Bengal, and this may be due to two factors: first, the fact that the British had done less to establish administrative and commercial control over that area, and, second, the greater durability of Hindu caste bonds, especially in the rural areas. The first factor springs from the fact that Bengal was conquered long before, while Bihar lies far away from the seaports; the second factor is confirmed by an examination of socio-economic relations in the Bihar countryside.

On the eve of the British conquest, there were three categories of tenants (more accurately, holders of land) in Bihar: the head rayats of villages; the rayats of the hudkasht type and the vast majority of tenants not included in these two groups. That is the conclusion drawn by S. N. Sinha on the basis of the data of the British tax administration, Colebrooke's data, Hunter'a later publications, and other similar testimonies. The Indian investigator lists the sources of enrichment which were opened up before the head rayats of villages by their status as tax-collectors in their villages, but says nothing substantial about the scale on which they carried on their own husbandry; land-holders under the right of hudkasht enjoyed its use by succession (provided they paid the fixed tax), while the rent paid by the other tenants was periodically reviewed.[53] Apart from these three higher categories of land-holders who leased their land directly from the zamindar, there were in Bengal and Bihar numerous subtenants and also day labourers hired to cultivate the lands of the rayats of the two main categories.

The principle of land-holding apart, tenants were divided according to property and social prestige into four categories: (1) ashrafs, (2) traders and milkmen, (3) chasa, or ploughmen, and (4) colats, or under-tenants. This classification, which has been borrowed from Buchanan, it not consistent in its grounds, which include caste, production and land indicators. S. N. Sinha accepts Buchanan's view that the ashrafs of Bihar did not keep ploughs, although they were allowed to engage in some operations, with the exception of the ploughing of land. The next two groups of tenants, while not enjoying a number of land privileges held out to the ashrafs, were frequently richer than the latter and had better farms. British land policy in the 1830s and 1840s helped to convert the hereditary land-holders, especially those of the hudkasht category into tenants-at-will.[54]

Unfortunately, S. N. Sinha gives no information about the husbandry of certain sections of the Bihar countryside, about their productive and consumer demands, market and direct connections with manufactures, and also about the activity there of merchant's and usurer's capital. Meanwhile, information about these aspects of life in the Bihar countryside may be gleaned from Buchanan's descriptions. Thus, he describes various types of land-tenure and husbandry in the countryside of the districts of Bihar and Patna. The ashrafs paid rent only for cultivated land, the amount being fixed by agreement with the zamindar landlords and well below the rent paid by the other categories of cultivators. One is left with the impression that the ashrafs enjoyed priority in leasing land directly from the zamindars, a privilege possibly due to the fact that they were a military stratum and, says Buchanan, before the establishment of British rule engaged in armed plunder, so that the zamindars' security depended on their numerical strength and loyalty.

At the same time, the ashrafs did not shun farming, with the exception of ploughing, because custom forbade them to lay hands on a plough; but it was the ashrafs who were the owners of the ploughs and the draught animals. With three sets of implements, an ashraf could lease from 30 to 40 acres of land, which brought him 190 rupees of income a year. The land was cultivated mainly by village servant-ploughmen, their wives and other members of the family. These lower sections of the countryside were rewarded with grain and in some instances with cash and a small plot which they cultivated by means of their master's implements.[55] The very durable communal traditions in Bihar led to a situation in which the local zamindars were as yet incapable of so oppressing the countryside, especially its "well-born" èlite, as they had done in Bengal. In this context, one of Buchanan's observations is very interesting. He wrote: "The tenants of Behar in general transact their own business with the agents of the Zemindars, and it is only among the rude tribe called Saungtar, and in the Bengalese parts of the district, that a kind of chief tenant is employed to transact the whole affairs of the community, a practice as I have mentioned that is common in Ronggopur, and which seems to have been once pretty universal in India; for the chiefs of villages, by whatever name (Mandal, Makaddam, Gauda, Shanaboga, etc.) known, seem to me to have been originally agents for the tenants, and not officers of government, or assistants of the Zemindars, as is now usually the case; and wherever the native customs have been carefully preserved, and well administered, the appointment of their officer is always regulated by the inclination of the tenantry. In Behar, as I have said, the tenantry have more confidence.... The Bengalese are more bashful; and it is only the Mandal that is gifted with the faculty of speech before a person of such consequence as the village clerk (Patwari); nor is it supposed that each Mandal should have audacity enough to find utterance before his landlord; so that on estates of any size there is a chief Mandal, who is spokesman for the others."[56]

The extent of economic differentiation in the Bihar countryside will be seen in part from the distribution of the farming implements among the various sections of the rural population. Thus, in the divisions of Purnea district the ploughs were distributed as follows (in shares): in Haveli "persons who rent land" had $\frac{3}{8}$, "those who cultivate for a share" $\frac{1}{4}$, "the servants and slaves" $\frac{1}{8}$ the under-tenants $\frac{1}{16}$, the servants of athoyars $\frac{3}{16}$; in Dangrkhora the figures were respectively $\frac{5}{8}, \frac{9}{32}, \frac{1}{32}, \frac{1}{32}$ and $\frac{1}{32}$; in Gondwara, $\frac{35}{64}, \frac{1}{16}, \frac{1}{4}$ 0 and $\frac{1}{8}$; in Dhamdaha, $\frac{21}{32}, \frac{1}{32}, \frac{1}{4}$, 0 and $\frac{1}{32}$, in Behadganj, $\frac{1}{2}, \frac{5}{16}, \frac{1}{8}, \frac{1}{16}$ and 0; in Krishnaganj, $\frac{1}{8}, \frac{5}{8}, \frac{1}{8}, \frac{1}{8}$ and 0.[57] We find that the higher tenants, that is, those leasing land directly from the zamindars, appear to be, even if not always, the strongest economic group. Now and again, however, the share of the lower sections in the countryside is fairly considerable as well.

In Purnea, as in Dinajpur, it was common usage among "poor farmers" to pool their implements in order to provide themselves with everything necessary for ploughing. This observation indirectly contradicts Buchanan's own assertion that in Purnea the cost of farming implements was trifling and was roughly similar to that in Dinajpur, and that in the northwest of the district, where the plough had no iron tip, it was altogether insignificant. He insisted that on the lands along the Ganges no ploughing was done at all. This may have implied the cultivation of light alluvial soils, which, did not, in effect, require any ploughing for a number of years and were only subjected to harrowing before sowing. The pooling of the implements may have been due to the extreme poverty of the lower sections, for whom even the "trifling" cost was exorbitant, and also the shortage of bullocks on the individual farms, especially in view of the fact that in Purnea ploughing (possibly when fallow land was upturned) had to be done with six bullocks.

The following data give an idea of the productivity and remuneration of agricultural labour. A ploughman with a boy-driver tilled with one plough pulled by six bullocks a plot of 45 local bighas, that is, 6 hectares. The grain yield was valued at 104 rupees 2 annas. Taking the price of unhulled rice in Purnea to be the same as in Rangpur (at 1 rupee for 115 kilogrammes), the crop yield may have come to 20 centners per hectare, so that the two cultivators—the man and the boy— could cope with a plot yielding 120 centners of rice.

But the production costs were not confined to the ploughing. The ploughing itself cost $37\frac{1}{2}$ rupees (with $\frac{9}{15}$ going into the maintenance of the bullocks, $\frac{4}{15}$ to pay the ploughman and $\frac{1}{15}$ each to the boy and to cover the cost of the impleaments, or in absolute figures: $22\frac{1}{2}$, 10, $2\frac{1}{2}$ and $2\frac{1}{2}$ rupees, respectively). The weeding and thinning were paid in grain worth 5 and $1\frac{1}{4}$ rupees. In addition, the seed cost $4\frac{1}{3}$ rupees, thus the cost of sowing came to $46\frac{1}{4}$ rupees. The outlays on harvesting and threshing were fixed at 1/7 of the harvest's value, which means here about 15 rupees. As a result, 42 rupees 14 annas was left for rent and income, or about 40 per cent of the gross product.[58] The structure of the price of grain was made up of the following elements: outlays on bullocks, seed and implements 28 per cent, payment of labour 32.4 per cent, and rent about 40 per cent. Here, the outlays on implements came to $\frac{1}{16}$ or $\frac{1}{17}$ of the rent.

Let us note that the area (6 hectares) cultivated in Purnea by the above-mentioned productive unit was three times as large as the "labour allotment" in neighbouring Dinajpur (2 hectares). The explanation will apparently be found in the fact that in the first instance it is the area which could be worked with one operation (ploughing), and, in addition, with the use of six bullocks (which, naturally, could not be kept on a plot of 2 hectares). The ploughing was followed by labour-intensive operations like weeding, thinning and harvesting. These could have never been carried out on a rice field of 6 hectares by one peasant family (two or three able-bodied persons). That is why Buchanan's example of productivity may apply only to the husbandry of the top section, where it was possible to concentrate and cooperate both the production funds (the bullocks in the first place) and the manpower of the lower sections. In other words, these calculations go once again to confirm that the husbandry of the upper sections ensured a higher rate of surplus-product than the efforts of the tenant on his "labour allotment" of 2 hectares.

But the transition to rural enterprise, apart from the restraining elements of traditional origin, was also blocked by rent obligations, and these, for their part, engendered indebtedness, a form of dependence which also spread to sections inclined to enterprise. In

Purnea, a large share of every type of produce—grain, milk, cocoons, indigo, etc.—"is usually spent before the person who rears it has brought it to market, so that the system of advances is carried to full as great an extent as in Dinajpur and a large share of the farmers, high and low, could not carry on cultivation without receiving them. A large proportion of the farmers are in debt, chiefly to merchants of various kinds who make advances for their produce, silk, indigo, grain and butter. The quantity of arrears of rent is considerable and the total loss by a deficiency of payment to the landlord is very trifling. Formerly, it is said, this loss was very heavy; when harvest came, the tenant could not sell his grain, and was under necessity of running away."[59] Buchanan says this was due to the fact that after the 1770 famine the numerical strength of the population had been re-established, and the demand for agricultural produce had increased. Thus, under the normal functioning of the existing system of rent and tax extraction, the ways to agricultural enterprise were blocked.

The total product raised on the cultivated land in the district of Purnea was valued (by the tax authorities, it would appear) at 21,100,000 rupees. Of these, the outlays on cultivation, Buchanan assumes, took up one-half, while one-quarter made up the tenant's net profit, the remaining one-quarter being, in his opinion, something like the amount of claims which the zamindar could reasonably lay. However, the revenues of the zamindars were multiplied by income from tax-free lands.

This amount and the proportions between its components are no more than approximate and preliminary if only because the very concept of "tenant"was extremely broad. Buchanan describes the basic categories of tenants as follows: from the actual owner of the land, who paid a small fixed rent to the zamindar, to the majority of the tenants who used the land under short-term contracts and, with rare exceptions, cultivated it themselves.[60] That is why the line between the outlays on the cultivation of land and the tenant's net income was very indefinite. The latter item frequently went to cover production costs, being partially added to the rent receipts, which with the addition of income from tax-free lands were clearly in excess of one-third of the agricultural product.

But for our purposes the important thing is not so much to specify these values as to compare them in general with the value of the handicraft product in the district of Purnea. Weaving, the major manufacture, turned out goods worth 1,600,000 rupees, of which the yarn cost over 1,100,000 rupees.[61] Thus, the components of the cloth price created by the labour of the artificer came to 600,000-700,000 rupees (3-3.5 per cent of the value of the agricultural product). Consequently, the surplus-product created by the weavers was not to be compared, either relatively or absolutely, with the product of agriculture.

The output of sugar-cane products in Bihar was also a direct continuation of the agricultural process. In the district of Shahabad the installation for the pressing and boiling of sugar-cane juice handled in a three-month season up to 4,725 seers, or 9,700 pounds (about 4,400 kilogrammes) of juice worth 176 rupees (that is, at 1 rupee for about 25 kilogrammes of juice), which suggests, perhaps, that gur was involved here and elsewhere. The outlays on equipment and the maintenance of four bullocks came to 14 rupees or 364 seers of juice (in kind)—under 8 per cent of the value of the original product. Each of the seven workers received $1\frac{1}{4}$ seers of juice a day, a total of 787 seers for the season, that is, under 16.7 per cent of the product. The other outlays consisted of the cost of the cane and the installation owner's profit.

In other words, here again the agricultural component clearly prevailed. But the source makes no mention of the owner of the installation. This may have been, as was the custom in India, the owner of the plot on which the sugar-cane was grown. An area of 6.4 acres (about 2.6 hectares) was required to grow sugar-cane to operate an installation in the course of a season.[62] Calculations show that one hectare of the crop yielded a product worth 45-50 rupees a year, or about 1,300 kilogrammes of gur.

In the neighbouring district of Patna, the structure of expenditures and incomes of those who owned installations for processing sugar-cane was the following: in the course of a month each of these produced 100 mans (8,234 pounds or 3,730 kilogrammes) of juice, which cost 100 rupees. The cost of processing consisted of the following items: transportation of the juice to the boiling vats 2 rupees; the cost of the vats 2 rupees 6 annas; fuel (manure) 4 rupees; pay for two workers 4 rupees; milk added in the boiling of the juice 2 rupees; plant used to condense sugar from the solution 2 rupees; rent for premises 2 rupees; packaging 1 rupee; and the owner's profit 29 rupees 10 annas; a total of 149. Against these outlays was the cost of the product: 50 mans (1,865 kilogrammes) of molasses 27 rupees; 30 mans (1,190 kilogrammes) of treacle 20 rupees; 17 mans (403.4 kilogrammes) of sugar 102 rupees; a total of 149 rupees. The season here continued for five months; the income of the establishment in that period came to 148 rupees, and together with the profits from the refining of sugar up to 160 rupees.[63]

We find, therefore, that there were definite distinctions in the activity of those who made sugar-cane products. One is left with the impression that the installation at Shahabad belonged to a land-owner and operated close to the field where the cane was grown. Evidence of this also comes from the large number of workmen (seven instead of two), some of whom could have been employed in the harvesting and delivery of the cane; they were also paid for their work in kind (juice), there is no information about the owner's profits, and the price of the juice is lower. In another district, the owner who bought sugar-cane and dried manure for fuel from the "farmers" was a petty entrepreneur, who carried on industrial production on his own, apparently in urban conditions. But there again the cost of the agricultural components came to three-quarters of the cost of sugar production. The entrepreneur's income could be classed as capitalist profit only with some doubt, because in annual terms they came to only about 13-14 rupees a month, which put the family in easy circumstances but did not provide the necessary basis for capital accumulation and extended reproduction.

The agricultural component in the cost of soap was also very large. In Shahabad, one lot of raw material (the process lasted four days) yielded roughly 45 kilogrammes of soap valued at 7 rupees $2\frac{1}{2}$ annas. Of these, 5 rupees went for fat and vegetable oil (about 70 per cent), 1 rupee 4 annas for soda, 4 annas for fuel and only $8\frac{1}{2}$ annas as pay for the artisan. When fully employed, he could earn 3 rupees 11 annas a month, but he hardly ever received more than 3 rupees.

The agricultural component in the price of vegetable oil was even larger. Thus, in the early 19th century, oil-pressers in Bihar processed $3\frac{1}{4}$ annas' worth of linseed a day, which yielded 4 anna's worth of oil and 1 anna's worth of cake. Thus the artisan earned $1\frac{3}{4}$ annas a day or not more than 3 rupees a month. But this amount also had to cover the maintenance of a bullock that set the press in motion, and the expenses for the repair of the latter. Because the bullock was fed on oil-cake, the artisan's earnings were reduced, and the share of the agricultural component in the cost of the product actually sold increased.

These data go once again to confirm my assumption that the peasants received from the handicrafts through the medium of commodity-money relations a product with a very large agricultural component. In other words, exchange in kind actually prevailed in what appeared to be commodity-money relations.

This also applied to cheap cloths which reached the countryside. Cotton, a purely agricultural product, already prevailed in the cost of the yarn. The very low pay of the women spinners added a relatively small share to the price of the yarn. Thus, according to Buchanan's calculations, there were about 160,000 spinners in Shahabad with an average annual output of 8 rupees per spinner. The cost of the cotton and its swingling apart, a spinner's net income came to $1\frac{1}{2}$ rupees a year.[64] Buchanan also estimates that in the districts of Gaya and Patna spinners earned $3\frac{1}{2}$ rupees. In the Bengal district of Dinajpur the spinners earned 4 annas a month or 3 rupees a year.[65] But even these additions to the cost resulted mainly from the efforts of the peasant women.

Weaving, the final operation, was carried on by professional craftsmen, but even then the agricultural component continued to prevail. Thus, in some areas of the district of Purnea the annual output of coarse cloth per loom was as follows (rupees and annas):[66]

Division	*Cost of cloth*	*Cost of yarn*
Sibgung[67]	112 8	73 2
Bhunis	120 0	82 8
Dangrkhora	112 0	68 0
Dulalgung	112 0	84 0
Bahadurgung	84 0	60 0
Gondwara	120 0	88 8
Haveli	120 0	97 8
Krishnagang	120 0	90 0
Dhamdaha	76 8	42 12
	1,089 0	765 8

Thus, the average output of cloth per loom came to 109 rupees a year, with about 43 rupees a year or $31\frac{1}{2}$ rupees a month going to pay for the work of the weaver and members of his family. Weaving in the district of Shahabad (Bihar) gives similar figures. Here, the annual average output per weaver was worth 78 rupees, of which the income of his family came to just ever 20 rupees.[68] Although the cost of the product and the incomes were smaller than in Purnea, the proportions were the same.

Judging by Buchanan's data, the conditions of workers in the spinning and weaving industries of Bihar in the first decade of the 19th century continued to worsen. The earnings of spinners, who turned out the lowest grades of yarn, dropped to $10\frac{1}{2}$ annas a month or by 20-40 per cent. But those who suffered most were the skilled women who produced the higher grades of yarn. Their earnings fell to $14\frac{1}{2}$ annas as compared with the 2-3 rupees 10 years earlier. This must have been due especially to the effect of the falling demand for costly cloths into which the yarn went. The earnings of weavers also declined somewhat, to $2 - 2\frac{1}{2}$ rupees a month.

It is interesting to note that Buchanan made his own calculations on the structure of the price of yarn and cloth, and that these were close to those given above. He held that in Purnea district 1,300 rupees' worth of yarn was produced every year, with the higher grades of yarn worth 357,000 rupees, and the cost of cotton not more than ten per cent of the amount. Incidentally, this percentage is minimised, for Buchanan also gives in the same place the ratio of 1:16 and even 1:17.5. The cost of coarse yarn was estimated at 947,000 rupees, of which he believed one half to cover the purchase of cotton.[69]

Nearly 160,000 women were employed in spinning in the district of Bhagalpur, each handling 34 pounds (15.3 kilogrammes) of cotton a year worth 11 rupees $1\frac{1}{2}$ annas, of which the cost of the cotton was 6 rupees $9\frac{1}{4}$ annas, and the wages 4 rupees $8\frac{1}{4}$ annas a year.

In the same district, there were 6,212 houses of weavers with 7,279 looms. The yarn came to $\frac{5}{7}$ of the cost of the cloth. However, the weavers worked not more than 10 months a year, the rest of the time performing as musicians, especially at weddings. That is why with an output of 7 rupees' worth a month, they turned out an annual product worth 70 rupees, of which 20 rupees constituted their income. Together with the money earned by their wives and by themselves as musicians (mainly in the form of food), the weavers received $2\frac{1}{2} - 3$ rupees a month.[70]

In the district of Patna, over 330,000 female spinners produced 2,367,000 rupees' worth of yarn a year. Subtracting the cost of the cotton (1,286,000 rupees), there remained the amount of their earnings: 1,081,000 rupees or an average of $3\frac{1}{4}$ rupees per spinner a year. But behind these averages were great discrepancies between the women, who spun in their spare time, when not engaged in their household and other chores, and the professional spinners, who turned out the higher grades of yarn.[71]

The distinctions between the weavers of the district in terms of skill and quality of cloth did not result in any differentiation in incomes. Buchanan gives the figure of 28 rupees as the average annual income of a weaver of any experience. He says this was due to the system of advance payments, which was inevitable in the ordering of costly cloths, producing indifference to the making "to a greater value". The system of advance payments, says Buchanan, was absolutely unnecessary, but it was being maintained by all the native dealers because it helped to keep "the workmen in a state of dependence little better, if so good, as slavery."[72] However, the weavers were plunged into such dependence not only by native dealers but also by agents of the East India Company. An advance payment to a weaver meant that he was forbidden to sell his goods to anyone before he fulfilled the Company's order.

The condition of jewellers in Patna goes once again to confirm the rule that the use of costly semi-finished products usually went to increase the dependence of Indian artisans on dealers. Buchanan noted that jewellers had no other capital apart from their tools. The merchants supplied the material and paid the workers depending on the quantity of labour.[73] The jeweller's earnings were very low, from 2 to 4 annas a day.

The workshops making palanquins and carriages in the district of Bhagalpur were something midway between a primitive manufactory and a workmen's team. There were about 30 such workshops in the centre of the district and about 40 in Monghyr. In each workshop there were from two to ten workers. Sometimes the master hired them and supplied them with materials and tools, on other occasions all the workers were partners. The working men were paid $1\frac{1}{2}$ – 2 annas a day, that is, $2\frac{1}{2}$ – $3\frac{1}{2}$ rupees a month. Three workshops in Bhagalpur and five in Monghyr had property worth between 1,000 and 3,000 rupees.

In Bhagalpur, charcoal was used by blacksmiths in Monghyr and iron-makers in Birbhum, and also exported to Jangipur and Murshidabad. Birbhum alone received up to 350,000 mans of coal (at 60 pounds a man, that is, about 11,000 tons) every year. The coal was produced by mountain tribes from whom it was purchased by petty traders and peasants owning carts, and sold in Birbhum at 1 rupee for 5-6 mans (135150 kilogrammes).

The makers of alcoholic drinks stood out among the artisans in terms of welfare. In Bhagalpur each made up to 60 bottles a day, which were sold for 1 rupee 13 annas, or 54 rupees a month. The costs were: 12 rupees for flour, 2 rupees 13 annas for fuel, 2 rupees to pay for the assistant, 155 annas for pots and 15 rupees for tax, leaving 21 rupees 10 annas as income.[74]

Buchanan mentions 90 paper-making installations in Shahabad, which belonged to 60 houses. Each turned out an average of 275 rupees' worth of paper a year, which came in four grades. Of this amount 137 rupees went for raw material, 16 rupees for fuel, $14\frac{1}{2}$ rupees for various parts of the equipment, $164\frac{3}{4}$ rupees for wages, and $41\frac{3}{8}$ rupees for profits,[75] that is, $3\frac{1}{2}$ rupees a month, which was not enough to class the owner as a petty capitalist. Meanwhile, judging by the components which went to make up the amount going into the payment of labour, these establishments had a detailed division of labour. Thus, each of the four permanent labourers preparing the raw materials received 25 rupees a year. Temporary operations were paid for separately: the stirring of the flour paste 12 rupees, polishing, cutting and packaging 10 rupees, shaping of the sheets by the craftsmen 25 rupees, hanging of the sheets on walls for drying 6 rupees, and three lesser operations about 10 rupees.

Buchanan asserts that the shaping of the sheets was done by the owner himself, and the mixing of the paste, polishing cutting and drying were done by the women and children of his own family. In that case, the family's total income increased to 100 rupees a year, which was two or three times higher than the earnings of ordinary artisans. These establishments were apparently somewhere between a large family workshop and a primitive capitalist manufactory. But the houses which had more than one installation could be confidently classed as petty capitalist enterprise.

Let us recall that Marx has the following observation about the paper industry as a subject of analysis: "In the paper industry generally we may advantageously study in detail not only the distinctions between modes of production based on different means of production, but also the connection of the social conditions of production with those modes: for the old German paper-making furnishes us with a sample of handicraft production; that of Holland in the 17th and of France in the 18th century with a sample of manufacturing in the strict sense; and that of modern England with a sample of automatic fabrication of this article. Besides, there still exist in India and China two distinct antique Asiatic forms of the same industry."[76]

For the Bihar districts, we do not have detailed data on the commodity structure of wholesale trade, but even there the prevalence of agricultural products is obvious. In the district of Purnea, the grain trade was very considerable; wheat was exported to Murshidabad in the East, and rice came in from Dinajpur and Nepal. But Buchanan gives no information about the methods by which the grain was extracted from the local rural population and sold on the market. This operation may have also been performed at the final stage through the merchants, who resorted to loans. The major grain traders in the district were called "Goldar mahajan" and were divided into two groups: Gharla and Bhusi. Of the seven banking houses of Purnea, two were branches of Murshidabad bankers —Jagat Seth and Lala Maghraj—and five were local bankers. The first two houses discounted and issued bills (up to 100,000 rupees), while the local bankers did business with land-owners, "keeping their rents, and discharging the taxes". Apart from this commercial and banking élite in Purnea, there were numerous communities and sub-castes of traders, shopkeepers, peddlers of the most diverse types and ranges of goods.[77]

Among the merchants of Bhagalpur, the grain merchants, the Goldars, were also prominent, and were followed by traders in cloths ("four houses of Moghuls from the West" imported goods worth 100,000 rupees) and importers of cotton. The retail trade, in which artisans of every trade were involved, was also specialised, as it was in Purnea. The lines of banking activity in the two districts also coincided. Their capital averaged 10,000-15,000 rupees. Each trade had a head who received small contributions from the members of his group, representing it before the authorities, regulating the cost of labour and articles, settling disputes and securing the necessary deliveries of articles during the passage of troops or the arrival of high-ranking persons. Although the British authorities did not give formal recognition to the rights of these heads, the latter retained their traditional status and power.[78] Still, the zamindar was in a position to erect a shed in the market-place, declare it the only place of trade and exact taxes from the sellers for the use of the place.

In Shahabad, the wholesale trade in grain was carried on by merchants who had a capital of up to 500,000 rupees. There were also considerable numbers of wholesalers in other lines. A group of merchants with capitals ranging from 1,000 to 25,000 rupees annually sent luxuries, costly cloths and salt to Ramgarh (Southern Bihar) worth 300,000 rupees. Together with overland trade Shahabad engaged in trade along the rivers. Some 560-570 boats with an average carrying capacity of 400 mans arrived in the district every year, carrying salt, rice, sackcloth and betel nuts, and taking out grain, blankets, vegetable oil and ghee. It is noteworthy that traders specialising in the sale of some handicraft goods had smaller capitals.

Thus, importers of paper operated with a capital of from 500 to 3,000 rupees. Cloth dealers had an even smaller capital: from 20 to 1,000 rupees, but then they numbered several hundred. Small-scale retail selling of cheap cloths for local markets must have prevailed in this line. Traders in footwear had 100-125 rupees, in metal dishes 20-200 rupees, in iron and tin from 5 to 30 rupees. Artisans of every trade sold their wares directly from their workshops: the soap makers had 15 establishments, the makers of glass ornaments 22, perfumery-makers 40, blacksmiths 54, potters 63, weavers 70, cotton swinglers 74, etc.

Shahabad's credit system rested on the mahajans, who made loans to the rural population and received in return the payment of debt and interest in grain. Their capital ranged from 500 to 30,000 rupees. In the early 19th century, these practices were still going on in the district: local bankers paid in almost all the tax in advance, while the tahsildars had agents who received the money due as tax and loaned it out on interest. On the average, the banker's capital fluctuated within the limits of 20,000-30,000 rupees, but the biggest of them had 400,000 rupees.

The structure of the trading and banking community in an ordinary district like Shahabad was sufficiently complicated both in terms of proprietary differentiation among its members and in occupational specialisation. The personal capital of village mahajans was not great: from 100 to 2,000 rupees, but it was said that over one-third of the rent in the district was paid with money borrowed from them.[79] Buchanan suggests that in Britain they could be called trading farmers, because they combined farming with money-lending (including grain loans) and trade. Special bepari traders handled the carriage of goods. Among them there were simple cart-owners who had several bullocks, and also persons with a capital between 500 and 5,000 rupees, who traded with Patna and Benares. The small shopkeepers bought grain from the bepari and sold it to the population. Their capital usually varied from 4 to 25 rupees, but some had 200 rupees.

The diversity of weights and measures was an additional factor which helped the trading community to build up its positions. In the Shahabad district, every town had its own weight: this meant the number of sikkas in a seer, and the number of seers in a maund. The seer usually contained 44 sikkas or 11,393 pounds, but some contained up to 88 sikkas. The maund contained from 40 to 52 seers. The measures of length and area were just as different.[80]

Information about the population in the central districts of Bihar in the early 19th century (Patna and Zillah-Bihar) gives the most general picture of the main elements of its social structure. Of the 3,364,000 population, over one-quarter (935,000) belonged to gentry, 92,000 to the traders, 242,000 to the artisans, and 2,094,000 to the ploughmen or day labourers. Of course, these figures are largely tentative: the borderlines between these groups were frequently vague, for some merchant and bankers were classed among the gentry, while the rural artisans connected with farming were not always easily distinguished from the ploughmen, etc. Still, the trading and handicraft population, making up a total of 10 per cent, came to only one-third of the size of the gentry, while the agricultural population was just over 62 per cent.[81]

Buchanan gives highly remarkable information about the structure and employment of the upper Hindu castes and the privileged groups of Muslims—the core of the gentry. For these two districts there were 25,890 persons who were born to use the pen; of these, 12,975 were employed, while 15,215 remained idle. Of the persons born to use the sword 1,150 persons were in the regular army, 11,452 served in the police and the tax agencies, while 28,630 were not employed under the British regime.

The following figures give an idea of the social and occupational structure of the population in the town of Patna. Of its total population of 312,000 people, 138,000 were gentry, 30,000 were traders, 78,000 were artisans, and 66,000 were ploughmen and day labourers.[82] Let me add that Buchanan gives his figures for Greater Patna, which includes the suburbs.[83] This explains the fairly high percentage of the agricultural population. As for the gentry, their numbers were not substantially increased by the enlargement of the urban limits, because they resided in the town proper (which evoked Buchanan's surprise, for he preferred the suburban residences to the over-crowded city). The attraction of the gentry to the urban centre was apparently due to their desire to be closer to their places of employment: the offices, the garrison, the temples and mosques (the higher sections of the Muslims were included among the gentry). The employment among the gentry will be seen from the following figures: of the 7,700 persons born to wield the pen, 3,300 found employment; and of the 4,400 born to use the sword, only 200 persons were enrolled in the Company's troops, 2,800 worked in the police and the tax agencies while 3,800 members of the military castes were idle in this colonial town of the post-despotism period.[84]

Profound diversification of the handicrafts and the services was characteristic of Patna, as it was of any major town in Mogul India. Buchanan names 147 urban branches and trades (altogether the district had 158). Most people were engaged in weaving: 23,400 in the town and 330,400 in the whole district. But with some exceptions, weaving was not a permanent occupation but a sideline. This becomes evident, by the way, from the fact that the number of women spinners was much greater than the whole handicraft population of the district. Of the handicraft trades proper, weavers prevailed—2,692 looms (the whole district had nearly 26,000); carpet-makers—128 looms in the town (209 in the district); blanket-makers—45 (564); tailors—258 (900); potters—350 (2,900); goldsmiths—583 (2,283); owners of oil-making establishments—881 (5,466); makers of sweetmeats—270 (1, 705), leather-dressers and cobblers—496 (3,543); brick-makers (probably, the owners of establish-ments)—47 (192); stonemasons—600 (990); carpenters making crude furniture and farming implements—441

(3,128), blacksmiths—209 (1,732) and armourers—30 (109).

Thus, the town of Patna does not appear to be the leading centre of manufacture in the district for any of the main handicrafts trades, with the exception of stonemasons (whose numbers in the district may have been understated). It is true that the data for the district also include the artisans of the town of Gaya, an all-India centre of pilgrimage, but even if we add the number of artisans in Patna and in the district of Gaya (there are no separate data for the latter town), we find a prevalence of artisans from the predominantly rural areas over their urban fellows. Only for some of the narrowly specialised branches turning out luxuries did Patna have a monopoly of production. Let us note that Patna did not concentrate within its limits any manufactures of considerable scale. Thus, and this is quite understandable, all the 36 sugar-boiling establishments and 7 indigo enterprises of the district were situated outside the town limits. Of the 64 paper-making enterprises in the district, only three were in Patna, and of the 481 distilleries, only 22.[85]

The prevalence in the town of the non-productive sections of the population, the relatively small share of its artisans in the total artisan population of the district (less than one-third), with a higher norm of consumption of handicraft products by the townsfolk, gave Patna a commodity deficit. The town imported goods worth 6,500,000 rupees and exported 3,260,000 rupees' worth, with some of the goods exported undoubtedly being transit goods. The Gaya area also had a trade deficit (imports 111,500, exports 29,000, deficit 82,500 rupees), but there 100,000 pilgrims and their companions annually spent vast amounts of money, quite apart from their costly offerings and gifts.

Those are some of the facts about manufactures in the districts of Bengal and Bihar in the early 19th century and their place in the social division of labour and social structure. I believe that they are also of additional interest because they refer to a period when the relations described were still largely to be seen as commonplace for the Mogul past of these districts. At the same time, they help to draw a conclusion about the stability of the pre-capitalist forms of social and economic life after a half-century of political domination by British merchant's capital.

The first thing that leaps to the eye is the fact that British capital was alien and did not mesh with the system of relations of production in India. Having established supreme ownership of land, it placed, only as an exception, some of its representatives as landlords with the rights of large-scale Indian zamindar holdings or those of the British private-property type. Nor was this a matter of the conquerors' being considerate, for in some instances they did not even have to resort to involved legal casuistry to take over the land because many zamindars in Bengal and Bihar were either their military adversaries or had failed to pay dutifully the land-tax. The main reason for the insignificance of British private land-ownership should apparently be seen in the organic integration of land and personal relations in India, in the fact that the hierarchy of the various sections of cultivators and land-owners was superimposed on the caste and community pyramid of the Indian society, with which it made up a single functional system.

Let us note that although earlier invaders had been alien in ethnic and religious communal terms, that had not been an obstacle to their penetration of the Indian system of social and land relations. Muslims of Turkic or Afghan origin successfully fulfilled all the functions of the zamindar (including the purchase of string for Brahmans) in the Hindu areas of Bengal or Bihar. There is also much confirmation in the sources of the presence of big Hindu or Sikh landlords in the predominantly Muslim parts of North India (chiefly according to the make-up of the rural élite and the cultivators). Of course, this discrepancy frequently served as a pretext for action against the upper sections belonging to other religions and ethnic groups, but their supplanting by native upper sections merely meant, in effect, a change in personal and group representation.

It was quite a different situation when the zamindar was an Englishman, representing a higher, capitalist society and being a member of the bourgeoisie—a higher product of this society in social, if not historical, terms—of which the Indian society was not yet aware. Of course, a reasonable bourgeois Englishman could "retreat into the historical past" and nominally exercise the functions of a feudal zamindar. But he was incapable of entering into the traditional personal relations with his subordinates in a zamindar establishment, let alone the toiling men, without converting these relations into a farce in action and a mockery in form. That is why there was no personal penetration by the British of the system of land relations in India. The lands made available to the British in the last quarter of the 19th century for tea plantations in the Himalaya foothills lay in areas that were virgin soil in social terms, and were not involved in the mature systems of India's land relations.

In whatever capacity, the British were vehicles of a different type of legal consciousness and a different legal order. No amount of study of Indian laws could turn a British administrator into a keeper of traditions in the eyes of the native establishment. But that was a society whose relations of production and the corresponding mode of production were in a state under which, as Marx put it, "tradition must play a dominant role.... It is furthermore clear that here as always it is in the interests of the ruling section of the society to sanction the existing order as law and to legally establish its limits given through usage and tradition. Apart from all else, this, by the way, comes about of itself as soon as the constant reproduction on the basis of the existing order and its fundamental relations assumes a regulated and orderly form in the course of time. And such regulation and order are themselves indispensable elements of any mode of production, if it is to assume social stability and independence from mere chance and arbitrariness."[86]

British merchant's capital had apparently no opportunity and did not ever intend to introduce in India the new, capitalist mode of production, nor was it capable of establishing the regulation and order designed to consolidate this mode of production. Moreover, its administrative, legal and political apparatus had to reckon with the form of social consolidation of the existing system of pre-capitalist relations which it found in the conquered country. That is why our old formula about British colonialism "conserving feudal relations (or survivals)" is incorrect in the sense that it invests with vigour and consciousness the actions of the British administration which actually amounted to a kind of conformity, an adaptation by the violator to the subject of violence.

Indeed, it is the regulation and order inherent in the social consolidation of the Oriental despotism, like the Great Mogul Empire, that signified the relative emancipation of traditional Indian society from the arbitrariness of the British conquest. Having seized the upper tier of the superstructure of this society, and the right to appropriate the rent-tax, British merchant's capital proved to be incapable of overcoming the resistance of the system of the underlying socio-economic relations and of destroying their well-regulated, constant and systematic character.

It is in the light of Marx's idea that one should also consider the very limited scope of the intrusion by British merchant's capital into the sphere of India's internal goods exchange or, to comprehend it by means of a more essential causal category, into the system of the social division of labour. Because that system, like the land system, was consolidated and regulated by the personal relations of domination and subjugation, intrusion into it was attendant with clearly defined functional duties and activity. The tax-farming banker, the middle-bracket grain-trading creditor, the petty money-lender who bought up grain in the countryside not only made up a functional vertical trinity but were also a part of the system of social relations, each on his own horizontal rung of the hierarchy. This dual vertical and horizontal subordination of the individual components of India's merchant's capital resulted in an equally organic interlacing of social, ideological and economic relations and functions, as it did in the relations in the personal and land sphere (let us recall, for instance, the goal of the Jain banker to erect a temple to crown his life time endeavours).

Let me add that if the penetration of personal and land relations still implied for representatives of British merchant's capital coalescence with the privileged sections of the oppressed society, the organic penetration of a trading and money-lending community would have entailed a social status very much lower than that long since attained by the merchants and the entrepreneurial bourgeoisie of the dominant nation. In other words, it would have been necessary not only to penetrate the social structure of the subjugated people, but also to hold within the limits of that structure far from the most honorable place, which meant paying a double price—ethnically and socially—for the right to make money on the internal goods exchange of the product alienated from the landholder.

In conclusion, here is a reproduction of the main elements of Marx's multi-stage formula for the system of precapitalist relations: the dominant role of tradition—the legitimised limitations (that is, the regulator of distribution)—constant reproduction of the basis of the existing order, regulation and orderliness as indispensable elements of the mode of production—its social stability and independence from mere chance and arbitrariness. We have here the whole mechanism of interaction and, in particular, its central element, which is usually ignored, namely, regulation and orderliness as necessary aspects of the mode of production. Only intrusion into this element, its destruction, deformation or transformation could have led to a break-up of the whole concatenation or to its essential modification.

We have already had occasion to see to what extent British capital had failed to do this with traditional Indian forms of social regulation and spheres of production, distribution and circulation. But this applied to the hinterland with its strong system of precapitalist modes of production. However, British capital could start its attack on "the constant reproduction on the basis of the existing order" by intruding into the relations of production in the coastal areas, implanting separate enclaves of capitalism and introducing new, bourgeois relations. If this occurred, the pockets of capitalism could become the initial centres drawing within the orbit of capitalism first the adjacent and then more distant areas. To what extent did this, in effect, occur? To obtain the answer, there is need to consider the relations between British merchant's capital and the merchants and artisans in India's coastal areas.

NOTES

1. R. Jenkins, *Report on the Territories of the Raja of Nagpur*, pp. 12-13.
2. *Ibid.*, p. 38.
3. *Ibid.*
4. *Ibid.*, pp. 37, 21-22.
5. *Ibid.*
6. *Ibid.*, pp. 35-36.
7. *Ibid.*
8. *Ibid.*, pp. 43, 45.
9. *Ibid.*, pp. 39-40.
10. *Ibid.*, pp. 41-44.
11. *Ibid.*, p. 46.
12. *Ibid.*, pp. 42-43.
13. *Ibid.*, p. 44.
14. *Ibid.*, pp. 26, 44, 46.
15. *Ibid.*, p. 45.
16. T. Marshall, *Statistical Reports...*, pp. 22-24.
17. *Ibid.*, pp. 21, 26.
18. *Ibid.*, p. 5.
19. *Ibid.*, p. 7.
20. *Ibid.*, pp. 19, 95.
21. *Ibid.*, pp. 22, 89.
22. *Ibid.*, p. 98.
23. *Ibid.*, pp. 91, 93.
24. *Ibid.*
25. *Ibid.*, pp. 91, 100-101.
26. *Ibid.*, pp. 97-98.
27. Ratna Ray, Land Transfer and Social Change under the Permanent Settlement, *JESHR*, vol. I, March 1974, pp. 35-36.
28. *Ibid.*, pp. 36-38.
29. *Ibid.*, pp. 38-41.
30. *Ibid.*, p. 45.
31. F. Buchanan, *A Geographical, Statistical and Historical Description of the District, or Zila, of Dinajpur in the Province, or Soubah, of Bengal*, Calcutta, 1833, pp. 67-68.
32. *Ibid.*, pp. 214-215.
33. *Ibid.*, pp. 68, 237.
34. *Ibid.*, p. 185.
35. *Ibid.*, pp. 203-205, 217-218.
36. *Ibid.*, pp. 236-237.
37. *Ibid.*, pp. 248-249.
38. *Ibid.*, p. 250.
39. N.K. Sinha, *The Economic History...*, vol. II, pp. 172-173, 175.
40. R.M. Martin, *The History...*, vol. II, p. 711.
41. *Ibid.*, p. 706.
42. F. Buchanan, *An Account of the District of Dinajpur...*, pp. 101-104.
43. *Ibid.*, pp. 279-281.
44. F. Buchanan, *An Account of the District of Purnea...*, pp. 529-531.
45. *Ibid.*, pp. 221, 531.
46. F. Buchanan, *An Account of the District of Dinajpur....*, pp. 281-282.

47. R.M. Martin, *The History...*, vol, II, pp. 707, 710-711.
48. There is a direct indication of this. See : *ibid.*, p. 353.
49. Ibid., vol. II, p. 706.
50. F. Buchanan, *An Account of the District of Dinajpur...*, pp. 73-74.
51. *Ibid.*, pp. 115-120.
52. *Ibid.*, pp. 120-131.
53. Ram Narayan Sinha, *Bihar Tenantry (1873-1883)*, Bombay, 1968, pp. 80-82.
54. *Ibid.*, pp. 91-94.
55. F. Buchanan, *An Account of the Districts of Bihar and Patna...*, vol. 1, pp. 547-559.
56. F. Buchanan, *An Account of the District of Bhagalpur....*, p. 463.
57. F. Buchanan, *An Account of the Disctrict of Purnea*, pp. 614-615.
58. *Ibid.*, pp. 431, 445-446.
59. *Ibid.*, p. 435.
60. *Ibid.*, pp. 437-439.
61. *Ibid.*, p. 543.
62. F. Buchanan, *An Account of the District of Shahabad...*, pp. 318-319.
63. F. Buchanan, *An Account of the Districts of Bihar and Patna...*, p. 661.
64. F. Buchanan, *An Account of the District of Shahabad...*, pp. 396-397, 401, 408-409.
65. R.M. Martin, *The History...*, vol. II, pp. 960-961.
66. F. Buchanan, *An Account of the District of Purnea...*, p. 243.
67. Apparently, Sahibgang.
68. F. Buchanan, *An Account of the District of Shahabad...*, p. 401.
69. F. Buchanan, *An Account of the District of Purnea....*, pp. 537-538, 540.
70. F. Buchanan, *An Account of the District of Bhagalpur...*, pp. 608, 616-617.
71. F. Buchanan, *An Account of the Districts of Bihar and Patna...*, vol. II, pp. 647-648.
72. *Ibid.*, p. 655.
73. *Ibid.*, p. 642.
74. F. Buchanan, *An Account of the District of Bhagalpur...*, pp. 589, 593, 627.
75. F. Buchanan, *An Account of the District of Shahabad...*, pp. 398-399.
76. K. Marx, *Capital*, vol. I, p. 381.
77. F. Buchanan, *An Account of the District of Purnea.....*, pp. 556, 577-583.
78. F. Buchanan, *An Account of the District of Bhagalpur.....*, pp. 631-637.
79. F. Buchanan, *An Account of the District of Shahabad.....*, p. 430.
80. Ibid., pp. 429-439.
81. F. Buchanan, *An Account of the Districts of Bihar and Patna...*, vol. I, p. 265, vol. III, p. 723.
82. *Ibid.*, vol. II, pp. 723, 738.
83. *Ibid.*, vol. I, p. 57.
84. *Ibid.*, vol. II, p. 738.
85. *Ibid.*, pp. 765-773.
86. K. Marx, *Capital*, vol. III, p. 793.

CHAPTER FIVE

BRITISH MERCHANT'S CAPITAL AND INDIAN TRADE AND HANDICRAFTS

In considering this subject, one should bear in mind, apart from the above-mentioned indifference of merchant's capital to the socio-economic level of the societies between which it acts as a mediating force, also some of the specific features of its mediation in the activity of the English East India Company.

Concerning the Company's Trade in India

Up to the end of the 18th century, the Company's main aim in its trade with India was to make use of its exclusive right to import Indian goods to the British and other European markets, making money on the difference in prices for these goods in India and Europe. According to the customs records, in the 17th century Britain imported from India medicines, saltpetre, silk cloths and yarn, diamonds, spices, chintz, indigo, skins, caskets, Chinese goods, cotton yarn, wool, gloves, muslins and Persian silks. The fashion for Indian goods turned out to be highly durable. It was said in a late 17th-century discourse that from the greatest dandies to the last kitchen-maids no one deigned to wear anything except Indian goods.[1]

A British writer of the mid-18th century so describes the prevalence of fashion for Indian cloths: "The general fancy of people runs upon East India goods so that the degree that chintz and printed calicoes which before were made use of for carpets, quilts, etc. and to clothe children and ordinary people became now the dress of our ladies; and such is the power of a mode as we saw our persons of quality dressed in Indian carpets which but a few years before their chamber maids would have thought too ordinary for them; the chintz was advanced from lying upon their floors to their backs, from the foot-cloth to the pettycoat."[2]

However, no demand for British goods was taking shape in India as a counter-tendency. That is why, if the East India Company had confined itself to marketing Indian goods in Britain, the result would have been only enrichment for the Company's shareholders at the expense of India's craftsmen and the British consumer, while British manufactures would have been hard hit by the competition from Indian imports. But that was not so. The mercantile-school discourse mentioned above, which on the whole gives an unfavourable characteristic of the Company's activity, admits that one-half the value of the goods coming from India was re-exported from Britain to European markets.[3]

A work by B.N. Ganguli contains extracts from a book by Thomas Man—"England's Treasure by Foreign Trade" (1684). He assessed the results of trade with India in the light of the mercantile theory. T. Man, for instance, claimed that the silver which went from Britain to the East for the purchase of luxuries was more than compensated for by the silver coming from continental Europe as a result of the sale of these goods there. He said that on one occasion the Company had spent 840,000 pounds sterling to purchase Indian goods which it sold in Europe for 4 million pounds. In that case it was enough to sell one-fifth of the goods outside England to recoup the currency earlier exported. This kind of operation was carried out by the Company, which had a capital of only 400,000 pounds. Thus, the observance of the mercantile principle of keeping Britain's balance of trade active depended on the high profits of trade with the East.[4]

Warren Hastings held that the Company's monopoly was necessary to make England "the emporium for supplying all the other countries of Europe with the productions and manufactures of India".[5] The heavy fines imposed on those who stored Indian goods or traded in them, Marx noted, led to a situation in which throughout most of the 18th century Indian manufactures were usually imported into Britain only to be sold on the continent, while the British market itself remained closed for them.[6] Thus, throughout the greater part (but not the whole) of the 18th century, the Company's monopoly of trade with India was a means of enrichment for the British bourgeoisie not only at the expense of the Indian artisans, but also at Europe's expense. In just one year—from July 1785 to July 1786—900,000 pieces of Indian cloths, mainly from Bengal, were sold in Copenhagen alone.[7]

One of the reasons for the difficulties encountered in selling European goods in India was the "revolution of prices": "In a treatise published in 1729 ... Thomas Prior commented that as gold and silver were more scarce in the East Indies than in Europe, it could be expected that wages and prices of commodities there would be lower than at home." This was the reason why "we export very few manufactures of that part of the world, but to purchase their commodities are obliged to send specie thither."[8]

Up until the beginning of the 19th century, every attempt on the part of English manufacturers to expand to any considerable extent the sale of their goods in India proved to be futile. The old frictions between the Company and the English manufacturers who felt the competition of Indian goods were being compounded by the latter's complaints that the Company's trade monopoly was limiting the sale of their goods on the Indian market. But I do not think that the Company's monopoly played the crucial part here because its management itself had an interest in making the exchange balance more favourable in order to expand British exports. Some restrictions on "strategic goods" (like the embargo on steel for hostile Maharashtra) were exceptions.

In 1793, the Company's board of directors even appointed a special committee to refute the petitions from the owners of woollen weaving-mills, who claimed that the Company's trade monopoly was limiting the sale of their goods. The committee declared that silk and cotton goods made in India were better and cheaper. As for woollens, even a lowering of the price would not increase their consumption in India which had so many substitute that were more suitable to her climate and more in accord with the customs and inclinations of the inhabitants.

The committee held that it was impossible to expand the sale of British goods in India because the latter had high quality raw materials, millions of industrious and skilled workers who toiled for a fifth of the wages paid in Britain. Besides, the garments of the Indians were much too simple and little subject to change, being determined by the rules of their caste or sect, to follow any special fashion.[9]

Testifying before a committee of the House of Lords in 1813, a Company's employee, who had served in Gujarat and Bombay for about 18 years, declared that he had not noticed any growth in demand for European goods among the native population. One exception were the Parsis, who used British fabrics, and also some small sections of the population in Bombay. On the whole, the Indians remained indifferent to British fashion so that chairs were offered only in houses which Englishmen visited.[10] Other testimonies also said that Manchester goods were sold in India at lower prices than local goods because the Indians did not show any preference for them.[11] The conviction was expressed that the situation would change with the technical reconstruction in Britain.[12]

At the same time, British witnesses claimed that by the second decade of the 19th century British steel had become of a better quality than Indian steel. But they also admitted that only a short while earlier Swedish steel alone had been superior. As for steel products, India still had better swords, while Britain had better knives and scissors. In the inland areas, however, there was a constant demand only for British firearms and only among the rulers who had decided to reorganise their troops on European lines.[13]

The demand among the Indian nobility for European durables was taking shape gradually. In 1809, B. Heyne, who met a local "polygarh" on the way from Cuddapah to Hyderabad, showed him his watch and to the latter's surprise mentioned that it cost 100 pagodas. He writes: "I am sure that he did not believe me, and equally sure that no zamindar, polygarh or any other Hindu, who styles himself a Rajah, in the country would give half the price for the best watch England can produce. They were always much pleased and ready to take a gun, a watch, looking-glass, etc., as a present, but they would never think of paying more for it than the value of the gold or silver about it. The Moormen (Muslims.—V. P.) are somewhat though not very different in this respect."[14]

The approximation in India of the cost of expensive materials going into the making of artistic goods with the final price (a phenomenon to be met with to this day) requires at least two explanations: first, it testifies to the fact that in many expensive articles the share of the artisan's labour inputs was relatively just as small as in a product like cheap cloths, sugar or vegetable oil; second, the properties of the use-value of such articles were so inactive that their acquisition functionally approximated the hoarding of treasure. Moreover, the fashioning of gold, silver or precious stones into objets d'art, to say nothing of ritual objects, established for these materials the function of hoarded treasures.

The relatively low value of the added handicraft labour with a very unreliable metal content of the Indian rupee of different coinage tended to consolidate that form of treasure which Marx designates as "its aesthetic form in the possession of gold and silver articles."[15] In other words, in India, as in other Asian societies, it was more reliable to hoard treasure in the "aesthetic form" of objets d'art than in the form of collections of coins that were of less than full and differing value; in addition, the former were easily disposed of at the first hint of uneasy circumstances. The export of treasure in finished jewellery form from Europe to India was, as a rule, impossible because of the different aesthetic standards and ritual purpose of the articles.

By the first decade of the 19th century, areas of production had taken shape in Britain specially designed for export trade with India, China and other Asian countries. Seeking to make His Majesty the King wary of the possible social consequences of any restrictions on this trade, the General Court of the United Company of British Merchants trading with East India said in its address on January 26, 1813: "An immense capital has been invested in establishments particularly adapted to the export trade between India and China: and that many heavy engagements have been entered into by persons in the city of London, and on both banks of the Thames, from London Bridge to Gravesend, the very subsistence of many of whom depends upon the continuance to the port of London of the export trade to India and China; and that nearly 10,000 industrious artificers, together with their families, would be in danger of beggary, in proportion as they would be thrown out of employment, by the removal of the export trade from its accustomed channel. This Court therefore conceives that it is of vital importance to the city and port of London, that the export trade to India and China should continue to be carried on as heretofore."[16]

This document clearly refers to the Company-controlled industries specialised to meet the demand of the Asian markets and the Company itself. It is also obvious that such vast markets could not be secured with a production apparatus of that size.

For a long time futile attempts were also made to convert India into a major producer of raw materials for British industry, although, as the Company's documents show, the appropriate efforts were being made in full measure by its management. Let us note that the Company's report on the production of cotton-wool (1836) declared that it was important to ensure delivery of good cotton-wool from East India for manufactures in Great Britain, and added that this had become the object of general concern roughly by the end of the 18th century. The great inventions and the improvement of all kinds of equipment for spinning and weaving, and also the improvements in the art of bleaching and printing chintz—from the first use of Arkwright's spinning-machine in 1769 to the establishment of the factory system in 1785—led to a steady rise in the demand for raw materials, so leading to a search for the means to secure their growing deliveries.[17]

But the export of cotton from India at once met with one obstacle, namely, the low and non-standard quality of the product, which was due to the short fibre of most Indian cotton varieties and also of the poor ginning. The best Indian cotton was grown on small areas in Bengal and was fully consumed by manufacturers in Dacca. Another area of high-grade cotton—the district of Nagpur—had been cut off by lack of roads until the 1860s. Only the cotton grown in Broach and Surat, which met the technological standards and was easily transported, was exported to Britain. However, it did not meet the demand of the British factories and in 1789, for instance, only 6 per cent of Britain's cotton imports came from India, the rest coming from the Ottoman Empire and the colonies of other powers.[18]

W. Silver lists in his book the measures taken by the British from 1788 to 1801 in order to expand the production of Indian cotton and to improve its quality. Among the earlier attempts was the use of seeds from Mauritius and Malta (1790), installations for cleaning cotton (1794), the growing of cotton on the plantation of one M. Brown in Malabar (1801).[19] But in subsequent years, there was a rapid growth in the importance of the South of the United States as the principal supplier of cotton for Britain's industry. Only in 1810, in view of the difficulties of US cotton supplies, was there an expansion of British imports of cotton from India to 27.8 million pounds, which was one-fifth of Britain's cotton imports. Even in that period, Indian cotton was being assigned the role as a kind of additional source for Lancashire, which still was not quite adequate in periods when British-American relations were strained. The extremely uneven demand for Indian cotton in Britain was reflected in the trade turnover of Indian merchants, but the hardest hit were the cultivators, who gained most in periods of favourable market outlook (for instance, in the record year of 1810, the Board of Directors insisted on a lowering of purchase prices) but bore the full brunt of the losses when exports fell. Even the Company's Board of Directors complained about the unreliable outlook.[20]

The export of raw silk from India, chiefly from Bengal, to Britain, began long before, but was insignificant until the mid- 18th century. Then, in the 1760s and 1770s steps were taken to encourage the production of raw silk and to raise its standards to the level of Italian and Spanish specimens. With that end in view, the Company set up several silk-winding establishments with improved treatment of cocoons. As a result, by the end of the 18th century Indian raw silk began to oust its European counterpart.[21]

The growing of indigo spread in India, in Bengal especially, after the formation of the United States of North America. But in 1789, of the 1,958,500 pounds of indigo imported to Britain, 846,500 was supplied by the USA, and only 371,500 by India. In the following years the export of indigo from Bengal increased rapidly and reached 3 million pounds in the 1795 season.[22] The specific feature of enterprise in indigo exports consisted in the fact that it was in the hands of private British dealers. Let us merely note that this type of agricultural enterprise was from the outset clouded by administrative coersion and had little in common with the introduction of capitalist relations into a subjugated society. That is quite natural because the indigo business was a mere continuation of operations by the selfsame merchant's capital.

European Trade with Gujarati Merchants

Although in the over two centuries of its rule in India British merchant's capital did not undergo any substantial change, British bourgeois society which it represented in economic terms had travelled the way from Elizabeth to Victoria, whereas India, by contrast, had forfeited some of its illusory military and political advantages in Akbar's reign. The balance of forces changed steadily in favour of the British establishment and to the detriment of Indian traditional strata. The bearing of the English invaders varied according to the historical take-off they encountered. In the 17th century, they were merchants, not very rich ones by Indian standards, who tried by flattery and bribes, to secure the right to trade and to establish their factories in the coastal areas. When Sir Thomas Roe had presented his gifts from the King of England to Jahangir, the latter told him: "Your presents have been inferior to those a merchant you have seen here has brought."[23]

Having established its political supremacy, the Company was still unable to bend to their will the system of commerce and credit which had been established, and so was forced to adapt itself to this system when entering into relations with Indian merchants on legally equitable terms. Especially firm and close economic links between Indian and European merchants existed in Gujarat.

When European vessels first appeared off the Western coast of India, Gujarat was economically one of the subcontinent's most developed parts and a natural centre of India's trade with the Middle East and East Africa. The transit trade from the Middle East to South-East Asia passed through the harbours of Gujarat. Tomé Pires was well aware of it: "Both Gujaratis and merchants who had settled in Combay sent many ships to every part of the world, to Aden, Ormuz, the Deccan kingdom, Goa, Bhatcal, to the whole Malabar coast, to Ceylon, Bengal, Siam, Pegu, Pedir, Pase and Malacca. They carried one cargo of goods there and returned with another, enriching and aggrandising Cambay. This town spread out its arms towards the most important points along the shipping lines, touching Aden with its right and Malacca with its left; the other places are less important."[24] Pires then goes on to list the goods sold in Gujarat (cottons, indigo, opium, leather as well as wheat and rice, which were grown in Cambay or imported from the neighbouring localities), and refers to the great number of Gujaratis in the main ports on the coast of the Indian Ocean and the adjoining seas; he says, for example, that "the Cambay merchants make Malacca their chief trading centre. There used to be a thousand Gujarat merchants in Malacca, besides four or five thousand Gujarat seamen, who came and went. Malacca cannot live without Cambay, nor Cambay without Malacca, if they are to be very rich and very prosperous."[25]

Permanent colonies of Gujaratis existed in the ports of the Red Sea and the Persian Gulf as early as the late 17th century. J. Fryer mentioned a Parsi merchant (in Surat), who, acting as a broker for the kingdom of Bantam (Java), became so rich that he built a magnificent house.[26] John Ovington, who visited Surat in 1690, writes about this port, the chief one in Gujarat, which had forced Cambay to take second place in the 17th century: "Surat is reckon'd the most fam'd emporium of the Indian Empire, where all commodities are vendible, though they never were there seen before."[27] The development of foreign trade brought prosperity to the handicraft industries, especially weaving. The numerous and rich towns of Gujarat were famous for the skill of their artisans. Trade with the adjacent regions of India was stimulated by the fact that Gujarat's agriculture could not satisfy the needs of the urban population. Grain, in particular, was imported from other parts of India.

The arrival of the Europeans did not, right away, affect the economic position of the towns in Gujarat, although the Muslim merchants, in whose hands maritime commerce was concentrated, became very soon aware of the fact that the European adventurer merchants dominated the sea lanes. But commerce did not come to a standstill because the Europeans pushed the Muslim traders aside. The establishment of direct trade links with Europe even stimulated to a certain extent artisan production in Gujarat. Ovington wrote that Surat craftsmen manufacturing silks exactly reproduced the finest and most beautiful specimens imported from Europe.[28] This not only serves to confirm the fact that local artisans had long and constantly worked on European orders but also the ability of Indian artisans to reproduce with their own means goods turned out on a different technological level. Still, this applied only to some consumer goods, and mainly cloths.

In the 17th century, Ahmadabad, the capital of Gujarat, flourished: "Ahmedabad was formerly celebrated for its commerce and manufactures in cloths of gold and silver, fine silk and cotton fabrics, articles of gold, silver, steel, enamel, mother-of-pearl, lacquered ware and fine wood-work. Excellent paper was also made here, and there were many artists in portrait-painting and miniatures. The trade in indigo, cotton and opium was very great."[29] The range of articles produced in Ahmadabad showed that its craftsmen worked for the feudal lords and foreign markets. In the early 17th century, 200 cart-loads of goods were sent from Ahmadabad to the ports every ten days.[30] Of course, this was not much in physical terms, but one must take account of the luxuries and valuables among the goods.

Commerce and money-lending in Gujarat had been in the hands of a few Muslim castes (Bohra and Khoja) and Hindu sub-castes (Bania and Bhattia) long before the boats of European adventurers appeared off the shores of India. The Hindu sub-castes specialised mainly in monetary, banking and money-lending operations and internal trade.

Early in the 17th century, the richest shroff of Gujarat, Shantidas, received the hereditary title of Nagar Seth, that is, banker of the city, from Jahangir for commercial services rendered to the Mogul court. In addition, the Treasury redeemed all his bills of exchange. From that time onwards, the head of the Nagar Seths became the chief of the Ahmadabad trading community and represented its interests with the Mogul administration.[31] "In 1725, the then Nagar Seth of Ahmedabad saved the city from plunder by the Marathas, and, in recognition of this, the combined guilds of the city assigned to him the perpetual right to levy a quarter per cent on all goods stamped in the municipal weighing yard."[32]

The territory through which the trade routes from the ports of Gujarat and Bombay ran was at first in the hands of the Mogul viceroys. In the first half of the 18th century, Gujarat became the object of a fierce struggle between the Marathas and the Mogul chiefs. Only in 1757 did Ahmadabad finally pass into the hands of the Marathas. Later on, the British invaders made raids into Gujarat, which formed a part of the Gaikwar's possessions. In 1780, Ahmadabad was taken by storm, but only in 1818 did the British finally succeed in capturing Gujarat and its capital. As long as a considerable part of Gujarat and Maharashtra remained under Maratha rule, the leading method employed by the Company's administration to enrich themselves in these regions was, naturally, their monopoly of foreign trade and not military plunder or taxation. Accordingly, the British had an interest in engaging the services of the native merchants. Thus, the opposition of the Marathas forced the Company to grant the most prominent Gujarati traders and bankers more advantageous terms for their collaboration than they offered, for example, to the Bengali merchants.

By the early 19th century, many Gujarati merchants from the coastal towns were acting as agents for the British trade monopoly. Nicholas Downton, one of the first Englishmen to set forth his impressions of a voyage to India (1614-1615), related that even at that time the English East India Company had long-established regular contacts with the Gujarati Banias as its agents, to whom it sold swords, knives, telescopes and other articles.

It is true that at first the Muslim merchants tried to keep the merchants of other creeds from establishing direct contacts with the Europeans. Thus, a prominent member of the Muslim merchants' community of Bohra was in a position, as late as the 1640s, to inflict punishment on a Hindu Bania for entering into trade relations with the English Company.[33] However, the Mogul viceroy of Gujarat communicated with the English through a Bania named Lakhandas. At first, the business contacts of the English merchants with the local population were apparently restricted to Banias, for some Englishmen believed that all Gujarati Hindus were Banias.[34] A century earlier, Pires wrote: "The Heathen (Hindus.—V.P.) of Cambay are called Banias."[35] Records belonging to a later period also confirm that local merchants acted as intermediaries between native princes and the European traders.[36] The above-quoted English mercantilist of the late 17th century says that treaties and agreements with the Indian princes could be concluded through their ministers, for the rulers were always prepared to conduct negotiations with any merchant and there was no need to approach the prince personally.[37]

As early as the 1670s, J. Fryer found that a system had developed in Surat under which Englishmen traded through the mediation of Indian merchants. For every transaction they concluded, the Indian merchants who acted as brokers received a commission of 2 per cent.[38] (Ovington, who went to Surat a few years after Fryer, gives the figure of 3 per cent.)[39] In addition, they secretely appropriated, according to Fryer, a part of the value of the goods they sold. It was difficult to check up on the brokers, for the Englishmen's knowledge of the Gujarati language was poor. Moreover, declares Fryer "ignorance is safer than to hazard being poisoned for prying too nearly into their actions."[40] That was the way, if we are to believe Fryer, the early contradictions between British capital and the ancestors of the Gujarati compradors were settled.

Fryer paints a very colourful picture of how the European merchant was received by the Banias of Surat, and their subsequent relationship: "As soon as you have set your foot on shore, they crowd in their service, interposing between you and all civil respect, as if you had no other business but to be gull'd; so that unless you have some to make your way through them, they will interrupt your going, and never leave till they have drawn out something for their advantage. At this time of shipping they present Governor of Surat, to license them to keep a mart here, which they make the European pay dearly for. Yet such is their policy, that without these, neither you nor the natives themselves shall do any business.... These generally are the poorer sort, and set on by the richer to trade with the seamen for the meanest things they bring (an example of the dependence of the poor members of a merchant's caste on the richer ones.—V. P.); and notwithstanding they take them at their own rates, get well enough in exchange of goods with them.... Enduring servilely foul words, affronts and injuries, for a future hope of gain; expert in all the studied arts of thriving and insinuation; so that lying, dissembling, cheating are their masterpiece. Their whole desire is to have money pass through their fingers, to which a great part is sure to stick: for they well understand the constant turning of cash amounts both to the credit and profit of him that is so occupied; which these Banias are sensible of, otherwise they would not be so industrious to enslave themselves."[41]

We find the British merchant, driven to distraction by the resourcefulness of the Gujarati traders, nevertheless trying to find an economic explanation of sorts for the enterprise of his Indian associates. For the time being, the European champions of primitive accumulation accepted the fact that the Indian merchant was, unlike the naive inhabitant of the West Indies or South America, a first-class businessman whose commercial shrewdness was not inferior to their own. But having conquered India, the British adventurers endeavoured to get rid of their Indian middlemen who traded on equal terms.

Almost all European travellers were unanimous in their admiration of the efficiency of the Indian traders, but opinions differed regarding their moral qualities. According to one description, "they are all cunning folk, and owe nothing to the people of the West, themselves endued with a keener intelligence than is usual with us, and hands as subtle as ours.... A cunning and crafty race: not, however, fraudulent, nor easy to deferred. And what is to be observed of all their manufacture is this, that they are both of good workmanship and cheap. I have never seen men of wit so fine and polished as are the Indians; they have nothing barbarious or savage about them, as we are apt to suppose.... In fact, the Portuguese take and learn more from them than they from the Portuguese; and they that come fresh to Goa are very simpletons till they have acquired the airs and graces of the Indies."[42] D. Pant quotes the following opinion of the Banias, given by William Finch: "They are as subtle as the devil, whose limbs I certainly persuade myself they are."[43] Thevenot takes a more moderate view, saying that the fourth caste in the Hindu hierarchy of castes were Ouens, or Banias, who were all merchants, bankers or brokers, and their purpose in life seemed to be the extraction of every possible kind of profit.[44] Fryer notes, however, how strictly the Banias observed the religious ceremonial and adds: "In cases of trade they are not so hidebound, giving their consciences more scope, and boggle at no villainy for an emolument."[45]

Mandelslo wrote this about the Gujarati Banias: "They never drive any bargain, but they endeavour to surprise and circumvent those they are to deal with. The Dutch and English know this by experience; whence it comes, that they make use of these people, as their brokers, and interpreters, that they may discover the impostures and cheats of others. There is no trade which they applied not themselves to; and there is no commodity but they sell it, unless it be flesh, fish, or any other thing that hath had life."[46]

Merchants from the Parsi community established especially close collaboration with the British. The Parsis are descendants of Zoroastrians who fled from Muslim persecution in Iran. The first of them landed in Sanjan, 94 miles north of Bombay, in the middle of the 8th century. At the close of the 17th century, the Parsis lived near Surat on the southern seaboard of Gujarat, in a district which stretched for 40 miles along the coast and 20 miles inlands.[47] They preserved the religion of their ancestors and did not intermarry with other communities. But after over a thousand years in Gujarat, the Parsis had established close connections with the economic and cultural life of the Gujaratis, and Gujarati had become their mother tongue. Only the caste system and religion had prevented their complete assimilatian. "Religion of a change of religion made no difference (in Gujarat.—V.P.). The Parsis, who orginally settled in Gujarat thirteen hundred years ago, may be considered as Gujaratis for this purpose. (Their language has long been Gujarati)."[48] However, such phenomena—individual castes or ethnic groups preserving their isolation—were rather frequent in India.

It would be incorrect to assume, as some do, that commerce has always been the only occupation of the Parsis. They had been agriculturists rather than merchants, although they also supplied the sailors with timber and water. The Parsis raised the famous Gujarat strain of cattle.[49] Among them were many skilful weavers.[50] Mandelslo asserted that in his day the Parsis grew tobacco, prepared palm wine, engaged in commerce, money-changing and the handicrafts, with the exception of smithery, an occupation their religion forbade them to follow.[51] The forefathers of Pestonjee Jahangir, the Bombay magnate (born in 1831), received from the Great Moguls a jagir near Surat and the titles of Nekshant Khan and Jabiar Khan.[52]

Prominent representatives of the Indian bourgeoisie, such as Dadabhai Naoroji and Tata, were descendants of land-owners. Land-owning Parsis had, of course, little in common with the soldiers of the Muslim nobility. Chand Kamdin, an ancestor of Naoroji, nine generations removed, won by his skill as perfumer the favour of Nur

Jahan, the beautiful wife of Jahangir, and in 1618 was granted 100 bighas of tax-free land. Consequently, the Parsis were not restricted in the choice of their occupation by religious prohibitions. D.R. Gadgil writes. "From early times, Parsis established connections as brokers with European traders. A remarkable feature to be noted about the Parsis is that their traditional occupations were not connected with trading or finance. In the accounts of the 17th century travellers, they are noticed chiefly as artisans, carpenters, weavers, etc. Their prominence in Bombay was also established in the first instance through their ship-building activity. Though they later became a dominant trading and financing community, like other Gujarat communities, their original artisan background is an important feature that deserves notice."[53] Fryer notes the low social position of the Parsis in Mogul Gujarat, who "having been curbed formerly by the Gentiles, and now by the Moors used as perfect slaves."[54]

After the European merchants came to India, brokerage became the main occupation of the rich Parsis. During the 17th century, the centre of the Parsi community was transferred to the English factory in Surat. When Surat's importance declined at the beginning of the 18th century, the Parsis began to move to Bombay; tradition has it that the first Parsi, Dorabjee Nanabhoy, settled in Bombay in 1640, while it was still in Portuguese hands. A Parsi, Modi Hirjee Wacha, possibly an ancestor of the well-known Wacha family, settled in the Bombay fort in 1617.

At first, the Muslim merchants of Gujarat were political and commercial adversaries of the East India Company. S. M. Edwardes says: "Though on the whole the Company looked with less favour on the Moors, than on the trading community proper (the Banias and the Parsis.—V.P.), they nevertheless showed them civility, by permitting them to travel on the Company's ships."[55] This was a peculiar arrangement because the traditional sea routes of the Muslim merchants had been cut by British pirates and the East India Company itself. That is why at first these merchants were unable to derive all the benefits from the spreading comprador trade. But beginning with the 18th century, the connection between the Muslim merchants and the British became stronger. The comprador operations compensated the Muslim merchants for their loss of such important clients as the Mogul chiefs. However, the contacts between the Muslim merchants and the Company were never as close as those of the Parsis and the Hindus. The Muslim merchants largely continued to conduct trade along the old lines: with the Middle East and East Africa. The two Gujarati castes of Ismailites (the Bohras and the Hojas) continued to play a leading role among the Muslim merchants.

English traders greatly appreciated the services of the Bania Virgee

Vora, the biggest merchant broker engaged in, commerce with the Europeans in Gujarat, who at the beginning of the 17th century captured the wholesale trade in English goods brought into Surat harbour. At the height of the hostilities between the Mogul authorities and the British, Virgee Vora granted the latter a loan of 200,000 rupees for trade purposes, and was executed by the Mogul Viceroy in Gujarat. Mandelslo wrote: "There are many rich people in Surat; a Bania called Vargivora, a friend of mine, possesses according to estimates, not less than 8 million" (apparently, rupees).[56] An English contemporary considered Virgee Vora the richest merchant in the world, and estimated that his fortune amounted to 8 million rupees.[57]

Virgee Vora was not the only creditor of the English merchants. A documentary source dating from the close of the 18th century refers to the practice of Surat bankers' financing English trading expeditions to China. Employees of the Company borrowed money from a Bania at a rate of 25 per cent, but if the expedition was shipwrecked on the way interest was not paid.[58] In the 1680s, the East India Company raised big loans from Indian bankers for the purchase of goods intended for Europe.[59]

A kind of hierarchy of Indian brokers working with European companies took shape. It was headed by bankers, or shroffs, who gave the Europeans credits and engaged in moneychanging. Sometimes they were even paid a nominal salary, for instance, 25 pounds sterling a year, but then they also provided loans of over hundreds of thousands of rupees, or tens of thousands of pounds sterling. The shroffs were followed by paikars, who supplied goods for money advanced by the Company. Finally, below them came the dallals or gomasthas, who were common agents of the Europeans.[60] Of course, depending on the circumstances of time and place, these agents could have different tasks to fulfil, but there is no doubt at all that the Europeans made use of the functional vertical arrangement of Indian merchant's capital.

Indian Traders and Artisans in the Company's Factories and Territories

A specific economic and social microclimate had undoubtedly taken shape at the factories of the British East India Company. It was determined not only by the good intentions of the Company authorities with respect to its early Indian subjects, but also by the need to reckon with the political situation taking shape round these early British possessions.

The British had especially strong commercial ties with Hindu merchants in Bombay, which became the Company's commercial and political stronghold in the west of India. In 1668, Charles II received as part of the dowry of his wife, the Portuguese Princess Maria Braganza, the small Island of Bombay and handed it over to the East India Company for a symbolic sum of 10 pounds. This was a very timely acquisition for the Company because its factories in the coastal towns of Gujarat, including the chief factory at Surat, were threatened by the Marathas. Bombay's insular situation facilitated its defence and made it possible to mount raids with impunity on the adjacent areas of Maharashtra. Besides, it had an excellent harbour. That is why in 1687, the Company's chief factory was transferred from Surat to Bombay, despite the fact that it lay in an unhealthy area.

In September 1668, the Council at Surat recorded the Company's intention: "It being the Honourable Company's desire that we contrive the best way for making Bombay a port for the exportation and importation of goods and persons to and from Persia, Mocha and other parts."[61] The document also expresses the desire to set up a shipyard in Bombay, where timber, iron works, carpenters' and many other materials "are very cheap, the buildings (meaning ships.—V.P.) far more substantial than in England". Besides, the thrifty merchants add, the money expended on pay for the ship-builders "will remain in the island and the people be the better able to pay those duties and rent annually received from them."[62]

In the 18th century, the ports of Gujarat began to lose their erstwhile importance. The economy of the towns and of inner Gujarat, Ahmadabad in the first place, was undermined by the decline of foreign trade and the feudal disorder. The trade routes were paralysed by countless transit levies and military raids.[63] In 1789, Forbes said that at one time everything had been in favour of Ahmadabad's trade, then an assemblage of merchants, handicraftsmen and travellers from various countries, in contrast to the scene of devastation and neglect which it now presented. In 1817, a British official reported that in Ahmadabad he found a sad scene of destruction.[64] The local merchants had also begun to move to Bombay. Because the Marathas held the areas with which Bombay traded, the brokerage of the local merchants in this trade became absolutely inevitable. That is why the Company was forced to allow the settlers to Bombay relatively advantageous terms. Thus, when in the late 17th century, the Company invited the Banias of Surat to move to Bombay, the latter bargained for and secured a number of privileges for themselves.[65] In the wake of the Hindu Banias the Parsis also moved to Bombay.

In a letter dated July 17, 1677, the Bombay factors request their colleagues in Surat to find a coiner by the name of Ratanji, who "is an able workman, which will be of great benefit in making all the money of a true and equal weight", and to send him as fast as possible to

Bombay as had been earlier agreed.[66] In the early 1740s, Coowasjee Kama, an ancestor of the well-known wealthy family of Lowjee Nassarwanjee Wadia, moved to Bombay among others and established the shipbuilding industry there, and so did Rustamjee Dorabjee, whom the British subsequently appointed the patel of Bombay.[67] S. M. Edwardes was obviously wrong when he said that Lowjee Wadia "had been connected with the island since the year 1692, when he assisted with a body of Kolis (a caste of fishermen.—V.P.) to repel the invasion of the Sidi. For this good work he was appointed by the government Patel of Bombay."[68] Wadia could not have performed such a feat in 1692—both because of his age (he died in 1774) and because of his status.

In 1773, the Parsis who had resettled from Gujarat were given a special tract of land on Malabar Hill in the centre of Bombay.[69] In 1780, there were already 3,000 Parsis in Bombay, and within ten years many more Parsis came to live in Bombay to escape the famine in Gujarat. In the 1770s and 1780s, the Parsis, according to Forbes, owned sizable areas of land and fine houses in Bombay. They either built the houses themselves or bought them from the British who were leaving for home. Incidentally, Forbes remarks on the Parsis' good knowledge of the political situation and also on their freedom from many caste prejudices, which were so characteristic of Hindu and Muslim merchants.[70]

The big merchants of Bombay in the early 19th century had the following ethnic and community composition: in 1805, 9 private leading European firms were registered in Bombay; 16 Parsi firms and 2 Parsi-Chinese agencies, 15 Hindu, 4 Muslim (Bohra), 3 Portuguese and 4 American firms.[71] Thus, out of 53 Bombay firms, 37 were owned by Indians. But despite the latter's numerical prevalence, British merchant's capital, relying on political power and higher organisation, controlled the commercial operations of the Indians.

The forms of cooperation between the Bombay merchants and the British were highly diverse. In the early 18th century, the Company traded in Bombay through its official brokers. Thus, in 1731, the Company rewarded its broker, Laljee, who had bought up all the woollen cloth, lead, copper and iron brought in from Britain by a ship a short while earlier, with an honorary present: a horse worth 800 rupees.[72] During the war between the Marathas and the Moguls, the Company prohibited its employees from selling goods in the inland areas, and entrusted these operations to Bombay and other Indian merchants.[73]

But as the ties between the local merchants were strengthened, the privileged broker began to hamper the British, and so the broker system was abolished in 1737. The Bombay Council motivated this decision by the assertion that its servants had never enjoyed "perfect freedom of trade ... being always obstructed by the power, interest and influence of the brokers." The Council believed that its "investment may be carried on better by contracting direct with the merchants." [74]

Many Bombay traders subsequently became partners of British firms. According to one source (1828), every European trading establishment had a Parsi partner, who usually provided most of the capital.[75] The dependent position forced the Indian merchants to pay a kind of tribute to the powers represented by the British partner. That British firms valued the services of their Indian associates will be seen from the following well-known incident: when, as a result of speculation, the Parsi Hormuzjee lost the huge sum of 200,000 pounds sterling (it is quite possible that the amount is greatly exaggerated), the firm of Charles Forbes, with whom he had close business ties, helped him to get back on his feet.[76]

Bombay merchants engaged in the provisioning of Bombay's garrison and fleet. A document dating from April 1738 speaks of the appointment by the Bombay Governor of three suppliers, modis, listed as Hirjee Jeejee, Bhikajee Jeejee and Manekjee Jeejee. Judging by their names, they were Parsis and brothers. They may perhaps have originated the rich family in which Jamshetjee Jeejeebhoy personified not the initial but the highest stage of prosperity. The duty of these three was to provision the Company's ships and factories with all things necessary.[77] In their private purchases of Indian goods, the Company's masters and officers used the services of Parsi agents, called dubashes.[78]

The building of a fortified wall by a man named Ramjee Parbhu, which was begun in the late 1730s, should be classed as a military contract secured by the Bombay Parsis from the British. As a reward for the work, which he assessed at 3,000 rupees, Parbhu requested 500 rupees in cash and the rest in land plots lying along the wall. The Bombay Council, considering that the land was lying waste, thought it right to do so when the work was over, and to pay the cash requested.[79]

Bombay merchants engaged in trade with the Middle East. In the early 18th century A. Hamilton met Indian Bania and Muslim merchants in the Persian Gulf ports.[80] This trade, which always shows a surplus for India, helped the British to compensate for the constant foreign-exchange deficit in their commerce with India. In the 50 years from 1710 to 1759, the Company exported from England to the Orient goods worth 9,248,000 pounds, while its coin and precious metals exports amounted to 26,833,000 pounds.[81] In this context, interest attaches to a petition filed by three Hindu merchants in 1741 to the Company's authorities. They complained that the recent decision of the Council abolishing the escort of men-of-war for convoys sailing to the Arabian Coast would seriously affect their old established commercial relations. "To your petitioners, the failure of the north trade will be fatal, as it is mainly with this money and from the profits of this trade that we are able to carry our business and maintain ourselves and families." But realising that the British administrators would not be moved by complaints about the cruel lot of their households, but by commercial reasons, the merchants stated: "By the loss of this beneficial trade from the north the Honorable Company would lose imports which contribute no trifling sum to the customs."[82] The Company could not withstand such arguments and reversed its decision. Let us note that the men-of-war were needed to protect the ships mainly against British pirates. Hamilton asserts that the chief pirate in the Bab el Mandeb Strait was the English Captain Avory.

In the 18th century the Gujarati merchants were engaged in extensive trade in Bengal. In the 1730s and 1740s, at their head was Molda Mohammed Ali of Surat, who traded along the Ganges and had a ship-repair yard near Calcutta. However, by the 1750s he had been ruined by his losses in Gujarat. Later, in the 1780s, Gujarati merchants—Hindus, judging by their names—were still buying Bengal silk, and also discounting bills in Kasimbazar.[83] However, by the end of the 1780s, the imports of Bengal silk to Gujarat fell to insignificant proportions.

Gujarat's trade with China was of special importance for the Company. The main item of this trade was the export of Indian opium and cotton. In the second half of the 18th century, Gujarat also exported large consignments of cotton to Bengal. This trade was controlled by the Bombay merchants, the British and the Gujarati, who concluded contracts with native merchants buying up the cotton in the villages.[84] An idea of these operations will be gained from the fact that in 1801 seven Bombay merchants bought a consignment of cotton worth 350,000 rupees for dispatch to China. Three of them were Englishmen and four Parsis.[85]

At the beginning of the 19th century commerce with China was the principal item in the turnover of Bombay. For example, in 1805, the export to China reached 6,473,600 rupees, and to Britain only 508,700 rupees.[86] But this did not mean that the China trade was an end in itself. In fact, the export of cotton, and later of opium, to China was the principal source from which the Company obtained its silver coins, so enabling it to purchase Indian export goods in Bengal and elsewhere.

The maritime trade with China and other Asian countries helped to raise Bombay's shipping. The Parsis began to take an interest in navigation in 1735. Readymoney was the first Parsis gentleman to reach

China in 1756. By 1792, the Parsis owned more than 20 big ships (mainly built in Bombay), two of them, moreover, having a displacement of over 1,000 tons. The biggest ship masters were members of the Wadia family, possessing six vessels, and members of the Readymoney family, who had three vessels. Bombay's richest ship master was also a Parsi, Rustomjee Cowasjee Banajee. Members of the Davar family—apparently the ancestors of K.N. Davar, the first mill-owner of Bombay—were also among the first ship masters of Bombay.[87] During the second half of the 18th century and the beginning of the 19th century, the principal source of the wealth the merchants of Bombay were amassing was shipping revenues.

At the same time, the Indian scientist A. Guha observes that there was direct discrimination against Indian shipping by the British Navigation Act and the Company's trade monopoly, which closed up the way for Indian ships and ship masters to the ports of Europe. Only in 1794, during the war and in connection with the shortage of ships for carrying raw materials, was a temporary— 18 month—permit issued to, use Indian-built ships not registered in British ports.

But the unprecedented appearance of Indian ships in London came as a shock to the ruling nation. Fears were expressed that the unflattering accounts the Indian seamen would spread upon their return home could have the most unfavourable effect on the minds of Asian subjects.

In order to avoid the restrictions and fines imposed on the owners of Indian-built ships, even British merchants began to refuse to use them. A Committee of the House of Commons heard this question in 1814: would it not be an advantage for British merchants to use ships which were as cheap as those of the Russian merchants? To this a British patriot replied that he would prefer to transfer to India the manufacture of woollens rather than ship-building. With the end of the Napoleonic wars, all the easements with respect to Indian shipping were abolished. The Navigation Acts that followed (up until 1848, when steam navigation became clearly superior) were aimed at preventing the appearance in European waters of ships built in India and manned by Indian crews. Even in trade with China, which was started by the Armenians (in 1722) and the Parsis, British ships had ousted their Asian; rivals by 1842. A. Guha concludes by saying that in this instance British policy in a sense allowed, however unwillingly, for the future and gradual revival of the cotton industry, but had deliberately killed ship-building.

The discrimination was directed not only against Indian ships and their masters, but also against their crews, especially non-European captains (mainly Muslims and Parsis). Thus, in 1797, Shamsuddin Razzak, the captain of "The Jahangir", desired to file a petition with the Canton authorities to recover debts from Chinese merchants, but the Company's representatives in Canton opposed this on the plea that such a petition would harm its long-term interests. Non-English merchants were not allowed, as English merchants were, to live in Canton for long periods. As a result, the number of Armenian residents in China fell from thirty in 1733 to one in 1809. The Parsis were still superior in numbers to the British merchants, but only at the cost of great effort. On the whole, Guha assumes that but for such obstacles Indian participation in trade with China would have been greater, and the Indians would have subsequently been able more successfully to resist the establishment of control by British agency houses.

These are some of the aspects of the collaboration between the Gujarat merchants and their British partners. While helping the East India Company to drain India, the Gujarat merchants acquired considerable wealth. The Englishman John Burnell, who visited India in 1711, wrote: "The Banias or merchants are not only rich and wealthy, but like the rest of the world are covetous after more, placing the height of their happiness in riches, which they will scrape together by mean and petty offices, some of them amassing prodigious sums of money, being accounted worth 90 or 100 lakhs, or so many times a Rs. 100,000."[88] Evidence regarding the enormous riches accumulated by the Gujarati merchants cooperating with the English is confirmed by documentary material. For example, in 1721, after the death of a well-known Company broker, the Parsi Rustomjee Manekjee, his heirs demanded the return of a loan amounting to Rs. 690,000 from the East India Company. After the Bombay Council of the Company refused to pay back the money, one of Manek's sons got the Board of Directors to agree to reconsider the matter. As a result, Manekjee's heirs received Rs. 564,000.[89]

Despite the fortunes they had made by the mid-18th century, the homes of the Bombay merchants were still far from the splendour they subsequently acquired. An English eyewitness reported in 1750 that many merchants' houses were badly built and inconvenient, having small windows and poor amenities; even the best of them had an air of squalor and low taste about them.[89a] It took decades for the Gujarat merchants to live down the oppression of their earlier rulers and to partake of the fruits of ostentation.

Thus, in the period of India's colonial exploitation by methods of primitive accumulation, the big Gujarati merchants of Bombay operated and made money chiefly as agents of British merchant's capital and so obtained the bulk of their profits. At the same time, the early seats of industrial enterprise appeared in Bombay. Up to the end of the 18th century, the British energetically implanted handloom weaving in Bombay, as they did in other factories throughout India.

In November 1678, a letter was sent from the Surat factory to Bombay recommending that weavers from Surat should be invited to Bombay to manufacture calicoes. The letter expressed the confidence that the invitation would be accepted by the weavers who had suffered from the consequences of the wars. By 1676, a regular industry had been established in Bombay. The Company imported raw silk and cotton and "distributed it to the weavers who worked under a muqaddam and were paid partly in money and partly in rice."[90]

The "Bombay Gazetteer" gives information on the handicrafts in Bombay during the 17th and 18th centuries. These documents help to form an opinion of the duties which the Indian middlemen, called muqaddam, performed. The documents of the Bombay Council of the East India Company show that in the 1730s the resettlement of the weavers in Bombay was preceded by negotiations in which the muqaddam put forward on their behalf a number of demands on the building of houses, supply of raw materials, etc. Through the muqaddam the Company recruited weavers, supplied them with raw materials, advanced money to them, collected the finished products and paid the weavers in cash and food-stuffs. The trust which the British placed in their agent was extremely great, for at times sums amounting to several thousands of rupees passed through his hands for which he did not have to account; the agent was only obliged to hand over a fixed quantity of manufactured goods.[91] Since the weavers completely depended on the muqaddam, he was able to exploit them in his own interest. Several muqaddams are mentioned by name in various documents. At the beginning of the 18th century, the chief master of the weavers working for the East India Company in Bombay was the Parsi Manna or Manak.[92]

The Bombay Council of the Company apparently acted with respect to the local weavers as general creditor and buyer-up, making use of the services of muqaddams. A document dated January 25, 1724, contains a request from the muqaddam Janojee and other weavers for an advance of 6,000 rupees for seasonal purchases of raw silk. Considering that their earlier debt had been paid off (apparently through deliveries of cloths), the Company agreed to make the amount available.[93]

Handloom weaving in Bombay apparently catered mainly for the European market. In 1670, the Company even sent English weavers, dyers and other artisans to India to show the Indians how to manufacture the goods which were most likely to find favour with the Europeans and which would therefore prove to be most profitable for the Company.[94] Some technical borrowings from Europe were used in Bombay. From 1724 to 1725, Cowasjee Rustomjee was in England with his family and brought back 12 tin pipe-coils and 3 stills for the making of alcoholic drinks. The first to use wine-making presses in the 1780s were the Parsis R. V. Wadia and D. Dadiseth.

However, all these capitalist-type endeavours are outclassed by the brilliant history of Bombay's ship-building. In the 1730, the East India Company set up a shipyard in Bombay. As we already knew, the first ship-building establishment of the East India Company on the West coast was in Surat, where, from 1673 onwards, the Parsis—whom A. Hamilton called excellent shipwrights—[95] built vessels for the Company. In 1735, a British officer taking over a ship built in the shipyards of Surat was struck by the skill and knowledge of the shipwright, Lowjee Nassarwanjee, and proposed that he should take charge of the work at the docks then under construction in Bombay.[96] But we also have a more modest version of the beginnings of Lowjee's career in Bombay. Maria Graham, who visited Jamshetjee Bakhman, the great-grandson of Lowjee in 1809, wrote that the latter "came to Gujarat to work in the dockyard as a day-labourer" and thanks to his great ability later became a shipwright.[97] In 1742, the Board of Bombay examined Lowjee's application for a loan of 1,000 rupees to build a house. Taking into consideration the merits of the applicant, testimonies of his capability, and his loyalty, the Board' decided to comply with the request of the mastercarpenter Lowjee.[98] When Lowjee died, he left a house and 3,000 pounds in cash to his heirs.[99] He was the ancestor of the Wadias, a family from which came many leading ship-builders of Bombay, and later on, at the end of the 19th century, a number of big mill-owners. The surname Wadia does not appear in any of the old sources which refer to Lowjee Nassarwanjee.

Lowjee's grandsons, Manikjee and Bakhmanjee, who died in 1790 and 1792, respectively, did not manage to leave large fortunes to their sons, Framjee, Manikjee and Jamshetjee Bahmanjee, who succeeded them.[100] In his work on the Anglo-Indian navy, published in three volumes, Ch. R. Low referred to the great services of J. Bahmanjee, who in 1802 launched the frigate "Cornwallis",[101] which was the signal for the East India Company to embark on a feverish building programme of big men-of-war launched in the dockyards of Bombay.

Information about the conditions in which Indian producers participated in the work of the shipyards is rather incomplete. It seems that the docks were, either entirely or to a considerable extent, the property of the East India Company. In any case, it is safe to say that Indians were not merely workers and foremen. The size of the inheritance bequeathed by Lowjee Nassarwanjee Wadia indicates that he probably was a contractor. Lowjee's great-grandsons owned a large tract of land in Bombay. Maria Graham wrote: "Pestanjee (a brother of J. Bakhmanjee.—V.P.) told me that he received not less than 15,000 pounds a year in rents, and that his brother received nearly as much."

An official document gives the following information with regard to the building activities in the shipyard of Bombay.[102]

Years	*Nos. of ships built*	*Years*	*Nos. of ships built*
1735-1744	7	1805-1814	38
1745-1754	10	1815-1824	26
1755-1764	2	1825-1834	33
1765-1774	17	1835-1844	35
1775-1784	14	1845-1854	36
1785-1794	22	1855	1
1795-1804	24	1856	2

The 84-gun battleship, "The Ganges", was launched in 1810, followed by several sister ships, costing 50,000-60,000 pounds. Vessels built in Bombay were notable for their great seawor- thiness and strength. Low quotes a letter written by the Chief Officer of a Bombay frigate to its builder, Jamshetjee Bahmanjee. It relates that a fleet of 17 British ships spent the winter of 1808-1809 in extremely difficult ice conditions in the Baltic Sea and that only the frigate which was built in Bombay escaped serious damage.[103]

British authors ascribe the successes in ship-building and other types of local enterprise to the business qualities of the contractors and the low cost of the raw and other materials. But there is no doubt that in the 18th century considerable benefit was already being derived from the exploitation of the non-free worker. It is true that the sources for Bombay say far less than the Bengal material about the bondage of the producers, but something can still be gleaned from them. A case in point was the position of the native inhabitants of Bombay island, fishermen of the Koli caste. A message dated February 21, 1717, from the Council of Directors contained a special reminder to the Bombay Council that the Koli were regarded by the statutes of the island as a sort of slaves for the British, so that when they complained about the small pay they should be told that they were slaves and had to work for the British for less pay than for the others.[104] It is true that in 1740 permission was given to raise the wages of the Koli to one-half a rupee a month.

Let us note, however, that the ordinary British practice of limiting wages applied to all categories of working-men in Bombay. In 1767, the Bombay Council noted with concern that the wages of workers in the various fields had become higher than a few years earlier. A special commission submitted recommendations, on the basis of which it was decided that a strong worker was not to receive more than 12 pice for a tenhour working-day, while workers who were not as strong or were older were to be paid less. This decision applied both to the Company's contracts and to those of private persons.[105]

On the whole, however, from the mid-18th century to the end of the Anglo-Maratha wars, the Company authorities could resort to extra-economic coercion in Bombay and the factories to a much lesser extent than in Bengal, where they already had political domination. Indeed, the number of artisans (to say nothing of the rayats) controlled by the Company was relatively small. Native industries were largely oriented not upon exports, as they were in Bengal, but upon catering for the navy, the army and the Company's administration and also the population involved in its activities.

Whereas in Western India British capital, engaged in primitive accumulation, made money up to the beginning of the 19th century chiefly from the monopoly of foreign trade, in Bengal and Bihar, which had been seized by the British earlier, first place from the mid-18th century went to the plunder of the rayats through taxation (on the basis of the supreme land-ownership appropriated by the foreign merchants), direct exploitation of the artisans by British trading capital and downright plunder of the people. Bengal in the second half of the 18th century provides tragic confirmation of the fact that merchant's capital, when dominant, constituted a system of plunder. What Marx said on this point applied above all to Bengal and in part to Southern India: "During the whole course of the 18th century the treasures transported from India to Britain were gained much less by comparatively insignificant commerce, than by the direct exploitation of that country, and by the colossal fortunes there extorted and transmitted to England."[106]

The tribute was transferred from Bengal to Britain in the form of export goods, which were paid for by the money coming in as tax.[107] In the 19 years from 1793 to 1812, more than 25 million pounds was extracted in the form of taxes and spent on the purchase of Indian goods for export and sale in Europe without any commercial compensation for India.[108] The merchants and bankers of Bihar and Bengal were, quite understandably, forced to collaborate with the East India Company in other forms and on other, less advantageous terms, than the Gujarati Banias.

The Company, which strove to increase tax receipts as much as possible, at first preserved and even extended the system of short-term tax-farming.[109] "The Bengal District Records of the 18th century show that the revenue was not paid by the land-owners to the revenue officers of the East India Company direct, but was collected through the agency of the indigenous bankers."[110] In 1765, when the Mogul authorities had to hand over officially the right to collect the land-tax in Bengal to the Company, Lord Clive appointed an 18-year-old descendant of the Jagat Seths as Shroff of the Company.[111] In the same year, Clive censured the Seths for ruining the zamindars. But it was the same Jagat Seths who, on the evidence of Bolts, played the decisive part in Lord Clive's notorious acquisition "or rather appropriation—of his jagir. In 1773, Warren Hastings established the Central Bank of Bengal and Bihar headed by Ray Dayal Chand, a member of the Jagat Seth family, and Huzuri Mal, a Calcutta merchant whose business it was to remit tax revenues.[112]

Rayat uprisings and dissatisfaction among the zamindars forced the East India Company at the end of the 1770s to discontinue the farming out of land-tax on a large scale. From that time onwards, the Company preferred to deal directly with the zamindars. The gradual exclusion of merchant's and usurer's capital from the sphere of tax-collection and loans to the Treasury as well as from foreign trade and, partially, from internal trade too, led to the decline of the big banking houses of Bengal at the close of the 18th century.[113] According to H. Sinha, the reason for this will be found in the fact that foreign trade slipped out of the hands of the Indians, while internal trade was for a considerable time also monopolised by the servants of the Company. As a result, the native bankers naturally lost their leading positions. The foremost banking house, that of the Jagat Seths, was but a shadow of its former self, although it still continued for some time to act as a medium for transmitting local revenue payments to Calcutta.[114]

The Jagat Seths remained bankers of the Company up to 1782.[115] They were then replaced by the Marwari banking house of Gopal Das, who was a member of a big Benares firm of Marwari bankers from the Agarwalla community. He and his brother moved to Calcutta in the 1770s and there acquired a great fortune. His son, Bhavanidas, was the supplier of the British army that invaded Mysore in 1799. How great the services were which Bhavanidas rendered to the invaders is evident from the fact that he received the sword of Tipoo Sultan after Seringapatam was taken by the British.[116] But these bankers were never able to rise to the position held by the Jagat Seths.

In the late 1780s, shroffs were no longer engaged in transmitting tax revenues. Local bankers, the Jagat Seths in the first place, had suffered great losses in the sphere of money speculations because the Company switched to the issue of its own coins, having seized the mint of the Jagat Seths.[117] The descendants of the Jagat Seths had the 12,000 rupees of pension paid them by the British for old services to live on.[118] In the 1860s, the Bengal Bania, B. Chunder, wrote that the descendants of the Jagat Seths still had their ancestral residence in Murshidabad, but had been altogether impoverished and until the British awarded them a pension had to live by selling off their family treasures.[119]

British capital, having noticeably supplanted Indian merchant's and usurer's capital in Eastern India, which operated in trade and tax-collection, gave it a kind of compensation in the opportunity to turn its accumulations into the acquisition of landed property. It was Hastings who admitted that the acquisition of landed property and loans taken out with land as security in the 1770s did not as yet have sufficient backing and ultimately were less gainful than investments in the securities of the Company's administration.[120] In order to make land property a reliable sphere of investment, there was need to establish the landowners' legal rights and to fix the land-tax, which was, in effect, done by the 1793 Permanent Settlement. The zamindars were legally recognised as owners of land, bound to pay land-tax at a fixed rate.

The old nobility proved incapable of meeting the great tax demands and in most instances lost their possessions. Within the first 20 years after the introduction of the Permanent Settlement, one-third or even one-half of the zamindar lands passed into the hands of new owners, who bought it at public auctions.[121] Marx noted that in Bengal, as a result of the Cornwallis Act, a large part of the landed estates passed into the hands of several urban capitalists who had free capital and who were willing to invest it in land.[122]

Tax-farmers and Company employees belonging to the highest Bengal castes, the Brahmans and the Kayasthas, prevailed among the new zamindars. Thus, in the mid-19th century, over 90 per cent of all zamindars were members of these castes in one of Bengal's districts.[123] The relatively insignificant participation by trading and money-lending castes, the Marwari among them, in seizing the landed estates is to be explained by the very tenacious caste traditions.

One gets the impression that up to the end of the 18th century, the Marwari and other bankers, who came not from Bengal but mainly from the upper parts of India, predominated in Bengal's trading and financial operations. But having started out in their business relations with the Company as independent brokers, they were gradually converted into its agents. D. R. Gadgil writes that "there were in Bengal communities like the Subarna baniks, who traditionally specialised in trade and business and who corresponded to the Banias in other regions. They do not, however, appear to have been important in Bengal banking or trade in 1750. In Bengal, in 1750, the situation appears already influenced in part by the advent of the British and other Europeans. An important indicator of this was the rise to importance of some elements in Indian society through association with Europeans. Here it is necessary to distinguish between relations of foreigners with Indians on the basis of businessmen to businessmen and relations of foreigners with Indians who acted as ... agents of the foreigners.... In Bengal, from the foundation of Calcutta onwards, the Englishmen sought chiefly administrative assistance and business agents. As a result, communities such as Brahmans and Kayasthas from Bengal who had no previous footing in business make their entry into it as the assistants and agents of British businessmen." During the latter half of the 18th century, "Bengali names in business are relatively unimportant and where they occur are mostly of the rising professional agent class and not those from indigenous trading elements."[124] N. K. Sinha also says that after the occupation of Bengal, Hindus of the upper castes predominated among the Company's brokers, whereas earlier on they were almost exclusively of the Vaishya caste.[125] The appearance of upper castes among the brokers was apparently due to the fact that with the occupation of Bengal the Company was in need of non-Muslims who were conversant with the collection of taxes and had sufficient social prestige.

Concerning the weakness of the local trading and money- lending castes in Bengal, N. K. Sinha says that this was due, in particular, to the fact that Vallal Sen, who was responsible for giving new ranks to different castes in Bengal in the second half of the 12th century, had placed bankers (the Subarna baniks) very low in the list. In the Mogul period, the low status of the local money-lenders led to the establishment in Bengal of newly arrived traders and bankers, who reckoned little with the local tradition concerning persons of their occupation. As an example, Sinha refers to the petition for the re-establishment of a mint in Murshidabad, which was signed, besides the Jagat Seths, by another seventeen local bankers, of whom only three were Bengali.

However, it is hard to explain the weakness of the trading and money-lending castes in Bengal on the strength of tradition alone. These same traditions did not, as Sinha himself observes, prevent Bengali Hindus of the upper castes—Mukherjee, Banerjee, Sharma, Tagore, Datta, Mitra, Ghosh, Sen—from predominating as the leading business section from 1757 to 1785. If by the early 19th century this group had somewhat withdrawn from commercial activity, this was due to the transfer of their funds into zamindar landed estates, land and house property in Calcutta, with a retention of a part of the financial operations.[126] However, up until the mid-19th century some Bengali of the upper castes were still represented in large scale enterprise.

Thus, enterprise itself, specifically money-lending, did not entail—at any rate in the 18th century—any conflicts with the caste regulations even for members of Bengal's upper castes. Besides, if Vallal Sen had lowered the Subarna banik caste for usury, the second biggest caste of Bengal Banias, the Gandha banik, was left by him in a place of honour within the caste hierarchy, it being assumed that they would confine their operations to the "pure" business of trading in grain.[127] But the status of the Gandha banik in Bengal's business world differed little, if at all, from the status of their more humble fellows. Both fell far short of the scope of operations carried on by the Gujarati and the Marwari Banias. The reason would seem to lie in the specific features of Bengal's land-tax system, where a ramified network of middlemen from among the land cultivators of various grades largely blocked for merchant's capital access to the surplus-product of agriculture. Besides Bengal's Mogul rulers preferred to deal with the richer bankers who came from the central parts of the Empire.

Although in the first few decades of British rule the bankers of Bengal still controlled a sphere of operations for accumulated money as loans to the government (now an alien one), Indian businessmen did not show any special inclination to purchase the securities issued by the British authorities. According to W. Hastings, there were not many Indian creditors, merely a few old Hindu families of the Presidency (that is, the landowning élite), whereas the majority of security owners were Englishmen.[128] After the conquest of Bengal, the East India Company established control over the wholesale trade—and to a certain extent also the retail trade—within Bengal, in addition to the monopoly of foreign trade which it already possessed. Romesh Dutt wrote about commerce in Bengal after 1757: "The Company's servants conveyed their goods from place to place duty-free, while the goods of the country merchants were heavily taxed in transit. The country traders were ruined."[129] Some merchants, however, were able to adjust themselves to the new conditions, they began to serve British merchant's capital and became agents of the East India Company. It was precisely with the help of these agents that the British laid their hands on a considerable part of retail trade in Bengal. The Nawab of Bengal Mir Kasim wrote to the Governor in 1762: "The Gomashthas and other servants in every district, in every Gunge, Perganah and village, carry on a trade in oil, fish, straw, bamboos, rice, paddy, betel-nut, and other things."[130] Indian agents, especially the Banias, displayed great cunning in the treatment of their British masters. Official documents of the East India Company record that Banias employed by Englishmen countenanced bad habits among young officials, involved them in debts and became the real masters of the situation.[131] However, I shall give below some examples of the converse.

Whereas under the dadni system the East India Company gave credits to the Indian buyers, private British merchants, especially employees of the Company, on the contrary, obtained credits from the Indian Banias. Those were the loans which enabled them to make large-scale purchases of Indian goods for shipment to Europe and also to live off the fat of the land, with expenses many times exceeding their salaries. The relations between the British debtor and the Indian creditor were formalised in a very peculiar way: the latter was employed by the former as his personal broker and was even paid a small remuneration for it.[132] In this way he was issued a kind of safe conduct which protected him against the arbitrary acts of the British administration and enabled him, for his own part, to act similarly with respect to his underprivileged compatriots.

By resorting to brute force, the Company arrogated to itself the exclusive privilege to conduct foreign trade in the principal commodities. An English author wrote at the close of the 18th century that "piece-goods, silk, saltpetre, opium, sugar and indigo pass almost wholly through the Company's hands."[133] In 1733, Hastings established the monopoly right of the East India Company to trade in opium. Merchants holding contracts were obliged to deliver opium at prices fixed by the Company. Thus, the position of opium merchants in conquered Bengal differed sharply from that of the Bombay traders who sold their opium direct to China. By the end of the 18th century, according to A. Guha's estimate, only 10 to 15 per cent of Bengal's foreign trade was in the hands of non-Europeans, which was far less than in Bombay and on the Western coast. This was due to the considerable concentration of Company employees in Bengal in 1828: 1,595 persons against 236 in Bombay and 116 in Madras.

At the end of the 18th century, the financing of foreign trade was taken over entirely by the East India Company and British banks. From the 1780s, the British began to set up their own banks in Bengal and these limited the activity of Bengal bankers,[134] but did not eliminate them. J. Taylor says that the dallals or brokers, and the poddars or shroffs formed "a wealthy and influential body" in Dacca. Through the dallals, the Company purchased cloths. The poddars "had extensive dealings with merchants and zamindars in the exchanges of coins and the remittance of money to different parts" of India. "Abolition of the Arcot currency, and the promulgation of the regulation which fixed the interest of money at 12 per cent" forced the poddars to reduce the volume of their operations.[135]

It is interesting to note that under the statutes of the General Bank, set up in 1786, anyone could be a shareholder, but only an Englishman a director.[136] In other words, the capital of Indian shareholders came under the control of the foreigners and was used by them for India's political and economic subjugation. By the early 19th century, there were close credit connections between British banks and local Marwari bankers. Local bankers made loans in the banks of the presidencies and acted as guarantors for the bank's Indian clients. When British private banks were set up at the end of the 18th century, the shroffs and the bill-brokers acted as guarantors.[137] Each system existed separately because it had its special functions. The native banker engaged in the granting of credits and the financing of the country's internal trade, while the first European banks confined their operations to the capitals of the three presidencies, accepting deposits mainly from Europeans, effecting remittances and financing foreign trade.[138]

The trade monopoly, especially in foreign trade, depended on the colonial exploitation of the enslaved artisans and peasants of Bengal. Francis wrote: "In order that the East India Company might avail themselves of their increased revenues, it was necessary that their investments should be enlarged.... This could not be suddenly done without a monopoly of manufactures; a monopoly supported by the numerous servants and agents, armed with authority which caused great oppression of the manufacturers."[139]

The Company used its extensive network of gomasthas to enslave the artisans. Before the conquest Bengal, like other parts of India, had, side by side with independent artisans, handicraftsmen working at home, who depended on the middleman. J. C. Sinha, who made a study of the economy of Bengal in the latter half of the 18th century, noted that the arrival of the British increased the power of the middleman. Before the East India Company established its rule, it exploited the artisans through the Bengal merchants, who, according to the contracts, undertook to supply the commodities specified in the agreement at definite periods and at fixed prices. After the conquest of Bengal, the British preferred to work through their direct agents, the gomasthas, who were given money by the Company, which they advanced to the weavers, enslaving them by usurious loans.[140]

In 1772, a Dutch merchant, W. Bolts, published in London a pamphlet against the East India Company. The author, who had scraped together a tidy sum (20,000 pounds sterling) during his service in Bengal from 1760 to 1768, later quarrelled with the Company's administration and was sent back to Europe. He claimed that the gomasthas forced the weavers to sign a bond for the delivery of a certain quantity of goods, at a set time and at a fixed price, that is, at a very low price; the weavers were given part of their wages in advance.[141]

Extra-economic coercion was added to debt bondage. "The assent of the poor weaver is in general not deemed necessary; for the gomasthas, when employed on the Company's investment frequently make them sign what they please."[142] J.C. Sinha quotes from the record of an English court sitting on April 12, 1773. According to evidence given by the weavers of Santipur "whose bona fides the judge had no reason to doubt—the weavers were forbidden to work for private traders and to manufacture any goods whatever apart from those ordered by the Company on pain of corporal punishment and confiscation of their property.[143]

Extra-economic coercion and the debt bondage of the artisans secured huge profits for the East India Company. Bolts wrote that the prices which the Company's gomasthas, and, in confederacy with them, the Jachendars (examiners of cloths), fix upon the goods were in all places at least 15 per cent and even 40 per cent less than the goods so manufactured would sell for in the public bazaar upon free sale. The weaver, therefore, desirous of obtaining the just price of his labour, frequently attempted to sell his cloth privately to others, this occasioned the English Company's gomastha to set his "peons" over the weaver to watch him, and not infrequently to cut the piece out of the loom when nearly finished.[144] The intensification of the artisans' labour apparently brought about a certain expansion of cloth production in individual areas. James Taylor held that trade in cloths in Dacca reached its zenith in 1787.

However, the isolation of the factory handicrafts from the internal Indian market and the extraction by the Company of the surplus-product produced by the artisans slowed down the growth of capitalist relations in these industries. Not only the manufacturer—the artisan, but also the merchant, who was in a relatively more favourable condition, failed to develop into an industrial entrepreneur. What Marx said about the ancient Asian forms of usury being able to exist "a long time, without producing anything more than economic decay and political corruption,"[145] is confirmed once again by the activity of the Jagat Seths and other banking dynasties both before and after the British conquest. As early as the second half of the 18th century there was evidence of the gap, which is characteristic of British India, between accumulation and the transformation of money capital into productive capital.

The incipient outflow of merchant's capital towards the coastal area for the purpose of fulfilling brokerage functions prevented the development of internal trade on the basis of the social division of labour that was taking shape in the 17th-18th centuries. Besides, in the second half of the 18th century, according to N. K. Sinha, the demand among the Mogul élite for luxuries fell not only because of the loss of Bengal, but also because of the invasion of the Afghans and the seizures of the Marathas, whose chiefs had simpler requirements.

However, the systematic and unflagging British control over the marketing of cloths, especially of the high-quality pieces, left their manufacturers no free outlet to the market. As a result, the earnings of weavers of all qualifications fluctuated about the level of 3 rupees a month, which ensured subsistence for the family but blocked the way to productive accumulation.

Meanwhile, the Company's profits were enormous. Thus the Company paid the weavers 3 rupees 9 annas for a piece of gurrah cloth, of which the weaver received only half a rupee. But in London, the same piece was sold for 45 s. 6 d. or 22 rupees 12 annas. Given a free market price, the weavers would have sold the piece for 7 rupees 6 annas. It is important to realise the amount of the profits that would have gone to Indian merchant's capital if it had had direct access to the markets of Europe, something that would have created the objective possibilities for enlarging the weaver's share in the price of the commodity.

However, even this relative welfare was coming to an end. N. K. Sinha assumes that Bengal owed its prosperity to the handicrafts and not to agriculture. As the artisan was increasingly forced to engage in farming, he not only lost his skill, but also that specific physical constitution which enabled him to produce his unique masterpieces.[146]

Direct coercion practised by the administrative and police bodies of the East India Company, and the binding of artisans through the Company's buyers-up and brokers were also common practice in other regions occupied by the British. A. Sarada Raju, who investigated the economic position in the Madras Presidency during the first half of the 19th century—on the basis of the Company's records—painted a dark picture of violence and arbitrary rule practised by the Company in its relations with Indian artisans.

In accordance with the demand of the European market, the Company's administration gave orders to its commercial residents for the supply of goods. The residents granted loans to local traders and middlemen, who distributed the money among the weavers as advance payments. The artisans were forced to accept these advances, which enslaved them, because orders from customers other than the Company came in very irregularly, for the traditional commercial links of the Indian artisans had been severed. As a result, many weavers were up to their neck in debt. The traders received a commission of 5 per cent calculated on the value of the goods, but their position was not too good either, for they had to bear the transport expenses as well as any losses that might occur.

"Early in the 19th century, the Committee of Reform reported that the weaver derived no gain by working for the Company, but had to supplement the meagre earnings thus obtained by producing coarse fabrics for sale in the market to maintain his family."[147] The Company's servants admitted that the artisans had to be compelled to work for them. According to a report made in 1802, commercial residents were constantly emphasising the fact that production for private customers was much more profitable than work for the Company, and that the artisans who worked for the Company did so not of their own choice but under compulsion.[148] The authorities of the Company did not, in fact, permit the weavers to accept any private orders until they had fulfilled those of the Company's. At one time, they were altogether forbidden to work for the private market. Weavers trying to escape from the colonial yoke by running away were brutally punished.

However, some weavers resisted the British authorities with success. Thus, in 1793, when the commercial resident in Dacca tried to lower the prices for the weaver's goods, they lowered the quality of their goods ... an effort to counter the reduction in price by economising on the quantity or quality of the yarn used. In general, there were several cases in the 1790s of weavers refusing to sign contracts, demanding higher prices because of the growth of prices for grain and cotton, and petitioning to be released from work for the Company.[149] N. K. Sinha cites many facts of resistance by weavers in Bengal to the extortions of the Company's servants and agents, and protests against the monopoly right to the purchase of cloths.[150]

Even if one abstracts oneself from the British coercion of the artisans and tries to give a general assessment of the consequences for the Indian handicrafts produced by roughly two centuries of work under European contracts, the result does not appear to be positive. First of all, the exports to Europe consisted almost entirely of the products of weaving, while the other crafts were ignored. The system and terms of the contracts were such that only the dealers among the Indians made money, while no elements of industrial enterprise were generated at all. According to T. Raychaudhuri, there is ground for the hypothesis that "the increase in exports in the early 18th century was partly generated by a shift in the centres of production" to the coast and "an increased appropriation of the surplus by a monopolistic company, and did not indicate a proportionate increase in production."[151] Thus, the temporary revival of one export industry did not lead to a general expansion of this type of production in India. Indeed, this export industry itself was not subjected to capitalist transformation as could have happened under equitable relations between the customer and the producer.

This hypothesis is highly fruitful in the sense that it draws attention to the need to study the changes of a territorial and sectoral order in the circulation of currency and goods caused by the beginning of the British conquest of India. These changes were most pronounced in Bengal. Although before the conquest the annual receipts into the treasury of the Great Moguls came to no less than 10 million rupees, there was no evidence of any actual outflow of coin or valuables. The point is, in particular, that the Jagat Seths' operations in transmitting the taxes were to a certain extent even beneficial for Bengal, because after 1728 these tax receipts were remitted to Delhi not in cash but in the form of bills (hundi). This could be done because their income outside Bengal was sufficient to meet their tax obligations to the

Moguls in this province. That is why the coin currency in the province was not reduced because of the remittance of the tax.[152] Besides, Bengal's foreign trade balance was invariably in surplus.

After the conquest of Bengal, although its new rulers did spend a sizable part of the tax receipts for the purchase of local goods, an outflow of coin began. About 45 million rupees was carried away from the Treasury by Mir Kasim (1764), and 50 to 55 million was plundered by British officers and employ- ees in the early years after the occupation of Bengal.[153] In the 1770s and 1780s, silver currency of the province was spent on Chinese goods, and also on fresh conquest in India—already outside the boundaries of Bengal—as well as on the import of indigo, cotton and other agricultural raw materials for subsequent export to Europe. As a result, by the end of the 18th century Bengal's annual balance of payments deficit reached 1.5 million rupees.[154] The shortage of cash and its concentration through the tax apparatus in the hands of the British weakened the positions of the local merchant's and banker's capital.

The surplus in India's trade with Britain became even more fictitious. The Company's administrators of the time, like Sir John Shore and Cornwallis, far from making a secret of the fact, in effect stressed it in discussions with their mercantilist-school opponents in Britain. Shore, in particular, claimed that India's trade surplus with Britain did not prevent the latter from extracting India's silver, until it was exhausted.[155] At the time, the outflow of silver and cash funds, and the concomitant rise in prices were especially felt in Bengal. The continuing outflow of silver and treasures was bound eventually to tell on the general process of accumulation in India herself. It is true that during the Napoleonic wars the situation changed temporarily. In 1806, speakers in the House of Commons noted that India had a surplus in her trade with Europe so that even the tax revenues no longer helped to offset it, and that this had once again led to the import of coin to India (through private merchants).[156]

Alongside the worsening of conditions for accumulation in the early 19th century, there were signs of a reduction in operations by Indian merchant's capital in marketing handicraft products. For instance, Bengal trading capital, largely ousted from the towns, streamed into landed property, although under favourable conditions it could have germinated industrial enterprise. In 1815, Governor General Moira, in a minute on the results of the introduction in Bengal of the Permanent Settlement, noted with satisfaction that merchant's capital and enterprise had been diverted towards the land.[157]

After its introduction, as before, Indian businessmen encountered, not only in industrial production but also in the key spheres of trade and credit, more and more competition and discrimination. Thus, the establishment of ship-building in Bengal helped a few merchants to acquire European-type ships, which gave them some independence (less than that of the Bombay ship-owners) in their overseas ventures. In particular, in the first decade of the 19th century, American firms preferred to collaborate with Bengal businessmen instead of the British agencies. One of these was Ramdulal Day, whose fortune was estimated at no less than half a million rupees. The Americans obtained large loans from him, although they complained that his interest was usurious. But after 1815, British firms, like Palmer and Alexander, took over trade with the USA. In 1813, R. Day had only one vessel, which was registered in the port of Calcutta (the Bengal ship-owner's last tragic jesture before his complete elimination, remarks A. Tripathi).[158] Parsi and Muslim ship-owners in Calcutta had more luck than the Bengali. A man named Dorabjee had three ships in 1803-1805, Dorabjee Biramjee six ships (1806), Buramjee Kovajee two (1813), Sayd Hussein and Sayd Mohammed had one vessel each (1803), etc.[159] The loss of direct connections with America, the decline of the coastal trade and the reduction in the export of some Indian goods forced the Bengal traders to engage in the selling of British goods, and this made them financially dependent on the shroffs in Upper India.

Let us note, however, that the native merchants of Bengal never fared as well as their fellows on the Western coast. By 1833, says Tripathi, hardly any group could be found in Bengal engaged in foreign trade, while coastal trade was limited. In the inland regions, competition from the British traders was crippling, and the decline was merely put off by the extension of British and American trade during the French revolutionary wars and the Napoleonic wars.[160] When these wars ended, private British merchants streamed to the shore of India, and the overseas trade of the Bengal merchants became unprofitable. They received some little compensation from the expanding internal trade, but there they encountered the archaic system of transit and municipal duties which presented a thousand obstacles. Besides, there, too, the Bengal merchants faced competition from British agencies which took the lion's share of the export trade in raw materials, especially indigo, and the import of British fabrics. It is true that a part of the local marketing of fabrics was in the hands of Indian wholesalers, like Ramratton Malik, Raj Madhab Bonarjee and Brajamohan Mukherjee. Indeed, the Indians prevailed only in the salt trade.

Being ousted from trade leading Indian businessmen took to usury and, what was even worse, the growing price of land induced them to invest in it, which, in turn, boosted prices still higher. The real tillers found themselves between the hammer of the zamindar and the anvil of the capitalist, who advanced credits for their production expenses.[161]

Merchant's and banker's capital in Bengal, apart from trading in agricultural produce and buying up land, including plots in the towns, especially Calcutta, engaged in subsidising European businessmen and entrepreneurs, participating as junior partners in British firms, and investing in the East India Company's securities, but did not invest productively in the indigenous industries.

In this situation, the appearance of the British manufacturer in India may seem to be somewhat unexpected at first sight. Indeed, by the early 19th century, some English manufacturers, who opened workshops and hired Indians, settled in India, mainly in Calcutta, Bombay and even in Madras. In 1813, during the debate on the East India Company's charter in the British Parliamentary committees, concern was expressed that the Indians, having studied modern technology under the guidance of their British masters, would be able to apply their knowledge as independent entrepreneurs or work for Indian businessmen. One speaker claimed that almost all local workers would prefer to work for Europeans rather than natives, partly because the former paid wages more regularly and partly because this provided better opportunities to study a craft faster.[162]

However, the last argument was not quite convincing be- cause the period of apprenticeship is bound sooner or later to run out. Indeed, the British themselves admitted that the Indian workers were highly skilled and enterprising. Colonel T. Munro declared that the inhabitants of India were skilled workers and were inclined to adopt any European craft for which they had individual capabilities, taking very little time to expand it to the point at which it met their own demand.[163] Concerning the hope that the Indians would long remain the hired workers of Europeans, another witness declared that as time went on those who were working for hire would soon set up shop on their own.[164]

But the committee members persisted in their attempts to prove that the Indians were unable to meet their own requirements in manufactures. An old Company's employee, Sir S. W. Mallett twice replied in the negative when asked whether he had seen instances of unsatisfied demand among the Indians for British goods. When asked whether the Indians were a trading and industrial people fully meeting their own requirements in goods, he replied unambiguously that they had an industry fully satisfying their requirements in goods. Committee members also asked leading questions, such as whether the Indians could be considered to be simultaneously an agricultural and industrial people. The reply was short and positive.[165]

Thus, the British industrial bourgeoisie, preparing for a broad offensive in India, was making a thorough study of the difficulties and opportunities to be encountered on that market. The possibility of British-type capitalist workshops being established on Indian soil—

first under foreign and then under Indian management—appeared to be a serious threat. However, one should not identify the yearnings of the British industrial bourgeoisie, on the one hand, and the oligarchy of the East India Company and its administrative and military personnel in India, on the other. For fiscal, strategic and even consumer reasons, the Company and its personnel were inclined to support some local industries designed to meet their demands (I say nothing here of the export industries). That is why, apart from ship-building, the Company took a favourable view of various other non-export industries (ship-building, incidentally, was to a considerable extent oriented upon export).

An early example of Indian enterprise in the Bengal Presidency supported by the Company was an iron works in Birbhum (Bengal). The first application for making iron on the basis of the rich local ore deposits by means of an improved method was filed in 1774 by Shudra Narayan. But the Company's Council set the rent too high (8,000 rupees a year), and the agreement was not signed.

Three years later, someone called Farquhar filed a petition with the Bengal authorities requesting the exclusive right to make iron in the Company's possessions west of the Burdwan meridian and to duty-free trade in the metal. It was proposed that controversial questions would not be within the jurisdiction of local officials, who engaged in trade as a sideline and could find themselves in the position of an interested party, but were to be settled on the level of the Governor's Council. Farquhar undertook to supply the Company shot and shells at 80 per cent of the price of the European product. Although his activity evoked resistance from the local jagirdars and rajahs, Farquhar obtained the Company's consent and was even granted an advance of 15,000 rupees in 1779 to complete the construction of his furnaces.

The subsequent ten years are reflected in the records mainly in the claims of the "natives", that is, the local zamindars, to the collection of taxes from Farquhar's works. His iron was also sold in Calcutta at 5 rupees, and English iron at 10 rupees 11 annas per maund (that is, in the first instance, 1 rupee for about 7 kilogrammes, and in the second, for half as much). In 1782, Farquhar withdrew from the iron-making business and contracted to manufacture gun-powder. In 1795, the property was seized by the zamindar, who laid duties on the production, and this opened a period of litigation.

We have no detailed information about what happened to the Birbhum works in the following half-century. Judging by a 1845 report (of which more below), metallurgical production was maintained on a technical basis which was higher than the traditional technology but which was already well below the contemporary level. In particular, charcoal was still used as fuel.[166]

Some additional information on the manufacture in India of goods according to European specimens will be found in a book by A. F. Tytler, who served in Bengal for eight years. In the pertinent section of the book, he set himself the task of showing private British businessmen that they would derive no sure or swift benefits from the abolition of the Company's monopoly on trade with India. Among the difficulties they were sure to face, Tytler gives general mention to the respect which the Company commanded among the local inhabitants because of its strength and energy, the inevitable competition of its employees, the advantages to be derived from the very scale of the Company's operations and its knowledge of the country's resources. Among the economic obstacles, he mentions the plight of the peasants and workers, a factor which was bound to slow the sale of European goods, and also the Indians' religious superstitions, customs and simplicity of furniture and clothing.

Tytler deals in greater detail with the competition European goods were bound to meet on the part of similar local goods, such as the footwear and harness made under European management in Calcutta and by natives in Kanpur and Dinajpur, fire-arms, knives and cutlery made in Monghyr, cutlery and locks in Balasore (Orissa), cloths and hair-powder in Chandernagar, utensils made under European management and without it, carriages and other vehicles built in Calcutta and elsewhere, and other smaller items imitating European specimens (including jam and adulterated wines). He says that the price of labour-power is so low that these goods, even when made of the best materials, could be sold wholesale to retailers for a quarter of the price paid for such goods of European make.

It is true that not all these goods were up to the standard of the high-ranking British, but their lowlier compatriots, the Portuguese, the Anglo-Indians, and also the wealthy Indians who were beginning to use European-mode goods were quite satisfied with the quality of local products. Tytler says that Indian-dressed leather, while being inferior to European leather in durability, was better in other respects: it was lighter and softer, and kept these qualities until the footwear became soggy. Even if Indian footwear was worn only half the time of European footwear, it was preferable, because a pair of shoes made under the supervision of a European craftsman, for instance, cost 2 to 3 rupees, and by a native shoe-maker $\frac{1}{2}$ to 1 rupee, that is, respectively, a quarter and an eighth of the price of a pair of shoes imported from Europe.[167] Other sources say that at first European-mode footwear made in India had low moisture resistance and caused discomforts to the wearer because of poor dressing, but that subsequently its quality improved[168]

In 1813, J. Malcolm mentioned a leather-dressing shop in Madras, which had been opened by a European gentleman who turned out delicate goods like buckskins for mounted artillerymen and gloves; he also mentions a fairly acceptable glass shop in Madras, the production of silver plates and carriages in Calcutta, which were of a higher quality than those coming in from Europe (however, many of the materials for these were imported).[169]

Shoe-makers turning out European-mode footwear had relatively high earnings—from 6 to 10 rupees, including all expenses, but of course, it was hard to start a business even on these earnings. The fact that their wives were engaged in tanning the leather shows that the families of such leatherdressers were not entrepreneurs.

Carriages, chaises and harness of every description made in Calcutta cost from 14 to 160 rupees, with the price going up because of the high cost of the components imported from Europe. It was the general opinion that Calcutta carriages were better than those brought in from Europe. Local wood better fitted the climate, while the artisans who worked under the supervision of Europeans displayed a high standard of workmanship. Three of four establishments in Calcutta supplied carriages for high-ranking persons, while numerous workshops run by "low" Europeans, and half-castes made cheap but fashionable chaises for the less opulent clients. All the ironwork, painting and other finishing were done on the spot and did not differ in quality from European workmanship. A carriage-maker and a blacksmith earned an average of 8 rupees a month, a painter 10, an upholsterer 7, and a saddler from 6 to 8 rupees.[170]

Carpenters, furniture-makers and silversmiths working for Europeans were, according to Tytler, equal to the best British craftsmen in skill.[171] An experienced joiner earned from 6 to 10 rupees, and a silversmith a little more. The tools were very simple: a wooden hammer, saw, plane, chisel, drill, a double-edged axe, which was also used as an adze.

European-type ships must have been built in Bengal with the use of similar tools. In Bengal ship-building originated later than in Bombay, but the period of their prosperity (late 18th early 19th centuries) coincided with the Napoleonic wars. An Indian scientist of our own period believes that European shipbuilding in Bengal was started in 1780 by Colonel Henry Watson, who obtained a tract of land in Kidderpur as a gift from the Company for the purpose of building docks fit for the construction, repair and equipment of naval and merchant vessels. The docks cost him 1 million rupees, but already in 1781 a 32-gun frigate was launched, to be followed by another frigate, the "Surprise", which in 1783 was chartered by the Company for 10,000 rupees a month to carry dispatches to Britain. The former frigate was used by the Company also to carry opium to China. Altogether from 1780 to 1800, at least 35 ships were built at the docks, which were later bought by James Kidd. In the last decade of the 18th century, when the export of Indian rice to Britain was started, there was an increase in orders for Indian-built ships. From 1800 to 1813, 146 ships with a total displacement of 65,000 tons were built; from 1814 to 1821, 96 ships with a displacement of 41,700 tons.[172]

Another Indian scientist dates the start of European ship-building in Bengal a decade earlier and connects it with Hooghly, from whose slipways, he says, at least 272 ships with a total displacement of over 120,000 were launched.[173] The concluding part of R. W. Mookerji's interesting study of Indian navigation in antiquity and the Middle Ages contains more detailed information about ship-building in Calcutta: 35 ships (17,000 tons) were built from 1781 to 1800; 19 ships (10,000 tons) in 1801, and 21 ships (10,400 tons) in 1813; a total of 237 ships with a displacement of 105,700 tons and a value of 20 million rupees, at an average of 200 rupees per ton, were built in Hooghly from 1801 to 1821.[174] These data are incommensurate either in time or place and do not help to give a precise picture of the total volume of ship-building in Bengal, but the large scale of this industry and the fairly big size of the ships (about 500 tons per vessel) are obvious. Although Indians worked on the docks, the technical management here, in contrast to Bombay, was provided by British masters. The ships were built of local timber, which was as fine as that used in Bombay.

But let us turn to the sources. During the Napoleonic wars, which increased the demand for ships and which simultaneously cut Britain off from continental Europe's timber, the interest in Indian ship-building was especially high. In November 1801, the House of Commons even discussed the question of moving the centre of British ship-building to India, where greater advantages were to be gained from the abundance of fine and low-cost timber.[175]

In 1803, A. Lambert published an article on ship-building in Bengal. It said that up to 1781 only two small vessels were built in Calcutta, but that same year Colonel Watson launched a 500-ton vessel capable of carrying 32 guns (according to the source, which shows that the differences between the data given by the Indian scientists are insubstantial). In the 20 years that followed, 38 ships and 39 small vessels valued at 3,600,000 rupees were launched, including a vessel built at Patna, and, together with the vessels built at Chittagong, Silhet and other places in the Bengal Presidency, the total comes to 53 ships and 93 small vessels with a total tonnage of 39,000 tons, valued at 5,100,000 rupees. Lambert noted, however, that Calcutta-built ships were of a truly high quality.

Lambert extolled the navigation qualities, strength and low cost of Bengal ships, which were usually sold at 30-50 per cent above the cost of production. "The scarcity of large ship timber in England will, it is to be hoped, direct the attention of the ministry of this country. Ships of the largest scantling can be built in Bengal cheaper in proportion than those of smaller dimensions; for the price of large ship timber does not rise here in the same ratio as at home: there being no scarcity to give it an artificial value, beyond the comparison of its solid contents to smaller timber."

Lambert cites many calculations to confirm the advisability of building British warships in Bengal. But he also adds: "Almost every article of ship-building, except the timber, would be procured from England, namely, iron and iron-work, anchors, cordage, sail-cloth, lead, copper, nails, bolts, shipchandlery, carvers' work, guns, gunners-stores, pump-gear, etc., which here constitute up to full two-fifths of the cost of a ship when fitted for sea."[176]

This line of reasoning is noteworthy, because it indicates that even when the situation was most favourable for Indian ship-building, its British patrons never forgot about the need to keep the colony technically dependent on the industry of the metropolitan country. However, official documents contain evidence that not only furniture, many iron, steel, gold and silver articles and almost all the leather goods but also iron-work for ships was manufactured in Calcutta in the early 19th century.[177] Full support for this branch of ship-building in Bengal and in Bombay could have paved the way for the construction of steamships.

Yet even the building of sailers in India, similarly to overseas navigation, aroused the stiff resistance of the British champions of laissez-faire policy. According to G. A. Taylor, a contemporary English observer, the arrival of Indian-built ships to the port of London at the end of the 18th century "created a sensation among the metropolitans, which could never have been exceeded if a hostile fleet had appeared in the Thames. The ship-builders of the Port of London took the lead in raising the cry of alarm. They declared that their business was on the point of ruin and that the families of all the shipwrights in England were certain to be reduced to starvation."[178] However, at that time the Select Committee of the House of Commons under the chairmanship of Sir Robert Peel declined their petition. It was noted that after six cruises the Bombay ships were in the same shape as the English ships after three cruises.

But towards the close of the Napoleonic wars the British authorities levied a double duty on goods brought on Indian-built ships,[179] and in approving the charter in 1813, the following stipulation was made: "The ships employed in private trade should be constrained to navigate with a certain number of Europeans outward, so as to prevent, as much as possible, the introduction of native seamen to this country."[180] In this way an end was put to the two golden decades of British indulgence for Indian ship-building.

Summing up our information on the manufactures introduced by the Europeans into India, mention must also be made of local printing. The first unsuccessful attempt here was made by B. Parekh in the 1670s. According to A. Guha, Rustomjee Kursetjee was the first Indian printer. In 1800, Danish missionaries set up a foundry in Serampur to cast Bengali type, and this was done by the blacksmith Pansanan Karmakar. In 1812, the Parsi F. Marzaban started the first printing-shop which used Gujarati type; the same year, another Parsi, Kikibhoi Chhargharr, also set up a Gujarati printing-shop. In Tanjur, a local rajah had several books printed in his printing-shop in 1815 in Marathi and Sanskrit. That same year, two religious books were published for Parsis. We have no information about how production in these printing-shops was organised, but it could be assumed that they were of the manufactory type.

Tytler believed that more and more Europeans would settle in India and that this would result in an improvement of production by local inhabitants, whose patience and persistence enabled them to reproduce any thing with the help of skilled craftsmen.[181] This was not borne out in two respects. First, there was no massive movement of small European industrialists to India; British capitalist production began to move into India in the form of large mills and only about 40 or 50 years later. Second, there was no marked development of Indian artisans, who turned out European-type goods, into the small-scale capitalists, for they did not have either the financial or the technical basis, while Indian merchant's capital showed no inclination to move even into European-type industrial production, being satisfied with the traditional, even if modified, spheres of activity.

The Social Status of Indian Merchants and Artisans under the East India Company

As I have said, the terms and scale on which local merchants were involved in the Company's operations differed in time and place, their political relations evolving accordingly.

Gujarati bankers provided the British with military-political services even in the early 17th century. They warned British merchants in Surat about any imminent attacks by the Rajputs.[182] As the European factories were fortified along the coast of Gujarat, they served as refuge for rich Indian merchants in time of internecine strife. Thus, in 1664 during Shivaji's raid on Surat, only the British and Dutch factories stood their ground with the aid of their artillery.[183] From the end of the 17th century, Bombay became the most reliable refuge for the Gujarati Banias. Fryer wrote in 1674 about the "Banias liking it better than Surat, living freer, and under milder taxations, which they put the present President in some hopes of complying with, could he open the way from hence up the country." But Fryer admits that this would depend on time, and to an even greater extent on the strength of the British.[184]

In the anxious days of the Marathas' struggle against the British colonialists, the Gujarati merchants behaved as the most loyal subjects of the East India Company, helping it with supplies and credits. Rich townsfolk frequently applied to the Company authorities with requests to extend its power and jurisdiction to their towns.[185] Gujarati Banias and Parsis served the Company's administration as advisers and agents. For example, two Parsi families of officials who had served the Peshwas for several generations took service with the new masters after the conquest of Maharashtra.[186] M. Elphinstone, Governor of Bombay from 1818 to 1827, when he was Resident at the Peshwa court at Poona (1811-1817), valued highly the services of Kurshatjee Modi, an employee of the mission. This Parsi had an excellent knowledge of local matters and served the British faithfully; he was apparently for that reason poi- soned by the Marathas.[187]

A. Hamilton explains frankly that a certain amount of protection against plunder in wartime was one of the main reasons inducing Indian traders to move into Fort St. George, around which subsequently the town of Madras arose. "The war carried on at Bengal and Bombay, by the English against the Mogul's subjects from 1685 to 1689, made Fort St. George put on a better dress than he wore before, for the peaceable Indian merchants, who hate contention and war, came flocking thither, because it lay far from those incumberers of trade, and near the diamond mines of Golconda, where there are, many times, good bargains to be made, and money got by our governors; the black merchants resorting to our colony, to secure their fortunes, and bring their goods to a safe market, made it populous and rich, notwithstanding its natural inconveniences."[188] The influx of Indian merchants helped to transform Madras into South India's major trading centre, even though its port had no convenient harbour.

During the first half of the 18th century, many Indian merchants settled in the shelter of the guns of Fort William on the territory of the future city of Calcutta. The most famous of the Indian businessmen of Calcutta was the Sikh Omichand (Amirchand), whom I have mentioned. His origins and activity were largely mysterious, until N. K. Sinha established the stages of his business career on the strength of the Company's records. He started out as an agent of the Seths from Sutanati, long working as brokers for the British in the purchase of goods. In 1752, he managed to trick his dying master into bequeathing his estate in his own favour. By 1755, he had become the owner of large tracts of land and many houses in Calcutta, which he maintained in such a state that they were a hazard to the life not only of the tenants but also of passersby. Towards the end of his life he amassed a great fortune, and in 1758 left a will under which his relatives received 160,000 rupees, and Guru Govinda 4,200,000 million rupees.[189]

Because Omichand belonged to the Sikh community, the following remark by D. R. Gadgil deserves mention: "In the earlier period of Sikhism, for example, the Khatris played a very important part and before Sikhism became a militant religion, Sikhs were reported to be important in trade, both internal and external. It is natural to assume that this was due to elements such as the Khatris among the Sikhs. The presence of Omichand, described as a Sikh, in Calcutta has to be interpreted in the light of this."[190]

In the mid-18th century, when the Company began its open territorial conquests in the Ganges valley, it received extensive financial and political support from the Jagat Seths and other Marwari and Bengali bankers. In 1749, the Jagat Seths granted the conquerors a loan of 1,200,000 rupees.[191] When Calcutta was captured by the nawab's troops in 1756, Omichand remained loyal to the defeated British to the end.[192] In 1757, before the battle of Plassey, which delivered Bengal into the hands of the foreign invaders, the Jagat Seths gave large amounts of money to Colonel Clive. An official English handbook admits that the Indian banker's rupees strengthened the sword of the British colonel, who overthrew the Muslim power in Bengal.[193] After the battle of Plassey, the Jagat Seths, Omichand and other bankers hampered the efforts of the nawabs of Bengal to free themselves from the British and to restore the subah's independence. On British instigation they conspired against Nawab Siraj-ud-Daula and refused to grant any loans to Nawab Mir Jafar. Just punishment was meted out to the Jagat Seths for their treachery: in 1763, when the British started a new war, Nawab Mir Kasim immediately ordered the execution of the two senior members of the Jagat Seths family. The British sent a protest but it was too late.[194] Omichand's role was equally treacherous. In 1757 he informed the British about Siraj-ud-Daula's intention to attack the British factory at Calcutta.[195]

In the mid-18th century, strong economic and political ties were established between the East India Company and Upper India's big merchant's and usurer's capital, and the history of the Rai family of Benares bankers from the Marwari caste of Agarwalla is indicative in this respect. The founder of the family, Partab, held various posts at

Akbar's court. All his descendants served the Moguls, until one of them, Hayaliram, was appointed to a high post in Patna, Bihar, where he struck up a friendship with the British and for his services to the Company was rewarded by Clive (on behalf of the Mogul Shah Alam!) with a jagir and the title of "Rajah Bahadur". The new jagirdar was in charge of setting up Bihar's colonial tax system. His son received more lands from Warren Hastings. In 1803, one of the Rai family negotiated on behalf of the Company with the nawab of Oudh, the maharajah of Gwalior and other feudal princes, and was rewarded with more jagirs and the title of Rajah.[196] Other Hindustani bankers also went to work for the British.

British "law and order" properly accorded with moral rules only to the extent that it did not clash with the self-seeking ends of the British conquerors. Here is the authoritative view of the Reverend Philip Anderson, who put out a book in the mid-19th century based on various sources and personal observations and giving a vivid description of the behaviour of his compatriots in India. One should bear in mind that friction between the Company and the Anglican Church was of a long- standing, dating back to the period when the House of Commons passed a bill putting the duty on the Company to carry a clergyman on board of every one of its ships with a displacement over 500 tons. This ideological supercargo turned out to be such a heavy load for the honorable Company and its personnel that until the end of the 18th century most of its ships were officially registered as having a displacement under 500 tons and any ship that was obviously larger had a displacement of 1,000 and more tons.

That is why Anderson undertook to substantiate the beneficial effect of the Anglican clergy on their compatriots, who were faced with imminent damnation among the swarms of pagans and Muslims and, what was even worse, the local Papists, especially female.

But what Anderson says suggests that the threat to moral values came rather from the subjects of the British crown themselves, and he admits that the Europeans had a bad influence on the people of India. Anderson refers to the view expressed by the president of the Madras factory, Pitt (early 18th century), who declared that it was the Europeans who had set the natives an example "of cunning, suspicion and disobliging behaviour". "When the Europeans first settled in India, they were mightily admired by the natives, believing they were as innocent as themselves; but since by their example they are grown very crafty and cautious."

Bribe-taking by Company employees was commonplace. "At the Hindu feast of the Divalee," says Anderson, "the Banias always offered presents to the President, Members of the Council, Chaplain, Surgeon, and others. To the young factors these gifts were of great importance as by selling them again, they were enabled to procure their annual supply of new clothes." But these young gentlemen were not satisfied with these traditional offerings and "had a clever way of enjoying practical jokes, and at the same time indulging their mercenary propensities", like entering a Bania's premises and pretending that they were shooting doves or sparrows. The Bania, who believed in the ahimsa doctrine and metempsychosis, was horrified and dropped in their hands a rupee or two to induce the visitor to leave. "There, reader, is a picture of the repre- sentatives of a high-minded nation, drawn by one of themselve," Anderson concludes.[197]

While sharing the Reverend Anderson's indignation at these petty extortions, one should not forget about the far more terrifying atrocities committed in time of war, for piracy fills a special chapter in the record of violence perpetrated against the Indians. The adventures of the above-mentioned Avery and others like him had been described in detail and need not be recounted here, but let us note the consequences that piracy had for the establishment of the Company's maritime monopoly. Only powerful escorts of warships could effectively resist the pirate vessels. The East India Company alone had such ships in the Indian Ocean, which is why Indians and private European merchants turned to the Company for protection from the pirates. This gave the Company additional opportunities to control navigation and trade.

Contemporaries may have discerned the connection between piracy and the Company's monopoly of the sea, and confirmation of this comes from the reprisals taken by the Indian authorities against the Company's factories in retaliation for the pirates' attacks. It is true that the Company's historiographers have labelled such acts as blind revenge, but public opinion in Britain took a suspicious view of the Company's assurances about it being uninvolved in the piratical operations, especially since there were grounds for such suspicions.

Summing up his study of British mores in India, Anderson wrote: "I can only say, that I represent the matter faithfully as recorded by the best authorities of the age . . . to be corrupt and corrupt others was the fashion.... Judge patiently, reader. Imagine yourself on the Bench for six months; see what culprits we shall bring before you, and then say whether you cannot form an opinion as to the statistics of folly and crime among Anglo-Indians in the Bombay Presidency at the opening of the eighteenth century."[198] He is echoed by T. Sidenham, who served in India for 20 years as military man and judge. In 1813, he told a Parliamentary Committee that he had cause to observe that the British were more inclined to resort to violence in foreign lands than any other nation and was sure that this held true with regard to India.[199]

Violence and extortion were not at all due to the low official remuneration of Englishmen in India. For instance, British officers in the Anglo-Indian army in the 1820s received the following annual salaries: a colonel from 1,250 to 1,467 rupees, a major from 635 to 777, a captain from 371 to 520, and a lieutenant from 224 to 333 rupees.[200] Senior employees were paid even more: a district collector received 20,000 rupees a year[201]—roughly a thousand times more than the average annual budget of a working Indian family.

A study by P. Spear under the characteristic title of "The Nabobs"[202] describes the life of the British in India in the 18th and early 19th century, showing the evolution of British society in India from a group of unscrupulous adventurers who were out to make money and enjoy themselves to a full-fledged ruling élite, held together by a sense of racial superiority and hypocritical morality. With its evolution all semblance of the human attitude to the Indian subjects disappeared, giving way to a haughty notion of the conquerors' superiority.

These examples—and they could be multiplied by numerous facts of the sacking and plunder of the conquered Indian towns—already suggest that the British "law and order" had its limitations. Indeed, its main function was to establish an order under which colonial exploitation would be carried on as a system of plundering the Indian people. This "law and order" applied to the Indian population only to the extent that it suited the interests of the conquerors.

The following fact shows that the British "law and order" was a far cry from the observance of the elementary norms. In 1752, J. Hallwell, manager of the Company's Calcutta zamindar estate, instituted proceedings against his assistant, Govind Ram, on charges of abusing his position, for with a monthly salary of 50 rupees he had been able to amass a fortune of 150,000 rupees. But the man was not imprisoned and was invited to explain himself. He did so willingly, saying that the money he had misappropriated was required for his equipment that traditionally befitted a man of his rank and position. His explanation was deemed to be convincing and far from being punished, he was allowed to save his fortune.[203]

But one should not assume that cordiality was the rule in relations between the European and Indian merchants. T. Raychaudhuri, who knows the subject very well, says that the Surat merchants strongly resisted British intrusion "in their Red Sea trade, and used their influence to stop the sale of textiles needed for this trade to the English until the latter forced the authorities to withdraw the restrictions."[204]

The fact that a section of the big merchants went over to the side of the British conquerors shows not only that they found feudal rule highly burdensome. With a few exceptions, Indian towns did not become politically independent bulwarks of popular resistance to the invaders. The stand taken by the merchants and other sections of the population in Indian towns during the conquest is important indirect evidence of the level of the urban economy in feudal India. Because trade and the handicrafts in the Indian towns were yet to escape from their dependence on the feudal lords, no politically separate plebeian and burgher opposition to feudalism had time to take shape in the main parts of India. "Though the Indian merchant and manufacturing classes were rich and spread out all over the country, and even controlled the economic structure, they had no political power.... Hence there was no middle class strong enough, or even consciously thinking of seizing power, as in some Western countries."[205] The feudal lord's military and political hegemony over the towns produced a situation in which the latter were unable to organise any independent resistance to the invaders whenever the ruler's troops suffered defeats.

Having established their domination, the British had no intention of setting up any municipal self-government, and as far as we are aware, the towns' upper crust did not make any such demands. The urban element proper (merchants, artisans and other working sections) did not apparently have enough importance in the social structure of the towns or in their social life to expect to secure leadership in self-government. As for the land-owners resident in the towns and the sections directly dependent on them, they were dominant in urban life, making use of traditional ties and relations of patronage. Of course, by passing laws which abolished the old system of land-holding stipulated by service and granted the zamindars the right of property in land, the British regime potentially laid the foundation for claims by the land-owning sections to participation in running the country, the towns in particular.

But it took the experience of almost a century for these claims to become accepted reality. Something like anticipation of this future is contained in Buchanan's interesting reflections:

"The goodness of the Company, in the government of Lord Cornwallis, has raised the zemindars to the rank which the European landlords obtained in the 10th and 11th centuries, when the fees of land became hereditary. The next step in improvement would be to give the towns and markets a privileged municipal government, the want of which in all eastern monarchies seems to have been the grand check that has hitherto prevented the people of Asia from making great advances in civilisation. Whether Bengal is sufficiently matured for such plan I will not venture to assert; but it must be recollected that in Europe the grant of a municipal government to towns followed immediately that of the hereditary right of succession to lands. Of course I would not propose to establish at once privileges similar to those which London or other great cities enjoy. Such must be the work of much time; privileges similar to those which were granted by early kings to their towns and cities would as a commencement be sufficient."[206]

One must also give Buchanan his due for the historical approach. He did not reiterate the vulgar views of his British contemporaries, who claimed that their Permanent Settlement had established something like the British system of relations between landlords and farmers at the end of the 18th century. A recollection of that period in the history of England, when hereditary land-ownership was taking shape and urban self-government was being established with the participation or even the domination of the big land-owning gentry,[207] may yield some productive analogies. But in England this process was a very complicated result of the clashes between the feudal barons, the knights and the upper sections of the peasantry with the participation of the towns. In Bengal, however, preference was given, by the will of the British administration, to one upper section, namely, the zamindars.

Under the existing balance of internal forces (even if one excludes a crucial factor like foreign domination) the strengthening of zamindar land-ownership did not have as a socio-economic consequence the self-government of the towns. Rather the reverse was true. Even under independence, the unilateral strengthening of the big feudal lords would have intensified their control over the towns and their economic life. Under colonialism, any notions of urban self-government were absolutely illusory. Let us note that although in 1790 the Company did nominally revoke the right of the zamindars to collect taxes in the market-place, the latter continued to levy such taxes under the pretext of collecting a land-tax in 1839, and to some extent even in the early 1870s.[208]

Today, Indian scientists are trying to assess the consequences of the first few decades of British rule. A. Guha says in his report at a seminar on social and economic history (Aligarh, 1968) that in 1815 India, like Japan by the 1860s, had an experienced commercial and banking community and also a narrow but sound foundation of Western knowledge. He added that in the last quarter of the 18th century, economic experiments were staged in some native states, like the establishment of a state monopoly on the pepper trade in Travancore or the establishment of a state bank in Mysore. He assumed that if India had had a government like the Meiji regime in Japan, her socio-economic development could have carried the country towards a revival, reformation and industrial revolution. But the national forces of progress turned out to be too weak to seize the initiative from the conservative elements and to derive advantages from the Great Uprising in 1857.

The analogy with Japan does not seem to be too convincing because by the mid-19th century many more bourgeois elements than in India had been accumulated in the Japanese towns and villages. Japan also surpassed India in the organisation of industry. But active and constructive intervention by the national state in economic life could obviously have carried India initially to the stage of the capitalist workshop at least.

In his paper, A. Guha also raised the question of why the industrial revolution did not occur in India after the conquest. Remarking on India's general technological unreadiness for such a revolution by the mid-18th century, he went on to consider the consequences of the conquest itself. Despite the funnelling from the country of 2 to 3 million pounds sterling annually, it continued to have big masses of cash capital. Thus, a British estimate said that about 160 million rupees was in circulation among the natives of Bengal from 1797 to 1801. Guha believed that the conquest had more effect on the interests of the merchants than on those of the zamindars and the bankers.

By the end of the 18th century, he says, the East India Company had two prospects: either to introduce the new factory machinery in the field of India's textile production, which it controlled, thereby keeping hold of some external market, or to switch investment to the export of agricultural products: opium, indigo, cotton, raw silk and sugar. For the sake of the common interests of the British industrial bourgeoisie, the Company opted for the second way. In 1786, Indian yarn was already no longer bought for export, and in the early 1790s a Glasgow merchant filed a petition with the British government to ban the export of textile equipment to India.[209] But the Company continued to step up the export of hand-made Indian cloths, which reached a peak of 3 million pounds in 1796-1799.

Indian weaving, even after the loss of its external markets after 1805, retained the internal market where, according to Guha's estimate, roughly $\frac{5}{7}$ of its products were consumed. I feel that this is an understatement because if we accept the above-mentioned figure for maximum exports, the internal demand comes to about 75 million rupees, that is, about half a rupee per head, which, according to family budget data, was a standard to be found only among the poorest sections.

Guha noted that from 1815 on, India, once an exporter of cloths, began to import them, and said that by this period the country already had an emergent class of entrepreneurs, a system of banking and insurance institutions, an expanding ship-building industry and, in addition, a high potential for accumulation. But despite these favourable factors India was unable subsequently to move to a dynamic economic system because of the operation of the mechanism designed to drain out its wealth through foreign political control of the economy, property and the administration.

Indeed, to return to the question with which we are immediately concerned, the pockets of incipient capitalist workshops introduced by the British turned out to be shortlived and did not provide the take-off for the subsequent formation of a sector of capitalist workshops, let alone factory production. In the Indian handicrafts the branches that suffered first were those in which mature petty-commodity and early capitalist relations had already taken shape. On the regional plane, accordingly, the commercial and handicraft centres on the coast, potential pockets of new social relations, were the first to feel most keenly the oppressive effects of colonialism. Indian scientists emphasised this point in their polemics with M. D. Morris.

From a statement of what happened one has to go on to assumptions—what could have happened if the British Raj had not modified the course of socio-economic, political, ideological and other transformation processes in India. There are several basic attitudes, which I find incorrect, to the formulation of such assumptions.

The first of these suggests that the inert character of 17th century Mogul society was transplanted to the 18th and 19th centuries. The point is that this inert character was breached in the early 18th century by the formation of the Maratha states and then of the Sikh state, Mysore and other states on the regional basis. Their historical potential can only be surmised because the foreign-policy factor, the British aggression, first began to tell on the course of affairs in Bengal, Mysore, Gujarat and Maharashtra, and then on the Punjab and the other more dynamic areas, thereby undoubtedly fortifying their military-administrative strata and, accordingly, weakening the householding strata. The need to muster the resources for the maintenance of troops intensified the tax pressure, especially the land-tax.

It is hard to say how relations between the states which emerged on the ruins of the Mogul Empire would have taken shape without the external intervention. But one thing is sure: European diplomacy did its utmost to cause sanguinary and ruinous strife between them, thereby inflicting much harm on economic and social progress. In this situation, which the invaders themselves created, the establishment of their power frequently appeared almost as release from "chaos".

Rejection of the idea that the colonial regime was beneficial does not imply adoption of the other extreme, that is, exagge- ration of the transformative potential of Indian society itself. The Japanese scientist T. Matsui remarks: "The British may be responsible as the holder of the power for doing nothing or for doing something in the wrong way, but it is too simple an argument to attribute the cause of slow growth solely to British rule, assuming the potentiality of the Indian economy to develop rapidly if only set free from the wrong doing of foreign rulers. For instance, one should not fail to notice that the economic surplus tended, in Indian hands, to be either spent for the large consumption of parasitic classes, or invested, when not hoarded, in land-ownership, usury or commerce, namely, in the non-industrial, half-traditional fields of investment. In short, there was want of the social spring which transforms the economic surplus into modern industrial capital." He denies that India's traditional elements—the village community, the caste system, Hinduism, etc.—were insuperable and puts forward this interesting idea: "Even when something seems to remain unchanged, its part, its meaning in history has changed fundamentally in a new social, economic, political, and cultural context, because the traditional in its entirety has not been preserved. If something seemed to stand petrified, the selective petrification itself was a new phenomenon under the modern colonial rule."[210] This approach appears to be sufficiently objective while being sufficiently dialectical.

The idea that the inertness of Mogul society was insuperable was expressed most vigorously by M. D. Morris, who set himself the task of proving that British rule did not do anything bad or, at any rate, did nothing worse to India. To substantiate his idea, M.D. Morris put forward several arguments. The first is that India's political history could be reduced to this short formula: "From chaos to chaos in three generations."[211] Possibly realising that this kind of assertion was relative (not to say arbitrary), M. D. Morris oddly enough refers to the British Marxist A. L. Basham, who recognises, as Marx did, the instability of the higher superstructural institutions in India, but there is no implication here of any periodical chaos after three generations.

The Marxist approach is more complex than M.D. Morris' reasoning, it only because it makes allowance for the vertical pluralisation of political climates in traditional Indian society. Marx pointed this out explicitly when he said: "However changing the political aspect of India's past must appear, its social condition has remained unaltered since its remotest anti-quity until the first decennium of the 19th century."[212] Indeed, it was the stable (and not the chaotic) character of the fundamental social conditions, Marx believed, that made it possible for the members of the village community to witness quietly "the ruin of empires" [213] This combination of political change at the top and social stability at the bottom provides food for more thought, but at any rate it will be easily understood that the Marxist assessment has nothing in common with the notion of periodic upheavals in Indian society every two or three generations.

Concerning M.D. Morris' subsequent assertions that India's

geography and climate prevented the formation of an effective system of communications and control, I can add nothing to my earlier considerations about the correspondence of the systems of production and distribution in pre-British India. But one argument of Morris' that cannot be accepted at all is that India's agriculture had a low level of productivity, together with his fantastic notion that it was "non-animal-powered" agriculture. The student is equally amazed, while the inexpert reader is tantalised, by the American scientist's view that crop yields in India were low because of the climate. It is hard to suggest these considerations for scientific discussion, whether it be oriented upon the past or the present. His statements about the low per capita income are of equally small interest. As we have already seen, comparisons of the surplus-product in agriculture and in the handicrafts and the results of the exchange between them are much more productive.

But I find the following idea of Morris' altogether too trivial: "My own general impression is that the traditional Indian society was supported at a lower level of real income per capita than was the case in early modern Europe or even in Tokugawa Japan."[214] What is the worth of this statement without an analysis of the system of production and distribution, the family budgets of various sections of the population and, most important, a clarification of the general reasons for the stability or, conversely, for the instability of socio-economic systems feeding on this or that mass of the surplus-product?

One could accept M. D. Morris' statement that the British did not take over a society already fraught with the industrial revolution. But why could the fact that India had reached precisely that historical point serve as ground for justification or condemnation of its conquest? Nor can more be gained by insisting, as Morris does, on the per capita rate of the national product as the yardstick of social development. As I have tried to show, relatively and absolutely large masses of the product in traditional Indian society were rather factors of stabilisation (and stagnation) in social structures than a take-off for their transformation. Reasoning on these lines, we find that the vast amount of surplus-value which is being appropriated, say, by the personnel of the present-day military-industrial complex in the USA also operates as a conservative factor. In other words, Marx's idea about the materialisation of the surplus-product becomes extremely important indeed, whether we apply it to the past or to the present.

M.D. Morris is right in objecting to the notion that the British conquest of India represented the triumph of the industrial revolution. In Marxist writings, the conquest of Bengal has been connected with to start of "the industrial revolution in Britain, but has never been identified with it. However, if we abandon the steam engine as an advantage of the conquerors, should we then go on the attribute it to "the organisational innovations of the Roman Catholic church, of the nation State, and of early modern military administration"?[215] Leaving aside the innovation in Catholicism, whose importance for India's conquest escapes me, I will agree with Morris that the state and military organisation of British bourgeois society was of considerable advantage in the colonial subjugation of other countries and peoples. But this organisation was itself a product of the protracted genesis of capitalism, which carried Britain not only to the steam engine but also to the industrial revolution. That is why in Marxist writings the periodisation of British colonial expansion in India has always been tied in with the stages in the genesis and development of capitalism in Britain. The industrial revolution undoubtedly enhanced the military advantages of the British, helping them to complete the conquest of India and to keep the subcontinent in their grip in the Great Uprising of 1857-1858.

In concluding his polemics with M.D. Morris, T. Raychaudhuri, who usually refrains from making any sharp political statements, writes: "Controversies in history have a particular tendency to get coloured by current political passions. The loss of empires and the struggle against colonial rule have generated attempts to rehabilitate the historical past of the imperial power .... It is difficult to consider such theses as the unprofitability of the colonies to the mother countries, absence of economic motives behind imperialism, long and continuous policies calculated to foster self-government in the dependencies, etc. as exercises in analysis uncoloured by political emotions,— though the fact does not necessarily invalidate them. The intellectual penumbra of the cold war and the earlier attacks on the theoretical basis of Marxism have included efforts to challenge all these implying exploitation of class by class and of country by country,—in fact the very concept of exploitation and class."[216]

NOTES

1. See : *A Discourse of Trade*, pp. 97-99.
2. See : *Hand-Spinning and Hand-Weaving*. An Essay published by the All India Spinners Association, Ahmedabad, 1926, pp. 50-51.
3. *A Discourse of Trade*, p. 98.
4. B.N. Ganguli, *Dadabhai Naoroji and the Drain Theory*, Bombay, 1965, pp. 5-7.
5. W. Hastings, *Memoirs Relative to the State of India*, London, 1784, p. 149.
6. K. Marx and F. Engels, *On Colonialism*, Moscow, 1965, pp. 38-39.
7. N.K. Sinha, *The Economic History....*, vol. I, p. 94.
8. See : K.N. Chaudhuri, Trends in Indo-European Trade in the Seventeenth Century, *IESHR*, vol. VI, No. 1, March 1969, p. 19.
9. See : B.B. Misra, *The Indian Middle Classes. The Growth in Modern Times*, London, 1961, pp. 118-119.

10. "Minutes of Evidence taken before Right Honourable the House of Lords, on the Lords Committee, appointed to take into Consideration so much of the Speech of His Royal Highness the Prince Regent as relates to the Charter of the East India Company", London, 1813, pp. 92-93.
11. *Ibid.*, pp. 19, 24, 37-38, 64, 92, 235.
12. *Ibid.*, p. 615.
13. *Ibid.*, pp. 411, 612.
14. B. Heyne, *Tracts....*, p. 301.
15. K. Marx, *Capital*, vol. I, p. 134.
16. "Papers Respecting the Negotiation with His Majesty's Ministries for a Renewal of the East India Company's Exclusive Privileges, for a Further Term after the 1st March 1814", London, 1813, p. 196.
17. "Report and Documents Connected with the Proceedings of the East India Company in Regard to the Culture and Manufacture of Cotton-Wool, Raw Silk, and Indigo in India," London, 1836, p. 2.
18. *Ibid.*, p. V.
19. W. Silver, *Manchester Men and Indian Cotton 1847-1872*, London, 1966, pp. 255-300.
20. *Reports and Documents....*, pp. XVII, 32, 39.
21. *Ibid.*, pt 2, pp. III, XXIV.
22. *Ibid.*, pt 3, pp. 23, 42.
23. J. Douglas, *Bombay and Western India*, London vol. I, p. 115.
24. [T. Pires], The Suma Oriental of Tomé Pires (An Account of the East from the Red Sea to Japan. Written in Malacca and India 1512-1515)...., vol. I, London, 1944, p. 42.
25. *Ibid.*, p. 45.
26. J. Fryer, *A New Account...*, vol. I, London, 1919, p. 231.
27. J. Ovington, *A Voyage to Surat...*, p. 131.
28. *Ibid.*, p. 166.
29. E. Thornton, *Gazetteer of the Territories under the Government of the East India Company and of the Native States on the Continent of India*, vol. I, London, 1854, p. 430.
30. *GBP*, vol. IV (Ahmedabad), p. 88.
31. B. Bhargava, *Indigenous Banking...*, p. 32.
32. D.R. Gadgil, *Origins....*, p. 27.
33. W. Foster, *English Factories in India, 1642-1645*, Oxford, p. 18.
34. [N. Downton], *The Voyage of Nicholas Downton...*, pp. 13, 24, 133.
35. [T. Pires], *The Suma Oriental of Tomé Pires....*, vol. I, p. 19.
36. *A Discourse of Trade*, p. 122.
37. *Ibid.*
38. J. Fryer, *A New Account....*, vol. I, p. 218.
39. J. Ovington, *A Voyage to Surat....*, p. 233.
40. J. Fryer, *A New Account...*, vol, I, p. 218.
41. *Ibid.*, p. 212.
42. Quoted from: D. Pant, *The Commercial Policy of the Moguls*, Bombay, 1930, p. 148.
43. *Ibid.*, p. 148.
44. [De Thevenot], *Voyages...*, pp. 184, 185.
45. J. Fryer, *A New Account...*, vol. II, pp. 107-108.
46. [J.A. de Mandelslo], *The Voyage...*, p. 51.
47. J. Fryer, *A New Account....*, vol. I, p. 293.

48. Jawaharlal Nehru, *The Discovery of India*, p. 310.
49. J. Fryer, *A New Account...*, vol. I, p. 295.
50. J. Ovington, *A Voyage to Surat....*, p. 219.
51. [J.A. de Mandelslo], *The Voyage....*, p. 59.
52. C.H. Rao, *Indian Biographical Dictionary*, Madras, 1915, p. 325.
53. D.R. Gadgil, *Origins....*, p. 20.
54. J. Fryer, *A New Account...*, vol. II, p. 115.
55. S.M. Edwardes, *The Rise of Bombay*, p. 136.
56. [J.A. de Mandelslo], *The Voyage...*, p. 51.
57. J. Douglas, *Bombay and Western India*, p. 114.
58. J. Ovington, *A Voyage to Surat....*, p. 391.
59. A. Hamilton, *A New Account of the East Indies...*, vol. I, pp. 199-200.
60. B.B. Misra, *The Indian Middle Classes*, pp. 76-77.
61. S.M. Edwardes, *The Rise of Bombay*, p. 107.
62. *Ibid.*
63. *GBP*, vol. IV (Ahmedabad), p. 89.
64. *Ibid.*, p. 90.
65. *GBP*, vol. XXVI (Materials towards a Statistical Account of the Town and Island of Bombay), pt. I, "History", Bombay, 1893, p. 46.
66. *Ibid.*, pt. II, *Trade and Fortifications*, Bombay, 1894, p. 208.
67. *GBP*, vol. I (Bombay), 1909, pp. 152, 154.
68. S.M. Èdwardes, *The Rise of Bombay*, p. 136.
69. Ch. Fawcett, *English Factories in India*, vol. I, Oxford, 1936, p. 79.
70. J. Forbes, *Oriental Memories...*, vol. II, pp. 385-386.
71. *GBP*, vol. I, p. 414.
72. *Ibid.*, vol. XXVI, pt I, p. 263.
73. *GBP*, vol. I, p. 408.
74. *GBP*, vol. XXVI, pt I, p. 268.
75. W. Hamilton, *East India Gazetteer*, vol. I, London, 1828, p. 261.
76. *Handbook for India*, pt I, p. 283.
77. *GBP*, vol. XXVI, pt II, p. 78.
78. S.M. Èdwardes, *The Rise of Bombay*, p. 239.
79. *GBP*, vol. XXVI, pt II, p. 281.
80. A. Hamilton, *A New Account of the East Indies*, vol. I, pp. 41, 91.
81. M.B. Morse, *The Chronicles of the East India Company Trading to China 1635-1834*, vol. I, Oxford 1926, p. 8.
82. *GBP*, vol. XXVI, pt I, p. 274.
83. N.K. Sinha, *The Economic History...*, vol. I, pp. 111, 125, 127.
84. J. Forbes, *Oriental Memoirs...*, vol. II, p. 65.
85. J. Douglas, *Bombay and Western India*, vol. I, pp. 241-242.
86. J.M. Maclean, *A Guide to Bombay: Historical, Statistical and Descriptive*, Bombay, 1880, p. 15.
87. W.H. Coates, *The Old Country Trade*, London, 1911, pp. 51, 90.
88. J. Burnell, *Bombay in the Days of Queen Anne*, London, 1933, p. 110.
89. *GBP*, vol. IX, pt I (Gujarat Population, Hindus), Bombay, 1899, p. 196.
89a. *GBP*, vol. XXVI, pt II, p. 444.
90. *Gazetteer of Bombay City and Island*, vol. I, Bombay, 1909, p. 462.
91. *GBP*, vol. XXVI, pt II, pp. 131, 132.
92. Ch. Fawcett, English Factories in India, vol. I, p. 57.
93. *GBP*, vol. XXVI, pt II, p. 158.
94. *A Discourse of Trade*, p. 99.

95. A. Hamilton. *A New Account of the East Indies*, vol I, p. 160.
96. *Handbook for India*, pt II, Bombay, 1859, p. 279.
97. M. Graham, *Journal of the Residence in India*, p. 44.
98. *GBP*, vol. XXVI, pt II, p. 191.
99. *Handbook for India*, pt II, p. 279.
100. *Gazetteer of Bombay City....*, vol. I, p. 391.
101. Ch. R. Low, History of the Indian Navy, vol. II, London, 1877, p. 176.
102. *Gazetteer of Bombay City*, vol. II, Bombay, 1909, p. 149.
103. Ch. R. Low, *History of the Indian Navy*, vol. I, London, 1877, pp. 278, 298.
104. *GBP*, vol., XXVI, pt II, p. 259.
105. *Ibid.*, pp. 252-253.
106. K. Marx and F. Engels, *On Colonialism*, p. 40.
107. *Minute of Lord Teignmouth*, 18 June 1789". See : "British Rule in India Condemned by the British Themselves", London, 1915 p. 17.
108. See : *Hand-Spinning and Hand-Weaving*, Ahmedabad, 1926, p. 95.
109. Ch. L. Jain, *Indigenous Banking in India*, London, 1929, p. 17.
110. *Ibid.*, p. 18.
111. W. Bolts, *Considerations.....*, p. 158.
112. J. Banerjea, *Indian Finance in the Days of the Company*, Calcutta, 1915, p. 67.
113. Ch. L. Jain, *Indigenous Banking in India*, p. 23.
114. H. Sinha, *Early European Banking in India*, p. 166.
115. *Ibid.*, p. 148.
116. *District Gazetteers of United Provinces, Benares*, Allahabad, 1909, p. 119.
117. *Selections from Unpublished Records*, vol. I, p. 165.
118. *Eastern Bengal District Gazetteers, Murshidabad*, Calcutta, 1914, p. 68.
119. B. Chunder, *The Travels of a Hindoo to Various Parts of Bengal and Upper India*, London, 1869, vol. I, p. 79.
120. W. Hastings, *Memoirs...*, pp. 18, 19.
121. See: S. Gopal, *Permament Settlement in Bengal and Its Results*, London, 1949, p. 3.
122. K. Marx, Khronologicheskiye vypiski po istorii Indii (664-1858), Moscow, 1947, p. 100.
123. E.N. Komarov, K voprosu ob ustanovlenii postoyannogo oblozheniya po sisteme zamindari v Bengalii, *Ucheniye zapiski Instituta vostokovedeniya*, vol. XVIII, 1957, p. 15.
124. D.R. Gadgil, *Origins...*, pp. 18-19, 21.
125. N.K. Sinha, *The Economic History....*, vol. I, p. 103.
126. See: *ibid.*, vol. II, pp. 224, 225.
127. F. Buchanan, *An Account of the District of Purnea...*, p. 217.
128. W. Hastings, *Memoirs...*, p. 18.
129. R. Dutt, *Economic History of the British India. From the Rise of the British Power in 1757 to the Accession of Queen Victoria in 1837*, vol. I, London, 1902, p. 19.
130. *Ibid.*, p. 20.
131. *Selections from Unpublished Records*, vol. I, pp. 462, 463.
132. N.K. Sinha, *The Economic History...*, vol. I, pp. 101-102.
133. H. Colebrooke, *Remarks on the Husbandry...*, p. 169.
134. H. Sinha, *Early European Banking in India*, p. 175.
135. J. Taylor, *A Sketch of the Topography and Statistics of Dacca*, Calcutta, 1840, pp. 186-187.
136. *Ibid.*, p. 14.
137. H. Sinha, *Early European Banking in India*, pp. 171, 173.

138. Ch. L. Jain, *Indigenous Banking in India*, p. 25.
139. See: J.C. Sinha, *Economic Annals of Bengal*, pp. 80-81.
140. *Ibid.*, p. 80.
141. W. Bolts, *Considerations....*, p. 193.
142. *Ibid.*
143. J.C. Sinha, *Economic Annals of Bengal*, p. 83.
144. W. Bolts, *Considerations...*, p. 193.
145. K. Marx, *Capital*, vol. III, p. 597.
146. N. K. Sinha, *The Economic History....*, vol. I, pp. 110-111, 177, 181.
147. A. Sarada Raju, *Economic Conditions...*, pp. 168-170, 173.
148. *Ibid.*
149. H.R. Ghoshal, Changes in the Organisation of Industrial Production in the Bengal Presidency up to the Early Ninteenth Century, in: *Readings in Indian Economic History*, p. 130.
150. N.K. Sinha, *The Economic History...*, vol. I, pp. 168-176.
151. *Readings in Indian Economy History*, p. 77.
152. N.K. Sinha, *The Economic History...*, vol. I, pp. 13, 232.
153. As early as the 1770s, a work was published specially dealing with the measures to prevent the outflow of coin from Bengal : [Sir James Steuart], The Principles of Money applied to the Present State of the Coin of Bengal: being an Inquiry into the Methods to be used for Correcting the Defects of the Present Currency for Stopping the Drains which Carry off the Coin; and for Extending Dit, [s.l.], 1772.
154. N.K. Sinha, *The Economic History...*, vol. I, pp. 232-234.
155. See: R.P. Masani, *Dadabhai Naoroji and the Drain Theory*, p. 31.
156. *The Asiatic Annual Register... for the Year 1806*, p. 26.
157. *Affairs of the East-India Company*, vol. III, pt I, suppl. 9 (Lord Moira of 21.IX.1815), London, 1832, p. 83.
158. A. Tripathi, *Trade and Finance in the Bengal Presidency 1793-1833*, Bombay, 1956, pp. 139-140.
159. *Ibid.*
160. *Ibid.*, p. 261.
161. Ibid., p. 262.
162. *Minutes of Evidence taken before the Select Committee... on the Affairs of East-India Company*, pp. 599-600.
163. *Ibid.*, p. 206.
164. *Ibid.*, p. 540.
165. *Ibid.*, 412, 497.
166. *Bengal District Gazetteer, Birbhum*, Calcutta, 1910, pp. 68-70.
167. A.F. Tytler, Considerations on the Present Political State of India: Embracing Observations on the Character of the Natives, on the Civil and Criminal Courts; *the Administration of Justice....*, London, 1816, vol. II, pp. 331-332, 340-342, 365-366.
168. *Minutes of Evidence of the East-India Company's Affairs*, 1813, pp. 475-476.
169. *Ibid.*, p. 114.
170. *Ibid.*, pp. 367, 369.
171. A.F. Tytler, *Considerations...*, p. 370.
172. S.B. Singh, *European Agency House in Bengal (1783-1833)*. Calcutta, 1966, pp. 18-20.
173. K. Datta, *Survey of India's Social Life and Economic Conditions in the Eighteenth Century (1707-1813)*, Calcutta, 1961, p. 110.

174. R.K. Mookerji, *Indian Shipping*. A History of the Seaborne Trade and Maritime Activity of the Indians from the Earliest Times, Bombay, 1959, pp. 181-182.
175. The Asiatic Annual Register, or, A View on the History of Hindustan, and the Politics, Commerce and Literature of Asia, for the Year 1802, London, 1803, pp. 253-255.
176. "The Asiatic Annual Register... for the Year 1803", London, 1804 (Miscellaneous Tracts), pp. 18, 19, 24.
177. *Minutes of Evidence...*, London, 1813, p. 709.
178. R. A. Wadia, *The Bombay Dockyard and the Wadia Master Builders*, Bombay, 1957, p. 178.
179. *Ibid.*, p. 185.
180. See : *Papers respecting the Negotiation... for Renewal...*, p. 125.
181. A.F. Tytler, *Considerations....*, p. 371.
182. [N. Downton], *The Voyage....*p. 116.
183. [J.B. Tavernier], *Les six voyages....*, p. 84.
184. J. Fryer, *A New Accounts...*, vol. I, pp. 181, 182.
185. A.K. Forbes, *Râs Mâlâ...*, vol. II, London, 1856, pp. 21, 80, 81.
186. "Minutes of Evidence taken before the Select Committee on the Government of Indian Territories", London, 1833, p. 294.
187. "Poona Affairs (Elphinstone's Embassy). English Records of Maratha History. Poona Residency Correspondence", vol. VII, pt I, Bombay, 1950, pp. 323, 324, 358-361.
188. A. Hamilton, *A New Account of the East Indies...*, vol. I, p. 360.
189. N.K. Sinha, *The Economic History...*, vol. I, pp. 239-241.
190. D.R. Gadgil, *Origins....*, p. 18.
191. D.R. Rau, *Present-Day Banking in India*, Calcutta, 1930, p. 250.
192. *Old Fort William in Bengal...*, vol. II, p. 98.
193. *Murshidabad...*, pp. 62-66.
194. B.R. Rau, *Present-Day Banking in India*, p. 251.
195. *Selections from Unpublished Records*, vol. I, p. 77.
196. *District Gazetteers of the United Provinces. Benares*, p. 118.
197. Ph. Anderson, The English in Western India; being the History of the Factory at Surat, of Bombay and the Subordinate Factories on the Western Coast. From the Earliest Period until the Commencement of the Eighteenth Century drawn from Authentic Works and Original Documents, London, 1856, pp. 270, 389.
198. *Ibid.*, pp. 339-340.
199. *Minutes of Evidence....*, p. 601.
200. *The East India Register for 1826*, p. LXVIII.
201. *The Asiatic Annual Register.... for the Year 1806. State Papers*, p. 38.
202. P. Spear, *The Nabobs*. A Study of the Social Life of the English in Eighteenth Century India, London, 1963.
203. B.B. Misra, *The Indian Middle Classes*, p. 82.
204. *Readings in Indian Economic History*, p. 74.
205. Jawaharlal Nehru, *The Discovery of India*, p. 263.
206. F. Buchanan, *An Account of the District of Purnea...*, pp. 585-586.
207. M. Weber, Gorod, Petrograd, 1923, pp. 61-62.

208. *Statistical Accounts of Bengal* (further referred to as "SAB") by W. W. Hunter, vol. V, London, 1875, p. 129.
209. N.C. Sinha, *Studies in Indo-British Economy Hundred Years Ago*, Calcutta, 1946, p. 28.
210. *IESHR*, vol. V, No. 1, March 1968, p. 30.
211. *Ibid.*, p. 4.
212. K. Marx and F. Engels, *On Colonialism*, p. 27.
213. *Ibid.*, p. 29.
214. *IESHR*, vol. V, No. 1, March 1968, p. 6.
215. *Ibid.*, p. 7.
216. *Ibid.*, p. 99.

SECTION THREE

INDIAN HANDICRAFTS AND ENTERPRISE IN THE EPOCH OF INDUSTRIAL CAPITALISM

New Methods of Colonial Exploitation and Socio-Economic Relations in India

A period of India's colonial exploitation by the British bourgeoisie proper opens with the completion in the early 19th century of the industrial revolution in Britain. The abolition in 1813 of the East India Company's trade monopoly marked the switch to India's exploitation by industrial-capital methods, a process which was accelerated by Napoleon's blockade of Britain, which was cut off from some of its markets and raw-material sources (hemp, raw silk, etc.). Thus, by depriving Britain of Italian raw silk, the blockade induced a step-up in the export of the raw material from Bengal.

Almost a quarter-century of anti-Jacobin and Napoleonic wars, says Engels, gave British industrial goods a virtual monopoly of all the trans-Atlantic and some European markets; when peace was re-established in 1815, England with her steam operated factories was able to supply the whole world, while steam engines were as yet almost unknown in the other countries. In factory production England had left them well behind.[1] In this quarter-century England achieved major successes in fighting her colonial rivals—France, Spain and the Netherlands.

The designation of the period of colonialism from the beginning of the 19th century to the 1860s and 1870s as a period of industrial capitalism requires the same reservations as those made earlier in considering the epoch of primitive accumulation. First, Britain apart, the other colonial powers, and not all of them either, entered that stage of capitalism only by the mid-19th century. Quite naturally, earlier colonial methods of the bloody dawn of capitalism still prevailed in their possessions. Second, in the British dependencies the methods of colonial exploitation were also being transformed slowly and with contradictory results.

The British mill-owners' economic ideal was a set of prosperous colonies with an effective demand for British goods and an abundant-supply of low-cost and high-quality raw materials for Britain. Actually, industrial capitalism and the type of colonialism it engendered had nothing in common either with welfare for the population of the colonies—the basis of effective demand—or with a boosting of the productive forces there—the basis of raw-material production by working men with incentives to do so. As merchant's capital before it, industrial capital used extra-economic coercion for its colonial exploitation.

It was the outstanding German revolutionary thinker Rosa Luxemburg who emphasised forcefully that coercion was inevitable as a factor helping to breach the self-sufficiency of the Asian and African countries for their inclusion within the system of the world capitalist market, adding that the capital accumulation cannot wait "for the completion of the natural slow erosion of non-capitalist forms in preparation for a transition to a commodity economy. Hence the constant military occupation of the colonies, native uprisings and colonial expeditions to put them down as a permanent feature of the colonial regime. Coercion in this case is the direct consequence of the clash between capitalism and subsistence structures which set a limit on capital accumulation."[2] She cited the example of the British appropriation of the right of supreme land-ownership in India and the eviction of Algerians from their lands by the French settlers.

Extension of extra-economic coercion against the producers of raw materials as a consequence of the industrial revolution in Britain and other advanced countries was inevitable because the revolution ran primarily in manufacturing, without introducing any essential changes in the technology of rawmaterial and food-stuff production. Machine production presented a growing demand for the types of raw materials which were either not produced at all in the metropolitan country (cotton, raw silk, jute and indigo) or were produced on a scale and at a price which did not ensure big industrial capital adequate profits. The lack or inadequacy of raw materials at home impelled these powers to obtain them on the usual commercial terms from countries which had such materials (e.g., cotton exports from the USA), or to import them from the dependencies in Asia, Africa and Latin America on whom inequitable terms of trade could be imposed. The former had, as a rule, a higher productivity of labour and lower production costs, while the latter were able to "offer" competitive prices only if extra-economic coercion was applied to the producer.

Marx blasted any illusions on this score in 1847, when in his work "The Poverty of Philosophy" he showed the connection between extra-economic coercion in the form of slavery and the raw-material requirements of large-scale industry. He wrote: "Direct slavery is just as much the pivot of bourgeois industry as machinery, credit, etc. Without slavery you have no cotton; without cotton you have no modern industry. It is slavery that gave the colonies their value; it is the colonies that created world trade, and it is world trade that is the precondition of large-scale industry."[3]

In some instances, the feudal-colonial system produced a lesser effect in the production of raw materials for factory industry than "direct slavery", and this was realised by the members of the House of Commons who represented in that lofty institution the interests of Lancashire. One of them, remarking on the falling cotton yields in the West Indies and Brazil following the abolition of slavery in the early 1860s, said with relief: "...In India alone free labour has been able to sustain a competition with that of slaves."[4]

This term "free labour" did not in any sense reflect the actual state of affairs in India. Under a subsistence economy the possession of money capital did not in itself as yet ensure the purchase of agricultural product. That is why the British authorities extensively applied coercion to force the peasants to grow the crops they needed (like indigo). Finally, the money form of the land-tax and its scale, which the land-holders found too burdensome when growing the usual food crops, forced them to switch to commercial crops (cotton, jute, indigo, sugarcane), which yielded a relatively large amount of return per unit of area. Additional guarantees that the peasant husbandries would specialise in raw materials were provided by merchant's and usurer's capital, which had secured control of the marketing of raw materials and the supply of food-stuffs to its producers, whom it held in debt.

Partial orientation by some Asian and African countries upon the production of raw materials involved coercion not only with respect to the direct producers but also to the countries themselves. The import of European goods, despite all the customs privileges, did not as a rule yield the returns that could cover the purchases of the necessary raw materials on a commercial basis. That is why a large part of the material values coming in from India was materialised land-tax, and was usually imported in the form of raw materials and semi-finished products, which replaced handicraft articles as the main export item. It is remarkable that a voluminous book about India's productive potential, published in 1840, makes no mention at all of its industrial products, the country being represented as a producer of agricultural produce alone.[5]

The elements that made up the tribute which India had to give will be seen from the following figures. In the five years from 1834/35 to 1838/39 India transferred to Britain through official channels 15,408,000 pounds, of which 3,160,000 pounds were dividends of the Company's stockholders, 2,495,000 pounds pensions for retired men of the Indian service, and 1,828,000 pounds interest on the "Indian debt" Other numerous items were mainly diverse military and civilian pensions. According to R. Montgomery Martin, apart from the annual remittances of over 3 million pounds to Britain, about half a million pounds was received in the form of private income and also profits from trade, a total of 4-5 million pounds.

Describing the mechanism by means of which the colonial tribute was transferred to the metropolitan country, James Melville, secretary of the East India Company, drew attention to the fact that it also included receipts in China from the sale of Indian opium and cotton which were subsequently spent in that country to purchase tea and silk. That is why, he said, the total value of the goods exported from India (directly or via China) came to 9 million pounds, of which a commodity mass worth 4 million pounds was a direct material embodiment of transfers by the Company and private persons. In addition, a part of the export earnings was brought to India from China in the form of treasures and coin. In 1830/31 to 1832/33, this import came to 7 million rupees a year and, in 1833/34 to 1837/38, it reached an annual average of 13.6 million (in 1937/38, 17.3 million rupees). The Opium Wars, we discover, had their own financial and currency history. Only the export of opium to China was worth 3.9 million pounds in 1836/37, and 2.9 million pounds in 1937/38.[6]

Apart from the extraction of raw materials, Britain's industrial capital also had another purpose, which was the forcible inclusion of India in the sphere of its market outlets. In addition to the gratuitous extraction of valuables from the colonies (or to some extent in place of it), there began the non-equivalent exchange which was carried on not through the mechanism of coercion, even if it did pave the way for such exchange, but through outwardly equitable commodity-money relations between seller and buyer. It was Marx who showed the essence of non-equivalent exchange when he wrote: "Capitals invested in foreign trade can yield a higher rate of profit, because, in the first place, there is competition with commodities produced in other countries with inferior production facilities, so that the more advanced country sells its goods above their value even though cheaper than the competing countries. In so far as the labour of the more advanced country is here realised as labour of a higher specific weight, the rate of profit rises, because labour which has not been paid as being of a higher quality is sold as such. The same may obtain in relation to the country to which commodities are exported and to that from which commodities are imported; namely, the latter may offer more materialised labour in kind than it receives, and yet thereby receive commodities cheaper than it could produce them."[7]

Consequently, the essence of non-equivalent exchange lies in the gap between the national levels of labour productivity in the advanced and the lagging countries. As a result, the former spend less socially necessary labour than the latter in creating the same exchange-value. That is why, when exploiting his worker, say, for an hour, the British manufacturer was able to sell on the world market the commodity produced in that time and to buy another commodity embodying the labour of many hours by an Asian or an African cultivator.

Even before the industrial revolution, the advanced countries of Europe had outstripped the Asian and African countries in labour productivity, especially in industry. The general spread of manufacture with its detailed division of labour, specialised tools and other implements, the use of simple mechanisation and of the energy of water and wind, the achievements of shipping and, finally, the greater physical strength of the average European worker as compared with that of the Indian artisan gave Europe an advantage in labour productivity in many key industries. But in some industries (especially in terms of quality and taste) the unsurpassed individual skills of the Indian artisans largely compensated for their technical lag.

The industrial revolution gave Britain the lead in labour productivity, paving the way for its non-equivalent exchange with other countries on an unprecedented scale. In "The Poverty of Philosophy," Marx gave the following calculations: "In 1770 the population of the United Kingdom of Great Britain was 15 million, and the productive population was 3 million. The scientific power of production equalled a population of about 12 million individuals more. Therefore there were, altogether, 15 million of productive forces. Thus the productive power was to the population as 1 is to 1; and the scientific power was to the manual power as 4 is to 1.

"In 1840 the population did not exceed 30 million: the productive population was 6 million. But the scientific power amounted to 650 million; that is, it was to the whole population as 21 is to 1, and to manual power as 108 is to 1.

"In English society the working day thus acquired in seventy years a surplus of 2,700 per cent productivity; that is, in 1840 it produced 27 times as much as in 1770."[8]

In some industries, the leap in labour productivity was even greater. Thus, in the cotton industry, whose products were becoming the chief item of British exports to India, the spinning jenny (invented in 1764) increased productivity 200-fold, and the loom (invented in 1785 and improved in the early 19th century) 40-fold. Nor did the growth of productivity stop there: from 1829-1831 to 1859-1861, the output of yarn per hour increased by 170 per cent, and of fabrics seven-fold. At the same time, there was a reduction of prices.

While the industrial revolution was advancing in some countries of Europe and in North America, there was stagnation and frequently even decline of the productive forces in Asia and Africa due to the colonial expansion, wars and disruption of long-standing economic ties. The incipient gap in productivity levels became disastrous for the countries of Asia and Africa, increasing their economic inequality even when commercial deals with foreign capital were nominally independent. R. Montgomery Martin estimated in the early 1840s that the British farmer had a five-fold superiority in labour productivity over the Indian cultivator, and the British weaver a six- or even ten-fold superiority over the Indian weaver.[9] But his figure for weaving appears to be clearly understated.

As was the case in Britain's efforts to include India in the world market as a producer of raw materials, Britain had to use force to breach that country's self-sufficiency in converting it into a mass market in order to realise its technical and economic superiority. The first act towards that end was the violation and, as the conquest proceeded, the total abolition of India's customs independence. By taking such forcible action under the pretext of promoting "free trade", the Western countries always made a point of protecting themselves from any Asian or African competition. Without going into the problem of discrimination against Indian goods on the markets of the metropolitan country, let us note that other countries also subjected Indian goods to tariff discrimination. Thus, in 1816, the USA introduced 60 to 70 per cent duties on Indian fabrics.[10]

But having breached the customs barrier, British capital came up against another obstacle in its trade expansion: the absence or inadequacy of needs for imported goods. As I have already said, the main reason for the narrow market demand lay in the fact that the vast majority of the Indian population, continued to live in the conditions of a closed subsistence economy or direct product-exchange relations. That is why the first branches of the Indian handicrafts to encounter British competition were those which had separated from the system of direct relations with agriculture. In other words, the most promising elements of the national economy were jeopardised. Accordingly, the foreign competition inflicted the greatest harm on the areas with relatively mature relations of production and social division of labour. The urban handicrafts which worked for the emergent all-Indian market and were going through initial stages of the genesis of capitalism suffered in the first place.

The village and local industries displayed a much greater power of resistance. An advantage of the former was their orientation upon the production of traditional agricultural implements, which did not change. Local industries turning out consumer goods relied strongly on traditional tastes and claims of the native population. The point is that the members of each caste in India had their own garments, head-dress, ornaments and special utensils, the use of these objects being traditional. Quite naturally local artisans had for centuries suited their labour skills and methods to the satisfaction of the diverse requirements of their consumers. This was a much more complicated task for the European factory with its standard and mass production. Only very slowly, partly adapting its goods to the tastes of the Indian consumers and partly standardising their demand, did the British mill secure control of the consumer market in India.

The competition of British consumer goods, however large-scale it may have been, resulted only in a reduction of output in some, but very important, branches of India's industry, without introducing any profound changes in the processes of reproduction. This competition depressed the native industrial enterprise, limited its accumulation of capital, but did not as yet subordinate it to foreign capital. The first important incursion by European industrial capital into the sphere of reproduction was the start of importation of factory-made yarn, metals, dyes and other factory materials which were used in the native handicrafts, first to India and then to China and other countries in the 1820s and 1830s. This meant not only a destruction of manual spinning, iron-making and other industries, but also the incursion of large-scale foreign industry into the very reproduction of many industries.

With the growing importation of foreign goods there was an extension of brokerage in marketing them, and this had a contradictory effect on native industrial enterprise. To the extent to which the middleman-merchant marketed consumer goods he was inflicting direct harm, and frequently actual ruin, on the local industries, but did not secure control of them. Whenever the merchant marketed industrial materials he ruined some industries and helped to press down the cost of production and improve the quality in others, thereby slightly enhancing their competitiveness with respect to the foreign factory production.

Having secured control of the supply of raw and other materials to the handicraft, the dealer established control over that handicraft, also handling the marketing of its products. In so doing, he extracted not only the surplus-product but also a part of the necessary product, thereby further hampering productive accumulation by the artisans. Because the dealer, with rare exceptions, did not invest capital in the outmoded equipment of small-scale production, the surplus-value he extracted flowed into the sphere of circulation, while reproduction in the handicrafts was effected on the old extensive basis. The preservation of archaic implements and a corresponding labour productivity resulted, under free competition with factory products, in a steady decline of the artisans' earnings and led to their impoverishment.

The gap that existed between the scale of accumulation of capital in the sphere of circulation and its application in the sphere of production in India was further widened in the period of industrial capitalism. Earlier on, the favourites of accumulation were the tax-farmers, and then the upper sections of the comprador merchants. The size of their fortunes has been witnessed not only by some of their contemporaries, who may have been too envious, but also by British fiscal agencies. Fortunes of several million rupees were not a rarity among the merchants of Bombay and to a lesser extent in other Indian towns. Even in the remoter areas, where British competition was less severe, merchants and bankers had capitals running to hundreds and thousands of times the aggregate value of handicraft equipment.

India's inclusion in the world market also had other dire consequences for its handicrafts. World prices for industrial goods were based on the market prices for factory products in the developed countries. Even with the manufacturer's super-profit and the cost of delivery and brokerage, factory goods were gainfully sold at prices well below the market price for native handicraft articles. To withstand the competition from factory imports, local handicrafts were forced to offer their wares at prices below their cost of production, with the dealer shifting the burden of the loss on to the shoulders of the artisans, depressing their incomes or share of the profits (where small-scale producers were concerned) to a level at which the artisans could hardly make ends meet. The export of cotton, raw silk, wool, vegetable oil and other raw matetials not only increased his costs but also made his purchases seasonal. Henceforth, if the artisans were to ensure themselves raw materials for the whole year, they had not only to make greater outlays but to spend the whole amount at once, which helped the merchant to tighten his grip on the producers and block their way to accumulation.

Colonial expansion not only undermined the accumulation of productive capital but also disrupted the course of extended reproduction in the peasant and handicraft economy which was deprived of the opportunity to improve its technical facilities on the basis of national production of the implements of labour. Marx completes chapter XII of Volume I of his "Capital", in which he deals with the division of labour and manufacture, with the following characteristic of the highest technical achievements of the manufactory period: "One of its most finished creations was the workshop for the production of the instruments of labour themselves, including especially the complicated mechanical apparatus then already employed.... This workshop, the product of the division of labour in manufacturing, produced in its turn—machines. It is they that sweep away the handicraftsman's work as the regulating principle of social production."[11]

One expression of India's lag, of which the first signs appear in the pre-British period, was that the production of instruments did not rise to the stage of the well-organised capitalist workshop. Only the establishment of such workshops capable of turning out mechanisms and machines could have stopped its growing backwardness in the period of industrial capitalism. But in the course of the 19th century there were no changes in the production of labour implements in any of the countries of Asia and Africa, excluding Japan and partly China. At the same time, the accumulations made in the first half of the 19th century enabled Britain to complete her industrial revolution and go on from the workshop-scale production of machines to factory-scale production.

Having traced the historical evolution of the machine basis for extended reproduction, Marx said: "Modern Industry had therefore itself to take in hand the machine, its characteristic instrument of production, and to construct machines by machines. It was not till it did this that it built up for itself a fitting technical foundation, and stood on its own feet. Machinery, simultaneously with the increasing use of it, in the first decades of this century, appropriated, by degrees, the fabrication of machine proper. But it was only during the decade preceding 1866, that the construction of railways and ocean steamers on a stupendous scale called into existence the cyclopean machines now employed in the construction of prime movers."[12]

Britain's industrial monopoly established by the mid-century implied above all that her bourgeoisie had at its disposal the bulk of the machine equipment for industry and transport. The British bourgeoisie had the opportunity to control the processes of reproduction on a modern technological level all over the world. For the capitalist countries where industrial revolutions took place in the 1850s-1870s, Britain's monopoly of the equipment market was soon over. With respect to the rest of the world, the capitalist powers, Britain in the first place, acted as a monopoly owner of modern implements of production and means of transport, thereby being able to exert a direct and vigorous influence on the economic development of the colonies and dependent countries, regulating the import into these countries not only of consumer goods but also of the instruments of production and the means of transport. Thus, by the second half of the 19th century, the conditions had been prepared for the export of capital in its productive form.

India's conversion from a supplier of cloths for the whole of Europe into a consumer of British fabrics was due above all to the technical superiority of the British mill over the Indian hand-weaver, and also to the British government's tariff policy, like the establishment of a prohibitive 75 per cent duty on the Indian goods imported to Britain. The East India Company went even further in its tariff and tax discrimination against Indian handicrafts. In the 1830s, it imposed the following taxes on native weaving: 5 per cent on the raw materials consumed; 7.5 per cent on yarn; 2.5 per cent on cloths; and 2.5 per cent on dyeing outside the workshop. Thus, the tax levies increased the cost of hand-made Indian goods by 15-17.5 per cent. Meanwhile, the customs tariffs on British factory-made goods came to only 2.5 per cent of their value.[13] This kind of tax policy created additional advantages for the export of the cheaper British factory-made fabrics and for the competitive struggle of Lancashire mills against Indian hand-weaving. Besides, this policy ensured British mill-owners more super-profits at the expense of the Indian consumer. (It should be borne in mind that the tax led to a rise in the market price of all the fabrics, including the British.)

Finally, the growth of mill industry in Britain also inflicted indirect harm on India's handicrafts: the export of cotton from India for working up in Britain led to a rise in the price of the cotton, thereby increasing the production costs of the artisans. The Board of Revenue said in 1818: "Either the actual improvement that had taken place in the manufactures of Europe, or the arrangements adopted by the different states on the continent to encourage such improvement, had operated to the disadvantage of the manufacturers in this country (India.—V. P.) by creating a demand for the raw instead of the manufactured material, a demand for cotton instead of cloth."[14] Table 2 gives an idea of the change in prices for British and Indian goods.

In the second and third decades of the 19th century, there was a crucial change in the balance of prices of English and Indian yarn, especially for the most popular grades. While the price of English yarn was halved, the price of Indian yarn remained unchanged. Because the price of raw materials remained stable, the change in the price of English yarn was due only to the new conditions in which it was manufactured. Indeed, the use of machines led to a vast saving of living labour (Table 3).

TABLE 2

Yarn Prices *
(thread per mile, pence)

Grade No.	*Prices of English Yarn*		*Prices of Indian yarn*
	1812	*1830*	*1812-1830*
40	1 1/2	3/4	2 1/8
60	1 3/8	3/4	2 3/4
80	1 5/6	3/4	2 3/4
100	1 1/4	1 3/16	3
120	1 3/16	1 3/16	3 1/4
150	1 1/2	1	4 1/16
200	2 3/8	1 3/4	5 3/8
250	3 3/8	2 3/4	8

* "Report from the Select Committee on East India Produce", p. 606.

TABLE 3

Structure of the Price of a Pound of Cotton Yarn in England and India, 1832*

Grade No.	*In Britain*			*In India*		
	cost of cotton	*cost of labour power*	*total price*	*cost of cotton*	*cost of labour power*	*total price*
40	1 s. 6 d.	1 s. 0 d.	2 s. 6 d.	3 d.	3 s. 4 d.	3 s. 7 d.
60	2 s. 0 d.	1 s. 6 d.	3 s. 6 d.	$3\frac{1}{2}$ d.	5 s. $8\frac{1}{2}$ d.	6 s. 0 d.
80	2 s. 2 d.	2 s. 2 d.	4 s. 4 d.	$4\frac{1}{2}$ d.	8 s. $10\frac{1}{2}$ d.	9 s. 3 d.
100	2 s. 4 d.	2 s. 10 d.	5 s. 2 d.	5 d.	11 s. 11 d.	12 s. 4 d.
120	2 s. 6 d.	3 s. 6 d.	6 s. 0 d.	5 d.	16 s. 0 d.	16 s. 5 d.
150	2 s. 10 d.	6 s. 6 d.	9 s. 4 d.	6 d.	25 s. 0 d.	25 s. 6 d.
200	3 s. 4 d.	16 s. 8 d.	20 s. 0 d.	6 d.	44 s. 7 d.	45 s. 1 d.
250	4 s. 0 d.	31 s. 0 d.	35 s. 0 d.	8 d.	83 s. 4 d.	84 s. 0 d.

* "Report from the Select Committee on East India Produce," p. 607.

Consequently, the low price of the raw material, cotton in this case, did not cover the vast losses involved in the traditional techniques of its working up. The prices of cloths were in a similar state. By the end of the 1830s, good shirting made in Britain was sold in India at 10 annas a yard, and coarse bed-sheet fabric from the USA at 3 to 5 annas, whereas the corresponding Indian pieces, even when made of imported yarn, were offered at double the price of the British fabric.[15]

Characterising the effects which the new methods of colonial exploitation exerted on the economy of India, Marx wrote: "England began with driving the Indian cottons from the European market; it then introduced twist into Hindustan and in the end inundated the very mother country of cotton with cottons. From 1818 to 1836 the export of twist from Great Britain to India rose in the proportion of 1 to 5,200. In 1824 the export of British muslins to India hardly amounted to 1,000,000 yards, while in 1837 it surpassed 64,000,000 yards."[16]

The crucial changes in India's foreign trade in textile goods occurred from 1813 to 1833 (Table 4).

TABLE 4

Foreign Trade in Textile Goods*
(rupees)

Year	*Cotton fabrics*		*Yarn Imports*
	Exports	*Imports*	
1813/14	5,281,458	92,070	—
1815/16	8,540,763	2,559,642	—
1825/26	5,834,638	4,124,159	124,146
1832/33	822,891	4,264,707	4,285,517

* "Hand-Spinning and Hand-Weaving. An Essay," Ahmedabad, 1926, p. 89.

The relatively rapid growth of British imports to India produced among some English businessmen premature hopes of full and rapid domination of the Indian market. The testimony of an English businessman, A. Seam, before the Select Committee on East India Produce (1840) is characteristic in this context. He claimed that a preference for English industrial goods, including luxuries and ironware, had been established all over India. He said that British-made iron agricultural implements had not been accepted in India, but added that British tools were used by artisans, notably carpenters, and also nails, screws, bolts, hinges and locks.[17] However, other sources do not confirm any massive switch in India to British imports.

In the early 1840s, British manufacturers and officials in India were still concerned about the dependence of Britain's key industry on

American cotton-wool. Thus, a report submitted by a Company official expressed anxiety over the fact that Britain bought 10 million pounds' worth of cotton from the USA annually, spending altogether 20 million pounds in the USA on materials which could be obtained in India. A corollary of this was the relatively small British export to India—a total of 6 million pounds—which was only a fraction per head of British export to the West Indies or Australia.[18]

British subjects were especially alarmed over the fact that the outflow of pound sterling to the USA was helping the US industry swiftly to become Britain's main rival on the world markets. By contrast, the inadequate use of India's potentialities for producing raw materials hampered the collection of land-tax in that country. That is why British officials put forward projects for growing more technical crops on larger areas, so as to increase the tax revenue. But this resulted in a kind of vicious circle, which could be broken only through a reduction in the land-tax. In 1838, Manchester's Chamber of Commerce and Industry noted that the land-tax revenues, which were being stretched to the maximum the producer could pay, ruined the incentives for improvement and greater efforts.[19]

In order to start the production of raw materials, bypassing the low-productive economy of the Indian husbandmen, the British authorities made an important effort to get British capitalists to settle on Indian soil. In 1830, the Bengal authorities offered special privileges to persons desiring to own low-lying lands near Calcutta. These lands were exempted from the landtax for 20 years, and in the subsequent period were to yield no more than a nominal tax (from 4 to 12 annas per bigha). According to the Acts of 1834 and 1837, any British subject could acquire land property in India on an equal footing with the Indians, it being assumed that indigo, cotton, coffee, sugar and other export crops would be grown on the newly acquired land. In other words, this was an effort to start capitalist-type plantations as a full-fledged system of land-tenure. However, the desired results were not achieved.

In 1840, a senior British official in India declared that apart from the production of indigo and sugar there was no area of any importance for British investment. Even the permission to buy landed estates made no difference. The British refused to buy the land because the country did not suit them, he declared.[20] Indeed, British industrial capital was still reluctant to own land with its attendant personal relations, the terms for recruiting manpower, its skill standards, the market structure, etc.; in other words, it refused to move to a historically lower stage.

But there were exceptions. There was the noteworthy activity of the British businessman Seam: the Company gave him 60,000 acres in the district of Gorakhpur. Seam refused to specify the actual amount of tax he was paying to the Company, but admitted that for the first gift of 55,000 acres he was paying only 7,500 rupees a year, a third or a quarter of the usual tax assessment. Seam set aside only 1.5 per cent of the area (800-900 acres) for indigo, sugar-cane and oats (possibly for his draught animals), leasing the rest of the land to rayats on the usual terms.[21] Seam may have prospered, but the broad spread of this kind of Anglo-zamindari status hardly met the general interests of the British regime. Indeed, there were other social and ideological obstacles, with which I shall deal later.

The failure of the project to set up British zamindar entrepreneurs made the British administration stage an experiment in the early 1840s to introduce modern techniques, notably US agricultural methods in the growing of cotton, in the rayats' husbandries. Several US specialists were invited to set up model farms to demonstrate to Indian rayats the advantages of US implements, cotton grades and soil cultivation, and also to improve the quality of cotton fibre through better ginning and unification of grade standards. Reports on the Americans' activity and their diaries contain many interesting facts about the Indian countryside in that period, the social mentality of some of its sections, farming techniques, the climate, etc.[22]

On the whole, the experiment turned out to be a failure and is in this sense highly instructive. The failure was partly due to the fact that the implements and the cultivation methods were not fit for India's natural conditions. But at the same time it turned out that India had no free farmers or slaves whose labour could be used to grow cotton, as was the case in the United States. It is true that the American cotton-growers discovered in the Indian countryside some sections which were reminiscent of these categories of the rural population in the US: the relatively well-to-do upper sections (according to the terminology adopted in the North-West Provinces, now the State of Uttar Pradesh, the Americans called them zamindars) and the landless rural sections (whom the Americans called coolies). The former watched with obvious interest how the US instructor swiftly and easily ploughed up the Indian soil, but showed no inclination to introduce the overseas novelties on their own fields. It may be assumed that the advantages of switching to commercial single-crop farming did not appear to them to be sufficiently obvious in order to break up the traditional system of production and social relations, which assured them of the jajman's status they claimed

As for the "coolies", they were hired to work on the model farms for 3 rupees a month. One of the Americans, T. Finney, said that after the farm servants learned to use the plough, they were given a rise of 8 annas. The Americans imagined that this would induce the men to start saving money to buy up land and cultivate it like farmers.

Naturally, nothing of the sort happened. Traditionally deprived of land, these toilers, who were accustomed to receiving remuneration in kind—the product which they had themselves grown, regarded the rupees they had earned as the fruits of an accidental venture by the foreigner (which it, in effect, turned out to be). Quite naturally, they spent these unaccustomed silver coins on entertainment and festivities, giving little thought to the opportunity of becoming an American-type farmer in India.

What is more, although the American cotton-grower paid his Indian "poor devils" the full rate (3 rupees 8 annas) in the inter-season period, when ploughing time came, the latter instantly demanded an increase of their pay to the incredible amount of 4 rupees a month. There again, the parties did not— and could not—understand each other. The American, accustomed to the annual hiring of farm hands, could not understand why the Indian "coolies" made such disloyal use of his heightened interest in their labour during the season, and the "coolies", unaccustomed to be paid in the off-season, could not understand why they could not have an increase of a half-rupee now that they were toiling from dawn to dusk. The fact is that the three or four months' work in the farming season provided the "coolies", the lowest section of the village servants, with sustenance for the year. Quite possibly, having rejected the Americans' explanation that the increase would deprive him of his profits and them of their work, they may have succumbed to the inducements of the zamindars or the traders and money-lenders, who were especially sensitive to the appearance of every extra coin in the village. Be that as it may, the diaries of the US planters abound in complaints about the lack of discipline among the Indian day labourers, who, as one American put it, were just as independent of the employer as the emancipated Negro in America.[23]

Apart from the socio-economic difficulties, the agricultural innovations also faced obstacles which stemmed from the absence in India of any serious agronomic research, for instance, in the sphere of vegetable selection. Thus, the Bourbon sugar-cane variety was introduced in Dinajpur in 1840. At first, the peasants displayed much restraint over the introduction of the new variety, but then, trusting the experience of some husbandmen, who had higher yields because of the new variety, and a better quality of juice, gave it preference over the local varieties. But by 1858, the Bourbon degenerated and the crop rotted in the fields.[24]

It would, therefore, be an oversimplification to maintain that the British administration had always and everywhere slowed down the development or even destroyed the productive forces of India. In a sense, even at that time they were rather interested in their development in some sectors of agriculture and even industry and transport, as I shall show below. But the attempts to create separate pockets of modernised production came up against the overall system of archaic socio-economic relations, which, far from being shaken by the British regime, were, in effect, compensated by it in some respects.

The point is that the switch to India's exploitation as a marketing outlet and a source of raw materials, as I have said, did not at all mean that the British had abandoned the idea of oppressing the country by means of their old methods. They continued to resort to armed plunder. But taxes were still the most important among the old methods of drain in the first half of the 19th century. The introduction of the Permanent Settlement in Bengal was the first link of the land-taxation system introduced by the foreign authorities, and this legislation has been fairly thoroughly studied, so I shall confine myself here merely to indicating the basic lines along which this civic legislation exerted an influence on India's socio-economic and socio-psychological evolution.

Marx pointed out that both the tax reforms carried out by the British (zamindari and rayatwari variants) combined "the most contradictory character—both made not for the people, who cultivate the soil, nor for the holder who owns it, but for the government that taxes it."[25] The land-ownership established by the British regime could not have been anything, in its initial form, except a caricature of private property, if only because the land-tax settlements stemmed from the establishment of the foreign administration's supreme ownership of land. Nor was this a legal proclamation but a real economic fact expressed in the extraction by the British administration of up to 50-60 per cent of the crop in the form of the land-tax (especially in some areas of "peasant" land-holdings—the rayatwari). Having established the land-tax on that level, the East India Company had, in effect, appropriated the claim to the rent-tax which belonged to the Oriental despotism. Because in some instances the tax absorbed not only the surplus-product, but also a part of the necessary product, the land decreased in price and partly lost its value altogether.

One British official, Robert Richards, presents this picture of the interconnection between the taxation drain and the reduction in the price of land or its total loss of value. In the Committee of the House of Commons of the East India Company's Affairs, he was asked: "You have stated that the tax is equal in some cases to the produce of the land; has land been a saleable value in any part of India where the taxes take away the whole of its produce?" Richards replied: "I am personally acquainted with instances where the revenue asessed upon certain lands has actually exceeded the gross produce.... Land, however, has a saleable value in those parts of India where our revenue systems admit of some rent being derived from the land by the land-holders or proprietor; but when the whole rent is absorbed by the government tax or revenue, the land is of course destitute of saleable value."[26]

The two main systems of land-taxation meant that the rayat, a member of the village community, was being deprived of his claim to own land, for the immense increase in the land-tax did away with the earlier traditional restrictions on the amount of rent—a necessary part of this claim. The rayat's land-holding privileges were also violated by the fact that the British administration confiscated the holdings of those who failed to pay the taxes, something that the diwanis of native rulers had not done. Even the top British official, H. Y. S. Cotton, admitted that the Mogul system of land-ownership was totally different from the British system and added that the revenue branches of the Mogul rulers, despite the acts of violence committed by them, never sold by auction the plots of those who failed to pay their duties, which the British did as a rule.[27]

For all the conservative features of the land-tax legislation, it undoubtedly exerted a revolutionising effect by its proclaimed defence of private property in land. "The zemindar and royotwari themselves, abominable as they are, involve two distinct forms of private property in land—the great desideratum of Asiatic society."[28] The land-tax settlements gave the Indian zamindars and rayats the legal ground for their confrontation with the arbitrary taxation imposed by the newly established British despotism. The struggle to establish private property in land was, I think, progressive in the sense that it defended the big landed estates against the growing claims of the British regime.

It is no mere coincidence that the immediate cause of the great Indian Uprising was the abolition of certain property rights of the feudal land-owners in Oudh by the British extremists, and that one of the results of the uprising was a pledge to safeguard the claims of the Indian landlords. I believe that the historical essence of the 1857-1859 Uprising for all-Indian social transformation lay in the fact that it assisted in bringing about the progressive consolidation of land-holding, although this process was not completed.

Up to the end of the 19th century, the oppression of the Indian peasants and artisans cannot be considered the basis of the process of primitive accumulation—the expropriation of the direct owner's means of production. In the countryside, the oppressed rayats were attached to the means of production by the traditions of their caste and the obligation to pay tax to the British Raj. The urban artisan was attached to his workshop through his enslavement by the usurer and (around the British factories) by the administrative prohibition to leave his place of origin. Finally, even if the cultivator or artisan tried to abandon his occupation, he could not find any free demand for his labour-power. Even after the direct producer lost his title to the means of production he remained bound to them by the semi-feudal conditions of enslavement. In other words, the oppression of the peasants and artisans in the first half of the 19th century did not entail the formation of a market of free labour-power.

In that same period, another condition for the capitalist system was also lacking in India: massive demand and a corresponding market for the implements of labour inherent in this production even in its earlier stages. The traditional tools of the farmer and the artisan were depreciated in the eyes of the promoter both objectively and subjectively, and could not attract the investment of capital, new capital, at any rate. Consumer capacities had been reduced in almost every stratum of the population. In this situation, the goods produced on the capitalist basis could be marketed only as a result of the direct expulsion of the same product turned out by the local handicraft production.

That is why the first to be hit by the British competition was petty-commodity mass production like textiles and then the making of vegetable oil. Still, the handicrafts in the small towns, having stronger bonds with the countryside, and the village community's industry on the whole withstood the blows administered by foreign imports. Here one should bear in mind that the 200-250 million Indians could not be clothed with the tens of millions of yards of cotton fabrics which Britain annually imported in the first half of the 19th century. Marx observed even later that despite the use by the British of direct political and economic power in India, they were able only gradually to dissolve the unity of industrial and agricultural production.[29]

The general decline of the native economy, the unreadiness of the sphere of circulation and the infrastructure fettered the transformation of the productive forces and held back the genesis of new relations of production in the field of industry. In such conditions there could, naturally, be no question of an Indian bourgeoisie rising not only from among the well-to-do master-craftsmen but also from among the dealers.

In this context, let us note the difficulties faced by British businessmen who tried to invest productive capital in India. One highly indicative instance is that of J. M. Heath, who had worked for the Company for 21 years and who in 1833 set up the Indian Steel, Iron and Chrome. This firm received a loan from the Company and lease-hold rights over four districts of South India (South Arcot, Koimbatore, Malabar and South Kanara). It succeeded in starting three enterprises—at Porto Novo (South Arcot), at Baypur (Malabar) and at Palampatti (near Salem). In 1840, Heath testified before the Committee on the

East India Produce. He dealt mostly with the British ferrous metal demand and the prospects of Indian pig-iron competing against Swedish and Russian steel. He spoke out most optimistically about the prospect for the Company's activity, and may have done so for the purposes of advertising. But what we are especially interested in is the information he gave about the work of his first unit.

It was situated on the sea coast 120 miles to the south of Madras. The idea of promoting these works first occurred to Heath when he studied the country iron-making, which used surface ore deposits, and was advised by prominent British experts that the ore was suitable for turning out first-class metal. Heath said the ore was to last to the end of the world. Although it was located within 150 miles of the works, the delivery was cheap because it came almost entirely by river-boat.

At first there were 32 British technicians, who headed all the technological branches. But by 1840 only two British foremen and one engineer remained to direct 3,000-4,000 Indians, who were employed at the enterprise itself, in the extraction of ore, the burning of charcoal, and their delivery. Heath gave a favourable account of the capacity of his Indian workers. Incidentally, he said, an experiment was made to hire 46 athletically built Ethiopians and Negroes from among those who worked in Bombay harbour on the loading of cotton bales. It was discovered, says Heath, that one of his own men was worth the lot. The excess of labour—Heath says that he could have hired a lakh of hands if he had wanted them—made it possible to pay them at the lowest rates: men and women working in the pit were paid 2 -2½ rupees a month, and at the enterprise itself high-skilled workers and foremen earned 5-7 rupees. These figures appeared to be so low that one member of the Committee even asked whether they included all types of remuneration.

The unit consisted of four blast furnaces operating on charcoal and yielding, at full capacity, 60 tons of pig-iron a week, a smelter with a capacity of 50 tons of ingots a week, and mechanical equipment. Now and again the initial power of the installation was exceeded many times over. But the marketing of products continued to be the key problem. For certain-reasons, the establishment was oriented exclusively upon the high-quality steel market of Great Britain, where its produce had to compete with Swedish and Russian steel. It may well be that there was no adequate or organised market in India for such products, especially since it was turned out in the form of pig-iron and subsequently re-worked into steel in Britain.[33] The orientation upon charcoal must have been a technical error of the producer, because coking coals were already being used in Europe. The attempt to switch to the new technology met with serious difficulties, because there was no coking coal in the area (nor has it been discovered in the south of India to this day). It had to be brought from overseas. The irregularity of the delivery by sea led to much idling, with the blast furnaces operating for not more than four months a year. That is why Indian pig-iron was unable to establish itself on the British market. The steel works at Sheffield decided not to use Indian pig-iron, while the stockholders, who expected to receive superprofits, never even got their proper dividends

At the same time, the technological results of this first experiment in modern metallurgy in India were quite satisfactory. In Sheffield, Indian pig-iron was classed as top grade and was sold for 6 pounds 10 shillings per ton. The steel made from it was used to build big bridges and gun carriages. A happier choice of site (close to hard coal) would have eased the transport difficulties and would have undoubtedly increased the profitability of the works.[31] S. K. Sen gives information, on the strength of official records, about the firm's subsequent lot. Because of the failure to secure capital from Great Britain, Heath turned for credits to the Madras Council, which lent him 571,000 rupees at 5 per cent per annum. But this did not save the firm. It never made any profits, while the British administration did not receive any interest on its loans.

In 1853, a new firm, the East India Iron Company, with a capital of 400,000 rupees but with a liability to pay the authorities under earlier credits 10,000 pounds—roughly onequarter of the capital—was set up under the sponsorship of the British authorities on the basis of the old firm. Although iron production was divided into four units in order to facilitate the supply of charcoal, the supply difficulties nevertheless resulted in the closure of the works at Palampatti in 1857, in Porto Novo and Baypur in 1866, and in 1874 the firm was dissolved.[32]

The early English manufacturers in India were employees of the East India Company, among them the man who founded the above-mentioned iron works. Incidentally, he ran the enterprises at Malabar and Salem through confidential agents, so that the losses they brought may have been due not only to the economic conditions, but also to the lack of control over the promoters and the managers. In the 1820s, Company officials also founded a spinning factory at Burdwan, but this enterprise turned out to be short-lived, too.

Britain's "liberal" sponsors of laissez faire were alarmed over these early and unviable offshoots of contemporary industrial enterprise, which were, moreover, not of Indian but of British origin. They expressed concern that the factory at Burdwan would be competing with the cotton mills in Britain. In order to calm his "benevolent" compatriots, a spokesman for the factory declared in 1832 that it had many serious complications, including difficulty with repairs and technical personnel, and mistrust on the part of the Indians for Indian factory-made fabrics. He told British manufacturers that he had great doubts about any factory in India ever being able to compete with factories in Britain.[33] These doubts were dispelled only a quarter-century later, but that required additional changes both in socio-economic relations and in the country's economic infrastructure.

Thus, even in the first half of the 19th century British capital intended to transfer to India mainly non-mechanised production. A. Guha notes as a historical curiosity, for which there were nevertheless good reasons, that in India the steam engine was first used not by the British but by the Nawab of Oudh who in 1819 installed an 8 h. p. engine on his pleasure boat. The following year, Danish missionaries installed a steam engine at a paper-making factory in Serampur, so inaugurating the use of steam as a source of energy in India. In 1828, Golok Chander, an ordinary blacksmith from Titaghur, fabricated a model steam engine and was awarded a prize of 50 rupees at an exhibition. But nothing was heard of him since.

It was Ardeshir Kursetjee Wadia (1808-1877) who began the systematic study of steam engines in India. With the help of a local blacksmith he first built a small steamboat (1838) and started the production of iron hulls for ships. From 1839 to 1841, Wadia studied marine ship-building in Britain, and was the first Indian to become a member of the Royal Society. Upon his return to India, he joined the Bombay Steam Factory and Foundry, and in 1857 became the chief engineer of a British shipping company on the Indus. Such were some of the opportunities, objective and subjective, for using steam as a source of energy in industry and transport in India even before the mid-19th century; but none were realised in the situation that then prevailed.

We find that the intentions of British capital rapidly and comprehensively to develop India as a market and rawmaterial source, to say nothing of converting her into a sphere of industrial enterprise, confronted great difficulties, which, in the most general sense sprang from the tenacity of the existing system of socio-economic relations resting on a corresponding technical and production basis. These relations and their basis are of interest in themselves and their consideration is a necessary premise for understanding the methods and consequences of colonial exploitation.

NOTES

1. F. Engels, *Sochineniya*, vol. 19, p. 270.
2. R. Luxemburg, *Nakopleniye kapitala*, Moscow, 1966, p. 260.
3. K. Marx, *The Poverty of Philosophy*, Moscow, 1966, p. 97.
4. *Hansard's Parliamentary Debates*, vol. 163, London, 1861, p. 178.

5. J.F. Royle, *Essay on the Productive Resources of India*, London, 1840.
6. *Report from the Select Committee on East India Produce*, pp. 2, 5, 279, 483, 485.
7. K. Marx, *Capital*, vol. III, p. 238.
8. K. Marx, *The Poverty of Philosophy*, pp. 86-87.
9. *Report from the Select Committee on East India Produce*, p. 281.
10. G. Guha, K. Marx and the Drain Theory, *Artha Vijnana*, vol. X, Nos. 3-4, September-December 1968.
11. K. Marx, *Capital*, vol. I, p. 368.
12. *Ibid.*, pp. 384-385.
13. A. Sarada Raju, *Economic Conditions...*, p. 175.
14. Quoted from: A. Sarada Raju, *Economic Conditions...*, p. 174.
15. *Report from the Select Committee on East India Produce*, p. 168.
16. K. Marx and F. Engels. *On Colonialism*, p. 27.
17. *Report from the Select Committee on East India Produce*, p. 71.
18. *Return: Cotton (India)*, pp. 80-81, 423-428, 467.
19. *Report from the Select Committee on East India Produce*, p. 11.
20. *Ibid.*, pp. 11, 36.
21. *Ibid.*, pp. 46-47.
22. *Return : Cotton (India)*, pp. 151-231.
23. *Ibid.*, pp. 168, 190.
24. *Statistical Accounts of Bengal*, vol. VII, p. 392.
25. K. Marx and F. Engels, *On Colonialism*, p. 78.
26. *British Rule in India Condemned by the British Themselves*, London, 1915, pp. 22-23.
27. H.Y. S. Cotton, *New India or India in Transition*, London, 1884, p. 55.
28. K. Marx and F. Engels, *On Colonialism*, p. 82.
29. K. Marx, *Capital*, vol. III, pp. 333-334.
30. See: *Report from the Select Committee on East India Produce*.
31. *The Second Industrial Conference*, pp. VI-VII.
32. S.K. Sen, *Studies in Industrial Policy and Development of India (1858-1914)*, Calcutta, 1964, pp. 44-45.
33. B.B. Misra, *The Indian Middle Class*, pp. 114-118.

CHAPTER SIX

MAHARASHTRA'S HANDICRAFTS, TRADE AND CREDIT SYSTEM IN THE 1820S-1850S

Maharashtra was finally conquered by the colonialists in a period when India's exploitation was already being switched to industrial capitalism lines. Only after three long wars did the British invaders manage, in 1818, to break down the fierce resistance of the Marathas. The confederation of Maratha states, which had earlier cut across the trade routes from Bombay into the heartland, disappeared from the map of India. A part of the Peshwa state, with the capital of Poona, was incorporated into the Bombay Presidency, while the eastern part of Maharashtra was divided between the Central provinces of British India and an old vassal of the East India Company, Hyderabad (Berar, a part of it, inhabited by the Marathas, was subsequently included in the Central provinces).

Maharashtra's economic history in the 1820s-1850s has been described by many scientists, with agrarian relations and British tax settlements after the conquest of Maharashtra being presented in the fullest detail. The heightened interest in this aspect of socio-economic life is quite understandable and was due to the following: first, the fact that the land-tax structure continued to be the determining factor of the overall socio-economic system and, second, the fact that M. Elphinstone and his subordinates had collected much information when the rayatwari system was prepared and established.

Among Indian scientists the agrarian relations in Maharashtra were studied by Romesh Dutt, D.R. Gadgil and D. R. Choksey. In Soviet writings, the greatest value attaches to the studies of I. M. Reusner. It is true that Reusner used the above-mentioned material (alongside earlier sources) to reconstruct socio-economic relations in the 18th century, but his line of thinking and methodology are a great help in understanding the processes going forward in the period under review. The data on Western Maharashtra's socio-economic system helped to gain an idea of the size and share of its product which was exchanged for the articles made by the artisans.

The surveys carried out after the British conquest clearly reveal an intention to embellish the position of the peasant husbandry. In 1828, an attempt was made to estimate the annual production costs and value of the product coming from 16 hectares (40 acres) of black soils in the Janau taluq in the district of Poona. The outlays for four bullocks were 19 rupees (interest on initial inputs and annual cost of maintenance); current expenditures on implements and interest on their value, 8 rupees; payment for a cart, 3 rupees; ropes, 1 rupee; seeds, 18 rupees; purchased fertilisers, 21 rupees; pay for two men and two women hired round the year, 85 rupees; remuneration for village servants, 28 rupees; for additional labour, 2 rupees; and donations, 5 rupees; a total of 190 rupees. The income was made up of the value of the wheat and gram—169 rupees, and millet—141 rupees.[1]

This was a relatively big husbandry with four full-time servants, but even there only 120 rupees was left for taxes and the maintenance of the master's family. Assuming the tax on 40 acres to be 90 to 100 rupees, we find that a rayat family had virtually nothing to live on. Still, considering that it was able to pay two servants (a man and a woman) 42 rupees a year, its own consumption must have been 50 or 100 per cent larger, that is, a product valued at 60 to 80 rupees. This money could have come from animal husbandry and secondary crops.

Under this assumption we find that the implements cost just over 3 per cent of the value of the staple crops, with 20-25 rupees, or another 6-8 per cent of the value of the crop, going into the use of handicraft articles by the families of the master and his labourers (possibly making up two married couples) and village servants. Let us recall that the implements were acquired chiefly through an exchange in kind with the village artisans, while the articles of consumption were bought and determined the market demand of the inhabitants of the village.

At the same time, Captain Robertson made another attempt to estimate the budget on a farm of 10.5 hectares (26 acres). The expenditures consisted of the following items: the purchase and maintenance of eight bullocks (apparently in annual terms), 16½ rupees; implements, 8 rupees; seeds, 10½ rupees, hired labourers (when members of the family took no part in the field work), 184 rupees; production expenditures totalling 219 rupees. Then followed the taxes—64 rupees, and contributions to the maintenance of district and village administrators and community servants—70 rupees; a total of 134 rupees. Such a farm was estimated to yield a product valued at 277 rupees. Thus, only 24 rupees, a clearly inadequate amount, was left for the maintenance of the peasant family itself.

Accordingly, Robertson looked around for items of economy which would help to create an impression of relative welfare. Thus, if the family had two men, the number of hired hands could be reduced, with a saving of 40 rupees; the growing of bullocks on the farm also gave another 3½ rupees; the sale of dairy produce 30 rupees; making up a total subsistence fund of about 100 rupees a year. However, even this optimal estimate merely emphasised the relative and absolute insignificance of the commodity consumption fund as a share of the aggregate product of the peasant farm and the impossibility of any marked expansion of the productive accumulation fund. However, Robertson recognised that the tax burden falling on the Maratha peasant was extremely heavy.[2]

The general economic decline was compounded by the fact that Maharashtra had been ruined by long wars. The existing system of socio-economic relations proved to be undermined by the abolition of the Maratha state system and the introduction of a new land-tax settlement by the British. Urban handicrafts engaged in catering for the court and the army were deprived of their customers, while the strengthening of market relations with the villages was hampered by competition from imported British goods, which were exempted from import duties and began their penetration of the country's markets. The greatest losses were inflicted on the producers of high and medium quality cloths. The manufacture of coarse cloths was better preserved in the villages, where the weavers used British yarn.

British competition brought about a situation in which the artisans "were soon to leave the looms for the plough, and, like the soldier, burden the land. The land was to supply the raw material for the steel giants of Manchester; the millions of India were to be bound to the soil to cultivate for the greed of their new masters that wealth which was to make England the richest country in the world, and the Indian rayat so poverty-stricken as to make it difficult to find a parallel in the world."[3] The drift of labour-power in Maharashtra from the handicrafts to agriculture was also admitted by the British administrators. One of them wrote in 1830 that many artisans in search of the means of subsistence were forced to turn to agriculture, although the burden on the land was, in his opinion, already too great.[4] Thus, in the first decade of British rule the progressive de-industrialisation of Maharashtra's economy had already begun. However, this phenomenon was common to the whole of India. Jawaharlal Nehru wrote: "The compulsory back-to-the-land movement of artisans and craftsmen led to an evergrowing disproportion between agriculture and industry; agriculture became more and more the sole business of the people because of the lack of occupations and wealth-producing activities."[5]

The artisans who continued in the occupation of their ancestors were doomed to semi-starvation. British administrators estimated that in the early 1830s a weaver's family had to spend 84 rupees a year only on cereals, usually the cheapest sort of millet, while having an annual income of about 108 rupees. Considering that human beings must have a number of other food-stuffs, clothing, fuel, utensils, etc., one can easily imagine the plight of the artisans. One should also bear in mind that this was the very early period of foreign rule, and that the condition of the artisans subsequently became even worse. Thus, a British official who surveyed weaving in Belgaum district in 1849 admitted that weavers' incomes had been reduced to one-third as compared to their incomes 20 years earlier. Indeed, in 1849 weavers in Belgaum district earned only 2 annas a day or about 36 rupees a year.[6]

We have no authentic information about the economic organisation of the Maratha handicrafts in the first half of the 19th century, but even before the colonial bondage the hired worker must have appeared alongside the dependent artisan in Western India. Thus, a British official reported in 1822 that a few years before the British conquest weavers working for hire had been paid half a rupee a day (apparently, a mistake or an overstatement). Weavers working under contract, that is, for a dealer, considered themselves to be in the black when they earned more than that amount, and in the red, when less.[7] Thus, the earnings of the hired man became a kind of criterion for the earnings on the dependent artisan. Still, on the basis of scattered data, one may assume that artisans dependent on buyers prevailed in the towns. This dependence was especially strong when costly articles were produced, because the dealers controlled the supply of the necessary raw materials and semifinished products going into the finished articles. From the 1820s on, the switch by artisans in Maharashtra, as in the whole of India, to the use of imported semi-finished products (yarn, metals) intensified the dealer's control over the small-scale industries. Thus while the loss of the feudal customer may have somewhat eased the power of the dealer, the switch to imported semi-finished products re-established it.

The condition of two towns, Bhagalcot and Poona, shows the destructive effect of the conquest for the economy of the Peshwa state.

Bhagalcot (extreme north of Kanara), according to T. Marshall, owed its prosperity in the past to the court of the native rulers and the general condition of the people, who were better off and thus created a demand for handicraft articles. Among the items formerly sold in the bazar were costly cloths, of which 50,000 rupees' worth were sold only on the occasion of one religious festival. People of high rank stopped all purchases, says Marshall, approximately by 1822, even those who could still afford expensive items, made do with cheap ones, because there was no occasion or incentive for persons deprived of their rank and position to dress up. A still greater number of people were altogether deprived of all means of sustenance.[8] British taxes dealt another blow at Bhagalcot's handicrafts and trade. Under the Indian rulers, 18 manufacturing houses paid 400 rupees in tax, the biggest of them paying 88 rupees. Under the British, the taxes on these establishments came, respectively, to 1,900 and 3,000 rupees. As a result, trade and handicrafts in the town declined.

In a report dated August 20, 1822, W. Chaplin wrote that in Poona "the mercantile and banking trades are perhaps those that have most materially suffered by the change from native to European government; the condition of the Sahookars is in consequence much deteriorated, it being computed that not two-thirds of the former capital are now employed in banking speculations." This was most noticeable in Poona and other big towns of the Deccan. Chaplin says that the decline of Poona's trade and credit operations was due to the fact that this city "has ceased to be the seat of government, the residence of a court and its numerous ministers and officers. A great stagnation of trade has ensued, since great purchases of jewels, and cloths, and diverse valuable commodities, are now no longer required to supply the demands of Oriental parade and luxury."

W. Chaplin believed that the banking business declined because of the changed tax system. The British authorities ousted the bankers and the money-lenders from the collection and remittance of taxes and established direct relations between the treasuries of the districts and the village administration.[9]

The decline of the handicrafts and trade brought about profound changes in the life of the towns and their population. To understand these changes, one must consider some general information about the towns of Maharashtra in the early years after its conquest. Soon after the capture of Poona, Elphinstone reported: "Poona may be reckoned to contain about a hundred and ten thousand inhabitants, having lost from a tenth to a fifth since the removal of Bajee Rao with his court and army. Nassick does not contain more than a fourth of this number. Punderpoor (Pandharpur.—V. P.) is still smaller than Nassick, and the rest all much smaller than Punderpoor."[10] As we see, this report, apart from admitting the decline of Poona, which began just after the conquest, also tells about the population of the main urban centres in that part of Maharashtra. In the early 19th century, this was a rural country with towns that were few and far between.

But other urban-type communities—the centres of small administrative units (kusbas) were also to be found in Maharashtra. In his report of May 1, 1821, Robertson describes the kusbas in the district of Poona: "There is no city excepting Poona in the whole district; but there are several very respectable kusba towns, which carry on an inland trade.... The principal articles of manufacture are coarse woollen and cotton cloths, and in Poona there are silk-weavers' looms, which vie with the manufactories of Peitun in producing silken surhees and dresses ornamented with gold tissue. The principal kusbas and other towns are Khair, Chacun, Sassore, Paubool, Gejooree, Powar, the two Tulligaums, Gera Nowlcombery, and Kendoor. The houses of these towns are comfortable buildings of stone and mud, covered with tiles, some of them two stories in height. They are inhabited by traders and bankers and Brahmans both of the Desh and of the Concan."[11]

Thus, these urban communities were not so much centres of the handicrafts catering for the cultivators (with the exception of the inevitable weaving) as administrative (with the existence of Brahmans), trading and money-lending centres through which taxes were collected from the rural areas. An 1822 census put the population of Poona at 81,000, of whom 8,701 belonged to the trading communities. Gujaratis (1,533), Marwaris (761) and Bohras (300) owned 271 shops out of the 1,407 shops in the city. This information gives an idea of the make-up of Poona's trading community in the last few years of the Peshwa state.

The decline of the city had an immediate effect on the privileged sections. The late Professor D.R. Gadgil, who came from Poona and was by origin a Konkan Brahman, described the Brahmans in the first few decades of British rule as follows: "The Brahmans adapted themselves quickly to new conditions and continued, though now in a secondary role, to hold positions similar to those held by them in former times. They supplied most of the administrative and clerical personnel for the British and manned the newly emerging professions. They maintained, as a consequence, their older status in the city to a large extent. The Kunbi-Marathas suffered in comparison. The well-to-do elements in this group under peshwa rule consisted of members of the nobility, landed gentry and military services. They were not to be found among the learned professions or in the administrative services. The nobility declined in wealth and importance, the landed gentry suffered in a similar manner and ceased also to stay in the cities, and higher military service became a closed profession to Indians. Consequently, the Kunbi-Maratha representation among the higher economic categories decreased enormously. The Kunbi-Marathas continued to form the bulk of the unskilled labour class, they also entered all the newer occupations or trades as unskilled or partially skilled or supervisory workers. They were also to be found in trade and business in a small way but they did not make their way in significant numbers to the higher ranks in them."[12]

Thus, the British conquest introduced important changes, in the condition of the Maratha caste, which was the chief one in the Maharashtra countryside and, perhaps, among the Maratha people as a whole. Under the peshwas, this caste was undergoing differentiation due to the impact of disintegration. Its top sections, originating from the élite of the village community, were taking shape as the military nobility of the Peshwa state. The next, more numerous section of the Marathas was taking shape as a section of small and middle landlords bound to perform military service. As time went on, these two groups would perhaps have finally separated from the householding Marathas to constitute a military land-owning group of the Rajput type, which they resembled in social status (but not yet by caste hierarchy).

The fall of the Peshwa state and the British conquest eliminated the military élite of the Marathas and markedly worsened the condition of the small and middle Maratha land-holders, subordinating them to the invaders' tax administration. In the stratification of this caste in the second half of the 19th century, the tendencies towards capitalist differentiation already prevailed. When dealing only with the towns, we find that the hired labourers consisted almost entirely of Marathas. More of the middle sections of the Marathas were small entrepreneurs and fewer were intellectuals. The claims among these new urban sections of the Marathas were incomparable with those of the Maratha élite under independent rule.

The general idea of the composition of heads of families among the middle and higher sections of the population will be obtained from the data on the occupational make-up of the communities and castes in Poona in 1822:[13]

Community	*Well-to-do*	*Traders*	*Artisans*	*Labourers and beggars*
Brahmans	2,748	240	—	220
Kunbis	1,223	534	270	2,947
Muslims	565	143	233	126
Parsis	—	13	—	—
Gujaratis	108	407	14	—
Pardeshis	239	125	5	141
Marwaris	10	194	—	29
Shimpis	156	383	221	221
Bohras	—	96	—	—

By "well-to-do" the census must have meant the land-owners, officials and priests resident in the city. Up to the end of peshwa rule, these feudal elements prevailed, at any rate numerically, over the traders. But subsequently the balance tilted in favour of the latter. Like other cities in India, Poona was gradually losing its feudal features and acquiring semicapitalist features.

Determining the effects of the fall of the peshwas, D. R. Gadgil insisted that the elements that suffered most were the military personnel and the retinues of the chiefs, the Brahmanical elements dependent on the service, patronage or bounty of the peshwas, and the craftsmen and traders especially closely connected with the court. The first quarter-century after the fall of the peshwas most probably witnessed a serious decline in the population and prosperity of the city in most aspects. The end of the 1830s may have witnessed the lowest point for Poona. "Towards the beginning of the forties, new forces seem to have made themselves felt which initiated a revival in certain sections."[14] However, the revival of the economy was incipient.

The state of Poona's trade and handicrafts has been described in an English work published in the mid-19th century as follows: "With the exception of grain-dealers, and those who trade in the raw products of the country, the mercantile classes in Poona are said to be declining in wealth. No market is now found for jewellery and precious stones, which were much sought after when Poona was the seat of native rule. The introduction of European piece goods has caused the disappearance of native fabrics, which could not compete with them in price, and Poona has now scarcely any manufacture except a very small one of paper."[15] Those are the fairly scattered data about the socio-economic condition of Western Maharashtra in the first three decades after the conquest. One is left with the impression that urban handicrafts were generally depressed and suffered more losses than the rural handicrafts.

There is no doubt that the upper sections in the villages which belonged to the Kunbi caste and engaged in farming, having lost their high status in Maratha society, while at the same time being subjected to British tax machinations, could expect the lower sections of the rayats, artisans and community servants to remain in traditional dependence on them, that is, to expect social inertia to continue. They had no inducements to recast the householding on any entrepreneurial lines. In the situation that took shape the Brahmans displayed a remarkably rapid adaptation to the new circumstances. By maintaining their special status in ideological institutions, they displayed a capacity to penetrate into the administrative and legal system of the British Raj.

It will be seen from the above that the transformative processes were insignificant even in these districts, which were separated from Bombay City only by the low Ghats. But if we look at the Kolhapoor state, which lay close to the southern borders of Bombay Presidency, such transformations were in general not to be observed at all at least up until the mid-19th century.

The Socio-Economic Structure of the Kolhapoor State

The "Statistical Report of Kolhapoor" was published by the political resident Major D. Graham in 1854. This source contains valuable and, with a few exceptions, highly authentic material on the socio-economic structure and productive forces in the state. With the destruction of the Maratha statehood, Kolhapoor was retained for the descendants of Shivaji as a dependent territory. By the mid-19th century, Kolhapoor had remained a feudal organism, whose economic ties with the outer world were still very insignificant and one-sided. It may be assumed that in this feudal reservation the traditional socio-economic structure was subjected to minimum change.

Graham's descriptions are thorough and sometimes almost meticulous. Although in his commentaries he seeks to present a picture of almost general welfare, his statistical and other factual material helps to form a more objective idea of the actual state of affairs. There is no doubt about Graham's competence in collecting his data. He must have had a knowledge of Marathi and Kanara. At any rate, his book contains not only numerous terms in these two languages but also expressions from local thieves' jargon. The accuracy of these statistical data is doubtful (Graham does not round off the long figures), but the fact that he had access to official records of the native administration and broad opportunities for personal interviews with local inhabitants makes his material authentic.

He gives a general characteristic of the social division of labour in the principality: "Possessing capabilities within her own boundaries to produce all the necessaries and all the usual luxuries required for Indian life, Kolhapoor has been long under the progressing efforts of a division of labour, though checked by constant wars and tyranny.

"From ancient times, the alluvial plain has been set apart from the grassy eminence, the forest from the orchard land, and a mutual exchange of proceeds has somewhat benefited the respective tenants of each locality. In the absence, however, of any extended foreign commerce, or finer description of manufacture, and also of any individual costly requirements, the movement (division of labour.—V.P.) has not yet progressed beyond that state of society where a mere maintenance is obtained by the lower classes, and where the superfluity of produce is wasted by the richer classes in providing for a host of idle dissipated retainers."[16]

That is a more or less common characteristic of an economically self-sufficient region of Indian feudal society. One specific feature (which was, however, to be found elsewhere as well) was the exchange of products between the agricultural population of the plain and the livestock-breeders of the "grassy eminence". But Graham does not back up his observations with any facts. He confines himself to giving some information about the cropping in the state, while animal husbandry is not mentioned even among the produce available at fairs and bazaars. Only skins are mentioned as raw material for leatherdressers. There were only 11,069 shepherds in Kolhapoor, while the rest of the agricultural populationcame to 276,456 out of the 546,165 subjects (at any rate, together with the members of their families).[17] That is why it is hardly worthwhile to exaggerate the scale of the exchange, mentioned by Graham, between the agricultural and the stockbreeding population (besides, the skins were supplied to the leather-dressers by Mhass, who were members of the village community—a predominantly agricultural unit). In the economics of Kolhapoor, there was no stock-breeding production as an important branch, and its role in the division of social labour was not more important than it was in the main regions of feudal India.

TABLE 5
Kolhapoor's Agricultural Produce*

Product	Maunds	Rupees
Rice	1, 002, 570	1, 450, 906 ½
Jowaree	626,904	835, 873
Nachnee and inferior grains	362, 561	362, 516
Wheat	109, 510	231, 678
Gram	128, 393	231, 678
Toor	54, 308	82, 757
Tobacco and cotton	36, 960	63, 976
Sugar-cane	343, 680	343, 680
Vegetables	—	231, 678
Total	2, 664, 886	3, 834, 742 ½

* D. Graham, "Statistical Report of Kolhapoor," Poona, 1854, p. 12.

Let us take a closer look at the social division of labour in the territory on the strength chiefly of the data about the aggregate social products. The figures for the main components of its agricultural produce (Table 5) evoke doubt at least on two points: first, the coincidence of the value of the wheat, gram and vegetables, and second, the relatively low price of a maund of tobacco and cotton, which are usually several times more costly than cereals per unit of weight; besides, 31,000 rupees and 16,430 rupees, respectively, went on the export of tobacco and cotton. That is why Graham's figures should not be regarded as precise (despite his claims) but as estimates.

The total production of cereals and pulses came to about 150,000-180,000 tons (the Kolhapoor maund equalled 2,5 bushels, or 50-60 kilogrammes of cereals) for half a million inhabitants, which could meet their requirements even if at a very low rate. The data for foreign trade, which are usually more precise, also indicate that Kolhapoor was self-sufficient in the staple food-stuffs. What is more, the major export items were rice (68,989 rupees), tobacco (31,110), hemp, (16,430) and cotton (16,287 rupees). Foremost among the imported goods were fabrics (533,893 rupees, including only 30,000 rupees' worth of European-made fabrics), salt (77,139) and coconuts (54,668 rupees).[18] Despite the importance of this trade, one could conclude, by comparison with the volume of local production, that the economic structure was characterised by self-sufficiency in food-stuffs, as in most of the major regions in India, and was in this respect typical of Indian feudal society.

This adds importance to the problem of the channels through which food and raw materials for the non-agricultural population were extracted, considering that it made up nearly one-half of the population of the state, and for the needs of the urban industry. Taxes and rent continued to be the main instrument by means of which the peasant was deprived of the surplus and of a part of the necessary product. The total tax revenue of the Treasury of the state and the jagir administration came to 1,933,426 rupees a year. The richest section of the population—the bankers and the money-lenders—paid small (nominal, as Graham puts it) taxes; many artisans were exempt from direct taxation (at any rate, Graham mentions these on only one occasion when he gives information about the elements of the price of handicraft production); the merchants paid insignificant taxes. That is why one must assume that the bulk of the taxes, roughly 1,700,000-1,800,000 rupees, was borne by the land-holders. This came to 40-45 per cent of the value of the staple produce of the agriculture. But the cultivators also had such duties to perform as the maintenance of about 14,000 sirdars and inamdars (including members of their families), and over 2,000 priests.

It is hard to say anything definite about the profits of the traders. Their profits may have been included in the cost of the farm produce. The incomes of the money-lenders from agricultural production consisted of two items: first, interest on the debts of 18,000 households, which came to 72,000 rupees a year, and, second, interest on the mortgaged jagirdar property, amounting to 102,000 rupees a year.[19] Thus, usurer's capital, which received a sizable share of the tribute from the cultivators, undoubtedly ranked second in their exploitation.

What, then, remained for the householder for the purposes of commodity exchange with the urban artisan? There is no adequate information about this. First, estimates of the agricultural product extracted by the landlords and the money-lenders are highly approximate. Second, in contrast to the British administrators of the neighbouring districts of Maharashtra, Graham was indifferent to the local village community, because it was not a part of his duty to levy taxes on it; that is why his descriptions of the right of the rural artisans to receive a share of the farm product are very terse. He only mentions that in the village the "requisite artisans, who are public servants, occupy their hereditary allotments and the Mahar, the Berud, the guide, the watchman, are all paid by a separate assignment of land."[20] In other words, up until the mid-19th century the archaic system of rewarding artisans and servants of the community with land allotments still remained in Kolhapoor.

It is very hard to say to what extent the peasant relied on the market products of the urban artisans. But we obtain some idea of the market demand among the rural population from the figures about the goods offered and sold at the fair annually held at Nursoba (Table 6).

TABLE 6

Annual Fair at Nursoba*

Names of articles	*Number of shops of each description*	*Value of merchandise brought for sale, rupees*	*Estimated value of merchandise sold, rupees*
Cloth	38	312,567	135,575
Brass and copper pots	30	24,597	13,184
Haberdasher's articles	14	809	427 ½
Glass bangles	17	1,459	655
Perfumery	7	357	161 ½
Confectionery	9	613	512
Articles sold by Jungurs	3	102	97
Pearls	13	33,445	5,439
Grain of every kind	—	3,000	2,000
Vegetables, fruit, etc.	—	1,000	700
Total	131	377,949	148,751

* D. Graham, "Statistical Report of Kolhapor", p. 248.

What is remarkable about this list of fair merchandise is the absence of any wares of the traditional community handicrafts, like pottery, carpentry, smithery and jewellery. Indeed, we find a prevalence of cloths, whose manufacture was not a prerogative of the community artisans. Nor did the community artisans manufacture any of the other goods offered at the fair. One is struck by the small volume of the sales of agricultural produce. The estimated figures for their sales and also the absence of any special shops warrant the assumption that this produce was sold by the peasants themselves through small-scale retail trade channels. At the same time, the large-scale purchases of cloths and metal pots suggest that these goods were in demand among clients, including peasants. The peasants may have paid for them with the money they had obtained in the village or from local money-lenders. One could, however, assume that the village traders themselves made wholesale purchases at the fairs for the purpose of retailing these goods in the villages later.

These details, which are important in themselves, do not modify the general impression that trade at the fairs satisfied the requirements of the rural population only in the consumer goods which were not manufactured by community artisans, and that the peasants had to produce a commodity equivalent (in the form of agricultural produce) of the value of the handicraft articles they purchased on the market (with the addition of trading and money-lending deductions).

The fair at Nursoba was the largest in Kolhapoor, but Graham's information about the other fairs suggests that the range of goods and the proportions between them were typical of all the trade fairs, which were a prelude to the extraction of a part of the agricultural produce through commodity-money channels.

One should not exaggerate the absolute and relative scale of this extraction. It was much smaller than the volume of the produce alienated from the land-holders in the form of feudal-tax services, and, besides, the peasants' market demand applied only to some consumer goods. That is why the social division of labour effected through trade between agriculture and the urban handicrafts in the regional framework of Kolhapoor was clearly less important than the social division of labour on a self-subsistence basis between the cultivators and the artisans within the community.

Table 7 gives an idea of the scale of industry in the Kolhapoor territory. Judging by the fact that a number of figures have been rounded off, Graham must have taken them from the Treasure. Because the taxes were levied on the products reaching the market, these figures do not include the cost of the articles turned out by the rural artisans and distributed in the community through natural exchange. This supposition is confirmed by the fact that the total value of the industrial products indicated by Graham is given under the head "Amount sold". Thus, these figures help to characterise only the commodity part of Kolhapoor's handicraft production.

To what extent could these handicraft goods be ranged against farm produce on the market? The non-agricultural population, making up nearly one-half of the total, and especially its well-to-do sections, including the community élite, were undoubtedly the main buyers of the handicraft goods. Besides, most of the peasant requirements were met by community artisans. That is why it is no exaggeration to assume that only one-third to one-quarter of the commodity products of the handicrafts was consumed by the peasants, or some 350,000450,000 rupees' worth in cash terms. This is 9-12 per cent of the value of the staple farm produce.

TABLE 7
The Quantity, Value and Net Profit of Kolhapoor's Manufactures*
(rupees)

Names of articles	*Amount sold*	*Expenses and wages*	*Profit*
Cotton	337,422	330,000	7,422
Cumblees	100,000	88,000	12,000
Numdas	3,600	3,240	360
Gur	120,539	90,406	30,133
Oil	120,000	100,000	20,000
Paper	12,000	9,600	2,400
Snuff	825	660	165
Liquor	24,681	19,745	4,936
Perfumery	2,500	2,000	500
Baskets, etc.	12,806	7,575	5,231
Carpets	1,040	825	215
Goonpats	875	526 ½	312 ½
Cotton thread	212,500	200,000	12,500
Pottery	281,220	209,591	71,628 ¾
Glass bracelets	1,800	1,254 ½	545 ½
Lac ditto	2,000	1,837	163
Charcoal	625	475	150
Leather	123,984	115,000	8,984
Iron	9,000	6,300	2,700
Total	1,367,417	1,187,071 ½	180,345 ¾

* D. Graham, "Statistical Report of Kolhapoor," p. 252.

Thus, if the feudal tax levies extracted 40-45 per cent, and the money-lenders took directly from the peasants 2 per cent of the value of the staple farm produce, only about 9-12 per cent of the volume (something like 4 million rupees) was realised by means of commodity exchange with the handicrafts. Let us bear in mind that these figures and calculations are approximate; moreover, one has to draw attention to the fact that the share of merchant's and usurer's capital in the social product is concealed in the feudal tax revenue (in the form of interest on the landlords' debts) and in the value of the mass of commodities (in the form of trading profits). But we are ultimately interested not in the distribution of the national product, but in its structure as a reflection of a definite level in the social division of labour. On the national (rather regional) scale, the social division of labour on a commodity-money basis apparently had a subordinate place. Internal community division of labour prevailed, and the urban (or, to put it broader, non-community) handicrafts existed mainly at the expense of the surplus and necessary product extracted from the land-holders by feudal methods (including the redemption of the noblemen's debts to the money-lenders).

Some idea of the state of the productive forces and the structure of material resources will be obtained from the following assessment (in rupees) of the main types of property.[21]

Houses	5,641,816
Cattle	3,425,500
Jewels	2,781,335
Cloths and foreign goods	405,000
Agricultural deadstock	1,492,857
Manufacturing deadstock	311,671
Artisans' tools	233,959
Copper pots and furniture	1,092,310
Carts	62,520
Total	15,446,698

While there is no assessment of land property, it can be approximately estimated. The real average profits on money-lenders' debts came to 12 per cent. But when rent extracted from landed property—the basis of high social status and political influence in feudal Kolhapoor—was capitalised (i.e., if the amount of rent was multiplied in accordance with the rate of average real profit), a lower interest rate should be taken than the local usurers managed to extract, especially since, according to Graham, the court instituted attachment for debt only up to 6 per cent interest a year (perhaps the rate close to the interest paid by well-to-do debtors, notably land-owners). That is why if we start from this more realistic rate of 6 per cent, the capitalised land property in Kolhapoor may be estimated at 27-28 million rupees, and with the prestige additions entailed by land-ownership—30-35 million, or an amount roughly equal to two-thirds of the value of property of all types. Because this included much property owned by the feudal strata (houses, jewellery, cloths, furniture, weapons, etc.), it may be assumed that feudal property in Kolhapoor in the mid-19th century dominated, as it did in earlier periods.

The stagnant nature of the economy was expressed in the prevalence of inert, non-productive property over the productive resources of agriculture (without land) and of industry. Finally, the mainly agrarian structure of the economy is reflected in the roughly ten-fold prevalence of the productive assets of agriculture (cattle and implements) over those of industry.

Thus, despite all the obvious and possible imprecisions and omissions in Graham's statistical calculations, they still help one to gain a coherent picture of the major indicators of Kolhapoor's economic system like the social division of labour, the structure of the national product and production assets. These make it possible to draw a preliminary conclusion to the effect that by the mid-19th century Kolhapoor had a society of the early stage of feudalism with a prevalence of self-sufficient relations.

What, then, were the internal socio-economic structure of the non-community industry in the state, the level of its productive forces, the scale of accumulation and the condition of the entrepreneurs and producers?

Graham gives information about employment in the various manufactures in Kolhapoor. He divides these into two big groups: those employing manufacturers and those employing artisans.[22]

Manufacture of product	*Numbers employed*	*Manufacture of product*	*Numbers employed*
Weavers of cloth	7,671	Gunny	267
Oil	3,842	Thread	566
Jagree and sugar	1,764	Ink	110
Distillery of liquor	2,850	Broad tape	264
Glass bangles	730	Dyeing	30
Paper	666	Snuff	154
Rope	235	Trenchers of leaves	2,293
Smelting iron	130	Cumblees	5,180
Bricks	313	Confectionery	526
Lime	344	Baskets	640
Charcoal	226	Pottery	3,711
Leather	715	Pefumery	265
Carpets	225		
		Total	33,997

Handicrafts employed	*Numbers*	*Handicrafts*	*Numbers employed*
Bricklayers and masons	931	Sikulgurs	286
Carpenters	5,475	Embroiderers	11
Shoe-makers	3,438	Coppersmiths	249
Goldsmiths	3,528	Sawyers	233
Tailors	1,505	Cotton- and wool-carders	356
Stone-cutters	1,456	Wood-hewers	253
Washermen	2,002	Tassel-makers	143
Barbers	2,387	Whitesmiths	213
Jingurs	463	Quarrymen	871
Blacksmiths	1,169		
		Total	24,969

Graham makes no direct classification for this division. Judging by the way production was organised in the basic lines of these two groups, the first included those where small establishments with a few workers prevailed, whereas the "handicrafts" were based on the individual labour of the artisans themselves. The petty-capitalist character of the "manufactures" is borne out by the fact that, in contrast to the "handicrafts", investments into which Graham limits to the value of the implements, the former have need of working capital. "A further sum Rs. 1,187,071 is requisite, for the purchase of the raw material used, together with the item on account of wages; and thus, altogether (including the value of the implements.—V.P.) a sum of Rs. 1,498,742 is annually invested as capital employed in the manufactories of the country."[23] Because, as in the "handicrafts", money-lenders' loans were used to finance the purchases of raw material in the "manufactures", their working capital can hardly be classified as purely capitalist. Conversely, there were elements of capitalist enterprise, connected with the functions of circulating capital, in the activity of merchant's and usurer's capital in the "handicrafts".

Graham must have also included the community artisans in his register, some of them at any rate. This will be seen from the numerous groups of carpenters, potters, leather-dressers and blacksmiths. At the same time, there is the fact that pottery is classed among the "manufactures", which runs counter to the usually individual character of the work of the community artisans. Graham must have started from the organisation of pottery production in the town. The same considerations apply to the classification of leather-dressers. Graham's classification of handicraft production could have been much better if he had brought out the community artisans in a special group. Unfortunately, they were ignored.

Graham's descriptions become more detailed and valuable as he moves to the higher forms of small-scale industrial enterprise, and this naturally has an effect on the reading of his facts. Because there is no special information about the community handicrafts, these cannot be studied. It is true that Graham provides detailed data about the artisan's implements, which is very valuable, but this does not reproduce a coherent picture of his status, his connections with the consumer or dealer, his financial dependence on the latter, etc.

Pottery, one of the earliest handicrafts, was also one of the most primitive in technical and organisational terms: 3,700 potters made 4,926,000 pots worth 99,900 rupees, and after covering their expenses of 87,412 rupees received a "profit" of 12,487 rupees. The potter's implements consisted of these components: one wheel (8 annas), one peg for supporting the wheel and one stick for turning the wheel with (1 anna 6 pice), one wooden piece for beating earthen pots with (2 pice), one bamboo frame for bringing earth in upon bullocks (3 annas), one iron hoe (4 annas), one large bamboo basket for collecting horse-dung (1 anna), one small bamboo basket (4 pice). Total value of deadstock, 1 rupee 2 annas.

Tanning was another lowly organised industry in Kolhapoor, although Graham does refer it to the "manufactures" (apparently assuming that an occupation of the low castes cannot be listed among the "handicrafts"). The tanners turned out 25,500 pieces of skin a year, and sold them to shoe-makers and saddle-makers for 40,242 rupees, receiving a "profit" of 8,984 rupees or 12 rupees per head. As in many other instances, Graham does not explain his methods of calculating the "profit". Because there is no mention of the existence among the tanners, as among the potters, even of petty entrepreneurs, their "profit" must have consisted of the difference between the proceeds of the sale of the finished product less the expenses of acquiring the raw materials and maintaining the family. It is hard to imagine any production realisation even of this tiny "profit" by the tanner, because his equipment was as primitive and cheap as that of the potter: one instrument to smooth skins (4 annas), one instrument for shaving hair off the skins (2 annas), one instrument for cleaning leathers after dyeing (3 annas), one piece of plank to smooth leather on (8 annas), two iron spikes to sew water-bags of leather (1 anna) and one hone for whetting instruments (1 anna); total value of these simple devices, 1 rupee 3 annas.[24] The potters and the tanners must have been mainly village communities' artisans.

Weavers had more complex and costly equipment. One wooden member of the loom cost 10 rupees, one brush cost 1 rupee 4 annas, and all the dead-stock, including another 26 items, was valued at 17 rupees 3 annas 6 pice. This equipment could be used by the weaver alone or with the occasional help from members of his family. However, there is one incongruity in Graham's statistics about weaving: there are over 7,000 "employed" for 1,642 operating looms.[25] This suggests that in some instances and perhaps as a rule the number of Graham's artisans corresponded not to the number of independent working-men, but to all the members of the families in the given caste. This assumption may be reinforced by the fact that the self-employed artisans numbering nearly 60,000 together with members of their families would add up to a population of 200,000-250,000, or nearly one-half of the population of feudal Kolhapoor, which is extremely doubtful.

The device for making oil, however simple, was in effect a mechanism. It consisted of a wooden trough that held the seed, and a wooden cylinder, about 4 feet high, fitted upright into the centre of the trough, with a heavy cross-beam above. By means of a system of attachments this mechanism was set in motion by a bullock. The oil-mill itself cost 12 rupees, and with its adjuncts 19 rupees 1 anna. Considering that a bullock cost another 10 rupees, the oil-maker could be classed among the relatively well-to-do "manufacturers". The total value of 4,000 candies (about 1,000 tons) of oil produced in Kolhapoor was worth 120,000 rupees, of which 100,000 rupees were expenses and the cost of the raw material. Of the remaining 20,000 rupees, each manufacturer received 7 rupees of "profit", that is, the 3,840 persons engaged in the making of oil were small-scale operators barely making ends meet.

Iron was produced by small entrepreneurs, with 180 persons employed to operate 30 furnaces. These produced about 200 tons of metal a year, worth 9,000 rupees, of which the profits came to 2,700 rupees. By the period under consideration, the condition of Kolhapoor miners had worsened. In former times, the miners had enjoyed the monopoly for supply of iron throughout the state, they received rent-free land from the government, together with an annual allowance of Rs. 1,000 for the supply of cannon balls, and were further entitled to subsistence from the villages adjacent to the scene of their operations. By the mid-19th century, says Graham, "the increased import of the cheaper and more easily worked material from England has greatly affected the condition of the Kolhapoor miners, who, however, contrive to eke out a subsistence obtained in mining by following the profession of itinerant blacksmiths. They, however, appear to be happy and contented, and the monthly wage of Rs. 5 which can be earned, is according to their ideas of comfort, fully sufficient for their support."[26]

Six persons worked at each furnace. Two men worked at the bellows, maintaining the necessary temperature, two brought up the charcoal and repaired the furnace when necessary, and two brought in the firewood for burning the charcoal and the ore.[27] I myself have seen an Indian popularscience film showing the "blast-furnace process"among the hill tribes. This showed roughly the same kind of labour organisation. The commentary stressed the importance of the blowing regime and the quality of the coal. The "blast furnaces" were in the form of clay cones about 120-130 centimetres high each. Every smelting produced a piece of iron mass weighing a few kilogrammes. The blacksmiths took over at this point and beat the metal into tips for tools and weapons. The technology of the Kolhapoor miners may have been higher than that of the present-day tribesmen, but their establishments were clearly more primitive than those in Mysore in the early 19th century.

One may assume that the profit went to the foreman, the man who headed the team. At any rate, on the strength of Graham's statement that each worker received 5 rupees a month and the furnaces operated only part of the year, their aggregate wages could have come to 6,000-

7,000 rupees a year, and the profits divided among the foremen at about 90 rupees a year.

Nearly 90 million tiles, worth a total of 179,820 rupees, of which 58,691 rupees was profit, was annually turned out in Kolhapoor. Considering that one establishment with three men employed turned out 400 double cylinder-shape tiles a day with 500 tiles worth 1 rupee, all the establishments together had to work nearly 225,000 days, from which it can he deduced that Kolhapoor had 800-900 tile-making establishments, about 2,5003,000 workers, and the annual profit of the master of each establishment was 60-70 rupees.

The petty-capitalist character of the tile-making establishments is confirmed by the organisation of production. First of all, five bullock-loads of clay, 5 head-loads of horse dung, and 2 head-loads of kiln ashes were mixed together in water and reduced to thick mud. One man prepared the mud, another gave the requisite quantity to be placed on the wheel, and the third turned the wheel and prepared the tiles in the shape of a hollow cylinder, tapering towards one end. While wet, two cuts were made with a piece of stone or wood on each side of the cylinder, leaving it, however, joined together at the upper and lower ends. When dry, the cylinders were baked in the kiln and sold to customers, who divided them into two parts longitudinally. Three men made 400 cylinders a day. [28]

Kolhapoor's biggest enterprises took shape in sugar and paper-making. Let us note that neither was a monopoly of the traditional specialised castes, so that the routine of caste technological regulations and hereditary limitations did not have any effect on either of these to the extent that they did on the traditional manufactures. Neither production (paper- making, at any rate) was a part of the system of village community's handicrafts.

The 18 paper-mills employed 666 persons, or 37 per unit. Paper was manufactured from hemp and gunny bags (apparently second-hand). The material was "reduced to a pulp in a machine called a Dung", which was run by three men. It took 20 hours to turn 4 maunds (over 100 kilogrammes) of material into pulp, which was thoroughly washed by two men. It was then dried and made into large lumps and left to bleach and putrefy. This was done by four men. The mass was then once again "put into the Dung" and washed in a tank. A men lifted the pulp from the tank with a mould; it was placed on a terraced floor and pressed to squeeze out the water. Thus, sheet after sheet was made and laid one over the other in a pile. The pile was then pressed again to squeeze out the superfluous water, after which the sheets were carefully separated one by one and plastered to dry on the house walls, which were in the first instance washed with white mud and water. As the water was absorbed, the paper dried and fell to the ground. The paper was put under a press, sized, polished and cut, and the edges made even.

There was no mechanisation despite the relative complexity of the technological process. The paper was made by a Muslim group of Kagdees. The deadstock of the establishment cost 29 rupees 14 annas, and the value of the annual product came to 12,000 rupees, of which 2,400 rupees was profit (133 rupees per establishment), 2,500 rupees went for the purchase of raw material, leaving 7,100 rupees to pay the workers (about 600 men without the owners) or 1112 rupees per man a year. However, Graham divides the whole amount of 9,500 rupees left after the outlays on raw material and the payment of the tax among the 666 employed, which gives a profit of 15 rupees per head.[29]

Some doubt may be expressed on this score because, what- ever the calculation, one worker received about half a rupee a month, which enabled him to buy only 30-40 kilogrammes of millet, an amount clearly insufficient to feed a family. The fact that Graham now brings out the profit, now lumps it together with the remuneration may be indirect evidence of the patriarchal methods used to exploit the members of the same caste. The notion that paper-making establishments were some kind of cooperatives manned by members of one caste is not borne out by any other analogy from India's economic life in that period. Perhaps the most justified assumption is that the paper-making establishments were primitive capitalist manufactories with considerable patriarchal caste elements in relations between the owner and the workers.

The paper went mainly to the Treasury (5,000 rupees' worth), as much was exported to the neighbouring states, and the rest (2,000 rupees' worth) was bought by local inhabitants. This orientation upon the Treasury subsequently ruined papermaking in Kolhapoor.

The boiling of gur was another branch in which establishments with a division of labour prevailed. They employed 1,764 persons, and so, because each unit had an average of 15 persons, there were about 115-120 establishments in the state. These turned out 4,296 candies of gur worth 120,529 rupees, of which the net profit came to 30,113 rupees, or 250-270 rupees per establishment, the highest profit for any Kolhapoor manufacture. This was due apparently to the very high value of the deadstock: 213 rupees 9 annas per establishment. There is, in general, some connection between the amount of capital invested in deadstock and the mass of profit per establishment.

Gur was made as follows. Four men were employed in cutting the cane and stripping off the leaves, and two men conveyed the cane to the establishment. One man was employed in dividing the sugar-cane into pieces about a yard in length. Seven men were employed at the installation itself. One applied the cane in a regular layer to the opening between two rollers, which seized and compressed the canes as they passed, another sat opposite to the feeder and received the cane as it passed between the rollers, an operation which was repeated three times, so that on leaving the roller the third time the canes were reduced to the form of dry splinters and were used as fuel in boiling the juice, which fell into an earthen vessel fixed at the foot of the roller. Two men were employed in driving the bullocks yoked to the installation. A fifth man conveyed the juice to the boiler. Two men tended the boiler.

It is hard to say whether the owner of the gur boiler was an entrepreneur, because his social status is unknown. But in the neighbouring districts of Bombay Maharashtra this industry was usually run by the village élite, who had large plantations under sugar-cane and employed dependent community servants to work there on the basis of giving them a share of the gur as reward. One could assume that this kind of traditional "hire in kind" was also practised in Kolhapoor.

Let us also note that bullocks were widely used in gur-making for conveying the material and for setting the installation in motion. Their value (16 bullocks at 10 rupees per head) made up "the bulk of the capital. The large iron pan (15 rupees) and the sugar-cane mill" (10 rupees) were the most costly items of the deadstock.[30] Thus, the devices used in gurmaking were highly primitive, and animals were the source of energy.

Let me say in conclusion that Graham estimated the cost of the deadstock on a peasant farm (without animals and carts) at 28 rupees 11 annas, that is, more than the dead-stock of a carpenter (11 rupees) and a blacksmith (23 rupees 1 anna).[31] Together with the animals and the carts, the cultivator's deadstock was considerably in excess of the value of the deadstock held by artisans, including members of the higher handicraft castes in the community. Together with the land-holding, this fact gave the peasants a higher social status than that of the artisans.

The review of the data about the socio-economic organisation of the handicrafts in Kolhapoor warrants the conclusion that entrepreneurial relations proper, even if they did exist, ranged over a narrow sect of secondary manufactures. Meanwhile, the basic manufactures were still either within the system of village community handicrafts, or were a variety of petty-commodity production. Information about the activity of merchant's and usurer's capital helps to some extent to specify our notions of the social relations in the handicrafts.

It is possible to judge about the network of trading and money-lending establishments on the strength of the data about the specialisation of trade and credits: there were 171 "houses of shroffs" (apparently money-changers only); Bania shops trading in grain and other goods—1,857; shops selling readymade cloth articles—178; betel leaves—276; copper and brassware—24; founders in metal—20, confectioners' shops—38; perfumers' shops—65; greengrocers' shops—68; shops selling opium and bhang—6; coarse hardware—40; paper—27; gold and silver-work—685; liquor—300; horse gear—48; fine metal-work—5, haberdashers' shops—14, shops selling silk goods—14; shoes and sandals—263; glass bangles—174; snuff dealers' shops—45; shops selling images of earth and stone—5; cumblees—364; baskets—98; and general stores—39.[32]

The great number of shops and the similarity of their specialisation with the structure of local manufactures, on the one hand, suggest that a number of shops were simultaneously establishments producing the corresponding goods, and, on the other, shows the extent of the buying-up of handicraft products. This is also borne out by the data on the artisans' dependence on the money-lenders. However, Graham has no description of the activity of the buyers-up.

The pyramid of usurer's capital has the following appearance :[33]

Number of banking houses	*Capital, rupees*	*Number of banking houses*	*Capital, rupees*
3	100,000	8	20,000
17	80,000	7	15,000
12	25,000	47	10,000
272	5,000		

Besides, there were 400 shroffs in the state, who must have operated mainly with loans from the richer bankers, in money-changing and the exchange of coins, and in small pledges; they had an income of 10 rupees a month.

Up until the establishment of the British protectorate, the Kolhapoor bankers "drove a thriving trade in lending money to the chiefs and sirdars" at exorbitant interest: 5 per cent premium and 24 per cent interest, even on the mortgage of a village and excluding "expenses attending the management of the mortgaged property". "Of late years," says Graham, "the custom of taking a premium has been discontinued, but the rate of interest still varies from 9 to 24 per cent, excepting among tradesmen, who in their dealings with each other seldom exceed 8 per cent."[34]

One should not assume that the British protectorate released the nobility from the claims of the bankers. This was rather some kind of compensation for the big landlords who had been deprived of the opportunity to limit the money-lenders' excessive claims by means of despotic violence. "Forcible and violent extortion of demand by personal torture and Dhurna have been discontinued, and the bankers are now more cautious in their speculations, and look more to individual character and security. The ancient abuse also has been abolished, which endured the contract system of collecting revenue, when the contractor, residing at headquarters, and subjected to sudden imperative calls from the Durbar, was forced into a league with some monied house to supply the urgent demand, which was always provided by the Saukar, but very dearly paid for by the oppressed rayat."[35]

The British "settled" the bulk of the sirdars' debts by inducing the mortgage of the greater portion of their estates and introducing regular installments in liquidation of the debt. This deprived the "banking community of large sources of profit in the items of interest and management of the mortgaged property". The Kolhapoor bankers had confined their dealings to "usurious transactions within the boundaries of Kolhapoor state. Some late trifling speculations in cotton, however, would lead to the hope that they are gradually becoming more alive to their own interests, and that ere long their capital will be employed in the manufactories and the produce of the country."[36] This prediction came true, but only decades later.

Meanwhile, in the mid-19th century, usurer's capital continued to operate in its traditional spheres. It is true that the tax measures put through under the British, notably the abandonment of tax-farming, resulted, as in the neighbouring districts of Bombay Maharashtra, in several bankruptcies among local bankers. But, Graham observes, in compensation of the loss sustained under these provisions, "the bankers contribute a mere nominal tax to the support of the State: they are now exempted from the forced levies which under the former government they were compelled to pay... on succession to property, or on other pretext."[37]

Graham assessed the banking capital of the state at 4,100,000 rupees, of which 400,000 could be written off as loss on account of bad debts, 600,000 as "shut up in jewels" and the balance bringing in the profit of about 380,000 rupees at 12-13 per cent annual interest. Nor is that the whole of the tribute paid by the population of Kolhapoor to the money-lenders, because "a further sum of about Rs. 3,700,000 has been advanced in former times from foreign Saukars, chiefly, however, to superior Jagirdars; and altogether the entire amount owed throughout the principality is not under Rs. 6,700,000."[38]

Incidentally, on the strength of this amount, and also of the fact that the value of all the property (without land) in the state came to 15,446,998 rupees, Graham draws the conclusion that property free of debt was valued at 8,746,998 rupees. But that is clearly an incorrect approach, because 4,700,000 rupees of debt fell either to the nobility (4 million) or to the land-holders (700,000), that is, the sections whose debts were secured mainly by land, either as property or holding. Taking my assessment of land property 30-35 million rupees), we find the total debt to the money-lenders equal to 15-18 per cent of the value of all the property.

The interest on jagirdar debt must have been somewhat lower because the state court only attached debts at 6 per cent a year. But even at this minimum rate total usurer's profit should be estimated at about 600,000 rupees. In other words, the income of the money-lenders came to nearly one-quarter of the feudal rent, but was three times the "profit" of all the manufactures taken together. These ratios show that usurer's capital operated in a profoundly feudal environment with the separate potential pockets of enterprise being very small and hardly subordinate to the overall socio-economic system.

It should be borne in mind that money-lending profit itself largely consisted of deductions from rent and the income of the handicrafts. With this kind of recalculation its share of the extracted surplus-product increases. According to Graham, the profits of local money-lenders consisted of 72,000 rupees obtained from the land-owners, 102,000 from mortgaged jagirdar property, and 205,900 from "handicraft labour".[39] If to the profit from the mortgaged jagirdar property is added the interest on "foreign Saukars", more than one-half of the total income of usurer's capital consist of deductions from feudal rent, one-eighth coming directly from the exploitation of the peasants and over one-third from the dependent artisans and indebted entrepreneurs.

One notable omission is the item of income from credits to merchants. This serves once again to show that the intracaste credit converted the crediting of trade into an internal affair of the members of the trading and money-lending castes and did not make it possible to separate trading and money-lending profit with sufficient clarity. These obscurities and also the absence of data on the size of trading profit tended to understate the true proportions of trading and money-lending operations.

Besides, despite the reform of the tax system it is doubtful that the money-lenders were entirely removed from the collection of taxes. Still, with all the possible correctives in favour of the actually stronger and broader positions of merchant's and usurer's capital in Kolhapoor economy, there is no doubt at all that it was on the whole subordinate to the landed nobility.

The material on the sources of profit gives an idea about the social-class environment in which merchant's and usurer's capital operated in Kolhapoor. Here are the main categories of debtors and the volume of their debt (in rupees).[40]

18,000	cultivators	700,000
89,000	individuals of other occupations	2,000,000
4,000	inamdars	300,000
	Total: 11,000 debtors	3,000,000

According to these data, all the inhabitants enjoying legal competence, that is, the heads of families, were in debt. It is impossible to make such an assumption for two reasons: first, not all were in need of credit and not all were allowed credit by the money-lenders; second, these figures show that only a part of the cultivators were in debt, because among the "individuals of other occupations" the debtors made up nearly 40 per cent of the total population, including women and children. The peasants must have applied to one money-lender in their village, so that the information gives the approximate number of debtors, while the non-farming persons could and had to turn to various money-lenders (especially in the towns). That is why one and the same person may be listed as a debtor by several money-lenders, which is what has confused the statistics. Finally, these data show only the lower section of the indebted landlords, and the amount of debt is much too small for the landlords to have paid the interest mentioned above.

After all these considerations about Graham's summarised data let us turn to his information about the enslavement of the toiling population by merchant's and usurer's capital in Kolhapoor. According to the data on the cultivators' debts, one could assume that most of the land-holders among them were debtors of money-lenders. When grain was advanced, the debtor paid a quarter more from the next harvest. On the whole, from each indebted husbandman 4 rupees a year of interest was collected, which came to about 5 per cent of the average annual income (84 rupees). But money-lending was only one side of the matter. "In every village, and in every individual shop, the real dealer manufactured, according to his ideas of honesty, his own weights and measures, from any material at hand, and used them without restraint, to his own profit, and to the disadvantage of all who dealt with him."[41] Commercial profit was undoubtedly a sizable addition to the usurious interest obtained from the cultivators.

Characterising the money-lenders' control of the artisans Graham says: "It is a matter of fact that in Kolhapoor a portion only of 5 per cent of the manufacturing body are men of any substance; the remainder borrow from the Saukar, and make the best terms they can according to their talent and ability." He then gives an interesting fact about the scale on which the money-lenders extracted the surplus-product from the "manufactures":

"After paying the expense of labour, the assumed net profit of Rs. 180,345 would admit of a payment of nearly fifteen per cent; but it is very problematical whether the bankers are contented with this return; and indeed they generally prefer extracting what they can, annually, on account, from the borrowing manufacturer.

"Thus, although the mere means of maintenance are obtained on sufferance, the manufacturer, who is generally forced to be content with the market profit (of the money-lender. V. P.), allows himself to be dipped further in the Saukar's books from year to year, on account of inordinate accumulating interest, and he can never hope to emerge from the condition of the hard-tasked journeyman."[42]

It is noteworthy that Graham makes no mention at all of the money-lenders' fulfilling the functions of suppliers of raw material or of buyers-up, a sphere of activity that could have been limited. The bondage of the producer sprang above all from his poverty, and compounded it. At the same time, it is interesting that Graham writes about debts in the "manufactures" only and says nothing about debts in the "handicrafts". Apparently, the more explicit petty-capitalist character of the "manufactures" and their connections with the market helped merchant's and usurer's capital to penetrate into them. The above-mentioned 5 per cent of producers who were "men of any substance" made up the small section of relatively independent entrepreneurs.

According to Graham, the number of Brahman bankers, saukars and traders in Kolahpoor was, respectively, 118, 1,130 and 24,442. Unfortunately, he does not give enough information about the ethnic and caste make-up of the community of Kolhapoor saukars, traders and money-lenders. It is true that he says that Gujaratis and Marwaris were frequently to be seen among the Banias and merchants,[43] but he does not specify either their numbers or status. It may be assumed that the Gujaratis and the Marwaris (as, incidentally, also the Maratha Brahman bankers of, say, Poona) were among the "foreign Saukars" who gave loans to the jagirdars. The fact that these communities were represented among the bankers of Kolhapoor is also borne out by the fact that only one banking house in Kolhapoor issued "hundies" to the amount of 5,000 rupees with the right of discounting these in remote towns, while the others made available hundies to the amount of 1,000 rupees only to Poona, Belgaum and Hyderabad in the Deccan.[44]

One is left with the impression that the occupational make-up of Kolhapoor's population (this information is considered separately below) was formed by Graham on a mixed principle: some categories included only those engaged in the given occupation, and others all the members of a caste specialising in that line. With this kind of approach the total population of Kolhapoor may be understated (not all the members of the families shown for the occupation are included among the members of the caste) or overstated (a double count of those included in the occupation and in the caste). On the whole, it appears that the total population of the state was, perhaps, understated, because of the usual statistical omissions, and also because there were more members of families than of those employed, and the omission of the former may not have been compensated by the double count of the latter.

This preliminary remark having been made, let us give the socio-occupational make-up of Kolhapoor's population in the form in which it is presented by Graham. Of the 546,156 inhabitants in the principality, 522,110 were Hindus and 24,046 were Muslims (small communities like the Jains are clearly included among the Hindus). The non-agricultural population was divided into the following socio-professional groups:[45]

Sirdars and 1st class inamdars	572
2nd class inamdars	13,149
Priests	2,379
Karkoons	7,792
Brahman bankers	1,187
Ditto servants	858
Ditto beggars and idlers	7,170
Saukars	1,130
Traders and shopkeepers	24,442
Manufacturers	33,717
Artisans	24,969
Sepoys	26,963
Labourers	45,869
Shepherds	11,069
Different professions	7,651
Gurkurees holding small inams	10,554
Beggars	4,977
Inferior and predatory classes	45,252
Total	269,700

The feudal establishment, itself sufficiently numerous, had a military force and a ramified ideological apparatus, consisting of Brahmans (among them the creed was spread not only by the temple priests but also the mendicant ascetics whom Graham so disrespectfully classes as "beggars and idlers"), which were fairly large considering the population of the state. When analysing the class make-up of the non-agricultural population, it is hard to imagine which section of the population could, in effect, constitute an important plebeian, let alone burgher, opposition to the feudal raj. The traders and the money-lenders were themselves in need of protection against the hatred of their debtors, constituting a majority of Kohlapoor's toiling population. Some pre-bourgeois elements among the manufacturing entrepreneurs depended on orders from the Treasury. The handicraft population was divided by the caste system, which classed some professions as "pure" and respected, and debased others to the status of "impure".

There remains the mass of the poorest. Graham calls them

"labourers" and "inferior and predatory classes", but says nothing about their status. It may be assumed that the "labourers" included porters, servants with unattractive jobs and all manner of ancillary workers. The "inferior and predatory classes" could have included, along with these same groups of working people, hill tribes and such inferior castes as musicians, etc. All these deprived people were despised not only by the upper sections but also by their fellow-workers from the "pure" castes. Of course, these people had nothing in common with any kind of "pre-proletariat" and constituted the lowest section of a traditional social structure.

A valuable addition to the sources on the socio-occupational structure of Kolhapoor will be found in the corresponding data for the city of Kolhapoor, a feudal centre of medium scale with 43,383 inhabitants, uncluding 20,235 women and children.[46] Although another 1,000 women are listed according to the occupations, it is still hard to assume that in such an old town new-comers were so numerous that adult men numbered over one-half of the population.

The social hierarchy of the city and of the whole state was headed by 40 top persons: 10 sirdars, 22 mankuri and 8 relatives of the rajah. Then came 16 first-class inamdars, who had whole villages for inams. Then followed the small inamdars, of whom only 12 had whole villages, while the other 500 had separate tracts of land as inams or watans. Characteristically, of these small inamdars, 300 Brahmans, and all the 16 major inamdars, are presented as "learned and other respectable Brahmans". In other words, the members of this caste clearly prevailed among the urban élite. All manner of Hindu priests numbered about 4,000. With all the distinctions in property status—from the big landlord to the mendicant ascetic—this unproductive part of the population (land-owners and priests) constituted nearly one-quarter of the male population of the city. In addition to this unproductive part of the population there were 300 shroffs; then came 3,000 Sepoys and the palace servants (1,600 persons). The idle sections of the feudal city also included 640 prostitutes, a figure which may perhaps indicate the high percentage of men coming to the city, and 25 "inferior dancing girls" (there were another 50 dancing girls and 25 singers, who had apparently something to do with art). Furthermore, there were 4,012 servants, and 2,735 traders at the bazaars and in the shops. Thus, of the 23,000 gainfully employed population about 17,000 were either rent-consumers or made up the personnel of the apparatus of coercion and administration, or all manner of servants and retainers.

This unproductive majority of the population (together with members of their households) was served by 2,077 artisans, 1,247 "manufacturers" and 1,200 "labourers". It may be assumed that the productive minority could not satisfy the needs of the city even in handicraft articles. For instance, 375 weavers could not possibly make enough goods for over 40,000 persons, many of whom obviously dressed lavishly. The same applies to the making of footwear, which was done by only 100 shoe-makers, and other important handicrafts. In other words, the handicrafts of a military and administrative centre like Kolhapoor did not have, or had very few, independent commodity contacts with the surrounding agricultural areas, were maintained through the redistribution of rent and depended on the bounty of the Treasury and the nobility. This implied the need to import not only farm produce but also handicraft articles which duly extended the operations of merchant's capital and strengthened its ties with the Treasury, the court, the supply department and the nobility.

It was the city of Kolhapoor, and its propertied sections, to be more precise, which were, in particular, the chief consumers of the sizable imports of cloths, because only the coarser cloths were made in the state itself. Artisans from the internal regions undoubtedly took part in supplying the city, because the cloths were the only major item of handicraft imports, and the city's requirements in these were not confined to cloths.

Let us consider in greater detail the occupational make-up of the city's handicraft population. There were 20 stone-masons, 80 bricklayers, 42 stone-cutters, 31 lime-makers, 200 tile-makers and 10 brick-makers. These 450 workers could have fully handled the city's building needs.

The working of metal was not sufficiently developed in the city, there being 40 blacksmiths, 15 tinsmiths, 15 coppersmiths 10 cutlers, 60 goldsmiths, 10 gunsmiths and 20 polishers of tools and weapons. A part of the metal articles (copperware and weapons) must have been imported. The city's requirements in wood-working were satisfied to a greater degree, involving 150 carpenters, 15 sawyers, 150 wood-cutters, 30 "makers of leaf trenchers", 15 basket-makers, 80 men who manufactured bamboo articles. Paper-making involved 37 persons—the number required for one establishment. Leather goods were made by 100 shoe-makers, 40 saddle-makers and as many tanners. Glass bangles were made by 90 artisans, pottery by 100.

The making of cloths and textile goods had many special lines. The above-mentioned 375 weavers were not the only group of such artisans. They included 50 cotton-spinners (very few for such a city); 35 artisans manufactured ropes, 15 cottontape, 40 gunny bags, 25 carpets, 25 silk fringe and tassels, 110 blankets; there were also 40 dyers of yarn and cloths and 400 tailors. The city had 50 perfumers, 150 barbers and 175 washermen.

In the food industry there were 24 men who parched the grain, 100 oil-makers and 50 confectioners. The small numbers of persons employed in this line were due to the fact that a large part of the produce was made in the small shops, which were both commercial and manufacturing establishments.

In Kolhapoor's trade, Graham brings out two of the most numerous groups: 800 "dealers in various articles" and 600 itinerant traders. The former must have had shops, and the latter were merely hawkers. Then comes specialised trade in goods: groceries 300, cloths 275, brassware 15, hay 25, betel leaves 45, tobacco 50, snuff, opium and bhang 5 each, and timber 65. There were 275 traders in rice who also hulled it before selling, and 25 who made and sold lanterns.

The lower sections of the trading people were either hawkers or small vendors who offered their simple wares in the open air. In shops (or shops cum workshops) there were 1,374 persons employed together with the owners. Among the biggest establishments were 20 shroff offices employing 150 persons, 28 shops selling cloths with 146 salesmen and 38 tailoring establishments employing 167 persons. Among the other establishments the more numerous were jewellery shops, which numbered 75, but which employed only 175 persons. Grain was sold in 104 shops employing 159, oil in 41 shops with 86 employees, liquor in 27 shops with 67 persons, confectionery in 19 shops with 43 persons; there were 14 smithies with 16 blacksmiths. This gives a picture of a bazaar with hawkers, stalls, petty shops, kiosks and workshops, and with the offices of shroffs and medium-size trading establishments rising above these here and there.

The city's traffic was handled by 100 persons who rented out carts, 75 persons who rented out horses, and 25 boatmen. For out-of-town trade bullock carts were used (the carrying capacity of a cart was even a kind of measure of weight for some goods).

There are some interesting facts about the intellectuals in the city. It had 100 scribes, whom Graham divides, much too precisely, into four linguistic groups of 25 persons each (Balbodh, Hindustani, Kanarese and Pharsi). In Kolhapoor there were 60 native doctors (who were helped in especially difficult cases by 25 exorcists) and 25 native teachers. In the period, these three professions had not yet entirely lost their connection with religion.[47]

Thus, summing up the review of Kolhapoor's economic and social structure, both of the state and the city, it is safe to say that in both instances we have a purely feudal organism with pockets of capitalist relations of the early manufactory type here and there. There is hardly any sign of the economic expansion of British capital as yet, and the very presence of the British has had an effect only on some "regulation" of the land-tax system and the tax-farming system.

The socio-economic survey of Kolhapoor could, in effect, have been tied in with the overall characteristic of India's historical development on the eve of the conquest (especially in view of the fact that Graham wrote his report on Kolhapoor only a few years after the establishment of the Eritish protectorate). The ground for this extrapolation into the past is provided by the confidence that Kolhapoor society had remained unchanged in form at least from the mid-18th century. Still I believe it necessary to place this material in the same chronological cross-section with the description of new phenomena and processes then originating in Bombay, Calcutta and other centres of British and Indian enterprise, however few.

The point is that in the first half of the 19th century there are signs of economic division and social disintegration of Indian society, that is, all the aggregates of formational characteristics which subsequently went to make up the multi-sectoral mechanism India had never known before. For a more distinct comparison between the extreme components of this mechanism, let us go on from Kolhapoor to Bombay, where the genesis of capitalism was already most pronounced on a colonial foundation.

Commercial and Industrial Enterprise in Bombay

The social and economic situation which had taken shape in Bombay by the early 19th century was unusual in historical terms. This had its own premises, including the break-up of the traditional social structure of the Indian town and its dislocation in favour of sections once depressed (Banias) or altogether neglected (Parsis). Alongside this aggregation of propertied sections, which was new to India, a new toiling section was taking shape, as various people dropped out from the conventional caste network.

The progressing deformative changes in Bombay could have led to corresponding changes in Maharashtra and Gujarat if this melting-pot had operated as an independent political, economic and ideological centre with respect to the traditional social groundwork on the adjacent mainland. Optimal development could have been expressed in a deformative and simultaneously constructive two-way influence, in the course of which there would have been a mutual and universal transformation of Bombay's social and economic structures which were in contact with, let us say, the neighbouring areas of Maharashtra. But—and here is the paradoxical distinction between "liberal" Bombay and oppressed Calcutta—it became a centralising, in the economic, political and ideological sense, component of its immediate hinterland only in the early 20th century. (This change may be tentatively dated to the period of the activity of Tilak, who was the first to express the unity of Bombay, Maharashtra and, largely, all-India interests and ties.) The strident statements by the British anthorities about Bombay's cosmopolitanism in the 19th century turned out to be negative in that they emphasised its alien character and incompatibility with the socio-economic structure of Maharashtra or Gujarat.

Indeed, in the period under consideration Bombay continued to be an outward rather than inward-oriented entity, oriented upon the metropolitan country and its interests in the Indian Ocean and the Far East. Bombay merchant's capital, being given an opportunity, with the British conquest of Maharashtra, to join in its commerce and credit relations, had long remained indifferent to Maharashtra's socio-economic condition, as something being given in advance, and even as hostile in its historically-rooted inertia. However, the Gujarat merchants had good ground to keep in their memories the legends, so real for their ancestors, about the raids of Shivaji and his successors on the towns of Gujarat.

In the first half of the 19th century, when Bombay city be- came the gate of trade routes which led deep into the heart of India, there were testimonies of a rapid growth of its foreign trade.[48] By the middle of the century, more than one-third of India's overseas trade passed through the Bombay harbour. The growing flow of British goods encouraged an ever greater number of Gujarat merchants of every section to act as compradors. Describing the Bohra merchants from Gujarat, who traded in Central India, J. Malcolm wrote: "The Bohras ... have imported the improvements of European settlements, even in the construction of their houses and furniture; they are the chief medium through which the trade in European articles is carried on."[49]

Maria Graham, an English traveller, who visited India in 1809, related her encounter with the Bania merchants of Gujarat as follows: "In Bombay (Presidency.—V. P.) there are a good many Banias or travelling merchants, who come mostly from Guzerat, and roam about the country with muslins, cotton cloth, and shawls, to sell. On opeining one of their bales, I was surprised to find at least half of its content of British manufacture (she speaks here of textiles.—V. P.) and such articles are much cheaper than those of equal fineness from Bengal and Madras. Excepting a particular kind of chintz made at Poonah, and painted with gold and silver, there are no fine cotton-cloths made on this side of the peninsula." Maria Graham's further account makes it clear that the British fabrics she saw in the bale of a Gujarat trader were factory-made. She went on to say how strange it seemed that cotton exported to England, worked up there and returned as cloth to India should sell here at a lower price than the local manufactures, where labour was so cheap. She believed that this was due to the unsettled state of affairs and the difficulty of sending goods to different parts of India, but the chief reason seemed to be the fact that England employed machinery.[50]

Gujarat merchants also made vast fortunes on the opium trade and were beginning to export cotton. In the 1820s, Gujarat compradors led by the prominent merchant, Jeejeebhoy, started, with the backing of Maratha traders, to export cotton. In the 1820s, Gujarat compradors led by the prominent merchant, Jeejeebhoy, started, with the backing of Maratha traders, to export cotton from Maharashtra.[51] Cotton export from Surat and Broach began even earlier and was almost entirely in the hands of Gujarat merchants. A British economist who studied the cotton trade in India said that the cotton trade between Berar and Bombay had been started and was still being carried on mainly by Indian merchants. He said that British merchant's capital in North-West India was weak because British merchants had a poor knowledge of the country, had no network of agents and had to face Indian competition.[52] But the main reason was, undoubtedly, the long resistance put up by the Marathas against the invaders, which had prevented them from establishing a control system over the local mechanism of distribution and exchange.

An English eye-witness gave the following description of the cotton trade in 1836: "The exporters of cotton to the coast are chiefly opulent individuals and native firms of Bombay. They have Gomasthas who had located themselves at Ramgaum (a cotton-growing area in Maharashtra.—V. P.) from whence they send out subordinates to the several pergunnahs, to make advances to patels and substantial rayats of villages about two months previous to the gathering, at 2 per cent, per month. They likewise purchase cotton from the mahajuns who are settled in the kusbas and almost every respectable village in the country, these mahajuns having made advances to the rayats in the similar way. When the cotton begins to come in, the principal taluqdars and mahajuns of large towns and points meet and fix what is called a sahukar's price and receive the wool from the producers (cleared from the seed) at the kusba or the village itself. They take a discount of one rupee per nug on account of the advances made by them."[53]

The penetration of commodity relations into the Indian countryside extended the function of trading and money-lending groups above all in the areas where commercial crops were grown. But in the first half of the 19th century, even in such a relatively prosperous area as Gujarat, the raw material was frequently funnelled by means of barter trade: in order to obtain a small quantity of oil needed for lighting, the peasant who had no ready money gave the local shopkeeper some cotton or grain in exchange, which the latter sold in the town.[54] Although the shopkeeper made use of every opportunity to control the consumer—such as the debt which the peasant incurred in the shop, the loss of his cattle, the failure of his crop, a wedding, and, finally, downright cheating and swindling of his illiterate customer—the self-sufficiency of the peasant household allowed the cultivator to retain some independence with respect to the trading and money-lending groups. Only much later did the gradual increase in the size of commercial produce in the peasant household bring about a situation in which the peasant was more and more frequently forced to borrow money from the money-lender, not as a consumer unable to satisfy his personal needs by means of his own subsistence economy, but as a small-scale cultivator having to turn to the money-lender chiefly because he depended on the market as a producer.

The transition of the land-holders in Western India to the growing of export crops as early as the 1820s and 1830s went hand in hand with the peasants' increased dependence on the dealers. The Gujarat peasants increasingly depended for their supply of grain on the merchants, who grew rich on this trade, especially in the period of crop failures. The population in the northern areas of Western India always suffered from great famines. The Bania merchants, who possessed big stores of grain, refused to supply any during the first famine year, in the hope that later their earnings would be enormous. The tax drain of the rayats went hand in hand with their domination by the money-lender. As I have already said, they were controlled by the Gujarat compradors through a network of middlemen and agents, consisting of urban money-lenders, the village élite and the village money-lenders. They were forced to give away their raw cotton at understated prices. In this way, the British industrial magnates obtained cheaper raw materials for their cotton mills through the medium of Indian landlords and money-lenders.

The East India Company's interest in the collaboration of the Gujarat merchants forced it even in the 19th century to allow them to join in the trade with China, an "exclusive monopoly" which the Company had jealously guarded against non-British European counterparts.[56] Opium cultivation in India was concentrated in the Benares and Patna areas, and in the Malwa region, whence it was transported via Bombay to Canton. But the merchants of Eastern India were unable to derive great benefit from the trade in opium cultivated around Benares and Patna, which the Company completely monopolised from 1799 to 1803. However, the merchants of Bombay sold opium and cotton to China, and imported tea and other goods, which were largely re-exported to Europe.[57]

That is not to say, of course, that the British authorities did not control the opium trade from Western India. After the final defeat of the Maratha confederation, the cultivation of opium was declared to be the exclusive privilege of the rajahs of Indore, Gwalior and other local rulers. But the buying up of opium was the monopoly of the East India Company, which brought opium to Bombay and sold it by auction to local merchants. In 1831, the British scrapped their agreement with the rajahs and abolished the monopoly which Malwa had had in the production of opium, while handing over the supplying of opium to private traders.[58] Large transit duties were levied on the opium being exported via the Bombay harbour. A pound of opium sold in Calcutta in the mid-19th century brought the East India Company 7 s. 6 d. of income, while the transit duties on opium going from Malwa gave the company 5 s. 8 d. per pound.[59] The trade in Malwa opium was carried on directly by the Gujarat merchants. One of them, Hathisinh, who was a descendant of the Nagar Seths, a noted family from Ahmadabad, regularly sent large consignments of opium, containing up to 2,000 chests, to China.[60] In the first three decades of the 19th century, the Parsi J. Jeejeebhoy, one of Bombay's richest merchants, made a vast fortune of 30 million rupees on the opium trade, and deposited these in an English bank in Bombay.[61]

It may be worth while to consider Jeejeebhoy's career in greater detail. Miss Postans, who visited Bombay in 1838, called him the wealthiest Parsi gentleman of Bombay. His way to success was highly typical of the Bombay merchants. He was born in 1783 into a family of scarce means; at the age of 12 he was apprenticed to his uncle, a glass merchant. But he did not remain long in his uncle's shops. His biographer, S. H. Ihabvala, wrote that opium, silk and similar expensive goods opened enormous prospects to the enterprising young man. Jeejeebhoy soon went to China, where he traded in cotton; he was unsuccessful and returned poor, in a pitiful state. But the failure did not discourage him; he made three more journeys to China and made a fortune. Even the French navy, which operated along the shipping routes and once seized a vessel with a cargo belonging to him, did not stop him. He was connected with one of the leading firms in Bombay, Crawford and Co. In 1824, he headed a group of Bombay merchants who began to export cotton from Berar. Lastly, he had investments in the shipbuilding industry and was the biggest dock-owner, employing on the average about 3,000 hands.[32] Many other merchants of Gujarat—the grandfathers of the future mill owners of Bombay and Ahmadabad—made their fortune by trading in opium.

This and trade in other goods with China led to the rise of Bombay's shipping in the first half of the 19th century. The official list of 49 ships with a total displacement of 27,274 tons, registered in the port of Bombay as of 1838, includes two ships (total displacement 2,002 tons) belonging to British companies. Twenty ships, and the biggest ones at that, were owned by Parsis. The other ship-owners were Muslims and Hindus. It is interesting to note that the masters of the 24 biggest ships were Europeans, who were also entrusted with another 9 ships (displacement of under 450 tons each). Finally, 16 ships with a displacement from 450 to 1000 tons had Muslim masters.

The ships registered in Bombay were built not only there (10) but also in Calcutta (5), Kochin (13), Daman (4), Surat (2) and Mazagaon (4). It is true that all the nine ships with a displacement of over 850 tons (and up to 1,500 tons) were built in Bombay or Calcutta. Only one ship was 40 years old, the average being about 20.[63] In the 1820s and 1830s, overseas ships were still being built in some Indian ports.

By 1840, that is, by the time of the Anglo-Chinese Opium Wars, the Parsis controlled the bulk of the opium trade. According to British estimates, Dadabhoy Rustomjee alone lost something like 2 million rupees through confiscation of opium by the Chinese authorities. Special clippers were built in Calcutta for smuggling opium. One of these, the well-known "Sylph", was owned by Rustomjee Cowasjee and could cover the distance between Calcutta and Macao in 16 days. That is why during the wars with China British troops were transported mainly on Parsi ships. Rustomjee Cowasjee alone made available 14 ships for that purpose.

In the first half of the 19th century, the Wadias were the biggest ship-owners in Bombay. From 1786 to 1842, the Wadias handled 16 big ships; Readymoney 7; the Kamas 7; Patel 8, and so on.[64] Among the biggest merchants and ship-owners in India were the sons of Cowasjee Banajee, a grandson of Banajee Limjee (d. 1734), one of the founders of the Parsi community in Bombay. The eldest, Framjee, bought a ship in 1807 (133,000 rupees, 679 tons), which managed to evade French frigates and deliver a consignment of cotton to China, which he sold at a high price. Having made a fortune, he opened a branch in Calcutta in 1811. In his closing years, he owned six ships. His younger brother, Rustomjee, was even more successful. Initially the head of the Calcutta branch, where he opened a firm in partnership with Robert Turner in 1810, he owned at least 27 ships, of which 15 were chartered by the British authorities during the first war against China at 115,000 rupees a year.[65] His enterprise in Calcutta will be dealt with below.

However, after the Opium Wars, many Parsi shipping companies declined, due to the fact that China switched to the cultivation and sale of her own opium and also to the development of steam navigation, from which the British endeavoured to keep away their Indian partners. It is true that in 1845 the Bombay Steam Navigation Company was founded with a capital of 1 million rupees; it had one steamship on the route to Ceylon and Karachi. The management of the company consisted of British and native Bombay merchants. But the big steamship companies set up in Bombay later, with the exception of the short-lived firms of the cotton boom period, were purely British. Steam navigation became a monopoly of British capital and a most important instrument of its control over India's economy. Only in 1906 did Bombay Muslim merchants, headed by Adamjee Pirbhoy, set up a steamship company which had nine old steamers. But after a number of disasters the venture was wound up.[66] The establishment of India's modern steam shipping was put off for several decades.

Although Gujarat and Maharashtra were the main fields where the Gujarat merchants carried on their internal trade, the Parsis controlled a large part of the marine trade of Karnatak and Kerala by the early years of the 19th century, and after these regions were occupied by the British they began to settle there in ever greater numbers. Apart from the Parsis, Gujarati Banias and also Marwaris began to settle in Karnatak and Kerala in that period.[67]

Modern Bombay and its suburbs, hemmed in by the sea and the Ghats, have always had extremely high land prices, for the city has had to fight the sea for tracts of land. That is why the possession of a land tract in Bombay became a source of income for its merchants, especially the Parsis. "The Parsis are the chief land-holders in Bombay. Almost all the houses and gardens inhabited by the Europeans are their property."[68] The Wadias were among the first to realise the prospects of owning the city's real estate. Back in 1826, the board of the Bank of Bombay included only one Indian, Dadabhoy Pestonjee Wadia, a man of unlimited means and the owner of vast tracts of land in Bombay area. In 1834, he was knighted by the British together with a group of another 12 Indians.[69] Miss Postans, who visited Wadia's family 30 years after Maria Graham, was amazed at the luxury of the Lowjee palace. She was told by the master of the house about the extensive trade with China and the value of some precious cargo which had just arrived in Bombay on his own ships. He also mentioned how much the Parsis owed to the protection of the Europeans in the establishment of their commercial activity.[70]

However, neither their fortune, nor their city estates, nor even the official honours bestowed upon them could eliminate the friction between the Wadias and the authorities. In 1805, when the British were very much in need of Bombay ships, they promised the Wadias new lands in Bombay. But the matter dragged on, and, in 1821, Jamshetjee Bomanjee on his death-bed gave Elphinstone a reminder of the promise. But the shilly-shallying continued until 1849, when three heirs of the family finally received two villages in the Salsett.[71] In 1965, I met Mrs. S. Wadia, who said, among other things, that to this day her husband's relatives received most of their income from the Bombay land plots.

In 1838, the "Asiatic Journal" said that Parsi artisans were employed at the Bombay shipyards, and that many of them had become rich ship-builders due to their capability and enterprise.[72] This also applies to the numerous members of Wadia's clan. But while the shipyards were fully owned by the East India Company, what were the Indian entrepreneurs doing there? The sphere of application of private Indian initiative was sufficiently extensive. According to an English writer, the shipyards were fully occupied by the Parsis who established an absolute monopoly there. The man supplying timber was a Parsi, the supervisor accepting ships was another.[73] Indeed, the timber was supplied by Parsis; this is borne out by an extant copy of a contract concluded back in 1741 between the East India Company and the Parsis Bhikhajee Ratanjee and Runjee Janjee for the delivery of timber.[74] The Bombay shipyards were apparently an enterprise whose fixed capital was owned mainly by the Company and the working capital by the Indian contractors.

But some shipyards were in the hands of Indians. Thus, A. Guha says that big sailing-ships were built at shipyards belonging to the merchant and banker Cowasjee Banajee (1790- 1832), a friend and partner of D. Tagore in several firms. The best clippers were built at his shipyards in Khidderpur, where one foreman was Junjeebhoy Rustomjee Wadia (1799-1854). The Mughal Dock of Mazgaon was owned by Aga Mohammed Rahim Shirajee. But following the collapse of the Union Bank and the bankruptcy of Banajee and the sale by Shirajee of his dock in 1847, Indian ship-building itself turned out to be doomed for at least a century, even though the Company's Bombay shipyards were kept going for another decade. In the period under consideration, they even multiplied the achievements of the earlier century.

In 1824, the largest man-of-war ever built in Bombay—the 84-gun "Asia" with a displacement of 2,883 tons—was launched; she took part in the battle of Navarin. Admiral P. Malcolm sent a message to the man who built the "Asia", Naorojee Jamshetjee, that the ship had played the main role in the battle and that the admiral was proud of her builders.[75] Altogether, according to the official data, from 1735 to 1835 the Bombay shipyards built 267 ships with a displacement of from 23 to 2,298 tons. Of these, 30 ships had a displacement of over 1,000 tons and four 2,000 tons.

The first steamer was built in Bombay in 1829 (displacement 411 tons). In 1838, a river-steamboat with an iron hull, the "Snake", displacement 40 tons, was built in Bombay. It was followed in 1839 by the first sloop, the "Victoria" (705 tons), and a 204-ton river-steamboat. Altogether from 1833 to 1857, 21 steamships were built in Bombay, the biggest of these being two steam frigates, the "Assaye" and the "Punjab", with a displacement of 1,800 tons each (1854).[76]

These brief data show that Bombay, in a sovereign India, could have become a major centre of modern ship-building. But from the outset the Bombay shipyards were subordinated to the interests of the British adventurers. The East India Company found it profitable to build good and cheap ships in India, especially since this yielded a large income. When the Company was wound up, Britain's industrial bourgeoisie, having obtained direct control over India, hastened to put an end to the Bombay shipyards, which it regarded only as a rival. After 1857, ship-building in Bombay was, in effect, discontinued. No more steamships were built at all, while only a few small coasting sailers were launched.[77]

The closing down of the Bombay shipyards cannot be explained entirely by economic reasons. Indian-built sailing ships were sturdier than British ones, and their cost was one-quarter less. Together with the savings on repairs, the running of an Indian ship for 50 years came to only a quarter of the cost of running a British ship.[78] The building of steamers with iron hulls naturally called for a new technology and different skills, but the first essays showed that these difficulties could well be overcome. Consequently, the decision of the Company's successors was based on this simple consideration: India had to be deprived of her own ship-building and the British monopoly of carrying goods by steamships consolidated. In this sense British capital managed to reach its goal. By the end of the 19th century, India had been deprived of her merchant marine, and this will be seen from the official data about the nationality of the ships calling at Indian ports (Table 8).

TABLE 8

Nationality of Ships Calling at Indian Ports*

Year	*Indian*		*British*		*Other nationalities*	
	No.	*,000 tons*	*No.*	*,000 tons*	*No.*	*,000 tons*
1857	34,286	1,212	59,441	2,475	—	—
1899	1,676	110	6,210	7,685	1,165	1,298

* W. Digby, "Prosperous" British India, London, 1901, p. 88.

Apart from ship-building, the Parsis established the manufacture of gun-powder for the East India Company, and there is documentary evidence that, in 1677, Munjee Dhunjee of Surat was awarded a Company contract, which he fulfilled, for the construction in Bombay of the first large gun-powder works. From the 1730s, Manokjee Manuwah was the Company's supplier of gun-powder (actually, even the powder-maker). In the 1780s, his sons took over the business. In 1797, the powder-maker was Bomanjee Hirjee, and in 1840 Marwanjee Rustomjee.

In the first half of the 19th century, the Company had a cannon works in Bombay, with the Parsi Sorabjee Shapurjee as a "foreman". His status must have been similar to Wadia's at the ship-building yards, for in 1852 he helped to build an iron works in Bombay. In order to purchase the plant, Shapurjee travelled to Britain in 1850. His wealth is confirmed by the fact that he was the first to build cotton-ginning and flour-milling enterprises in Bombay. His grandson became a big supplier of textile equipment and a mill-owner.[79]

Bombay also had an industry turning out luxuries for the British and the propertied sections of the Indian population which imitated the British fashion. In 1808, the Parsi Pallonjee Bomanjee opened a carriage-making establishment, with an initial investment of only 500 rupees. He took the name of Pankhiwalla ("palanquin-maker"), and soon grew rich. His workshop became a fairly large establishment, possibly run on capitalist lines. At any rate, he was known to pay his workers 15-20 rupees a month, and his European-type carriages were sold not only in India but also in Europe, Afghanistan and Singapore. The enterprise began to decline only with the arrival of motor-cars in the 20th century.[80]

The shroffs' credit business was an important branch of Bombay enterprise, because British-founded banks could not and would not meet all the credit requirements among the city's merchants. The sheriff of Bombay gives the names of 21 shroffs who went into business in 1809-1845. Judging by their names, none of them were either Parsis or Muslims. According to the sheriff, the shroffs issued bills for any point in India from Peshawar to Travancore. The Bank of Bombay incurred almost no losses from working with any of them. What is more, the sheriff made mention of the timely support given to the British by the Bombay shroff Bunsilal Abichand during the 1857 uprising.[81]

In the first half of the 19th century, Indian firms in Bombay underwent some organisational changes. Family firms continued to be the rule, while joint-stock companies were not the leading form for capital accumulation by Indian businessmen. At the same time, as A. Guha notes, Indian joint-stock companies with unlimited liability made their appearance, involving persons of different nationalities and communities. The Parsi ship-owner, S. M. Readymoney, had for his partner a Konkan Muslim, Ali Bin Mohammed Husein Rogay; H. Bomanjee owned several ships together with Forbes and Co.; up to 1835, J. Jeejeebhoy had the Hindu, Motichand Amichand, for his partner.

Indeed, the whole of Bombay was inhabited by people of different nationalities, castes and religious communities. In 1848, "The Bombay Times" wrote: "Our shop-keepers are nearly all Parsis—so are our furniture-makers also—but the workmen employed in the manufacture of Bombay furniture of such exquisite design ... are nearly all men from Cutch and Gujarat. Our best shoe-makers are Chinamen; our armourers and perfume dealers are mostly Persians; our horse dealers are Afghans and Baluchis. Our potters form a regular organised craft (i. e., occupational caste.—V. P.) and pay homage to a deity presiding over them...."[82]

On the whole, the terms on which big Gujarati merchants collaborated with British industrial capital were favourable even in the first half of the 19th century, and the sphere of their collaboration (comprador trade, export of opium, credit, ship-building and other manufacturing in Bombay, etc.) was fairly extensive. Probably no other group of Indian merchants established such sound relations with the British. Here is what the Indian Industrial Commission, which included descendants of the leading merchants of Bombay, says about these relations: "If the cause be sought (of the activity of the Indians in the Bombay industry.—V. P.), some indication of it may be found in the fact that Indians have held a large and important share in the trade of Bombay since the city first came into English hands. The Mahommedans of the west coast, especially, traded by sea with the Persian Gulf, Arabia and East Africa from much earlier times. The Parsees and Hindus from the northern Bombay coast districts (i. e., from Gujarat.—V. P.) are recorded, at the beginning of the British occupation, as taking ... a most important share in the trade of the port as contractors, merchants, financiers and ship-builders, and have throughout shown themselves little, if at all, inferior to the Europeans in enterprise, and usually in command of more capital."[83]

We find that the social content of Bombay was Indian with a small upper echelon consisting of Englishmen. However, although at first sight the population of Bombay comprised the traditional communities and castes, the make-up and proportions of these components were unusual for a major urban centre of the pre-British period. That is why there was no institutional mechanism of the traditional Indian city in Bombay, as was the case in Calcutta and Madras. Besides, the origin of the surplus-product on which Bombay grew in its first century and a half, and accordingly the mechanism of redistribution, were not at all typical of India (and therein lies its distinction from Calcutta where many absentee rent-consumers always lived). The decisive importance of merchant's capital and its profit predetermined the overall irreversibility of the entrepreneurial tendencies which had emerged in the city by the mid-19th century.

NOTES

1. See: G. Keating, *Rural Economy in the Bombay Deccan*, London, 1912, pp. 168-169.
2. *GBP*, vol. XVIII, pt II, pp. 331, 352.
3. See: D.R. Choksey, *Economic History of the Bombay Deccan....*, pp. 34, 165.
4. See: *Ibid.*, p. 213.
5. Jawaharlal Nehru, *The Discovery of India*, p. 277.
6. D.R. Choksey, *Economic History of the Bombay Deccan...*, pp. 306, 311-312.
7. See: *ibid.*, p. 305.
8. See: *ibid.*, pp. 305, 307.
9. *Selections of Papers from the Records at the East India House...*, vol. IV, pp. 516-517.
10. *Ibid.*, p. 139.
11. *Ibid.*, p. 405.
12. D.R. Gadgil, *Poona...*, p. 26.
13. *Ibid.*, pp. 46-49.
14. *Ibid.*, p. 18.
15. See: E. Thornton, *Gazetteer of the Territories..*, vol. IV, p. 160.
16. D. Graham, *Statistical Report of Kolhapoor*, Poona, 1854, p. 253.
17. *Ibid.*, pp. 140-141.
18. *Ibid.*, p. 268.
19. *Ibid.*, pp. 274, 283.
20. *Ibid.*, p. 162.
21. *Ibid.*, p. 274.
22. *Ibid.*, p. 142.
23. *Ibid.*, p. 257.
24. *Ibid.*, pp. 241, 256.
25. *Ibid.*, pp. 162-163.
26. *Ibid.*
27. *Ibid.*, pp. 223, 243.
28. *Ibid.*, pp. 234-235.
29. *Ibid.*, pp. 223-226, 252, 253.
30. *Ibid.*, pp. 142, 219-221, 254.
31. *Ibid.*, p. 258.
32. *Ibid.*, p. 141.
33. *Ibid.*, p. 272.
34. *Ibid.*
35. *Ibid.*, p. 273.
36. *Ibid.*, p. 274.
37. *Ibid.*, p. 275.
38. *Ibid.*, p. 274.
39. *Ibid.*, pp. 273, 274.
40. *Ibid.*, p. 273.
41. *Ibid.*, p. 269.
42. *Ibid.*, p. 257.
43. *Ibid.*, pp. 141, 147.
44. *Ibid.*, p. 272.
45. *Ibid.*, pp. 140-141.
46. *Ibid.*, pp. 115-118.
47. *Ibid.*, pp. 45, 46.
48. The Value of Bombay's exports and imports (million rupees) : in 1800-1809

56.0, in 1810-1819 46.7, in 1820-1829 56.6, in 1830-1839 82.2, 1840-1849 192.4, and in 1850-1859 262.0 (*Gazetteer on Bombay City*..., vol. I, Bombay, 1905, p. 416).

49. J. Malcolm, *A Memoir of Central India*..., vol. II, London, 1832, pp. 111-112.
50. M. Graham, *Journal of the Residence of India*, Edinburgh, 1813, pp. 32-33.
51. *Buldana (Central Provinces District Gazetteers)*, Calcutta, 1910, p. 276.
52. J. Chapman, *Cotton and Commerce of India*, London, 1860, p. 15.
53. *Ibid*., p. 90.
54. A.K. Forbes, *Râs Mâlâ*..., vol. II, p. 248.
55. Postans, *Western India in 1838*, vol. II, London, 1838, pp. 222-223.
56. See: K. Marx, *Capital*, vol. I, p. 752.
57. At the Indo-Soviet Symposium on Economic and Social Development of India and Russia from the 17th to the 19th century, held in Moscow in May 1973, Prof. Amalis Tripathi gave a subtle analysis of the role India's trade with China had played in the remittance of the colonial tribute to the metropolitan country (in 1840, Melvill, the Secretary to the Company, calculated the home charges to be 3.2 million pounds sterling and private remittance to be 0.5 million pounds each year). "For the time being remittance through China was not only more lucrative, it was almost imperative", Tripathi noted.
58. F.S. Turner, *British Opium Policy and Its Results in India and China*, London, 1878, pp. 55-56.
59. J.W. Kaye, *The Administration of the East India Company*, London, 1858, p. 683.
60. *Indian Textile Journal*, February 1931; F.S. Turner, *British Opium Policy*..., p. 56.
61. S.H. Ihabvala, *Sir Jamashedji Jeejeebhoy*, Baronet, Bombay, [s.a.], p. 20.
62. Postans, *Western India in 1838*, vol. I, p. 122.
63. *Report from the Select Committee on East India Product*, pp. 613-614.
64. W.H. Coates, *The Old Country Trade*, pp. 51-52, 59, 137-145.
65. K.N. Banaji, *Memoirs of Late Framji Cowasji Banaji*, Bombay, 1892, pp. 13-15, 18-19.
66. W.H. Coates, *The Old Country Trade*, pp. 159-160, 203.
67. A. Sarada Raju, *Economic Conditions*..., p. 188.
68. M. Graham, *Journal of the Residence in India*, p. 45.
69. J. Douglas, *Glimpses of Old Bombay and Western India*, London, 1900, pp. 111-112.
70. Postans, *Western India in 1838*, vol. I, p. 106.
71. R.A. Wadia, *The Bombay Dockyard and the Wadia Master Builders*, Bombay, 1957, p. 251.
72. *Gazetteer of Bombay City*, vol. II, Bombay, 1909, p. 149.
73. W. Hamilton, *East India Gazetteer*...., vol. I, London, 1828, p. 261.
74. *GBP*, vol. XXVI (Materials Towards....), pt 2, p. 190.
75. *Ibid*., vol. II, Appendix, p. 4.
76. *Ibid*., p. 326; Ch. R. Low, *History of the Indian Navy*, vol. I, p. 4.
77. Ch. R. Low, *History of the Indian Navy*, vol. I, pp. 540, 541.
78. W. Digby, *Prosperous" British India*, London, 1901, p. 87.
79. [S.M. Rutnagur], *Bombay Industries*: The Cotton Mills, Bombay, 1927, p. 725.
80. *Gazetteer of Bombay*, vol. I, p. 478.
81. J. Douglas, *Glimpses of Old Bombay*, p. 119.
82. Quoted from: S.M. Edwardes, *The Rise of Bombay*, p. 269.
83. *Indian Industrial Commission*, vol. I, London, 1919, p. 65.

CHAPTER SEVEN

BENGAL AND BIHAR: ECONOMIC CONDITIONS, HANDICRAFTS, TRADE AND ENTERPRISE

From the 1810s to the 1850s, Bengal and Bihar continued to have many of the features which distinguished them from Western India and other parts of the country as well. The historical features in the development of the area considered above, the influence of the relatively earlier British conquest and the socio-economic measures taken by the new authorities, as well as all the old but still distinctive natural conditions and resources of Bengal and Bihar continued partially to tell. As I have already done, I intend here to bring out from the complex of land and tax relations only those which through the economic activity and consumption of the various rural sections exerted a direct influence on the condition and economic ties of the separate spheres of industrial production. Meanwhile, the British authorities and British capital, as I have said, began to form pockets of production catering for their immediate demands and requirements.

Industrial Production

The economic history of Bengal and Bihar in the first half of the 19th century has been a subject of growing interest, above all among Indian scientists. Attempts have been made to regard the results of development in that period as more complicated than had earlier been believed, when the decline of Dacca and other old cities, with its tragic social consequences, did in fact screen some of the positive processes.

However, this kind of approach now and again becomes something of a partial rehabilitation of British rule and enterprise.

A highly contradictory assessment of the consequences of the British administration's policy in Bengal and especially of the Permanent Settlement is contained in "Trade and Finance in the Bengal Presidency 1793-1833", a work which resulted from the two-year stay of the Indian scientist A. Tripathi at the School of Oriental and African Studies, London University. The author cast doubt on the established notions about the drain of India's national wealth as the most obvious evidence of her exploitation by foreign capital, and also as the root cause of stagnation in the Indian economic life.

One of his arguments is that the decline of Bengal's cotton production was compensated by the three- of four-fold growth (in terms of value) of the commercialised part of agricultural raw materials: indigo, raw silk and opium. It is true that Tripathi does not point to the danger latent in such a one-sided orientation, because any decline in world prices immediately had an effect on Bengal's welfare. Besides, the harvest prices of indigo were fixed at such a low level that the producer found it much more profitable to grow, say, rice to which he was well accustomed.

The fixed land-tax and the growing commercialised part of agricultural produce under mounting competition from British factory-made goods inevitably tended to push native capital into land-ownership. In the circumstances, the upper sections of the village able to extend their husbandries turned to money-lending and the lease of land, so evolving from a potential entrepreneurial opposition to the zamindars into their allies in oppressing the lower sections of the peasants. Tripathi admits that the growing income from land was absorbed by the un-restrained rise of rents. "The peasantrv lost the margin of profit which was rightfully theirs. Worse still, zamindars, taluqdars and middling farmers turned money-lenders as the spread of money economy and increase of production raised the need for rural credit. The union of the zamindar and the money-lender in the same person was an unmitigated disaster for the country's economic development. It deprived industry and trade of capital and it shackled agricultural improvement by taking away the only incentive before the peasantry."[1]

As a result, agriculture developed mainly the extensive way, through an increase in the area of farmland and not through higher levels of production and lower cost. Tripathi admits that, apart from the zamindars, this went to benefit only their agents and those who acted as middlemen in the lease. He points out that F. Buchanan observed that in Bengal "the wealthy farmers are considered as mere flayers of the poor and no people privately join more earnestly in the cry than the landlords. In public, however, they court the wealthy farmers and it is alleged often purchase their assistance to enable them to fleece the poor tenantry." Buchanan stresses high-interest loans, primarily rice loans for nutrition and seeds.

The Company's Charter (1833), Tripathi assumes, paved the way for the import of British capital, while the ruin of local industry and the effects of the Permanent Settlement produced a numerous section of landless labouring-men. "Apparently, the time seemed ripe for an Industrial Revolution in Bengal under British management, financed by the joint resources of the British and the native capitalists, which would open avenues of employment to the middle classes, divert capital from land to industry and take off the increasing pressure of population on land. Apparently, again, the time seemed ripe for a protectionist policy, which would guard the interest of that Industrial Revolution from foreign competition and the interest of the peasantry from the planter, the rentier and the money-lender. This, however ... did not happen." The next chapter of India's industrial potentiality, says Tripathi, saw "the frustration of the Indian middle class and the deterioration of the Indian peasants' conditions."[2] Such is the conclusion drawn by this scientist, who emphatically sought to take an objective look at the results of British policy.

Even while switching to the export of agricultural raw materials, India encountered discrimination on the British markets. For instance, after 1836, Britain's duties on Indian sugar were higher than those on the West Indian product. The British government seemed to think that the interests of British plantation-owners were more important than those of British exporters, to say nothing of Indian producers.

A. Guha does not deny that some progress was achieved in the generation before and after 1815 in some fields of the economy: the production of indigo, cotton, silk, ship-building, and internal and foreign trade. But he argues with those of his colleagues who, having first exaggerated the scale on which the handicrafts were ruined in that period, swung to the other extreme by allowing the idea of a general rise in the economy. Guha, in particular, draws attention to the flow of investments from the highly productive to the less productive branches (for instance, from the production of muslins to the production of coarse cloths).

He recalls the view of an authoritative witness of these events, namely Rammohan Ray, who said in 1831 that the reason for the growing wealth was the actual rise in the value of real estate (the reference here is to zamindar estates). That is why, Ray believed, only the land-owners and the merchants got rich.[3] The bulk of the surplus-product extracted went to the metropolitan country, the rest going to the land-owners and merchants.

But let us look at the concrete context of these problems as presented in the sources and scientific writings. Let us start with weaving, which was rather a subject for sentimental sympathy than for scientific research. It is true that the circumstances of the decline of Bengal weaving beginning from the mid-18th century were already considered in detail by H. R. Ghosal: Maratha raids and internal disorders, oppression by Company agents, a reduction in orders from the Indian nobility, the French Revolution and the Napoleonic wars, the start of British factory competition on the European market and the transfer of this competition to India's own market.[4] But he gave no analysis of weaving as an aggregation of production relations.

Meanwhile, even British sources contain material for judgments on this subject. The most reliable witness of the condition of textile production in Dacca in the 1830s and 1840s, and also a great authority as regards its past, continues to be James Taylor, the British surgeon who spent eight years in the city and made a direct study of various sections of the population and of official records. He gives information about the steady reduction from the early 19th century of the textile investments in Dacca by the Company and other exporters. In 1761, the Company purchased in Dacca goods worth 2,200,000 rupees (other expenses by the factory in Dacca came to 56,000 rupees). In 1787, the collector of the district estimated its trade at 10 million rupees, of which 3 to 4 million rupees were purchases for export to Europe. But in 1807, cloths worth only 861,800 rupees were exported to Europe, in 1810 557,000 rupees' worth, and in 1813 only 338,100 rupees' worth. In 1817, although exports increased somewhat with the end of the Napoleonic wars, the post of the Company's commercial resident in Dacca was itself abolished and it may be said that from then on the export of cloths to Europe was discontinued. To be more precise, the total export of cloths from Dacca declined rapidly in subsequent years: in 1817/18 it came to 1,524,000 rupees; in 1821/22 1,216,000; in 1825/26 629,000; and in 1831/32 360,000 rupees.[5]

According to Taylor, the decline in Dacca's external trade began in 1785, when the production of British muslins, "which appear to have rivalled the common qualities of Indian muslins", reached half a million pieces. "From this time, the foreign trade of Dacca began to be affected, and from the heavy duty of 75 per cent which was afterwards imposed upon its staple, it declined, in proportion as the manufactures of Britain increased in value. The general prosperity of the place has still more seriously been affected by the importation of British yarn and cloths of late years."[6] The first great importation of cotton yarn into India took place in 1821, but it was not until 1828 that it really hit this district. Indeed, by 1831, the importation of British yarn reached considerable proportions—6,624,000 pounds. "The manufacture of thread, the occupation in former times of almost every family in the district, is now, owing to the comparative cheapness of English thread, almost entirely abandoned, and thus the arts of spinning and weaving, which for ages have afforded employment to a numerous and industrious population, have in the course of 60 years, passed into other hands that supply the want not only of foreign nations, but of the rivalled country (India.—V. P.) itself."[7]

The general social effect of Dacca's weaving has been calculated by K. N. Chaudhuri from the data of the East India Company for 1783.[8] Altogether, the city had 25,200 weavers. They were supplied with cotton by 33,300 cultivators who worked six months a year, and with yarn by 80,000 women. Another 5,000 women embroidered the cloths, and about 3,000 artisans were occupied in dyeing and other ancillary operations. The labour activity of these 145,000 people was controlled by 750 traders and their employees.[9] Thus, the employment ratio per weaver was approximately 1:6, and this has to be taken into account when assessing the social implications of the decline of weaving in the second quarter of the 19th century.

More detailed information about Dacca's market connections in the 1840s is given by the acting commissioner in Dacca, In May 1844, he drew up a report on the weaving in the city and claimed that he had interviewed native manufacturers and dealers, and also old residents in the city among the British (including Taylor). The report says that the demand for Dacca muslins began to decline in 1789 (the effect of reduced demand for luxuries on the Continent in connection with the French Revolution). In the early 1840s, goods went only for internal consumption, with the exception of some small export to the Middle East. The finest muslins (grade 250 yarn), made up at English mills or locally, were produced to the small amount of 50,000 rupees and were supplied to the courts of Delhi, Lucknow, Lahore and the King of Nepal. These figures are indirect evidence that the erstwhile sumptuousness of these courts was becoming a thing of the past.

The most important weaving products were now medium-grade fabrics made by Hindu weavers from British yarn (grades 40 to 200). These were used by the higher and middle groups of the district, and were also exported to Calcutta, Murshidabad, Patna, Rangpur, Dinajpur and other districts. The value of these goods came to half a million rupees, but after the cost of imported yarn was subtracted, the weavers were left only 330,000 rupees. Besides, embroidered cloths were manufactured in Dacca from British cotton and Assamese silk yarn, and these went mainly to the Middle East. Their total value came to 200,000 rupees, but of these only 90,000 rupees' worth was produced by local weavers (30,000 rupees) and embroideresses. Besides, 16,000 rupees' worth of turbans and 20,000 rupees' worth of shawls were made in Dacca.

Finally, cheap cloths, made from the lower grades of British yarn, were produced in Dacca and the surrounding towns. The value came to 150,000 rupees, of which 50,000 went into the purchase of yarn. The cheap cloths were made by the lower castes of Hindu weavers, and also by Muslim weavers from the caste of Julah. The sale of cheap cloths was handled by the merchants of Dacca. Altogether, the artisans of Dacca turned out a new value (including the profits of middlemen) of 550,000-600,000 rupees a year. Bearing in mind that in the second half of the 18th century weavers, spinners and other artisans created a new value of over 3 million rupees a year, it will become obvious that overall textile production in Dacca had dropped to one-fifth or one-sixth by the 1840s. On the other hand, by then Dacca annually imported 300,000 rupees' worth of yarn and 150,000 rupees' worth of fabrics made in Britain.[10]

The once grand city was rapidly declining. Its population, numbering 200,000 in 1800, was down to 68,000 in 1838. "Poverty has increased in a far greater ratio than population has decreased, a fact which is ascertained from the records of the chokeedaree or assessed police tax (the only available criterion for judging of the general condition of the population.—V. P.), which show that from 1813 to 1833 the collections have fallen from Rs. 31,300 to Rs. 10,000. In consequence of all these changes, many families who were formerly in a state of affluence are now reduced to comparative poverty, while the majority of the people belonging to the lower classes are from want of work in a very destitute condition, and are glad to procure any employment, however unsuited to their previous habits, to enable them to earn a subsistence for themselves and families."[11] A great number of houses were unoccupied or in a state of ruin while the suburbs were being overrun with jungle.

Still, those who survived from Dacca's great community of weavers continued to toil in the old tradition of skills and techniques. Here is how Taylor described the dead-tock of spinning and weaving: "The total number of implements used in converting the raw material into thread, and weaving the latter into the finest muslin is said to amount 126. They are all made of small pieces of bamboo or reed tied together with twine or thread, and are of a style of workmanship so rude and simple that almost every weaver can make them himself, although to save time and trouble they are usually sold ready made in the bazars."[12] Each Hindu and Muslim caste of weavers made its own range of goods, with the castes specialising in the making of cheap grades regarded as lower castes.[13]

In the late 1830s, weavers and, which is even more amazing,

spinners continued to turn out cloths and yarn unrivalled in the West. Taylor says: "...Even in the present day, notwith-standing the great perfection which the art of weaving has attained in Britain, these fabrics are unrivalled and in point of transparency, beauty and delicacy of texture are allowed to excel the most finished productions of the loom in any country of the world." Taylor then goes on to quote the opinion of Dr. Ure, the author of a work on the cotton industries in Britain (1836), who says that the Dacca yarn was much finer than the highest number made in England, "spun by the distaff and spindle, or woven afterwards by any machinery."[14]

The skilled craftsmen were doomed to bondage and poverty. "Few of the class of artisans work by the day. Formerly the weavers manufactured muslins on their own account, and it is mentioned by Mr. Bolts, that in the time of Alverdi Khan, it was no uncommon occurrence for a weaver to bring at one time as many as 800 pieces of muslins to a merchant. In the present day they work by contract, receiving thread and an advance of money from the merchants or their agents, the pykars. The average amount of wages of the few that work by the day or month, is estimated at rupees 2-8 (2 rupees 8 annas.—V.P.) a month."[15]

It is true that if a weaver worked over the allotted time in order to prepare the warp, he could make another 10 annas. A weaver's apprentice of 10 or 12 years of age got 4 annas a month after having been two years in the business, an amount generally increasing every year, until he received 12 annas the last year. This small payment led to the further decline in the weavers' living standard. The plight of the women spinners was even harder, for the most skilled of them could not earn more than 16 rupees a year. Thus, the monthly wages of Dacca's artisans fluctuated from 12 annas to just over 2 rupees. This meant that even nominally the wages of high-skilled craftsmen in Dacca were lower than those of artisans in the remoter centres and rural localities. But the situation was compounded by the fact that in Dacca food prices were higher than the average. At least one-half of the food consumed in the district was imported from outside, in consequence of which rice was dearer there than in the surrounding country.[16]

The ruined artisans were used to do the lowest-paid work by the day, and the women of their families were employed in work like the hulling of rice. Let us note that in the late 1830s steam-driven grain-cleaning and mustard-oil making machinery was installed, "but after a short time, the projectors found they could not compete with the native manufacturers, and accordingly the speculation was abandoned."[17] The mechanised enterprises suffered a defeat from the primitive devices set in motion by women.

Of course, there could be no question of any productive

accumulation in this depressed industry. A modern Indian analyst says that in contrast to the broad cloth-makers, who heralded the industrial revolution in Britain, the Indian weavers did not have the barest savings. They were mere hired workers receiving 2-3 rupees (5-6 shillings) a month, while a man with an income of 48 pounds was ranked as a member of the middle classes even in the 1830s. That is why the production of the highest-quality goods depended on advance payments from time immemorial.[18] Let us note that the comparison here is between the condition of Indian artisans and the British cloth manufacturers whom Marx cites as an example of merchants directly controlling production.[19] Neither the Indian artisans (at any rate, the more well-to-do among them) nor their creditors ever showed any inclination to intervene directly in production, which was conserved in technical and organisational terms.

It took little effort to ruin Dacca's weaving industry. I have had occasion to admire some of the specimens deposited in India's museums. Of course, they were much too costly to be used for the clothes of even well-to-do people. But Dacca's weaving could have very well, and should have been, preserved as an art craft turning out decorative articles. Its destruction is one of the crimes committed by the British regime against India's art. If it is possible in sovereign India to gradually restore the art crafts and to ensure the marketing of their products, despite the growing technical superiority of machine production and the standardisation of taste, there were no objective causes for destroying them in the first half of the 19th century. The decline of cotton-weaving was only slightly compensated by the growing production of silks, but that was a purely British enterprise with large workshops, which were first owned by the East India Company and in the second half of the 1830s passed into private British hands.[20]

The decline of the traditional industries, especially of weaving, could have been compensated, if not in social terms then in terms of production through the development of news industries on an early capitalist (manufactory) or even powerloom mill basis. As we shall see, the Bengal entrepreneurs operating in partnership with the British or on their own, did expect such compensation. Let us start with the oldest "new branch", the coal industry.

The earliest attempts to start the working of coal deposits in Raniganj were made in 1771 by the collector of Chota Nagpur, and another employee of the East India Company. They secured the exclusive right to extract coal within the administrative borders of Bengal. But although the coal was being mined in five places, it did not reach the market in sufficient quantities to enable the new enterprise to make a profit. Besides, its founders had other duties to perform, and soon the mining was stopped.

Only in 1808, 30 years later, did the East India Company show any interest in resuming the mining of coal in the Damodar valley, but no practical steps were taken until 1815-1817, when an Englishman resumed mining, after receiving from the Company a credit of 4,000 pounds at low interest. But he, too, was unsuccessful, and in 1830 the mines passed to Alexander and Co., an agency which had acted as surety under the Company's credit. In the 1820s, several other British mineowners appeared. In 1835, following the bankruptcy of Alexander and Co., its mines and equipment, including steamengines, were taken over by D. Tagore for the small amount of 7,000 pounds. Together with several British and Indian businessmen he set up a new firm and enlarged the business by buying operating mines and building new ones.

The Bengal Coal Company, which included the enterprise earlier established by D. Tagore, was founded in 1843 and became the leading coal-mining company. In 1846, 91,500 tons of coal was mined in Raniganj, and in 1857-1860, following the opening of a railway, 385,000 tons of coal was mined annually. In the early 1870s, Raniganj coal was sold in Calcutta at 11-13 rupees per ton. But by then, all the large coal mines in Raniganj were already in the hands of British businessmen. One exception was constituted by the pits at Siarsol, opened in 1846 by the local zamindar, Govind Prevad Pandit. The workings included pits ranging from some equipped with steam engines and producing 60,000-70,000 tons to small pits only a few metres deep and employing half a dozen miners to turn out some 750 tons a year.[21]

The destiny of Bengal's metallurgy was sadder. As I have said, in 1845 W. Jackson published a report on the production of iron in Birbhum. It was carried on by local inhabitants and had 30 furnaces. The smelting took four days and yielded 25 maunds of iron worth 17 rupees. Charcoal was the fuel, and this was ruining the forests in the district. Taking the maund as the standard one (38 kilogrammes), the weight of one smelting came to a ton, so that about 60 kilogrammes of iron cost one rupee.

In 1853, a new report on the ores of Birbhum and the Damodar valley was submitted. The author of the report, Dr. Oldham, had the special duty of deciding whether it was possible to use the local metallurgy in building railways. His assessment of the ore resources in the area turned out to be understated as compared with subsequent studies, but the interesting fact is that the technology of iron-making in Birbhum differed from the conventional one accepted throughout India.

Indeed, the record shows that local furnaces were relatively very productive and that they were highly concentrated within a limited area. Thus, there were 70 furnaces in Cutch, with the smelting done by Muslims, and the purifying of iron by Hindus—worthy cooperation in such an important industry. Each furnace annually yielded 34 tons of iron. Recalling that Jackson's report has each furnace yield over 0.9 ton in the course of a four-day process, this must have referred to furnaces of similar productivity (considering the time going into the preparation of the furnace, transportation of the raw material, inevitable seasonal interruptions, etc.). Altogether, 2,300 tons of metal were smelted a year, and in quality it was up to the level of good pig-iron. The expansion of production was hampered by the shortage of charcoal.

Nevertheless, in 1855, MacKey and Co. of Calcutta founded an iron-making enterprise with several furnaces (whose technical data are, unfortunately, unknown). This enterprise did much harm to the local iron-makers, but within a few years it, too, proved to be unprofitable and was closed down on several occasions. The shortage of coal and the heavy rentals for the working of the subsoil led, according to an official source, to the ruin of Bengal iron-making. In 1870, there was only one big furnace still in operation. Within two years, the local zamindar, who took over the MacKey enterprise, attempted to re-open it, but failed.

With that failure, "the most complete indigenous system of iron manufacture ever practised in Bengal was for the time put a stop to."[22] Apart from the reasons given in the source for its ruin, there was undoubtedly the competition from British metal which was being produced at more powerful furnaces. As for Bengal metallurgy, although it did reach the level of a well-developed capitalist establishment, its inability to evolve into large-scale blast furnace production on hard coal had a fatal effect on its viability.

Finally, a few words about the participation by zamindars and other wealthy Bengalis and Biharis in the growing and processing of indigo. In 1810, Buchanan discovered in the district of Purnea seven indigo establishments owned by natives. Several establishments were owned by the Bengali zamindar, K. Roychaudhuri, who paid 30,000 rupees of land-tax a year. Siaram Sanyan founded 24 establishments, the banker M. Sen had seven, etc. But in the growing of indigo, the preference given to British plantation-owners also led to a situation in which, as one British official put it, it was hard to find a zamindar planter in East Bengal who was not ultimately either completely ruined or forced to allow a more powerful neighbour to participate in his affairs.[23] Even the independent enterprise of the zamindars who engaged in the production of the export crop was reduced to naught by the British. Indians were similarly discriminated against in the production of tea. The first Indian to have a tea plantation was Maniram

Dewan, who by 1853 owned two small plantations and paid full land-tax from these, while his British rivals enjoyed privileged concessions. Dewan turned out to be involved in the 1857 uprising and was executed the following year.[24]

Large-Scale Enterprise in Trade and Industry

In the situation, Bengal's banking and merchant's capital still refused to display any serious intentions of going beyond the servicing of British enterprise and local zamindar estates. A key sphere of these services in the 1840s was trade in agricultural produce, which ensured the receipt of taxes and rent, and also proceeds from export products. Thus, in the district of Dacca, according to J. Taylor, the following system of grain trade was in existence: "From their command of capital they (the merchants.—V. P.) are enabled to regulate the price of grain in the bazars, and as the rayats generally borrow from them at an exorbitant rate of interest, the latter, in order to liquidate their debts, and to pay their rents to the zamindar, are generally obliged to sell the produce of their fields immediately it is reaped and at a price ... which yields but a small profit." If the peasant was free of debt, when the crop was good he tried "to lay aside a sufficient quantity of grain for one year's consumption", lending out the remaining grain to his neighbours (apparently, the non-agricultural sections of the village, or the indebted peasants). "This is a common practice, I believe, throughout India," says Taylor.[25] Although this evidence is not sufficient to draw any final conclusion, one is left with the impression that, as compared with the 1780s, Bengal's merchant's and usurer's capital had strengthened its positions in the extraction of grain from the village and its marketing in the town.

Merchant's capital had to intensify its participation in marketing food-stuffs because, if anything, the scale of Bengal's internal trade had shrunk in the first half of the century. As a result of the influx of British yarn, the importation of cotton from other parts of India declined (as regards Dacca, it probably did not amount "to one sixtieth of the quantity imported in 1787").[26] Taylor reported: "The only articles of commerce which have been introduced into the district by Europeans, and which may be considered as supplying the loss of its manufactures, are indigo and safflower. These two dyes have been cultivated for foreign markets since the year 1800, but the aggregate value of both products (as raised within the limits of the district) is not more than 4 lacs of rupees a year, or one-eighth of the capital employed in the purchase of cloths for the English market in 1787."[27] Let us add that British capital had dominated the production and marketing of dyes from the outset, so that native merchants found it hard to enlarge their operations. Additional and indirect evidence of the fact that the local merchants were still being prevented from carrying on foreign trade on their own was the decline of the Armenian and Greek trading communities, which could also have been connected with the steady reduction in the export of Indian cloths to the Ottoman Empire and Iran.[28]

In the situation, native merchant's capital did not display any productive potentials in Bengal's industries, although it did extend credits for indigo production. "The transactions of poddars are confined at present to granting hundies on Calcutta, Patna, Murshidabad, Benares, Sylhet and Mirzapore. They advance money to indigo planters on bills drawn on Calcutta, and loans to the inhabitants on mortgages of houses and land, and on jewels, gold and silver articles, etc. left in pledge with them."[29] There is every reason to assume that the above-mentioned planters were British capitalists (and this is borne out by other sources), because it was quite logical for them to issue bills upon Calcutta banks.

British capitalists took loans from local bankers at an interest rate close to that of British banks—6-7 per cent per annum. But whenever local banking capital turned to manufacture, it at once lost its proper European features. Taylor goes on: "Many of them (Dacca poddars.—V.P.) import English thread from Calcutta and retail it to the weavers, but this article is purchased in largest quantities by the merchants who visit Calcutta in the cold season. Pykars form another numerous class of persons connected with the manufactures and trade of the place. They are agents who make purchases of country thread in the different bazars in the country and procure cloths for the merchants in the city. An advance of money is made by the merchant, and the pykar enters into an agreement to deliver to him a certain number of bales of cloth of certain dimensions, quality and number of thread within a specified time. He distributes the money among the weavers and superintends the work, and for his trouble receives a small commission of about 2½ per cent" (of the value of a given order).[30] There was a similar system in the finishing of cloths.

As I have already said, the rise in the prices of zamindar land property, which was due to the growing appropriation of rent by the zamindars through the fixed land-tax and the increasing share of commodities in the rayats' farm produce was the decisive factor behind the movement of capital in Bengal in the first half of the 19th century. The Bengali weekly "Bangadoot" reported in 1829 that over the three preceding decades the price of an acre of land had risen from 15 to 300 rupees.[31] Still, as I have already shown in part, Bengal capital now and again sought to extricate itself from being bogged down in real estate and the marketing of the product extracted by its owner. But the efforts of Bengal capitalists did not rise above brokerage for British firms. The Bengali historian Dipesh Chakrabarty speaks of Bengal's leading businessmen of the 1820s-1840s in the following outspoken terms:

"When Mutty Lall Seal or Dwarkanath Tagore or Ram Gopal Ghosh entered business in 1819, the 1820s and in the 1830s, respectively, they had before them a set of investment choice presented by the economy of Bengal. The existing investment pattern was already colonial, i.e., specialising in the production and export of primary products, like, mainly, indigo, raw cotton, opium, sugar, oilseeds, etc. A study of the business preferences of Dwarkanath or Mutty Lall or Ram Gopal will show that they never chose outside this range of choices presented by the colonial economy. In this sense they were all dependent on colonialism. The investment-choices of the British mercantilist really fixed up for them their possible areas of investment.

"Mutty Lall traded in cowhides, 'was the founder and promoter of the first indigo mart which was established here under the style of Messrs. Moore, Hickey and Co.,' was hired by English merchants for his sound judgments on indigo, sugar, rice, and saltpetre. He exported indigo, silk, saltpetre, sugar, and rice to Europe and imported from England cotton-piece goods and iron. He also became 'a large ship-owner'. Besides, he was a Banian to a number of agency houses, including his own Oswald, Seal and Co. and Ram Gopal's Kelsall and Co., when the latter was still an assistant there. Perhaps Oswald, Seal and Co. also invested in indigo in a large way.... If Dwarkanath's or Mutty Lall's or Ram Gopal's dependence on colonialism was an economic fact, it was an ideological fact too. This ideology expressed itself in a native sharing by the Bengali intelligentsia of the Free Trader's faith in the 'do good'ing missions of British capital in India."[32]

The specific features of the propertied classes in Bengal were most pronounced in the structure of Calcutta's urban élite. The Bengali student, Benoy Ghose, has noted that the development of commercial agriculture round the towns of Bengal, notably Calcutta, in the first half of the 19th century engendered a lively trade in agricultural produce, extended the trade ties between town and country and opened up various opportunities for Bengal enterprise. "The commercial activities of Bengal entrepreneurs like Madan Dutta, Ramdulal Dey, Dwarkanath Tagore, and others, created a favourable situation for the gradual growth of industrial capitalism in Bengal. But the situation thus created could not be adequately exploited by the infant Bengali 'bourgeoisie' owing to various political and economic handicaps." Ghose also assumes that the history of these outstanding representatives of Bengal enterprise merely shows "how indigenous commercial enterprises were willynilly forced to be diverted to immobile and unproductive channels, and consequently to ruin."[33]

To back up his view, Ghose tells the story of R. Dey, D. Tagore and their immediate heirs. Ramdulal Dey began as a skipper,[34] but his star rose only with the formation of the United States of America, when "Ramdulal exhibited the greatest spirit of commercial adventure and imagination in alluring the United States to the shores of Bengal. He liberally advanced money to the captains of American ships, loaded their vessels with cargo after careful calculation and sold their imports at the highest price and profit.... Obviously the bulk of American business passed through Ramdulal's hands in Bengal." Stressing the great confidence the Americans had in Ramdulal, Ghose gives a long list of Boston, New York and Philadelphia companies, which was discovered in Ramdulal's account books after his death in 1825. One touching feature was the christening of an American ship after Ramdulal, in his lifetime. His US admirers presented this subject of the British Company with a life-size portrait of President Washington.

However, Ramdulal's US orientation did not prevent him from collaborating with the British as well. Thus, he was broker for the leading British company, Fairley Fergusson. He managed to make a fortune that ran to millions of rupees. Despite the fact that shortly before his death he had lost about 5 million rupees in speculations and through other firms' bankruptcies, his funeral cost half a million rupees, and his heirs donated several lakhs of rupees to charities. Still, the capital of this wealthy Bengal merchant did not assume productive form and was invested by his heirs "in buying real properties in Calcutta and zamindaris in rural areas."[35]

Referring to East India Company records, B. B. Misra estimated Dey's fortune at 4 million rupees. His son, A. Dey, was a receiver of Palmer and Co., which went bankrupt in 1830, and then became a director of the Calcutta Union Bank. He was also a Bania of large companies like Charles Cantor, Rally Brothers and Charles Forrester.[36] Thus, he did not confine himself to owning real estate, but maintained close ties with the British business world.

Ramdulal was succeeded as the richest Bengali businessman by Dwarkanath Tagore who was appointed diwani of the District 24-parganas in 1823, at the early age of 29. In 1828, Tagore became the only Indian director of the Commercial Bank; and the following year, diwani to the East India Company's Customs, Salt and Opium Board, and the founder of the Calcutta Union Bank. Finally, in 1834, he resigned his service under the Company and was the first Bengali to "enter into mercantile business in Calcutta on the European model". In partnership with W. Carr and W. Prinsen he established the firm of Carr, Tagore and Co.

In 1842, he had the honour of a brief sketch of his life and activities appear in the "Colonial Magazine", which said, in part: "Ever anxious to set before his countrymen an example of enterprise and improvement, Dwarkanath established indigo factories on all his estates, and subsequently introduced the system of sugar-cultivation practised at Mauritius. In the joint capacity of hereditary zamindar, landed proprietor and planter, his varied occupations brought him into constant intercourse with the revenue department of the Government, and with almost every mercantile firm in Calcutta. His wealth and extensive credit enabled him to take a leading part in the origination and management of the Union Bank, of which he became afterwards the sole proprietor...."[37]

Let us add that Tagore ran an experimental 600-bigha sugar-cane plantation, but obtained only a few seers of sugar. He then bought a steam-operated sugar-cane press and switched to growing another variety. This time he obtained a fairly large crop, but it proved to be unprofitable because his production costs were twice as high as the price of traditionally produced sugar. Tagore lost 200,000 rupees on his sugar experiments, and finally switched to buying up gur from the peasants, to learn that this yielded sugar at only a quarter of the cost. That marked the end of his agricultural enterprise and mechanised processing of the product.

In 1836, Tagore paid 70,000 rupees at an auction for a pit founded in Raniganj in 1812 by a British firm. But in mining Tagore soon began to collaborate with British capital, establishing the Bengal Coal Co., which in the mid-19th century was the leading producer of coal in Bengal (50,000 tons in 1840 and 200,000 tons in 1860).[38]

After the death of Dwarkanath Tagore in 1846, his son and heir, Dobendranath, sold all the industrial establishments, pits and his share of Carr and Co., but the zamindar estates were retained and provided the basis for the welfare of the Tagore clan over the following decades. However, during the Swadeshi movement, one of the Tagores undertook a short but vigorous essay into industrial and steam-shipping enterprise.

Thus, in the first half of the 19th century, Indian industrial enterprise in Bengal possibly equalled Bombay's in scale and maturity. This may largely be explained by Bombay's lack of an adequate hinterland until the 1820s. But it subsequently out-stripped Bengal in national industrial development, especially since there was, in effect, nothing to compete against, because the Bengal capitalists were abandoning even the existing industrial ventures. This may be partially due to the orientation of native banking capital.

Some details about European banks in Bengal in the first half of the 19th century are given by A. Guha in a paper presented to a seminar on social and economic history. In his view, these banks were unable to function without collaboration with native bankers and shroffs.

Among the shareholders of the Bank of Bengal, founded in 1809, were many Armenians, while the Maharajah Sikhanoy Roy was on the board of directors, although only British subjects were usually members of such boards. Among the leading shareholders of the Commercial Bank (1824-1830) were Palmer and Co., and Tagore. Of the 202 shareholders, 73 were Indians and the rest Europeans. But, Guha remarks, the Indians' share of capital was relatively larger in proportion to their numbers. In 1842, the bank's loans and credits were allocated as follows: indigo 59.1 per cent, silkwinding 1.6 per cent, coal-fields 2.9 per cent, traders 4 per cent, municipal services 2.6 per cent, goods 21 per cent, and stock 8.7 per cent. We find that the bank's operations clearly inclined to spheres in which British capital had direct or indirect interest.

Pointing to these and other examples of collaboration between British and Indian capital (for instance, in Bombay), A. Guha noted the legal privileges enjoyed by British businessmen in India, where they could be tried only by the courts in the capitals of the presidencies. Consequently, when the commercial interests of Europeans and natives clashed, the latter were unable to secure swift and effective justice. In this way, the judicial system indirectly produced a situation in which business practice under an Indian-British or British signboard was more attractive for Indians than an independent business. The patron-client relationship dominated the Anglo-Indian business world.

One of the reasons for the frequent losses incurred by Indian shareholders, especially in the remoter areas, was the unwillingness of the British authorities to introduce the principle of limited liability for joint-stock companies (among which British-controlled companies prevailed). That is why in any crisis the Indian shareholders were the first to pay. Thus, this principle was not introduced in the 1845 and 1850 acts.

Smaller but more tenacious businessmen from the trading castes soon came to succeed the bigger entrepreneurs of high origin, like the Tagores, the Deys, and Ram Gopal Ghosh.[39] Remarking on the decline of the landed aristocracy in Bengal's urban life throughout the 19th century and the emergence in its place of "an educated Bengali middle class" linked with service in the British administration, Benoy Ghose said: "Bengal had practically produced no industrial family in the 19th century for reasons we have indicated before, and none of the families in the upper layer had been able to climb up there from the working class, the artisan class, or from the peasantry. The ancestors of the upper an middle class family-founders in the urban area of Calcutta had, almost without exception, come from the middle and lower-middle strata of the old decadent society, and what is perhaps more important, from the traditional upper castes like the Tantubaniks, Gandhabaniks, Subarbaniks, etc."[40]

Let us note that he classifies these three castes of Bengali usurers in the highest bracket, whereas the Statistical Accounts for the districts of Bengal cast doubt even on their membership of Vaishya. This may be due to the two factors: first, in Calcutta, they had more favourable opportunities for enrichment and enhancement of their social status than in the districts; second, Ghose must have expressed his personal or, at any rate, later conclusions about the status of these castes as they rose with their wealth.

Indeed, according to B. Ghose, in the course of the 19th century the traditional trading castes of Bengal making use of the neglect of trade by the landed aristocracy and "the educated middle class", slowly but surely secured control of the local sphere of circulation in Calcutta. Many small traders developed into big ones, while the once opulent rent-receivers led an idle life and were gradually impoverished. In 1853, the Bengali newspaper "Sambad Prabhakar" criticised the "economic parasitism" of the traditional middle classes in Bengal as follows: "The middle class people are now seeking a secure shelter under Government employments, and the Government also is not very liberal about it towards them. The retreat of this class from the field of trade and commerce is really shameful.... The traditional caste-taboos also operate actively against the free movement of trade, as nobody is free in our society to choose his trade according to his will. . . Unfortunately, the rich people who have enough money, have indeed very little courage and vision to lunch a business. They would prefer to get the job of a mutsuddi or a banian under a foreigner, by offering lakhs of rupees as security deposit and loan, rather than to invest that amount in any independent business. They are very eager to invest their money in Government securities for earning a fixed interest and are not at all willing to risk it in any adventurous enterprise."[41]

Basing himself on Bengali and some Calcutta reference works of the late 1850s, B. B. Misra drew up the following table of the national and religious communal origins of the leading businessmen and financiers in Calcutta:[42]

Year	*Leading European merchants and agents*	*Leading Hindu merchants and shroffs*	*Leading Muslim firms*	*Bengali traders*	*Bengali agents or Banias*	*Parsis*
1815	23	34	15	29	—	—
1835	61	29	11	14	24	1
1855	151	41	31	145	45	8
1858	173	52	35	159	66	10

British businessmen, who prevailed not only numerically but also in their relative individual influence, obviously had the leading role to play. It is not quite clear whom Misra includes under the head of Hindu merchants, who could have been both Bengali and Marwari.

At any rate, in the mid-19th century the Bengali still held a leading position among the upper section of the Indian business community in Calcutta. Thus, in 1853, only five of the 103 members of Bengal's Chamber of Commerce were Indians, but four of them were Bengali. Of the three managers of the Union Bank, two were English and one Bengali, and of its 12 directors, eight were English, three Bengali and one Parsi. In 1853, 129 of its shareholders were Europeans, 70 Bengal Hindus, two Muslims and one Parsi.

However, these figures should not be automatically applied to the overall balance of forces within the Indian business community. The point is that Marwari capital, more than Bengal capital, inclined to independent operations, even if only in nominal terms. Besides, Marwari bankers adhered to traditional forms of business organisation in virtue of caste usage and relative lack of education (in the European sense). That is why in subsequent decades the Marwari on the whole tended to stay away from British joint-stock companies.

Thus, while at the end of the 18th century independent industrial enterprise by Bengali capitalists had been insignificant, by the mid-19th century it had dwindled drastically, in absolute and relative terms (as compared with other spheres where Bengali propertied classes made their fortunes). There was no sign of a national capitalist sector taking shape in Bengal's industry. Some establishments engaged in the processing of agricultural raw materials (as a rule, owned by Englishmen) merely helped to funnel them out of the country. But the relatively large market share in Bengal's agricultural product paved the way for the formation of a petty-commodity sector on that basis. A necessary condition for its formation was the introduction of "protected" tenancy with fixed rent that would limit to some extent the extraction of the products from the land-holders (rayats) by the zamindars.

The early elements of Bengal's bourgeoisie found refuge in the income they derived from their zamindar estates and also turned to service in the British and native administration and the professions. Reflecting on the untapped possibilities for the industrial revolution. A. Guha made the significant remark about a generation of men after 1815, whose early attempts at industrialisation proved to be futile because of the pressure of the colonial system and their apprehensions about joining with Indian peasant uprisings for the sake of a different political system. It appears, indeed, that Bengal's industrialisation was impossible without the elimination of the Permanent Settlement and its after-effects.

In the first half of the 19th century, the Gujarat merchants and the Bengal land-owners constituted two groups which had obtained the greatest privileges from the British regime as compared with other propertied sections in British India. Significantly, this does not apply to the merchants of Bengal or to the land-owners of Gujarat and Maharashtra. In other words, even with respect to India's propertied sections, the British pursued a varied line.

It may appear at first sight that the distinctions—frequently formal and sometimes fairly essential—in British policy on the territory of every presidency were due to adaptation to local conditions. This was undoubtedly one of the reasons; but the distinctions were to a greater extent the result of a deliberate line aimed to maintain and expand a system of distinctions and divisions in Indian society to produce a countless multiplicity of cells isolated from each other. This line was substantiated, for instance, by R. Jenkins, a member of the Company's Board of Directors, who expressed his own view during the negotiations with the British Cabinet in 1833 concerning a new charter for the Company. He said: "The natives of the several Presidencies of India are, I conceive, as different in manners, usages and feelings, in languages and institutions, as the inhabitants of the different kingdoms of Europe, and by leaving the power of legislation, as at present, in the Local Governments, we do more justice to them than we can possibly do by a generalising system. On this subject I feel ... the impolicy of endeavouring to eradicate the national distinctions existing between the natives of our different Presidencies, and which, besides contributing to the happiness and well-being of the people themselves, are one main ingredient of our strength. If we could achieve that uniformity in the laws so much talked of, which can only be operative through a similar uniformity in the manners and modes of our Indian subjects, we should not keep the country for a day."[43]

There were fairly substantial differences of social consciousness among the Bombay merchants and Bangal zamindars. Among the former contacts with the life of their compatriots, apart from the population of Bombay, a city of unique social make-up, were casual and indirect. Bombay merchants could be much more aware of affairs in Canton than in Allahabad or Delhi. Besides, because Bombay merchants belonged to the Parsi community, to the Muslim communities of Khoja and Bohra and even to the Hindu trading and moneylending castes, they were variously alienated from the real needs and aspirations of their own people. Jealously safeguarding their religious and caste traditions and notions, they took a pragmatic and conformist attitude to social affairs, without giving too much thought to the growing contradictions of their own being. That may be why the Bombay merchants, among whom there were many striking personalities, failed to produce any politician, before Dadabhai Naoroji, to express the all-India aspirations and even the self-seeking interests of their groups.

But the position of the Bengal zamindars was different. As a section intermediate between the British tax press and the cultivators who toiled on the land, their position inevitably involved them in the main social contradictions of British India, those between the peasant, who produced the bulk of the national surplus-products, and the British regime, which extracted various proportions of that product.

Bengal zamindars sought to maintain their privileges with respect to these two opposed parties, that is, to secure the fixed land-tax and a sliding rent, which they collected from the landholders. The duality of this attitude made them, on the one hand, claim to represent the national interest vis-à-vis the British regime, and on the other, rely on that regime as a guarantor in extracting the rent from its producers, that is, a majority of the nation which they claimed to represent.

Most of the zamindars accepted their dual position because the attendant costs in terms of national pride and social prestige were more than compensated by material welfare and a higher social status among their compatriots. But it is the Bengal zamindars who brought forth Rammohan Roy, the first Indian to rise to a conscious expression of national requirements and interests. While accepting the British regime and the Permanent Settlement, he insisted on essential correctives. His economic views are highly relevant to our subject. Thus, he said that both the main land-tax systems were upsetting the limitations, fixed by tradition, on the rent extracted from the rayats, thereby undermining the potentialities for accumulation in agriculture. That is why he proposed that the land-tax in the rayatwari areas and rent payments in the zamindari areas should be fixed.[44]

I have failed to find in Roy's writings any concern for the lot of Indian handicrafts, but Bipan Chandra tells us that the call to buy Indian goods instead of imported goods was carried in 1849 by the "Prabhakar", which was published in Poona; and in his lectures in Poona in 1872 Ranade explained that Swadeshi meant preference for Indian-made goods even when these were more expensive and of a lower quality than the best foreign goods.[45] Although the time of this statement lies beyond the period under consideration, the formula had undoubtedly matured within its limits.

In the first half of the 19th century, big traders and money-lenders continued, as a rule, to act as reliable political supporters of the British rulers. Lieutenant-Colonel W. H. Sleeman, who served in India for many years, declared: "There is no class of men more interested in the stability of our rule in India than that of the respectable merchants; nor is there any upon whom the welfare of our government, and of the people, more depends."[46]

During the Great Uprising, many big native bankers, irrespective of their nationality and caste, continued to serve faithfully those who were persecuting the insurgents. The gazetteers of those districts of the United Provinces that were the scene of the uprising were full of reports about the "loyalty" of the top strata of the native merchants and money-lenders. For the services they rendered during the uprising—making available money and provisions and organising troops to fight the insurgents—many traders and money-lenders were rewarded with estates and titles.[47] Among the recipients of such rewards was Abirchand Daga, a forefather of the present-day capitalists of the same name.[48] The merchants of Panipat supplied grain to the British forces around Delhi.[49]

It is true that some merchants in Delhi gave financial support to the government of Bahadur Shah. In one day alone, bankers contributed 100,000 rupees to the coffers of the insurgents. But Bahadur Shah had to apply strong pressure to obtain these loans. In one such incident, Bahadur Shah ordered that two bankers be brought to his palace and asked them for a loan; when the bankers declared that the war had ruined them, he gave them an angry reminder of the fact that one of their partners had already given the British 30,000 rupees. Thereupon, the bankers loosened their purse-strings and handed over 50,000 rupees each. Towards the end of the uprising, some of the insurgents' chiefs simply imposed levies on the bankers to pay the Sepoys.[50] The merchants of Delhi showered Bahadur Shah with complaints about the losses they suffered from requisitions made for the needs of the insurgents.

But far from all the merchants of India supported the foreign regime. Anti-British sentiments appeared to be still rather strong among a section of the merchants, especially in the interior of the country, where their broker operations were less instrumental in compensating them for the loss of their traditional business.

On the basis of documentary evidence, D. R. Gadgil notes that commerce and the handicrafts declined in Lucknow, the capital of Oudh, after the annexation of that state by the British and the suppression of the uprising. The section of the population that had been attracted by the special conditions existing for commerce under the native government, left the town.[51]

There is some information, rather scanty, it is true, about the participation of merchants in the Great Uprising. For in- stance, letters from Punjab Banias addressed to Sepoys have been discovered. These letters announced that a day for the uprising would soon be fixed and urged all the Sepoys to come out against the British regime. When the uprising broke out in Delhi, shops in the Punjab became centres of discussion about the need for a repetition of the Delhi events.[52]

The question of why some of the merchants and bankers of Hindustan and the Punjab supported the uprising has still to be investigated fully, but at any rate their assistance to the insurgents, whether voluntary or involuntary, was not at all due to the fact that their own economic contradictions with the British regime had become sharper or had developed farther than those between the regime and the emergent bourgeoisie in British India's old colonial centres, like Bombay or Calcutta. Their attitude during the uprising was determined by the fact that the age-old links between the merchants of Delhi, the Punjab and Oudh, on the one hand, and the native rulers and the feudal economy as a whole, on the other, were still relatively strong. This feudalmerchant patriotism was an offshoot of feudal patriotism and was destroyed together with it in the fire of the uprising.

In historical terms, the future belonged to the early, weak and sometimes twisted shoots of bourgeois nationalism, which began to make their way to the surface of India's political life from the mid-19th century, however timidly. A serious study of this development requires an examination of the periodicals of that period, but lacking such an opportunity, I shall have to confine myself to a few examples.

In 1853, when the British Parliament was debating a new bill on the government of Indian territories, many public bodies and private individuals in India sent petitions to the House of Commons expressing their wishes about the political and economic line to be pursued by the British regime. The petition submitted by the Bombay Association requested the House of Commons that it should grant India a constitution retaining the "best elements" of the existing system but making the administration less cumbersome and less secret, and at the same time more responsible, efficient and acceptable to the Indians.[53] Seeking to limit the powers exercised by the oligarchy of the East India Company, the Bombay merchants suggested that the Council for Indian Affairs should be directly responsible to the House of Commons. With some reservations, the petitioners also requested that the salaries of the British officials in India should be reduced. Furthermore, they declared that the time had come "when the natives of India are entitled to a much larger share than they have hitherto had in the administration of the affairs of their country." They therefore proposed that Indians be admitted to the provincial councils and to judicial and administrative bodies. The Bombay Association also stressed that the industry of the Presidency was in need of railways and highways and of an extension of harbour facilities. Finally, they pointed out that it was wrong to spend a mere 12,500 pounds on the education of 10 million inhabitants of the Presidency, while the land-tax alone exceeded 1 million pounds.[54]

The Madras Native Association stressed in its petition that the amount of land-tax levied by the administration was without parallel in India's history and asked that at least a part of the revenue be used for irrigation and the road-building. It was said in the petition that thanks to the rayat's labour money was always available to wage wars of self-aggrandisement, to pay the personnel of the Indian civil service excessive salaries and grant them pensions of 300 pounds per annum, and to pay dividends of 10 per cent to the stockholders of the East India Company, but when the rayat needed a new road to improve his condition he was told that he must build it himself.[55]

The British Indian Association of Bengal, among whose leadership rich Bengali zamindars dominated, but which also included Parsi and other non-Bengali merchants, asked in its petition for a reduction of the land-tax, encouragement of commerce and industry, public works, the abolition of the huge monopoly of the East India Company and a restriction of the "free trade" that led to a decline of the native industry. The petition suggested that the appointment to the higher administrative posts should be based on the candidates' personal experience, ability and a knowledge of the country's languages and laws. This was obviously in the interest of the upper strata of Bengal, for, if promotions were made under those conditions, their representatives would undoubtedly have advantages over the young civil servants sent from Britain. The petition expressed a desire to alter the administrative system of India, because the Board of Control and the Board of Directors of the Company were not subjected to any control. The familiar requests to lower the officials' salaries and to abolish the salt and opium monopoly were not forgotten either. But the Bengal merchants would have been fully satisfied if opium was sold as "freely" as in Bombay.[55]

The petitions submitted by the representatives of the wealthy strata of the three Indian presidencies contain no essential differences and this suggests that they had been coordinated. They all expressed loyalty to the British regime, both in form and substance. None of them expressed any desire for home rule, even in a limited form which would preserve the sovereign power of the British Empire. The petitioners merely asked that the absolute rule of the Company's Board of Directors and Board of Control should be somewhat restricted. They undoubtedly took into account that, in this respect, their request coincided with the aspirations of the British industrial bourgeoisie, who were also urging their representatives in the House of Commons to secure for them direct government of this major colony of the British Crown. The urge to lower the salaries of the colonial officials did not affect the British industrialists either, for the Indian civil service was staffed chiefly by the sons of impoverished aristocrats.

The economic wishes amounted to a request for a lower land-tax (the taxes levied on trade were quite small) and a rather vague reminder that some encouragement ought to be given to native industry. It is hard to say to what extent these loyal petitions reflected the real interests of the merchants in major ports like Bombay, Madras and Calcutta, but it is quite possible that at the time their aspirations went no farther than to be rid of the Company's restrictions and to become independent in their dealings with British industrial and commercial firms.

Bholanath Chunder's book "The Travels of a Hindoo to Various Parts of Bengal and Upper India" helps us to understand the views of the rising Indian bourgeoisie. At first, the work appeared in an English newspaper printed in Calcutta, and was then published in London. The author, a Bengal merchant, made his travels—or, to be more exact, his business trips—from 1845 to 1866. The whole book is written in good English and is shot through with loyalty to the colonial regime. It opens with a dedication to Sir John Lawrence, the Viceroy of India. The author glorifies British law and order, the administration and the railways. The table of contents, an enumeration of the highlights on the author's travels, leaves one with the impression that he was trying to look at his country through European eyes.

The author wrote with bitterness about the neglected state in which he found the palace of the Jagat Seths and about the decline of the urban handicrafts, something that a European traveller could also have noticed.

But only an Indian entrepreneur could deplore the fact that the Indians were obliged to wear garments made exclusively of British textiles and looked forward to the day when their sons and grandsons would wear garments made entirely of Indian cotton cloth produced by Indian manufacturers.[57] He reproached the colonial authorities for their extravagance in building sumptuous administrative edifices and residences in Calcutta.

But this newly-fledged Indian bourgeois still laboured under various feudal ideas. He cherished no more than a faint hope that perhaps in the 20th or 21st century the Indians would be able to sink mines and build factories, despite the fact that at the time Indian capitalists already had mills in Bombay. He believed that India's industrial future depended on the dissemation of knowledge and enterprise and not on national liberation. These considerations were not set out merely in deference to colonial censorship, for the author said in his conclusion that Indian thinking had never known and had never tried to understand any other form of government except despotism. Claiming that neither constitutional monarchy nor republic were appropriate to Indian conditions, he suggested that the Indian rajahs should be taught the elements of good government and good conduct.[58] There is no doubt at all that mid-19th-century India was not prepared for a constitutional monarchy, to say nothing of a republic. In the early 18th century, Indian society, I believe, entered upon a long period of transition from the Oriental-type macro-centralisation to the monarchy of midi-centralisation (the Peshwa and Sikh states). In the course of subsequent development the relevant social forces, a national division of labour, and the multiplicity of internal exchanges could well have taken shape—the very basis on which alone a uniform system of administration and the rule of general law can be created that are required of the transition to an absolute monarchy.[59]

Japan's experience shows that in the 19th century absolutism was the only state system that was realistic for the East in historical terms and capable of preserving the national sovereignty and progress through the Genesis and development of capitalism. But Indian society had lost its independence before it managed to reach the absolute-monarchy level. The rajahs, the pitiful relicts of the Oriental despotism retained by the British regime, were incapable of performing any historical feat, regardless of however well they were trained in good administration and good conduct.

NOTES

1. A. Tripathi, *Trade and Finance in the Bengal Presidency 1793-1833,* Bombay, 1956, pp. 253, 260.
2. *Ibid.,* p. 266.
3. *Rommohan Roy on Indian Economy,* Calcutta, 1965, p. 22.
4. H.R. Ghosal, *Economic Transition in the Bengal Presidency (1793-1833),* Patna, 1950, pp. 26-45.
5. J. Taylor, *A Sketch...,* pp. VI, 190-191.
6. *Ibid.,* pp. 307-308.
7. *Ibid.,* p. 365.
8. *Ninth Report from the Select Committee 1783,* Appendis 51.
9. *IESHR,* vol. XI, Nos. 2-3, June-September 1974, p. 163.
10. *Return : Cotton (India),* pp. 272, 273.
11. J. Taylor, *A Sketch...,* pp. 566-567.
12. *Ibid.,* p. 174.
13. *Ibid.,* p. 175.
14. See: *ibid.,* p. 164.
15. *Ibid.,* pp. 311-312.
16. *Ibid.,* pp. 310-312.
17. *Ibid.,* p. 234.
18. See: B.B. Misra, *The Indian Middle Classes.*
19. See: K. Marx, *Capital,* vol. I, p. 337.
20. For Details, See: H.R. *Ghosal, Economic Transition...,* pp. 46-63.
21. *Statistical Accounts of Bengal,* vol IV, pp. 112, 122-125, 136.
22. *Bengal District Gazetteer,* Bribhum, pp. 69-71.
23. H.R. Ghosal, *Economic Transition...,* po. 78-79.
24. A. Guha, Colonisation of Assam: Second Phase 1840-1859, *IESHR,* vol. IV, No. 4, December 1967, pp. 307-308.

25. J. Taylor, *A Sketch...*, pp. 294, 296.
26. *Ibid.*, p. 165.
27. *Ibid.*, pp. 308-309.
28. *Ibid.*, pp. 365-366
29. *Ibid.*, pp. 186-187.
30. *Ibid.*, pp. 312-313.
31 *Readings in Indian Economic History*, p. 146.
32. D. Chakrabarty, *The Colonial Context of the Bengal Renaissance..., IESHR*, vol. XI, No. 1, March 1974, pp. 96-98, 100.
33. *Readings in Indian Economic History*, p. 138.
34. B.B. Misra cites some additional details about the origin of Ramdulal Dey's wealth. He started out as an ordinary gomastha at 4-5 rupees a month, and then became a clerk at Farley and Co. of Calcutta, Having obtained the necessary business knowledge, Dey struck out as an independent broker and middleman for US merchants (B.B. Misra, The Indian Middle Classes, pp. 82-83).
35. See: *Readings in Indian Economic History*, pp. 139, 140.
36. B.B. Misra, *The Indian Middle Classes*, pp. 83, 103.
37. See: *Readings in Indian Economic History*, p. 141.
38. R. Dutt, *India in the Victorian Age. An Economic History*, London, 1904, p. 114.
39. B.B. Misra, *The Indian Middle Classes*, p. 106.
40. *Readings in Indian Economic History*, pp. 143-144.
41. *Ibid.*, pp. 146-147.
42. B.B. Misra, *The Indian Middle Classes*, p. 103.
43. *Papers Respecting the Negotiation...*, London, 1813, p. 360.
44. Rajah Rammohun Roy, *The English Works*, vol. I, Allahabad, 1906, pp. 272, 278, 281-282. For details, see : E.N. Komarov, *Ram Mohan Roy—prosvetitel i provozvestnik natsionalnogo dvizheniya v Indii, "Obshchestvenno-politicheskaya i filosofskaya mysl v Indii*, Moscow, 1962, pp. 50-54.
45. Bipan Chandra, *The Rise and Growth of Economic Nationalism in India*, p. 123.
46. W.H. Sleeman, *Rambles and Recollections of an Indian Official*, London, 1844, vol. II, p. 143.
47. "Ghazipur", p. 110; *Banda*, p. 109; *Allahabad*, p. 189; *Moradabad*, p. 168 (*District Gazetteers of United Provinces series*, Allahabad, 1909-1911).
48. *Central Provinces Provincial Banking Enquiry Committee*, vol. II (Nagpur), 1930, pp. 495-496.
49. C.T. Metcalf, *Two Native Narratives of the Mutiny of Delhi*, Westminster, 1892, p. 155.
50. *Ibid.*, pp. 113, 174, 200.
51. D.R. Gadgil, *The Industrial Evolutions of India...*, p. 9.
52. *The Crisis in Punjab, from the 10th of May until the Fall of Delhi (by a Punjab Employee)*, Lahore, 1858, pp. 17-18.
53. *Minutes of Evidence taken before the Select Committee on the Government on Indian Territories* (Parliamentary Papers), vol. 33, London, 1853, p. 228.
54. *Ibid.*, p. 132, 229, 231.
55. *Ibid.*, p. 212.
56. *Ibid.*, pp. 216, 217, 258.
57. B. Chunder, *The Travels of a Hindoo to Various Parts of Bengal and Upper India*, vol. I, London, 1869, pp. 64, 65, 140-141.
58. *Ibid.*, vol. II, pp. 273, 408, 409.
59. See: K. Marx and F. Engels, *Sochineniya*, vol. 10, 1958, p. 432.

CONCLUSION

The material put together in this book provides an opportunity to reconsider the problem of primitive capital accumulation in India in the first half of the 19th century. The first thing one must say is that on the eve of the British conquest and in the first few decades after it the traditional socio-economic structures of India were preserved. It is true that the Sikhs and the Marathas had cleared the despotic Mogul strata from the areas they controlled, but the upper tier of the social-class pyramid of the Indian society, which those strata had earlier taken over, turned out to be largely filled by a new section of victors. Accordingly, the British Permanent Settlement merely resulted in some personal changes among the landlords, but did not eliminate them.

Mid-19th-century India had yet to reach the social maturity of early 16th-century Britain where "the old nobility had been devoured by the great feudal wars. The new nobility was the child of its time, for which money was the power of all powers."[1] The numerous sections of Indian rent-receivers maintained the traditional way of life and notions of its meaning and social values. Let us bear in mind that "the might of the feudal lords, like that of the sovereign depended not on the length of his rent-roll, but on the number of his subjects...."[2] The European vassal system undoubtedly had no direct analogies in India, but there the relations of patronage were as much in the way of primitive accumulation as vassal relations in Europe had been.

The redistribution of rent under the control of the zamindar landed estates tended to prolong the historical being of the socially conservative and economically parasitic elements of India's society, of all the retainers, the countless "relatives", priests, big and small tax-collectors, watchmen and guards. In the areas under the Permanent Settlement there was no disbandment of the feudal military retinue, an important condition for primitive accumulation in the social and purely financial sense. The countless idlers continued to consume the surplus-product produced by the cultivators, without feeling any (let alone imperative) need for a leap from one (feudal) to another (capitalist) formation.

Things were somewhat different in the rayatwari areas, where the upper echelons of the traditional structure had been largely eliminated first by the Marathas themselves and then by the British authorities. There, the upper strata in the countryside were given more room for carrying on independent husbandry. But the way here was hampered by the excessive land-tax, which sharply increased the land-holders' debts to the money-lenders. In other words, the rayatwari areas lacked the crucial condition for the genesis of the capitalist farmer—the long-term lease with fixed cash payments and a steady rise of farm prices.[3] But one could also get the impression that the upper strata of the rural community combined the land and the implements of labour they owned with the labour-power of the village serfs, who had no land and frequently no households.

Although some information has been cited in this book about the conditions for such a combination, I must admit that the most essential aspects of the problem have yet to be studied. Still, it is safe to note the circumstances favouring the conjunction of labour-power with the means of production on the capitalist basis. First, the lower strata of the countryside (in Bihar, for instance) were also able to own implements and draught animals, which they used to cultivate the owner's land; second, there is no evidence that even local markets of free labour power were taking shape in the rural areas; work was remunerated in kind at the traditional rates, which to some extent fixed the rate of exploitation.

The socio-economic structure of the Indian countryside potentially transferred the separation of the real producer from the means of production into a highly specific sphere, because some part of the agricultural population, which differed here and there but was almost always fairly large, had long been deprived of the land and frequently also of its draught animals and implements, fully or to such an extent as to be unable to carry on farming on its own. This section of the Indian countryside had always existed off the remuneration to be obtained from labour inputs in the husbandries of fellow villagers. It could be emancipated only from the traditional right to employment, especially in season and for a correspondingly higher renumeration.

The failure of the cotton-growing farms on capitalist lines showed that this right also had a reverse side to it: it demon-strated that the village population that had no households was affixed to the traditional sphere of employment with the corresponding farming implements, labour skills and principles of remuneration. That is why the social and production status of these toilers could have been changed only with the entrepreneurial transformation of this sphere of their employment, which would have meant conversion into a "surplus population" for a sizable section.

But the land-tax situation in the first half of the 19th century ruled out this kind of transformation, because both the Permanent Settlement and the rayatwari reform had disrupted or even eliminated the traditional restrictions on rent-extraction either directly in favour of the British Raj or indirectly through the medium of the zamindars. Without deciding the question of whether the upper strata in the countryside had any economic entrepreneurial potential, let us note that the rate of extraction of the agricultural product established by the British regime in itself blocked the way to any realisation of this kind of potential. What is more, one is left with the impression that the British land-tax system impelled the rural upper sections to resort to unproductive methods of gain, like subleasing land, money-lending and trade.

In this situation it never occurred to the upper rural strata to do anything to clear the land, and, on the contrary, the fact that they made available to the tenant not only the land but also the draught animals, the implements and the seeds showed that they were cutting back on their own economic activity and that they were abandoning their functions in the production process in favour of the direct producer. Only a special study will show how widespread this was, as also the husbandry with the labour allotment, in the various parts of India. It appears, however, that in Maharashtra the upper rural strata continued to be more involved in independent husbandry than they were, say, in Bengal.

Nor can the ruin of the rayats by excessive tax-rent claims or high money-lenders' interest be regarded as a part of the process of primitive accumulation, because this amounted, in effect, to no more than a substitution of one producer for another with a similar-type husbandry. There was no fundamental change in the identity between the old and the new productive unit because of any possible quantitative differences (more or less cattle, implements, etc.). Although the degree of ultimate commercialisation of the agricultural product did apparently increase under the pressure of rent-tax and money-lending demands, the preservation of traditional economic methods ruled out any commercialisation of the production process itself on any substantial scale. The seed, cattle and implement loans made available to the cultivators ultimately made it harder for them to acquire these elements of production through market relations.

On the whole, India's agriculture in the period under consideration appears to have remained on the level of a patriarchal-subsistence feudal sector. There is no reason to assume that in that period there was any noticeable extension of the area under cotton, jute, sugar-cane or other commercial crops. As for indigo, its cultivation tended rather to ruin the peasant than to provide a basis for commercialising his husbandry. Some pockets of agricultural enterprise, like the processing of sugar-cane, were yet to separate from agricultural production and its inherent production and social relations.

There is no evidence of any marked change in the handicrafts catering for agriculture, because the latter did not modify its demand either in quantitative or qualitative terms. At the same time, the traditional nature of farming techniques rid these branches of the dangers of foreign competition. It is true that with the importation of British steel the smithying industry became to some extent dependent on the import of its main material, but this had no negative effect on the condition of the artisan himself.

Weaving, the major branch of the petty-commodity sector, was a different matter. Together with the decline of the sections which manufactured high-quality goods, there was also evidence of change in the conditions of production and marketing of mass consumption goods. The switch to imported yarn lowered the cost and improved the quality of cloths and even appeared to have somewhat eased the condition of the weavers (apart from the losses suffered by the families in the making of yarn). But this gain was reduced by the looming competition of low-cost British factory products. With the introduction on the Indian market of the price of production operating at English factories as the basic price for fabrics, the possibility of entrepreneurial accumulation in local handweaving disappeared. Making use of the weavers dependence on imported yard, the buyers-up began to secure ever greater control of the marketing of their goods. But accumulation among the buyers-up, as I have already said, did not actually materialise in productive capital.

A whole group of artisans making all manner of utensils from metals, ceramics, wood and cloths, and also clothing and expensive footwear, each responded differently to the changes taking place in the country. The most to suffer were the handicrafts catering for the refined tastes of the nobility, both native and foreign. But even the crafts catering for the employed and non-aristocratic land-owning sections also began to face difficulties (even if not everywhere). The condition of this group of artisans was determined mainly by the changes in the effective demand of its traditional clients. Because in the period under consideration these changes in different parts of India cannot be compared, it is impossible to make any overall statement about the condition of artisans in these handicraft branches. On the whole, it had undoubtedly worsened, although in varying degree (with the difference ranging from Maharashtra to the Punjab). Here again, merchant's capital confined itself to a formal subordination of labour, making use of the difficulties faced by the artisans in purchasing materials, especially the more expensive ones.

Enterprises turning out European-type goods, which had arisen mainly in the centres of the presidencies, were an exception. The extensive use of wage-labour and the technology borrowed from Europe implied not only cooperation but also a detailed division of labour. But such enterprises, which may have numbered several hundreds, were concentrated in a few centres, and in a country of India's size they did not constitute a national manufacturing sector. About the "transplantations" of this sector by British business, the following may be said: during the period in which the metropolitan country was completing the industrial revolution it was a hopeless business to export obsolete hand-operated equipment even into the colonies. Besides, the range of goods that capitalist workshops in India could turn out was swiftly taken over by the British factory (with a few exceptions, like carriages).

The ventures by British capitalists (on their own or in partnership with Indians) in the traditional Indian industries— iron-making and ship-building—appeared to be more promising, but there again pre-factory technology and the discriminatory line pursued by the metropolitan country either tended to ruin the enterprises or to make them superfluous. Coal mines were an exception, but that was a new industry catering for the British fleet. Besides, in that industry manual labour by workers mainly of "impure" origin was maintained at least until Independence. The combination of a semidependent labour force and primitive technical facilities allows one to classify these mines as capitalist manufactories only with great reservations .

If one also takes into account the ruin or decline of industries with workshops based on a detailed division of labour (the making of arms, paper), one will realise that there is no ground for any notions of some kind of petty-capitalist or manufactory sector existing in India in that period. In the absence of the basic process of primitive accumulation and genesis of capitalism it was naturally impossible to speak of the rise of the capitalist as representing an emergent class.

The enrichment of some merchants and bankers as well as landlords should be seen as a premise for the formation of a capitalist sector in the future. The sad experience of those of them who made attempts to start industrial enterprise in ship-building, coal-mining, iron-making and even in the processing of indigo shows that there were no objective economic or political conditions for the formation of a national capitalist industry in the India of that period. For the cash accumulations of the Indian propertied classes to be materialised in the means of capitalist production there was need of a new situation, and this arose after the Great Uprising, entailing changes in the land-tax policy, railway construction and the start of India's conversion into a sphere of British capitalist investment.

The formation of a capitalist sector in India began without a number of key premises for the new formation. In the social and institutional spheres society was not purged of the inert elements of the traditional structures, whose links were weakened or disrupted but not broken, while the prerogatives of the relevant institutions were largely reduced or restricted, but not eliminated. In the sphere of ideology, rationalism did not become even a superficial, élitist philosophical trend, while fideism continued to reign, even if in different forms, in every section of society; there was no change in the claims to material and spiritual goods, but many sections had to be satisfied with less. In the theoretical and applied sciences and in the arts there were no fundamental changes in the cognition and comprehension of nature, society and man; the great achievements of the past were dogmatised and became the highest standard. In the sphere of technology there was no systematic or purposeful transformation of implements, no changes in the methods and organisation of labour; both exploiters and exploited maintained the traditional attitude to work.

The absence of the key premises of the genesis of capitalism in India or their immaturity ruled out any spontaneous movement of this mode of production to the level of a sector, let alone one that was formationally definitive. But in the second half of the 19th century, the state in a number of countries which, like India, were late in entering upon the capitalist path, set about actively to shape a system of its premises which had not taken shape in the course of spontaneous historical development. Some of this work in India was done by the British regime, including the establishment of some administrative centralisation with a place "law and order", railway construction, and the beginnings of modern education and publishing. But these measures lacked the most essential elements without which the separate undertakings did not amount to the complex change in the whole of society. Moreover, the British regime, by maintaining and even supporting stagnation in such key aspects of India's social life as agrarian relations, the caste system, religious and communal disintegration, the rajahs' states, etc., tended to conserve precapitalist inertia in the social being of the vast majority of the Indian population*. That is why the labouring sections suffered not so much from the genesis and development of capitalism as from the inadequacy, incompleteness and deformation of these processes.

NOTES

1. K. Marx, *Capital*, vol. I, p. 718.
2. *Ibid.*
3. *Ibid.*, p. 743.

INDEX

I

J

K

L